Austrian Economics and the Political Economy of Freedom

NEW THINKING IN POLITICAL ECONOMY

Series Editor: Peter J. Boettke
George Mason University, USA

New Thinking in Political Economy aims to encourage scholarship in the intersection of the disciplines of politics, philosophy and economics. It has the ambitious purpose of reinvigorating political economy as a progressive force for understanding social and economic change.

The series is an important forum for the publication of new work analysing the social world from a multidisciplinary perspective. With increased specialization (and professionalization) within universities, interdisciplinary work has become increasingly uncommon. Indeed, during the 20th century, the process of disciplinary specialization reduced the intersection between economics, philosophy and politics and impoverished our understanding of society. Modern economics in particular has become increasingly mathematical and largely ignores the role of institutions and the contribution of moral philosophy and politics.

New Thinking in Political Economy will stimulate new work that combines technical knowledge provided by the 'dismal science' and the wisdom gleaned from the serious study of the 'worldly philosophy'. The series will reinvigorate our understanding of the social world by encouraging a multidisciplinary approach to the challenges confronting society in the new century.

Recent titles in the series include:

Explaining Constitutional Change
A Positive Economics Approach
Stefan Voigt

Ethics as Social Science
The Moral Philosophy of Social Cooperation
Leland B. Yeager

Markets, Planning and Democracy
Essays after the Collapse of Communism
David L. Prychitko

Governance and Economic Development
A Comparative Institutional Approach
Joachim Ahrens

Constitutions, Markets and Law
Recent Experiences in Transition Economies
Edited by Stefan Voigt and Hans-Jürgen Wagener

Austrian Economics and the Political Economy of Freedom
Richard M. Ebeling

Austrian Economics and the Political Economy of Freedom

Richard M. Ebeling

Ludwig von Mises Professor of Economics, Hillsdale College

NEW THINKING IN POLITICAL ECONOMY

Edward Elgar Publishing

Cheltenham, UK • Northampton, MA, USA

© Richard M. Ebeling, 2003

Published by
Edward Elgar Publishing Limited
Glensanda House
Montpellier Parade
Cheltenham
Glos GL50 1UA
UK

Edward Elgar Publishing, Inc.
136 West Street
Suite 202
Northampton
Massachusetts 01060
USA

A catalogue record for this book
is available from the British Library

Library of Congress Cataloguing in Publication Data
Ebeling, Richard M.
    Austrian economics and the political economy of freedom / Richard M. Ebeling.
        p. cm. – (New thinking in political economy)
    Includes bibliographical references.
    1. Austrian school of economics–History–20th century. 2. Free
enterprise–History–20th century. 3. Economics–History–20th century. I. Title. II.
Series.

HB98 .E24 2003
330.15'7—dc21

                                                                    2002041382

ISBN 1 84064 940 2

Printed and bound in Great Britain by MPG Books Ltd, Bodmin, Cornwall

For Anna,
with love and appreciation

Contents

Acknowledgments

Almost all of the essays included in this volume were written during the 1990s, following my appointment in 1988 as the Ludwig von Mises Professor of Economics at Hillsdale College in Hillsdale, Michigan. This position has given me the delightful opportunity each year to teach a two-semester course on Austrian Economics that has stimulated me constantly to rethink and refine my understanding of the 'Austrian' approach on a wide variety of issues and topics in both theory and policy. This has been reinforced by a two-semester course on the history of economic thought that I teach each academic year.

Another pleasurable role as the Mises Professor has been my participation in Hillsdale College's annual Ludwig von Mises Lecture Series. In fact, seven of the ten essays included in the present volume were originally prepared for these lectures and first appeared in the Hillsdale College Press *Champions of Freedom* book series, for which I serve as the editor. These are Chapters 1, 2, 3, 7, 8, 9, 10 in the present volume. Hillsdale College has been a most generous supporter of many of my scholarly activities over the years, for which I am deeply grateful.

Two other essays, Chapters 4 and 5, were originally delivered at conferences organized by the Ludwig von Mises Institute of Auburn, Alabama and appeared in volumes sponsored by them. The Mises Institute, with whom I am affiliated as an adjunct scholar, has for 20 years performed meritorious service in preserving and advancing the ideas of the Austrian tradition from Menger to Mises. I wish to thank the Mises Institute and its president, Lew Rockwell, for allowing these two essays to be reprinted in the present volume.

The remaining essay, Chapter 6, was originally prepared for a 1993 symposium on 'The End to "Isms"? Reflections on the Fate of Ideological Politics after Communism's Collapse', organized by my late colleague and dear friend, Alexsandras Shtromas, who had served as a professor of political science at Hillsdale College for almost ten years, until his untimely death in 2000. It subsequently appeared in a volume with the same title as the symposium that was published by Blackwell Publishers. I wish to thank Blackwell for permitting this essay to be reprinted here.

Thanks are also owed to my secretary, Carol Kratzer, who has helped with the retyping and preparing of these essays in their present revised forms for publication. The Hillsdale College library staff has been consistently helpful with inter-library loan and photocopy requests and assistance in tracking down various reference materials.

I would also like to mention that, if it had not been for my friend, Alex Shtromas, I would never have had the good fortune to meet my wife, Anna. In 1991, Alex and I made several trips together to the former Soviet Union as consultants on political and market reform and privatization to the newly elected democratic government in Lithuania and for the city of Moscow. On one of these trips, in May 1991, we attended a memorial conference in Moscow in honour of the Soviet Nobel Laureate and dissident, Andrei Sakharov. It was there, through a friend of Alex, that I was introduced to Anna. We were married on 24 December 1991.

It is to Anna that I dedicate this book. A PhD scholar in political science and history from Moscow State University in her own right, as well as a successful business executive when I first met her in Moscow, she has been the source of everything good and right in my life ever since. She has been my constant supporter, partner and collaborator in all of my professional activities. Without her assistance my recent work on the 'lost papers' of Ludwig von Mises, which we unearthed in a formerly secret Moscow archive, would have been impossible. This dedication is but a small reflection of everything that I owe her.

Introduction

THE AUSTRIAN ECONOMISTS AND NEOCLASSICAL ECONOMICS

The chapters in this volume attempt to explain some of the theories and apply some of the policy implications of the Austrian School of Economics. The Austrian School had its beginnings with the publication of Carl Menger's *Grundsätze der Volkswirtschaftslehre* in 1871. He is best known for having formulated a version of the theory of marginal utility, along with the two other founders of the marginalist approach, William Stanley Jevons and Leon Walras. Jevons and Walras structured their variations on the marginalist theme in the garb of mathematical notation, with an emphasis on the conditions and requirements for the existence of equilibrium states.

Menger, on the other hand, presented the theory in a framework that gave greater emphasis to the roles of uncertainty, imperfect knowledge, and causal and time processes of economizing and production. He was also more interested in explaining the logic behind the process of price formation, rather than the particulars of a specific equilibrium end-state of affairs in the changing conditions of the market. And, in addition, he emphasized an aspect of the social process that neither of his two marginalist co-founders gave any serious attention to: the evolution and formation of spontaneous social institutions. Menger's mode of exposition lead Frank H. Knight to comment in 1931 that, 'In fact, the entire theory is much more convincing in the loose, common-sense formulation of Menger than it is in the more refined mathematical version of Jevons and Walras.'[1]

The Austrian School, however, established its place in the mainstream of economic thought in the 1880s and 1890s through the contributions of Eugen von Böhm-Bawerk and Friedrich von Wieser. The two, who were also brothers-in-law, had come across Menger's book when they were students and devoted a good portion of their scholarly efforts over the coming years to developing and extending Menger's ideas. They wrote widely on the topics of value and price, capital and interest, imputation and factor pricing, and opportunity cost. Böhm-Bawerk was the careful methodical logician who assisted in getting Austrian ideas noticed by the economics profession by his willingness to enter into extensive debates in the pages of the economics journals, both in German and in English. Wieser was more of an introvert who shied away from debates and argument for the most part, but attempted to incorporate some of the Austrian ideas within his second field of interest, historical sociology, in which he formulated a theory of entrepreneurship and leadership for understanding the nature of social and political processes.

During these first decades of the school's existence, the most visible battle lines of debate and disagreement seemed to be primarily with the German Historical School. The latter's proponents rejected an essentially logical-deductive approach to economic analysis for what often appeared an almost purely atheoretical focus on statistical and historical fact gathering from which they believed period-specific economic 'laws' might be derivable. In the wider economics profession, the 'Austrian' approach seemed to many to be merely one variation on the common marginalist theme. In the 1890s and 1910s, the most heated area of argumentation between Austrians like Böhm-Bawerk and 'neoclassical' economists like John Bates Clark often seemed to be over 'technical' issues of how one should think about capital and capital goods; that is, as concrete, discrete produced means of production that are way stations through time leading to the completion of a finished consumer good (as Böhm-Bawerk argued), or as a self-sustaining 'fund' of capital in which the role of time and a period of production could be set aside as not very useful concepts (as Clark insisted).

It is true that, below the surface, points of methodological difference were present. Thus British neoclassical economist Francis Y. Edgeworth could chide Böhm-Bawerk for missing some nuances in the logic of price formation because of his failure to construct his theory in mathematical form,[2] while, in turn, both Böhm-Bawerk and Wieser could take a young Joseph A. Schumpeter to task for rigidly adhering to a mathematical and 'positivist' approach that led him to reason in circles and fail to appreciate the uniquely 'mental' aspects to all economic phenomena and their understanding.[3]

But at this time, in general, these differences in 'method' and 'approach' of exposition seemed more a matter of temperament and training than something central or crucial to the reformulation and development of economic theory on the basis of the marginalist concept. The Austrians began to become more conscious of distinctive features in their approach during the 1920s and, especially, 1930s. In 1932, Hans Mayer, successor to Wieser's chair at the University of Vienna, contrasted what he referred to as the 'functional' and 'causal-genetic' theories of price. The functional theory, at the core of the mathematical school that had grown out of the work of Jevons and Walras, focused on a detailed description of *the conditions and requirements for states of general equilibrium*. Mayer also highlighted the distinctly artificial assumptions that were frequently postulated in the formulations of the functional approach. The causal-genetic theory, that had emerged out of Menger's contributions, focused on explaining *the logical processes of price formation out of the interactions of market participants on the basis of their subjective valuations and choices.*[4]

At the same time, in 1931, Ludwig von Mises also argued that 'Within the field of modern economics the Austrian School has shown its superiority to the School of Lausanne and the schools related to the latter, which favor mathematical formulations, by clarifying the causal relationships between value and cost, while at the same time eschewing the concept of function, which in our science is misleading.'[5] It was misleading in the social sciences, including economics, Mises had argued earlier in 1929, because it directed attention away from that unique property of the human sciences that is the ultimate causal factor at work that sets the sequence of social events in motion – men's intentional and volitional will. It also gave the false impression that quantitative predictability was possible in the social sciences in the same manner that it was believed possible in the natural sciences. Mises insisted that 'Economics too can make predictions in the sense in which this ability is attributed to the natural sciences. The economist can and does know in advance what effect an increase in the quantity of money will have upon its purchasing power or what consequences price controls must have. ... However, this knowledge is not quantitatively definite', because it depends upon the subjective valuations, judgments and expectations of the interacting market participants. And these were always subject to change and modification owing to the volitional character of such valuations, judgments and expectations. Hence the laws of economics referred to qualitative logical relationships, and not quantitative empirical relationships. 'This is the reason why history cannot predict things to come and why it is an illusion to believe that qualitative economics can be replaced or supplemented by quantitative economics,' Mises reasoned. 'Economics as a theoretical science can impart no knowledge other than qualitative. And economic history can furnish us with quantitative knowledge only *post factum*.'[6]

It is nonetheless true that what separated the Austrians from the neoclassical economists was not easy to see on the surface, especially following Lionel Robbins' 1932 *Essay on the Nature and Significance of Economic Science*, in which he attempted to synthesize what he saw as the common elements in the 'Austrian' and 'Lausanne' Schools in terms of a refined and general conception of the universal logic of human choice under conditions of scarcity.[7] The critical references to and analyses of the mathematical or 'functional' approach by Austrians like Mayer and Mises have sometimes confused the issues involved. Neoclassical economists have often presumed that the Austrians were opposed to their method of analysis because of a lack of proper mathematical training or a failure to appreciate the centrality of a careful formalization of the equilibrium concept for any successful economic reasoning. And as the Austrian economist Ludwig M. Lachmann once observed, 'Unfortunately, they [the Austrians] never were able to show, with the cogency their case required, the incompatibility between the idea of planned action, the very core of Austrian economic thought, and an analytical model which knows no action, but only reaction.'[8]

For the neoclassical theorist, man is the 'chooser' within a set of superimposed 'given' constraints. He is assumed to already have a set of given ends which have been ranked in order of importance, an endowment of given means technologically known to be usable for certain uses and applications, and to be confronted with various terms-of-trade in the form of market prices at which he may trade off the alternatives amongst which he must choose. Given his tastes, means and price constraints, the individual merely calculates what has to be the only rational and optimal 'choice' in his objectively known circumstances. All the individual's decisions are in principle predictable, in fact, preordained, in this 'Logic of Choice', since any choice other than the one dictated by the 'given' conditions would be by definition suboptimal and therefore contrary to the purpose of utility maximization.

For the Austrians, however, this is beginning the analysis one step removed from its causal origin in the mental processes of the individual actors. The Austrians, in other words, ask, from whence come the givens the neoclassical approach takes as its starting point? They argue that the individual creatively imagines a future state (or states) of affairs, conceives of ways in which the objects of the world might be usable as means to attain it (or them), tries to discern causal relationships in the use of those means, and weighs the worth to himself of giving up one goal possibly to achieve some other. Thus 'ends', 'means' and 'trade-offs' arise from and are brought into existence out of the minds of men; they do not exist independently and separately from the human minds that generate them. This is the basis for the Austrian conception of a wider notion of subjectivism than merely an agent's given tastes and preferences. These intentional activities of the mind are a reason why the Austrians often refer to their approach as a 'Logic of Action'.

The uniqueness of Austrian subjectivism, in contrast to the neoclassical subjectivism of given tastes and preferences, therefore, is its intentionalist starting-point. Man is not merely one of the many quantitative variables the simultaneous interactions of which produce a general equilibrium solution. Man, instead, is the focal, the Achimedian, point around which the social world revolves and comes into being. Man is, in the words of the American 'Austrian', Frank A. Fetter, not merely the passive evaluator of goods, but the 'doer of acts'.[9] From Menger through Mises, the Austrians have seen man as the being that gives meaning, order, structure and significance to the world. Ends and means, costs and benefits, 'sooner' or 'later', finished consumer good and factor of production, profit and loss, friend or foe – all are ultimately concepts and relationships that are creations of the human mind. The alpha and omega of social phenomena is the subjective world of acting man. The laws of nature and the physical environment may be the limits within which human endeavours are possible of accomplishment, but it is the human actor's conceptions and perceptions of the desirable, possible and attainable that serve as the divining rod for actions initiated, productions undertaken and social relationships formed.

This also helps to explain why, for the Austrians, human action and the events of the social world seem far more unpredictable and far less deterministic than they appear to many neoclassical economists. Having assumed the 'givenness' of the ends–means structure and the constraints out of which any choice will arise, the logic of that choice and its rationality under the circumstances can all be predictively and deterministically explained. Because the decision maker saw these as the alternative ends from which he would want to or could choose, and that these were the available means and their uses, and given that these were the trade-off options as he saw the possibilities before him, the individual came to - had to come to - the conclusion that 'this'was the only logical thing he could - or would - do under the circumstances.

The Austrians see the logic of choice as emerging out of a forward-looking mental process through which an individual *creates in his mind* the elements and options out of which a future choice might arise. Out of the individual's potential fields of interest, some particular interest (desire, want, 'urge', attraction) comes to be the focus of his attention. He imagines some future moment when this interest would be satisfied, fulfilled or completed if he were to act to bring it about. He pictures in his mind what such a state of satisfaction or fulfilment would look like or require. He then mentally brings himself back nearer the present and imagines ways and means by which he can bring that desired or wanted projected future state of affairs into existence. He may undertake any number of such mental projections into the future, imagining various sets of ends and means that are then competing options vying for accomplishment, and from which he may decide to choose.

He may retrace the mental steps of some previous imagined project to incorporate things he has 'learned' and thought of in fantasizing about other imaged projects, and then reshape this earlier goal and plan of action. He begins to weigh and compare the alternatives, and thinks what each is worth to him - what is the valued benefit of each and what costs in terms of forgone projects and uses of means he might be willing to pay - as the price to bring any one of them to fruition. All of this is occurring in time and takes time. And each represents a purpose and a plan about the actualized outcome of which he cannot be perfectly certain.

Herein lies the inherent unpredictability of choice and decision making in the Logic of Action. The analyst cannot know with predictive certainty what the actor's choice will be, *ex ante*, because the actor does not even know what the alternatives are or how he will evaluate and rank them independent of the temporal 'fantasizing' process out of which a choice may be made. In this sense, our future choices are hidden not only from the social and economic analyst, but from ourselves as well. We can never really know our own choices until we make them. Thus knowledge about our own choices always awaits us in our own future, whether that future is a moment from now or decades away.[10]

This is part of the reason behind the Austrian resistance to and often rejection of the 'mathematical' method in economics. In the neoclassical scheme of things, man is reduced to being one of the 'data' in the form of his given tastes and preferences, the quantitative aspect of which now makes its contribution to the determination of general equilibrium outcomes. As Pareto expressed it, 'The individual can disappear, provided he leaves us this photograph of his tastes.'[11] Man becomes merely one of the dependent variables in a system of interdependent equations for an economic equilibrium. Or, as the Swedish economist Gustav Cassel once visualized it, man is now 'merely fate determined, like wind-blown shavings raised and lowered on the curves of mathematical determination'.[12] There is no place in this conception of man for acting men who know best their own interests, who can evaluate best their own local circumstances, or who can judge how to pursue their own interests and use their local circumstances to the best effect in the face of profit opportunities as they may see them. Man becomes inanimate matter manifested in the form of relative amounts of various combinations of goods 'chosen' when confronted with a 'given' set of prices.

As an extension of this view of man, in general neoclassical economists have been far more receptive to admitting the possibilities for government intervention, regulation and control than have been the Austrians. With man viewed as a passive responder to his given circumstances, and with a misplaced confidence on the part of a growing number of economists that they had the ability to master not only qualitatively but quantitatively the interconnected relationships between all of the factors at work in the economic system, it became in the 20th century an easy step to conclude that men and their 'choices' were capable of manipulation in the name of attaining more 'optimal' outcomes than when men were left on their own in the market. This was an attitude that was increasingly held by economists on both the 'left' and 'right'. The professional economist possessed the theoretical and quantitative tools to remake, or at least modify, the economic terrain, because of the higher plain from which the neoclassical economist claimed to be able to see the workings of the world.

Many Austrians have, instead, adopted as their conceptual starting point

Max Weber's use of the idea of 'purposeful action' as human behaviour to which 'the acting individual attaches a subjective meaning', and 'social action' as an action by an individual in which he 'takes account of the behavior of others and is thereby oriented in its course'.[13] In this Weberian framework, individual and intersubjective meanings that the actors assign to their own conduct and the reciprocal conduct of others define the meaning and context of social actions. Thus an 'exchange' is determined by the meanings the actors see in their mutual conduct, said Weber, and 'Without this "meaning" we are inclined to say that an "exchange" is neither empirically possible nor conceptually imaginable.'[14]

Especially following the writings of Ludwig von Mises, the Austrian economists have argued that a theory of human action should be constructed on the basis of the qualities and characteristics that common-sense reflection suggests are the natural conditions under which the human actor chooses and acts. Thus the Austrians have emphasized imperfect knowledge, decision making under uncertainty, and the possibility of error. Furthermore, as we have seen, they have argued that 'choice' should not be viewed as fully predetermined or predictable from some prior 'data' of the 'given' situation. Instead, choice emerges out of mental processes in which the actor, in a fundamental sense, creates the 'ends' and 'means' and the terms-of-trade in the context of which a choice will be made. Hence the 'givens' of neoclassical theory in which choices are made are, in fact, not given to either actor or analyst prior to the actual choice-making process itself.

The Austrian economists have also assigned crucial importance to understanding the role of the entrepreneur as initiator and coordinator of enterprising activities, and the processes through which multitudes of human plans in the market may or may not be successfully coordinated through the institutions of market competition and the price system. Their emphasis has been less on the final state of any general equilibrium and more on the processes of creation, adjustment and change in temporal sequences of market interaction. A hypothetical equilibrium state has served more as a conceptual reference point to explain the circumstances under which there would no longer be incentives or opportunities for further profitable actions by either demanders or suppliers. The task of market theory, in the view of most Austrians, has been to explain logically and trace the implications and consequences of the process by which market actors discover potential gains-from-trade at particular moments in time and through time, and initiate actions that take advantage of them.

The Austrian emphasis on active intentionality on the part of individual decision makers has led a number of the members of the school to give especial emphasis to the evolution and development of institutions and societal patterns that are the unintended consequences of human action. From the interactions of multitudes of individuals, each pursuing their own particular ends, Austrians such as Menger and Hayek have clarified how a complex social order emerges, forms and sustains itself, without either prior design or directed central plan. Through evolved rules and codes of interpersonal conduct, and customs and patterns of social and market interaction, individuals may retain a wide latitude of personal freedom in their actions, while, at the same time, constantly having incentives for constructing and adjusting their respective plans in ways that tend to be harmonious with and mutually beneficial for many of the other members of society.

Finally, the Austrians have drawn various economic policy conclusions from their theoretical explorations into social and market phenomena. Their fundamental argument is that a complex economic order cannot successfully function for purposes of mutual coordination of multitudes of human plans without the institutions of private property and market competition. Only in a setting in which individuals may own goods and resources and buy and sell them will they have the incentives and opportunities to evaluate and appraise their usefulness for the attainment of competing purposes for which they could be applied. Out of these valuations and appraisements emerge gains-from-trade that manifest themselves in the form of market prices in consummated transactions. And these market prices, expressed in the common denominator of money offered to buy and sell goods and resources, then serve as the device for economic calculation which make possible the efficient use of the scarce means of production and the economizing of dispersed information for the coordinating of those multitudes of individual consumer and producer plans.

The Austrians concluded that both socialism and political intervention within the free competitive market process prevent or impede effective use of people's abilities and knowledge for the greater mutual benefit of all the members of society. Traditional socialism abolishes private property, eliminates private buying and selling of goods and resources, and imposes centrally directed planning on all economic activity. By doing so, socialist central planning does away with all the mechanisms for discovering what the members of the society consider worth buying, how best to produce the goods desired by the consuming public, and how to balance the plans of production with those of consumption for a rational apportioning of men and material among their alternative uses. Political intervention in the market through regulations, controls and prohibitions does not do away with the competitive process in the same radical manner as comprehensive socialist planning, but it prevents the free choices and decisions of individuals from determining what actually gets produced, in what productive manner, at what prices and costs and for whose mutual benefit. If, as the Austrians have argued, more knowledge and information is dispersed among the various members of society than can ever be fully mastered, appreciated and integrated in a single mind or among the best of a handful of minds, then both socialism and political intervention in the market must reduce the effectiveness and efficiency of the way the economic order works and its results.[15]

OUTLINE OF THE BOOK

Chapter 1, on 'How Economics Became the Dismal Science' compares the older 18th and 19th centuries' classical economic tradition with the neoclassical school of the late 19th and 20th centuries. It is argued that, in spite of their many limitations and misconceptions, central to the classical way of thinking was the discovery that economic order was possible without political design. The human actor was seen as the discoverer of gains-from-trade, the initiator of market transactions for mutual benefit, with market competition and the system of prices being the institutional framework through which the activities of all the members of the global community were brought into balance and patterned structure. They were confident in having unearthed the socioeconomic regime that could provide both freedom and prosperity. And the chapter explains how different was the neoclassical approach, with its narrow conception of man reduced to passive responder to given, known constraints.

Chapter 2, on 'The Significance of Austrian Economics in 20th-Century Economic Thought', contrasts the alternative conception of economic theory and method developed by the Austrian economists from Menger and Böhm-Bawerk to Mises and Hayek. The emphasis is on man as active imaginer and creator, who initiates action and brings about the market process. It is shown that the Austrian meaning to and emphasis on time and production, capital and interest, money and unintended consequences follows logically from the school's starting premises concerning man and his circumstances. The significance of unintended consequences is highlighted and the limits of planning and regulation are explained within the Austrian framework.

Chapter 3, on 'A Rational Economist in an Irrational Age: Ludwig von Mises', offers a fairly detailed exposition and analysis of some of the core ideas to be found in Mises' writing. Particular emphasis is given to understanding and appreciating his insistence that the central concepts in economic reasoning are inescapably derived from introspective reflection on the logic of our own actions. The chapter explains the significance of economic calculation in Mises' system and how it forms the foundation for his argument concerning the workings and superiority of the market economy over either socialist planning or various forms of production and price intervention by government.

Chapter 4, 'Economic Calculation under Socialism: Ludwig von Mises and his Predecessors', is an exploration in the history of economic thought, and demonstrates that there was in fact a small handful of economists before World War I who had cogently and insightfully made many of the same criticisms of socialist central planning made famous by Mises and Hayek in the middle decades of the 20th century. It then discusses Mises' criticisms of socialist planning in relation to these earlier criticisms, both in his early writings on socialism in the 1920s and in his more mature restatement of the argument from a more consciously 'subjectivist' perspective in the 1940s.

Chapter 5 on 'Ludwig von Mises and the Gold Standard', discusses the Austrian theory of money and the monetary system. Building on the earlier contributions of Menger on the market-based origin of money, Mises developed a theory of the value of money and its purchasing power that was constructed on strictly methodological individualistic lines. Thus we find in Mises' exposition a microeconomic foundational approach to what in the 20th century became known as macroeconomic change and fluctuations. Mises also questioned any monetary and macroeconomic goal of price level stability, precisely because the very notion of a 'stable' price level was inconsistent with an insight into the 'dynamics' of money's effect on the 'real variables' of the economy. Instead, Mises advocated what he referred to as 'sound money', by which he meant a commodity-based monetary standard, such as the gold standard, and one not open to the discretionary and disruptive influences of government manipulation and control.

Chapter 6, on 'Liberalism and Collectivism in the 20th Century', explains how and why the liberal market order came to be undermined during that century by socialism and interventionism and what its consequences have been on society. World War I, more than any other event, brought about the demise of the liberal social order that prevailed in many parts of the world before 1914. Private property, freedom of trade and commerce, sound, gold-backed money, international freedom of investment and movement of people came to an end. The state grew strong and the individual grew smaller and weaker in comparison. As the chapter suggests, all of the major ills of society can be traced back to the transfer of power and authority away from free, private individuals interacting in the market-place to the halls of government – most especially the undermining of the free and spontaneous institutions of civil society that in the earlier liberal market era served as the means for individual moral responsibility and social activity to solve the problems of poverty and the poor, and for the fostering of a sense of 'social duty' by free men.

Chapter 7, on 'The Political Myths and Economic Realities of the Welfare State', discusses how this shift away from individual, private action to organized state control came about and with what effects. It attempts to explain how the modern welfare state began in late 19th-century Imperial Germany as an attempt by the monarchy and the ruling political groups to pre-empt the rapid growth of the socialist movement, by undermining the appeal of socialism, and how it both created an elitist planning mentality among a wide number of intellectuals and social scientists and bred a politicization of society whose web of privileges and favours through state action is far more intricate and difficult to break than anything under the old mercantilist system of government management and control.

Chapter 8, 'The Free Market and the Interventionist State: the Political Economy of Public Policy', applies the Austrian approach to a critique of three rationales for government intervention in the market economy: the ideal of 'perfect competition', 'social justice' and the 'public interest'. It develops the Austrian position that the perfect competition framework offers a poor basis from which to evaluate the 'efficiency' of market outcomes, as well as arguing that the 'social justice' critique of the market economy fails as both a benchmark and an 'operational' policy tool from which to advocate redistributive changes in society. Finally, the chapter tries to show that a market process approach can show how many supposed social and public goods problems can be solved in the private, competitive arena.

Chapter 9, on 'The Limits of Economic Policy: the Austrian Economists and the German ORDO Liberals', discusses two of the leading market-oriented schools of thought in the 20th century. It seeks to bring out those areas of diagnosis and prescription the two schools shared for understanding the collectivist tragedies of the 20th century. But it also traces where their views on the evolution and impact of historical capitalism diverged and therefore lead them to significantly different conceptions of the role of government in the free society.

Finally, Chapter 10, on 'The Global Economy and Classical Liberalism: Past, Present and Future', offers a political–economic account of the rise and decline of the system of free trade in the 19th and 20th centuries. It discusses the connection between restrictions on international trade and the emergence of the interventionist welfare state, and suggests the policy changes that would be necessary and appropriate for the 21st century to produce a truly integrated, open, peaceful and prosperous global economy.

Together, I hope these chapters offer a clearer conception of the ideas and policy prescriptions of the Austrian School of Economics and show the potential for freedom and prosperity in a political and market order in which men are at liberty to use their knowledge and abilities without unnecessary political restraint and control. The people of the 21st century deserve better than the political and economic ideas and policies the 20th century gave to the world.

NOTES

1. Frank H. Knight, 'Marginal Utility' [1931], reprinted in *The Ethics of Competition* (New York: Harper & Brothers, 1935) p. 160.
2. Francis Y. Edgeworth, 'Professor Böhm-Bawerk on the Ultimate Standard of Value' [1892], reprinted in *Papers Relating to Political Economy*, Vol. III (London: Macmillan, 1925) pp. 59–64.
3. Eugen von Böhm-Bawerk, *Capital and Interest*, Vol. 3 (South Holland, IL: Libertarian Press 1959) pp. 228–9; and Friedrich von Wieser, 'The Nature and Substance of Theoretical Economics' [1911], in Israel M. Kirzner (ed.), *Classics in Austrian Economics*, Vol. I (London: William Pickering, 1994) pp. 285–303.
4. Hans Mayer, 'The Cognitive Value of Functional Theories of Price' [1932], in Israel M. Kirzner (ed.), *Classics of Austrian Economics*, Vol. II (London: William Pickering, 1994) pp. 55–168
5. Ludwig von Mises, 'On the Development of the Subjective Theory of Value' [1931], in *Epistemological Problems of Economics* [1933] (New York: New York University Press, 1981) p. 165. Attention has been drawn to Mises' comment the following year, at a meeting of the *Verein für Sozialpolitik* in Dresden, Germany, in 'The Controversy Over the Theory of Value' [1932], ibid., p. 214, that 'Within modern subjectivist economics it has become customary to distinguish several schools. We usually speak of the Austrian School and the Anglo-American Schools and the School of Lausanne ... these three schools of thought differ only in their mode of expressing the same fundamental idea and ... are divided more by their terminology and by peculiarities of presentation than by the substance of their teachings', to suggest that Mises did not at this time really and fully see the difference between the Austrian and neoclassical approaches. But considering his comment the year before, in 1931, a more reasonable interpretation is that at the meeting of the *Verein* he was emphasizing to an audience made up of some Marxists and a large number of members of the German Historical School that the great divide was between all those who understood the logic of the laws of economics along the 'marginalist' line regardless of the different approaches, and those like the Marxists who still adhered to the Classical labour theory of value or the German Historicists who rejected any universal and theoretical laws of economics.
6. Mises, 'Sociology and History' [1929], ibid., pp. 116–8.
7. Lionel Robbins, *An Essay on the Nature and Significance of Economic Science* [1932] (London: Macmillan, rev. edn, 1935).
8. Ludwig M. Lachmann, 'Methodological Individualism and the Market Economy' [1969], in Walter E. Grinder (ed.), *Capital, Expectations, and the Market Process: Essays on the Theory of the Market Economy* (Kansas City, KS: Sheed Andrews and McMeel, 1977) p. 164, n. 9.
9. Frank A. Fetter, *Economic Principles* (New York: The Century Co., 1915) pp. 171–2.
10. I have attempted to develop some aspects of this intentionalist approach and a complementary Austrian theory of expectations formation in the market process. See Richard M. Ebeling, 'Human Action, Ideal Types, and the Market Process: Alfred Schutz and the Austrian Economists', in Lester Embree (ed.), *Schutzian Social Science* (Norwell, MA: Kluwer Academic Publishers, 1999) pp. 115–34; 'Austrian Subjectivism and Phenomenological Foundations', in Peter J. Boettke and Mario J. Rizzo (eds), *Advances in Austrian Economics*, Vol. 2 (part A) (Greenwich, CT: JAI Press, 1995) pp. 39–53; 'Expectations and Expectations-Formation in Mises' Theory of the Market Process', in Peter J. Boettke and David L. Prychitko (eds), *The Market Process: Essays in Contemporary Austrian Economics* (Brookfield, VT, US/Aldershot, UK: Edward Elgar, 1994) pp. 83–95; 'Cooperation in Anonymity'; 'Toward a Hermeneutical Economics: Expectations, Prices, and the Role of Interpretation in a Theory of the Market Process', in David L. Prychitko (ed.), *Individuals, Institutions, Interpretations: Hermeneutics Applied to Economics* (Brookfield, VT, US/Aldershot, UK: Edward Elgar, 1995) pp. 81–92 & 138–53; and 'What is a Price? Explanation and Understanding', in Don Lavoie (ed.), *Economics and Hermeneutics* (London/New York: Routledge, 1990) pp. 177–94.

11. Vilfredo Pareto, *Manual of Political Economy* [1927] (New York: Augustus M. Kelley 1971) p.120.

12. Quoted in Eric Englund, 'Gustav Cassel's Autobiography', *Quarterly Journal of Economics* (May 1943) p.474.

13. Max Weber, *The Theory of Social and Economic Organization* (New York: Oxford University Press, 1947) p.88.

14. Max Weber, *Critique of Stammler* (New York: Free Press, 1977) p.112.

15. I have discussed some additional aspects of Austrian views on public policy in essays not included in the present volume. I have explained the development and content of Ludwig von Mises' various policy writings in Austria during the years 1918-38, when he was a senior policy analyst for the Vienna Chamber of Commerce; see Richard M. Ebeling, 'The Economist as the Historian of Decline: Ludwig von Mises and Austria Between the Two World Wars', in Richard M. Ebeling (ed.), *Globalization: Will Freedom or World Government Dominate the International Marketplace?* (Hillsdale, MI: Hillsdale College Press, 2002) pp.1-68. I have explained Mises' ideas concerning post-World War II European economic reform and reconstruction in the context of his general system of ideas in Richard M. Ebeling, 'Planning for Freedom: Ludwig von Mises as Political Economist and Policy Analyst', in Richard M. Ebeling (ed.), *Competition or Compulsion? The Market Economy versus the New Social Engineering* (Hillsdale, MI: Hillsdale College Press, 2001) pp.1-85. I have also discussed the Austrian theory of money, monetary policy and the business cycle in the context of the Great Depression and in contrast to Keynesian economics, and in comparison to the ideas of Joseph Schumpeter, in Richard M. Ebeling, 'The Austrian Economists and the Keynesian Revolution: The Great Depression and the Economics of the Short-Run', and 'Two Variations on the Austrian Monetary Theme: Ludwig von Mises and Joseph A. Schumpeter on the Business Cycle', in Richard M. Ebeling (ed.), *Human Action: A 50-Year Tribute* (Hillsdale, MI: Hillsdale College Press, 2000) pp.15-110 and 149-87. For a comparison of the similarities and differences between the Austrian and the Swedish economists on money, monetary policy and the business cycle, see Richard M. Ebeling, 'Money, Economic Fluctuations, Expectations and Period Analysis: The Austrian and Swedish Economists in the Interwar Period', in Willem Keizer, Bert Tieben and Rudy van Zip (eds), *Austrian Economics in Debate* (London/New York: Routledge, 1997) pp.42-74.

1. How economics became the dismal science: the classical economists and 20th-century economics

THE 19th-CENTURY CRITICS OF CLASSICAL ECONOMICS

Economics was first called 'the dismal science' by the 19th-century English essayist and man of letters, Thomas Carlyle. He wanted to capture in a phrase all that he thought was wrong with the ideas of the economists of his own time. Carlyle focused all his literary venom on the proponents of the free market. He first used the phrase in an 1849 essay where he referred to economics as 'the Social Science ... which finds the secret of this Universe in "supply and demand", and reduces the duty of human governors to that of letting men alone ... Not a "gay science," I should say, like some we have heard of; no, a dreary, desolate, and indeed quite abject and distressing one; what we might call by way of eminence, the *dismal science*'. In Carlyle's mind, 19th-century economics was a 'self-cancelling Donothingism'. He deplored 'all this Mammon-Gospel of supply and demand, Competition, Laissez-faire, and Devil-take-the-hindmost, [which] begins to be one of the shabbiest Gospels ever preached, or altogether the shabbiest'.[1]

Carlyle much preferred the world before the classical liberal era in which he was living, an older time of class distinction and political paternalism in which everyone in the society knew his place and everyone was secure in his station in life. The newer world of free enterprise industrialism and free market competition disturbed him. Where was the Archimedean point that gave orientation and certitude to life and one's place in the world? The free market order was, in Carlyle's words, 'anarchy plus the policeman'.[2]

His associate, John Ruskin, was also disturbed by the idea of man as a free, autonomous agent, following his own interests under the guidance of the profit opportunities of the market. 'All this misery,' Ruskin declared, 'has come of the spreading of that thrice accursed, thrice impious doctrine of the modern economists, that "to do the best for yourself, is finally to do the best for others."'[3] Ruskin could not understand how order could come without design. Leaving men to their own individual designs surely could only mean Carlyle's anarchy plus the policeman. Even when that design was the customary, traditional order-of-things, it at least provided structure and continuity to the world – each man knew what was supposed to be important and what he was supposed to sacrifice and turn aside from for a higher social good.

THE 'JOYFUL' SCIENCE OF THE CLASSICAL ECONOMISTS

What people like Carlyle and Ruskin saw as the dismal science, the proponents of a free market economy saw as a liberating and joyful science. In 1836, Henry Fairbrain, a fellow Englishman, looked into the future, and this is how he viewed the triumph of the ideas championed by the free market economists:

> Seeing then that in the natural order of things the triumph of Free Trade principles is now inevitable, magnificent indeed are the prospects that are opening on mankind. Nations will become united in the golden bands of peace; science, liberty, and abundance will reign among the inhabitants of the earth, nations will no longer be seen to descend and decline, human life will become prolonged and refined; years will become centuries in the development of the blessings of existence.[4]

He was joined in this joyful spirit a few years later by the French economist, Frederic Passy, who concluded, 'Some day all barriers will fall; some day mankind, constantly united by continuous transactions, will form just one workshop, one market, and one family ... And this is ... the grandeur, the truth, the nobility, I might almost say the holiness of the free-trade doctrine; by the prosaic but effective pressure of [material] interest it tends to make justice and harmony prevail in the world.'[5]

The economists of the late 18th and early 19th centuries considered theirs to be a joyful science – I am reluctant to use Carlyle's term and call it a 'gay science' because of the subtle changes in the meaning of words in more recent times – because they were sincere in the confidence that they had discovered aspects of the human circumstance that could have revolutionary significance for the human condition, if only learned and appreciated by the members of society. What they saw was the possibility for men to live together in peace, prosperity and freedom. If their rhetoric sometimes was dramatic and exaggerated, it needs to be kept in mind that the world they lived in was the exact opposite of the one they conceived as possible. Wars, great and small, seemed unending; poverty and wretchedness existed everywhere for almost everyone; and governments, to the extent that their coercive power permitted, tried to intrude into and control what seemed to be almost every aspect of life.

What the economists of over two hundred years ago began to discern and explain was the possibility of social order without political design. And, not only was such a politically unregulated order a possibility, but its outcome would be one more conducive to creating the wealth of nations than any attempt by governments to try to plan such prosperity. Indeed, the very basis for the existence of society could now be shown to emerge out of the natural characteristics of men. This was, of course, explained in the opening pages of Adam Smith's *Wealth of Nations*. Through a division of tasks in which men took advantage of their comparative skills, abilities and potentials, the productivity of all would rise, raising the standard of living for the community as a whole. And men discovering these possibilities would also discern that there were profitable gains from trade by exchanging their specialities in the market arena.

In the division of labour and the mutual gains from trade, the early economists saw the essence of society. In the words of Count Destutt de Tracy, in his 1817 *Treatise on Political Economy* (a work considered so important by Thomas Jefferson that he supervised its translation into English from French): 'Society is purely and solely a continual series of exchanges ... And this is the greatest eulogy we can give to it, for exchange is an admirable transaction, in which the two contracting parties always both gain; society is an uninterrupted succession of advantages, unceasingly renewed for all its members.'[6]

And if the social benefits arising from a division of labour within a nation were true, the same principle demonstrated its validity among peoples whom historical accident had placed in different countries. For the early economists, it overthrew the mercantilist notion that the nations of the world were in perpetual conflict with one another. Another nation's prosperity did not mean the impoverishment of one's own. Indeed, the greater the wealth of one's international neighbours, the larger the market for one's own productions through an internationalization of the division of labour. Thus David Hume, in his essay, 'Of the Jealousy of Trade', boldly told his countrymen in 1752, 'I shall therefore venture to acknowledge, that, not only as a man, but as a British subject, I pray for the flourishing commerce of Germany, Spain, Italy, and even France itself.'[7]

War, therefore, was seen by these early economists not only as destructive but as contrary to the long-run economic well-being of all the belligerents because it disrupted the existing or potential bonds of the division of labour from which the prosperity could come that would replace the poverty of mankind. 'War,' declared Frederic Passy, 'is no longer merely a crime; it is an absurdity. It is no longer merely immoral and cruel; it is stupid. It is no longer merely murder on a large scale; it is suicide and voluntary ruin.'[8]

If mankind was to take advantage of the potential improvements that could come from a division of labour, it was necessary also to realize that with division of labour came a division of knowledge. And only those to whom the knowledge belonged would have the full incentive to bring that knowledge to bear in productive ways that could benefit their fellow men through trade. Thus individuals had to have the economic liberty to apply their knowledge to production so that, while motivated by self-interest for personal gain, it could at the same time be utilized for the good of the society. This was a theme emphasized by Adam Smith.[9] But let me quote Jeremy Bentham, from his 'Manual of Political Economy', written in the 1790s:

> The interest which a man takes in the affairs of another, a member of the sovereignty for example in those of a subject, is not likely to be so great as the interest which either takes in his own; still less where that other is a perfect stranger to him ... A first Lord of the Treasury ... or of Trade, or any other member of the Legislature, is not likely in the instance of any one of the many thousands of trades existing in the world, to form relative to the best mode of carrying on that trade a choice so good as that would be formed by a person embarked, or intending to be embarked, on the trade in question: still less in the instance of every one of those trades.[10]

For the early economists, this insight served as a powerful argument for the recognition of and respect for individual freedom. Not only, in their view, was human liberty an end in itself that gave each man the latitude to develop his potential to the fullest as he, the individual, saw fit, but human freedom was also a means to a social good – the means through which the rest of the society could benefit from all he might contribute to the general welfare.

But men would have the incentives to make this contribution only when they were allowed to benefit from their own efforts. Hence there emerged the uncompromising case for the sanctity of private property in the arguments of all the early economists. And their defence of private property began with the right of the individual to his own labour. A man's right to property is not secure, argued John R. McCulloch, one of the great 19th-century popularizers of economic principles, 'when he is prevented from using the powers given him by nature, in any way, not injurious to others, he considers most beneficial for himself. Of all the species of property which a man can possess, the faculties of his mind and the powers of his body are most particularly his own; and these he should be permitted to enjoy, that is, to use or exert, at his discretion'.[11]

Nor can society gain from a man's discretionary use of his own mental and physical labour unless he may also keep the fruits of his effort. 'Nothing, it is plain, would ever tempt any one to engage in a laborious employment,' McCulloch pointed out, adding, 'he would neither domesticate wild animals nor clear and cultivate the ground, if, after months and years of toil, when his flocks had become numerous and his harvests were ripening for the sickle, another were allowed to step in and rob him of the fruits of his industry.' In truth, he concluded, property is 'the foundation on which the other institutions of society rest,' because, 'Where property is not publicly guaranteed men must look at each other as enemies rather than as friends.'[12]

Consequently, McCulloch insisted, 'Let us not, therefore, deceive ourselves by supposing that it is possible for any people to emerge from barbarism, or to become wealthy, prosperous, and civilized, without the security of property. Security is indispensable to the successful exertion of the powers of industry. Where it is wanting, it is idle to expect either riches or civilization.'[13] Furthermore, McCulloch argued, the right to property benefited all in the society: 'The right of property has not made poverty, but it has powerfully contributed to make wealth ... it is mere error and delusion to suppose that the rich have been benefited at the expense of the poor. The right of property gives no advantage to one over another. It deals impartially by all ... The protection afforded to property by all civilized societies, though it has not made all men rich, has done more to increase their wealth than all their other institutions put together.'[14]

But the right to property and a system of voluntary exchange were not merely an avenue for enhancing the material well-being of the society. They also served as methods for civilizing men, if by civilization we at least partly mean courtesy and respect for others, and an allegiance to honesty and the fulfilling of promises. Let me allow Adam Smith to explain how the market economy helps foster such conduct in men:

> When ever commerce is introduced into any country, probity and punctuality always accompany it ... It is ... reducible to self-interest, that general principle which regulates the actions of every man, and which leads men to act in a certain manner from views of advantage ... A dealer is afraid of losing his character, and is scrupulous in observing every engagement. When a person makes perhaps twenty contracts a day, he cannot gain so much by endeavoring to impose on his neighbors as the very appearance of a cheat would make him lose . . . a prudent dealer, who is sensible of his real interest, would choose to lose what he has a right to, than give any ground for suspicion.[15]

When men deal with each other on a daily and regular basis, they soon learn that their own well-being requires of them a sensitivity for those with whom they trade. Losing the confidence or trust of one's trading partners can result in social and economic injury to oneself. The self-interest that guides a man to demonstrate courtesy and thoughtfulness for his customers, under the fear of losing their business to some rival with superior manners or etiquette to his own, tends over time to be internalized as habituated 'proper behaviour' to others in general and in most circumstances. And through this means, the other-orientedness that voluntary exchange requires of every trader, if he is to attain his own ends, fosters the institutionalization of interpersonal conduct that is usually considered essential to a well-mannered society and cultured civilization.[16]

While the 19th-century economists provided people with the insight that peaceful trade is more profitable than war and conflict, while they taught the importance of respect for human freedom and private property, and while they enhanced our appreciation of the way that the principle of voluntary exchange helps inculcate honesty and good manners among men, was there no injustice in the world, was there no exploitation of men by their fellows in society?

Yes, there has been and there is. To understand how some of these early economists and economic liberals analysed these immoralities, it is necessary to turn to another French economist of the early 19th century, Charles Dunoyer. In a series of articles published in *Le Censeur Européen* in 1816 and 1817, Dunoyer distinguished between two groups in society. One of them he called the *'Nation of Industrious Peoples'*, composed of

> farmers, merchants, manufacturers, and scholars, the industrious people of all classes and all nations. In the other, there are the major portions of all the old and new aristocracies of Europe, office holders and professional soldiers, the ambitious do-nothings of all ranks and all nations who demand to be enriched and advanced at the expense of those who labor. The aim of the first is to extirpate from Europe the three scourges of war, despotism, and monopoly, to ensure that men of every nation may freely exercise their labors, and, finally, to establish the forms of government most able to guarantee these advantages at the least cost. The unique object of the second is to exercise power, to exercise it with the greatest possible safety and profit, and, thus, to maintain war, despotism, and monopoly.[17]

In other words, society is composed of one set of people who work and save and who produce and exchange, and another set of people who wish to acquire and consume what others have saved and produced. The latter group acquires the wealth produced by those others through political means - taxation, regulation and government-bestowed privileges that interfere with the natural course of free market forces. And this source of injustice and exploitation is the same in every country. In our own era, those who want 'to be enriched and advanced at the expense of those who labor' are, of course, the welfare statists, the economic interventionists, and the proponents and supporters of every other form of collectivism.

The 19th-century economists, therefore, were suspicious of all attempts to extend governmental control over economic activities. The potential for corruption and political exploitation was presumed to exist always, even in democratic regimes. This was stated forcefully by the French economist, Jean-Baptiste Say, in his *Letters to Mr. Malthus*:

> I know that certain governments, corrupted and corrupting, stand in need of monopolies, and custom duties, to pay for the votes of the honorable majorities which pretend to represent nations: I am not so unreasonable as to expect them to

govern so entirely according to the general interest, as to be able to obtain votes without paying for them; but, at the same time, why should I be astonished that such systems have deplorable consequences?[18]

The 19th-century economists warned of the various indirect and long-run dangers to be expected from state paternalism, even when instituted in the name of concern for one's fellow man. It would be exaggeration to claim that they were unreserved advocates of *laissez-faire* and uncompromising opponents of all forms of state intervention. Scholars of the period have shown that this was most certainly not the case.[19] But they were persuaded that, in general, the burden of proof in arguments over the introduction of any government intervention or regulation fell upon the proponent of such a policy.

An American economist in that era, Thomas Cooper, was admittedly one of the more consistent advocates of an unregulated market economy. His 1826 volume, *Lectures on the Elements of Political Economy*, was one of the widely used and influential textbooks in economics courses in both the United States and in England during the first half of the 19th century. As a result, the following passages capture the general spirit of the age and the ideas that economists wished to convey to young students and the rapidly expanding literate adult population:

The true principles of Political Economy teach us that a system of restrictions and prohibitions on commercial intercourse cuts off the foreign market, diminishes the number of buyers, and the demand for our national produce: hence, the consumer is compelled to accept less for his produce, while he is compelled to pay more to the home monopolist. Hence, the wealth of the nation is wasted; every consumer is abridged of comforts that he might otherwise procure, and his means of purchasing even home-commodities are diminished. They teach us also, that men should be permitted, without interference of government, to produce whatever they find it in their interest to produce; that they should not be prevented from producing some articles, or bribed to produce others. They should be left unmolested to judge of and pursue their own interest; to exchange what they have produced when, where, and with whom and in what manner they find most profitable and convenient; and not be compelled by theoretical statesmen to buy dear and sell cheap; or to give more, or get less, than they might if left to themselves, without government interference or control. That no favored or privileged class should be fattened by monopolies or protections to which the rest of the community is forced to contribute. Such are the leading maxims by which Political Economy teaches how to obtain the greatest sum of useful commodities at the least expense of labor. These are indeed the maxims directly opposed to the common practice of governments, who think they can never govern too much; and who are the willing dupes of artful and interested men, who seek to prey upon the vitals of the community ... Make a man a statesman or a legislator, whom experience and reflection has not yet made a cautious man and diffident of himself, he takes for granted that he is not only invested with the office, but intuitively also with the knowledge necessary to conduct it ... He is apt to interfere in concerns wherein he has no knowledge or experience, from an irresistible inclination to exercise all hazards the power conferred on him ... In fact, a legislator might as well direct the analysis of the chemist, or the manipulations of the pin maker, as the pursuits of the planter, the manufacturer, or the merchant. From the time of Colbert to the present, every fact has tended to establish the reasonableness of the request. *Laissez-nous faire*; let us manage our own business.[20]

For the classical economists of the 19th century it was the market economy that was the liberating force of society – the market with its principles of human freedom, private property and voluntary exchange. These principles were not limited to any one nation or one people. Their validity, importance and value applied to all men in all places. Eventually, they hoped to see these principles applied everywhere and, when they were, the world would be one community of free and prosperous men. For them, this is what made economics the antithesis of a 'dismal science'.

In praising the classical economists of the 19th century, we should not discount their errors and limitations. For the classical economists, from Adam Smith through David Ricardo to John Stuart Mill, the assumption was that the quantities of labour devoted to the production of goods determined the relative values of those goods in the market. The common denominator behind all economic goods desired by consumers on the market, they believed, was the necessity for the application of various amounts of labour for their production. The value possessed by goods was, therefore, inherent in them and reflected the relative amounts of labour devoted to their material creation. It is true that some classical economists attempted to modify the theory in various ways during the 19th century when faced with various contradictions and anomalies. But it is nonetheless the case that their 'labour theory of value' generated one logical end in Karl Marx's view that, since labour was the source of all economic value, if the worker did not receive an 'appropriate' wage – reflecting the 'full value' of what his labour had produced – this was proof that he was being 'exploited' by the employer who kept for himself a part of what belonged to another.

It took the Austrian economists of the late 19th century to demonstrate successfully the fallacy in the 'labour theory of value' and its Marxian offspring.[21] For more than a hundred years now, economists in general have understood that value is not something inherent in goods; rather, value is something imputed or assigned to desired objects by a human evaluator who sees in an object useful qualities to serve his personal goals or ends. Value, like beauty, is in the eyes of the beholder and is not something inherent in the thing itself.

Secondly, some of the classical economists created a caricature called 'Economic Man', who was viewed as narrowly self-interested, guided only by a desire to maximize monetary profits and unconcerned with 'non-economic' ends.[22] It was not until the early decades of the 20th century that economists came to see that the unifying and universal concept behind all human action was the necessity to choose among alternative ends desired when the means at man's disposal were limited or scarce in relation to the purposes for which they could be applied.[23]

But in spite of these shortcomings – and their seriousness cannot and should not be discounted – the classical economists tried to develop, and to a great extent succeeded in developing, a theory of market phenomena that was highly realistic and insightful. They viewed economic science as a tool for comprehending how the world actually worked. And, with their theory of market phenomena, they proposed economic policies they believed could assist in eliminating poverty, foster opportunities for individual and social improvement, and create a political environment in which men could be free – free to be independent, choosing human actors and free to use their knowledge and abilities in ways that also would serve the common interests of mankind. The way they, in general, wrote, thought and argued demonstrates this beyond any doubt. A student picking up one of their treatises or textbooks would be challenged to think in a serious and disciplined fashion; but their economics, no matter how abstract or demanding, almost always had a commonsensical and relevant tone to it. The classical economists' self-assigned task was to understand and explain the way the world worked, and a student could feel confident that he would have gained such an understanding when he had successfully completed his course of studies.

THE 'DISMAL SCIENCE' OF 20th CENTURY 'MAINSTREAM' ECONOMICS

In our own day, economics and economics textbooks have a different 'feel' than they did in the 19th and early 20th centuries. For one thing, today's economics textbooks confront the student with a dizzying array of diagrams and mathematical notations that intimidates many of them from the moment they begin the first chapter. It is worth recalling that this is a relatively new phenomenon. Until about 75 years ago, geometry was hardly ever found in books on economics and mathematical notations and equations were practically non-existent. As late as 1932, a professor of political economy at Johns Hopkins University, a Dr Broadus Mitchell, could make the following lament in his own economics textbook, when he came to the discussion of supply and demand:

> I hate graphs, anyhow. They are the only pictures economics books have in them, and they are mighty poor substitutes for comic strips. And the letters and symbols with which they are generally encumbered get me all mixed up. You see things like this: 'Drawing a straight line from the point k on the vertical axis OY, to the point

of intersection P, and dropping a line from P to the horizontal axis OX, we clearly perceive that the quantity demanded, etc., etc.' I clearly perceive nothing except that the author has failed to realize that I have something better to do than to look up his old big letters and little letters and big italics and little italics. As though this were not enough, he often uses not only 'the line DD', but 'the line D'D',' and 'D"D".' That last is beyond human endurance.[24]

But there is a more serious side to this mathematization of economics to which a number of prominent economists have drawn our attention over the years. First, there is the German economist, Wilhelm Röpke, who despaired in the 1950s that:

Whereas formerly a good economist was a man who knew how to assess the relation of the actual economic forces and whereas formerly judgment, experience, and a sense of proportion were rated higher than the formal skill in handling certain research techniques introduced illegitimately from the natural sciences into economics – today, glory goes to him who knows how to express more or less hypothetical statements in mathematical symbols and curves.[25]

And, more recently, in the 1980s, Nobel Laureate James Buchanan made the following criticisms:

Economics, as a discipline, became 'scientific' over the quarter century, but I put the word in quotation marks and I deliberately use it pejoratively here. As it is practiced in 1983, economics is a science without ultimate purpose or meaning. It has allowed itself to become captive of the technical tools that it employs without keeping track of just what it is that the tools are to be used for. In a very real sense, the economists of the 1980s are illiterate in basic principles of their own discipline ... Their motivation is not normative; they seem to be ideological eunuchs. Their interest lies in the purely intellectual properties of the models with which they work, and they seem to get their kicks from the discovery of proofs of propositions relevant only to their own fantasy lands ... Our graduate schools are producing highly trained, highly intelligent technicians who are blissfully ignorant of the whole purpose of their alleged discipline. They feel no moral obligation to convey and to transmit to their students any understanding of the social process through which a society of free persons can be organized without overt conflict while at the same time using resources with tolerable efficiency.[26]

James Buchanan's charge is a particularly harsh one. Can it be true? Every quarter, the *Journal of Economic Literature* (a publication of the American Economic Association) contains within its pages the tables of contents of practically every economics journal in the world in which there appear articles in English, along with brief summaries of what are considered the more interesting or important of these hundreds of articles. The following are a few random samples taken from the September 1993 issue of the *JEL*:

'Ants, Rationality, and Recruitment', *Quarterly Journal of Economics* (Feb. 1993): This paper offers explanation of behavior that puzzled entomologists and economists. Ants, faced with two identical food sources, were observed to concentrate more on one of these but, after a period, they would turn their attention to the other. The same phenomenon has been observed in humans choosing between restaurants. After discussing the nature of foraging and recruitment behavior in ants, a simple model of stochastic recruitment is suggested. This explains the 'herding' and 'epidemics' described in the literature on financial markets as corresponding to the equilibrium distribution of a stochastic process rather than to switching between multiple equilibria.

'Non-linearities and Equivalence Scales', *Economic Journal* (March 1993): This paper focuses on the estimation and testing of equivalence scales in the context of a demand system with nonlinear logarithmic expenditure effects in its budget-share equations. The authors show that such nonlinearity enables one to identify the scales of demographic separability restrictions on preferences and to avoid false rejection of the hypothesis that the scales are independent of the base utility level. The empirical analysis is based on micro data drawn from the U.K. Family Expenditure Survey.

'A Pseudo-R^2 Measure for Limited and Qualitative Dependent Variable Models', *Journal of Econometrics* (April 1993): A pseudo-R^2 measure for limited and qualitative dependent variable models is proposed. A consistent estimator for the variance of the disturbance term is also suggested. The pseudo-R^2 measure is shown to have the same asymptotic limit as the conventional R^2. The measure is adapted to the logic model in an empirical example of female car-owning modeling. The pseudo-R^2 is applicable to a wide set of limited and qualitative dependent variable models and offers a valuable tool for model evaluation.

'The Value of Money in an Overlapping Generations Model: A Note', *Journal of Economic Theory* (Feb. 1993): In this paper, a simple overlapping generations model with N perishable commodities, no intrinsic uncertainty, one agent per generation with an intertemporally separable utility function, and one asset – money – is constructed. To this basic model, two extrinsic states of nature (h is equal to 1 or 2) are added at date 2. Sufficient conditions are found to ensure a continuum of rational expectations equilibria exist with the property that money is worthless if h is equal to 1. The result is then extended to money becoming worthless with positive probability for a finite number of dates.

'The Interaction between Time-Nonseparable Preferences and Time Aggregation', *Econometrica* (March 1993): This paper specifies and empirically analyzes a continuous-time, linear-quadratic, representative consumer model with time-nonseparable preferences of several forms. Within this framework, the author shows how time aggregation and time nonseparabilities in preferences over consumption streams can interact. The behavior of both seasonally adjusted and unadjusted consumption data is consistent with time-nonseparable preferences if consumption goods are durable and if individuals develop habits over the flow of services from the good. The data do not support a version of the model that ignores time nonseparabilities in preferences and focuses solely upon time aggregation.

'The Equity Premium and the Risk-Free Rate: Matching the Moments', *Journal of Monetary Economics* (Feb. 1993): The authors investigate the ability of a representative agent with time-separable utility to explain the first and second moments of the risk-free rate and the return to equity. They generalize the standard calibration methodology by accounting for the uncertainty in both the sample moments to be explained and the estimated parameters to which the model is calibrated. The authors find that the first moments of the data can be matched for a wide range of preference parameter values but the model is unable to generate both the first and second moments of returns that are statistically close to those in the sample.

Can there be a more devastating demonstration of the distance modern economics has travelled since its happier days in the 19th century? Is there a more damning proof of how much economics has become a 'dismal science' possessing almost no connection to either the problems of the real world or the actual human beings who populate it, and which economics is supposed to assist us in understanding?[27] Saying this is not meant to be a criticism of either abstract theorizing or even the usefulness of 'unrealistic assumptions' if their use enables us to return to the real world and comprehend it better. For example, among the Austrian economists, Ludwig von Mises is usually considered the one who was most insistent that economics is an *a priori* science that reasons from 'self-evident' abstract axioms from which are derived logical conclusions that are claimed to have validity in explaining aspects of the real world. Yet he once reminded his fellow economists:

A theory of [human] action could conceivably be constructed on the assumption that men lacked the possibility of understanding one another by symbols, or the assumption that men – immortal and eternally young – were indifferent in every respect to the passage of time and therefore did not consider it in their action. The axioms of the theory could conceivably be framed in such universal terms as to embrace these and all other possibilities; it would be conceivable to draw up a formal praxeological system patterned after the science of logic or the science built upon the axioms of, for example, Hilbertian geometry. We forgo these possibilities because conditions that do not correspond to those we encounter in our action interest us only in so far as thinking through their implications in imaginary constructions enables us to further our knowledge under given conditions ... Because we study science for the sake of real life ... and not as a form of mental gymnastics, we generally do not mind forgoing the gratification that could be offered by a perfect, comprehensive system of the axioms of human action, a system so universal that it would comprise all thinkable categories of the conditions of action. Instead, we are satisfied with the less universal system that refers to the conditions given in the world of experience.[28]

How and why did this turn of events happen with economists? In his book, *The Counter-Revolution of Science*, F.A. Hayek gave, in its essentials, the generally correct historical explanation: the successes of the natural sciences in the 18th and 19th centuries in developing a set of analytical and empirical tools for understanding and predicting an increasing variety of physical phenomena – and their impressive application for solving problems in engineering, biology and industry – intimidated and persuaded a growing number of social scientists that, if their fields were to be 'real' and 'true' sciences, they had to adopt and apply these same scientific methods and techniques to their own disciplines.[29] And economists were among those social scientists who came to suffer most of all from an inferiority complex in relation to the natural sciences.[30]

In the last three decades of the 19th century and the first decades of the 20th century, economists, therefore, searched for ways to see their own field in the context of mathematics and the natural sciences. William Stanley Jevons, one of the most highly regarded economists of the late 19th century, argued, for example:

> I do not write for mathematicians, nor as a mathematician, but as an economist wishing to convince other economists their science can only be satisfactorily treated on an explicitly mathematical basis ... I contend that all economic writers must be mathematical so far as they are scientific at all, because they treat of economic quantities, and the relations of such quantities, and all quantities and relations of quantities come within the scope of mathematics ... To me it seems that our science must be mathematical, simply because it deals with quantities. Wherever the things treated are capable of being greater and less, there the laws and relations must be mathematical in nature. The ordinary laws of supply and demand treat entirely of quantities of commodity demanded and supplied, and express the manner in which the quantities vary in connection with the price. In consequence of this fact the laws are mathematical.[31]

The father of what is referred to as a general equilibrium theory in economics, Leon Walras, argued the same at the threshold of the 20th century:

> The whole theory [of economics] is mathematical. Although it may be described in ordinary language, the proof of the theory must be given mathematically ... [T]he twentieth century, which is not far off, will feel the need, even in France, of entrusting the social sciences to men of general culture who are accustomed to thinking both inductively and deductively and who are familiar with reason as well as experience. Then mathematical economics will rank with the mathematical sciences of astronomy and mechanics; and on that day justice will be due to our work.[32]

Francis Edgeworth, in his *Mathematical Psychics* (1881), declared:

> Where there are data which, though not numerical are quantitative – for example, that a quantity is greater or less than another, increases or decreases, is positive or negative, a maximum or a minimum, there mathematical reasoning is possible and may be indispensable ... The conception of Man as a pleasure machine may justify

and facilitate the employment of mechanical terms and Mathematical reasoning in social science ... 'Mécanique Sociale' may one day take her place along with 'Mécanique Céleste', throned each upon the doublesided height of one maximum principle, the supreme pinnacle of moral as of physical science.[33]

In this emerging view of man and his actions reduced to mathematical and quantitative dimensions and methods, the final stage was reached with the conclusion of Vilfredo Pareto. In his *Manual of Political Economy*, he stated that the only function the human being played in the economist's analysis of quantitative relationships was to provide information about his relative desires for goods, after which he could be disposed of: 'The individual can disappear, provided he leaves us this photograph of his tastes.'[34]

This severing of economic analysis from the everyday experience and common sense of human activity – this elimination of the human actor from the centre stage of economic understanding – was even praised as the highest perfection to which economic science could aspire. In a lecture delivered in Japan in 1931, Joseph Schumpeter delighted in pointing out that, with the full mathematization of economic science, 'The severance from every day forms of thought is perfect, and the general reader is made to realize that the thing is beyond his reach.'[35] In Schumpeter's eyes, economics had become a true science now that it was approaching incomprehension by the ordinary, informed and interested reader. How exactly the opposite of the classical economists of the 19th century! In the introductory chapters of their treatises and textbooks, the classical economists always emphasized to their readers that economics was a difficult subject and that the reader would have to accept the intellectual discipline to follow long and often complex chains of reasoning. But they always assured the interested student that at the end he would have mastered the subject, learned valuable lessons about the workings of the economic system, and would then be able to make informed decisions about the various public policy issues of the day.[36]

Economics now began leaving the ordinary student and the interested citizen dismally in the dark; but far worse was the impact that this new approach to economics had on the way economists began to think about the economic order. Economists now came to believe that they had the capacity to control and plan an economic system. In 1937, an economist named Alan Sweezy wrote an article entitled, 'The Economist in the Socialist Economy'. He argued that there, in the midst of the Great Depression, any economist had to feel a deep sense of frustration. The economies of entire nations were out of joint, with massive unemployment and vast amounts of idle resources while the wants of multitudes went unmet. Every economist knew that the problem was that economic relationships between supplies and demands were out of balance, that prices and costs were not in harmony. The economist knew this and he also knew what 'correct' relationships could set everything right again.

He possessed the theoretical knowledge to tell what the relationships should be to bring the economy back into equilibrium; and with the appropriate statistical data he could feed the numbers into the mathematical equations to find just the right solutions. But under a private enterprise economy, the economist possessed no authority to collect the data or implement the changes to restore full employment. Under socialism, however, the economist would have just such authority:

> It thus appears that from a narrow professional point of view the economist can expect to gain heavily from the victory of socialism. He can look forward both to expanded opportunities for developing his science and to an entirely new influence in the formulation of economic policies ... With their present knowledge and analytical equipment, economists and production managers could formulate price-output policies which would be more in the social interest than those adopted by enterprises in the capitalist world. Perhaps even more important is the fact that in cooperation with production managers economists would have hitherto undreamed of opportunity for getting the data and carrying out the experiments necessary to equip them more adequately for their job ... [With] the establishment of socialism ... the economics profession is likely to acquire unprecedented usefulness and prestige.[37]

Nor has this confidence in the quantitative and mathematical method been confined to those on the political left. In his 1964 Presidential Address to the American Economic Association, Chicago School economist, and later Nobel Laureate, George Stigler hailed the new 'golden age' of hyperquantification and the vistas it offered to the economist:

> The age of quantification is now full upon us. We are now armed with a bulging arsenal of techniques of quantitative analysis, and of a power - as compared to untrained common sense - comparable to the displacement of archers by cannon ... It is becoming the basic article of work as well as of faith of the modern economist that at a minimum one must establish orders of magnitude, and preferably one should ascertain the actual shapes of economic functions with tolerable accuracy ... It has been a slow development, contributed to by an early development in some natural sciences but mostly by the demonstrated successes of the [economic] pioneers of the quantitative method ... It is a scientific revolution of the very first magnitude ... I am convinced that economics is finally at the threshold of its golden age - nay, we already have one foot through the door ... This is prophecy, not preaching.[38]

Whether economists admit it or even reflect upon it, the mathematization and quantification of economics has resulted in an increasing tendency to reduce and treat human beings as variables assumed to possess particular functional properties for the purpose of constructing and solving sets of mathematical equations. Man, in other words, is reduced to a mathematical function. Man becomes merely part of the economic 'data' of the economic system. Even more, man is transformed into a 'dependent variable'. In other words, given his assumed preferences for various goods and services and his 'reaction' to changes in such things as relative prices and income, he comes to be viewed as a passive responder to the constraints and 'trade-offs' with which the economist confronts him in his economic models for purposes of prediction and control of market and social outcomes.

Once this view of man becomes imbedded as part of the tacit mental process of the economist – based upon the way he is trained to think about his economic theorizing and comes through habit to do his professional work as an economist – it is a small step to viewing man as something to be manipulated to obtain the outcomes he, the economist, considers to be desirable. He does not directly command human beings to get them to move in the directions he desires; instead, he manipulates the parameters in which they act to get the response he, the economist, considers 'preferred' or more 'optimal'.[39]

THE 'JOYFUL' VERSUS THE 'DISMAL' ECONOMICS

Economists like James Buchanan have made the distinction between end-independent and end-dependent rules.[40] End-independent rules specify the general procedures or guidelines within which actors are permitted to undertake courses of action. As long as the actors 'obey the rules', they are free to construct their own goals, strategies and judgments concerning what ends to pursue and which means seem most useful and efficient to attain their individually chosen purposes. End-dependent rules, on the other hand, specify the particular goals to be pursued and the methods actors are to utilize in their actions because the permitted goals and methods to be applied are designed to ensure that the outcomes produced are the ones the rule makers desire to see attained.

What made the economics of the 19th-century world of the classical economists a 'joyful science' was their view of the human actors as autonomous, creative beings, who knew their own interests and circumstances better than any planner or regulator. They argued, therefore, for end-independent societal 'rules of the game'. Within the general rules of private property, voluntary exchange and unregulated competition, each and every individual was left free to determine his own purposes, devise what he considered the best means to attain them and search out on his own those mutual gains from trade with his fellow men that were evaluated by him as most advantageous. And they argued that the cumulative result from the free actions of this multitude of men would be an outcome – though unplanned and often unimagined – more conducive to the generation of wealth and human satisfaction than if the political authority tried consciously to create it.

What made the economics of the 20th century a new 'dismal science' was the view of men as dependent variables possessing certain quantitative properties within a system of mathematical equations. Their particular qualities and characteristics as variables in the systems of equations are whatever the economist finds useful or 'interesting' to assume for purposes of his analysis. Men are viewed as being interchangeable with ants; it is as permissible to study ant behaviour to draw conclusions about human action as it would be to study men (with whatever behavioural characteristics the economist chose to endow them) for an understanding of the 'choices' made by ants. Most 20th-century economists, therefore, had little hesitation in assuming and often proposing end-dependent societal 'rules of the game'. The economist designs and the human variables respond. He provides the guiding hand and expert knowledge to tell the political authority how to construct policies to overcome presumed market failures and fluctuations in output and employment. And have no fear, in doing so, the economist is happy to assure the rest of us that he has entered his 'golden age' of quantification that will enable him to measure and specify us in a functional form so he will know better how to control us. He has even prophesied it!

For all their often pompous rhetoric and exaggerated moralizing tone, how different were those classical economists of years gone by! They better understood what they did not know and could not know, and they therefore usually possessed fewer pretensions concerning what they as economists could claim to do. Today, for the most part, economics programmes at institutions of higher learning grind out graduating classes of dull economic technocrats, masters of the minutiae of statistical methods and abstract model building, but with little appreciation of the nature of man or the actual workings of the social and economic order.

At the end of his Nobel Lecture in 1974, F.A. Hayek gave the following warning to his fellow economists concerning their tendency towards a 'pretence of knowledge':

> There is a danger in the exuberant feeling of ever growing power which the advance of the physical sciences has engendered and which tempts man to try, 'dizzy with success', to use a characteristic phrase of early communism, to subject not only our natural but also our human environment to the control of a human will. The recognition of the insuperable limits to his knowledge ought to teach the student of society a lesson in humility which should guard him against becoming an accomplice to man's fatal striving to control society – a striving which makes him not only a tyrant over his fellows, but which may well make him a destroyer of a civilization which no brain has designed but which has grown from the free efforts of millions of individuals.[41]

Only a full appreciation of what Hayek wished to convey in this passage can free economics from its present status as a dismal science. It remains to be seen if economists will ever learn.

NOTES

1. These quotations from Carlyle's writings are taken from Fritz Machlup, 'The Dismal Science and the IIIth of Nations', *Eastern Economic Journal* (April 1976), 59–63, where the original source references are given; see also David M. Levy, *How the Dismal Science Got Its Name* (Ann Arbor, MI: University of Michigan Press, 2001) pp. 3–28.
2. Quoted in Charles Gide and Charles Rist, *A History of Economic Doctrines: From the Time of the Physiocrats to the Present Day* (Boston: D.C. Heath and Co., 1927) p. 511.
3. Machlup, op. cit.
4. Quoted in Francis Edwin Hyde, *Mr. Gladstone at the Board of Trade* (London: Cobden-Sanderson, Ltd., 1934) p. 104.
5. Quoted in Edmund Silberner, *The Problem of War in Nineteenth Century Economic Thought* [1947] (New York: Garland Publishing, Inc., 1972) p. 105.
6. Count Destutt de Tracy, 'Treatise on the Will and Its Effects', in *A Treatise on Political Economy* [1817] (New York: Augustus M. Kelley, 1970) p. 6.
7. David Hume, 'Of the Jealousy of Trade', in *Essays: Moral, Political, and Literary* (Indianapolis, IN: Liberty Fund, 1987) p. 331.
8. Silberner, op. cit.
9. Adam Smith, *An Inquiry into the Nature and Causes of the Wealth of Nations* (New York: The Modern Library, 1937) Book III, Chapter II, p. 423.
10. Jeremy Bentham, 'Manual of Political Economy' [1793–5] in *Jeremy Bentham's Economic Writings*, Vol. 1 (London: George Allen & Unwin, 1952) pp. 229–30.
11. J.R. McCulloch, *The Principles of Political Economy*, 5th edn [1864] (New York: Augustus M. Kelley, 1965) p. 29.
12. Ibid., pp. 27–8.
13. Ibid., p. 33.
14. Ibid., p. 35.
15. Quoted in Edwin Cannan, *An Economist's Protest* (New York: Adelphi Co., 1928) p. 425.
16. For a restatement of this Smithian argument in a modern economic form, specifically in game-theoretic terms, see Robert Axelrod, *The Evolution of Cooperation* (New York: Basic Books, 1984).
17. Charles Dunoyer, 'On the System of the Balance of Power in Europe', *Le Censeur Européen*, Vol. I (1819), pp. 93–142, from an unpublished translation.
18. Jean-Baptiste Say, *Letters to Mr. Malthus* [1821] (New York: Augustus M. Kelley, 1967) pp. 9–10.
19. See, for example, Lionel Robbins, *The Theory of Economic Policy in English Classical Political Economy* (London: Macmillan & Co. Ltd, 1952); A.W. Coats (ed.), *The Classical Economists and Economic Policy* (London: Methuen and Co. Ltd, 1971); and D.P. O'Brien, *The Classical Economists* (Oxford: Clarendon Press, 1975), pp. 272–92.
20. Thomas Cooper, *Lectures on the Elements of Political Economy*, 2nd edn [1830] (New York: Augustus M. Kelley, 1971), pp. 27–31.
21. Carl Menger, *Principles of Economics* [1871] (New York: New York University Press, 1985); Eugen von Böhm-Bawerk, 'Unresolved Contradiction in the Marxian Economic System' [1896], in *Shorter Classics of Böhm-Bawerk* (South Holland: Libertarian Press, 1962) pp. 201–301; Böhm-Bawerk, *Capital and Interest*, Vol. I, pp. 241–321 and Vol. II, pp. 121–256 (South Holland: Libertarian Press, 1959); also H.W.B. Joseph, *The Labour Theory of Value in Karl Marx* (London: Oxford University Press, 1923).
22. See, for example, John Stuart Mill, 'On the Definition of Political Economy; and the Method of Investigation Proper to It', *Essays on Some Unsettled Questions of Political Economy*

[1844; 2nd edn, 1874] (New York: Augustus M. Kelly, 1974) pp.120-64; and Walter Bagehot, 'The Postulates of English Political Economy', *Economic Studies* [1879; 2nd edn, 1888] (Clifton: Augustus M. Kelley, 1973) pp.1-27. But for less rigid and more realistic conceptions of man by classical economists, see Nassau W. Senior, 'An Introductory Lecture on Political Economy' [1827] and 'Four Introductory Lectures on Political Economy' [1852], in *Selected Writings on Economics: A Volume of Pamphlets 1827-1852 by Nassau W. Senior* (New York: Augustus M. Kelley, 1966); and John E. Cairnes, *The Character and Logical Method of Political Economy* [1875; 2nd edn, 1888] (New York: Augustus M. Kelley, 1965).

23. Philip Wicksteed, *The Common Sense of Political Economy* [1910] (London: Routledge & Kegan Paul Ltd, 1933); Hans Mayer, 'Untersuchung zu dem Grundgesetz der Wirtschaftlichen Wirtrechnung' ('Investigation into the Fundamental Laws of Economic Calculation'), *Zeitschrift für Volkswirtschaft und Sozialpolitik*, Bd. 2 (1922) pp.1-23; Richard Strigl, *Die ökonomischen Kategorien und die Organisation der Wirtschaft* (*Economic Categories and the Organization of the Economy*) (Jena: Gustav Fischer, 1923); Ludwig von Mises, *Socialism: An Economic and Sociological Analysis* [1922; 2nd edn, 1932] (Indianapolis, IN: Liberty Classics, 1981), pp.99-109; Ludwig von Mises, 'On the Development of the Subjective Theory of Value' [1931] and 'Remarks on the Fundamental Problem of the Subjective Theory of Value' [1928], in *Epistemological Problems of Economics* [1933] (New York: New York University Press, 1981) pp.146-82; and Lionel Robbins, *An Essay on the Nature and Significance of Economic Science* [1932; 2nd edn, 1935] (London: Macmillan, 1972).

24. Broadus Mitchell, *A Preface to Economics* (New York: Henry Holt and Co., 1932) p.96.

25. Wilhelm Röpke, 'The Problem of Economic Order' [1951], in *Two Essays by Wilhelm Röpke* (Lanham, MD: University Press of America, 1987) pp.3-4.

26. James M. Buchanan, 'Political Economy: 1957-1982', in *Liberty, Market, and State: Political Economy in the 1980s* (New York: New York University Press, 1985) pp.14-15.

27. See Geoffrey M. Hodgson, *Evolution and Institutions* (Cheltenham, UK and Northampton, MA, USA: Edward Elgar, 1999) pp.1-9.

28. Ludwig von Mises, *Epistemological Problems of Economics* [1933] (New York: New York University Press, 1981) pp.14-15.

29. F.A. Hayek, *The Counter-Revolution of Science* [1952] (Glencoe: The Free Press, 1955); also Wilhelm Röpke, *Citivas Humana: A Humane Order of Society* [1944] (London: William Hodge & Co. Ltd, 1948) pp.53-6 and 67-72; and Eric Voegelin, 'The Origins of Scientism', *Social Research* (Dec., 1948) 462-94.

30. Fritz Machlup, 'The Inferiority Complex of the Social Sciences' [1956] and 'Are the Social Sciences Really Inferior?' [1961], in *Methodology of Economics and Other Social Sciences* (New York: Academic Press, 1978) pp.333-67.

31. William Stanley Jevons, *The Theory of Political Economy*, 5th edn [1911] (New York: Augustus M. Kelley, 1965) pp.xiii-xiv and xxi and 3-4.

32. Leon Walras, *Elements of Pure Economics* [1900] (New York: Augustus M. Kelley, 1969) pp.43 and 48.

33. Francis Y. Edgeworth, *Mathematical Psychics* [1881] (New York: Augustus M. Kelley, 1967) pp.2, 12 and 15.

34. Vilfredo Pareto, *Manual of Political Economy* [1927] (New York: Augustus M. Kelley, 1971) p.120.

35. Joseph A. Schumpeter, 'The Crisis in Economics – Fifty Years Ago', *Journal of Economic Literature* (Sept., 1982) p.1057.

36. For a rejoinder in the 1930s to the type of argument that Schumpeter made (though not directed specifically at him), see Edwin Cannan, 'The Need for a Simpler Economics', *Economics Journal* (Sept., 1933) pp.367-78.

37. Alan Sweezy, 'The Economist in the Socialist Economy', in *Explorations in Economics: Notes and Essays Contributed in Honor of F.W. Taussig* [1937] (New York: Augustus M. Kelley, 1967) pp.422-33.

38. George J. Stigler, 'The Economist and the State' [1965], in *The Citizen and the State* (Chicago: University of Chicago Press, 1975) pp.55-6.

39. Cf. Chapter 2 in the present volume; also Richard M. Ebeling, 'Austrian Subjectivism and Phenomenological Foundations', in Mario Rizzo and Peter J. Boettke (eds), *Studies in Austrian Economics*, Vol. 2, Pt A (Greenwich, CT: JAI Press, 1995) pp. 39–53.

40. Geoffrey Brennan and James M. Buchanan, *The Reason of Rules* (Cambridge: Cambridge University Press, 1985); see also Norman P. Barry, *The Invisible Hand in Economics and Politics: A Study in the Two Conflicting Explanations of Society: End-States and Processes* (London: Institute of Economic Affairs, 1988).

41. F.A. Hayek, 'The Pretense of Knowledge' [1974], in *New Studies in Philosophy, Politics, Economics, and the History of Ideas* (Chicago: University of Chicago Press, 1978) p. 34.

2. The significance of Austrian economics in 20th-century economic thought

SOCIAL ENGINEERING AND ECONOMIC ENGINEERS

The 20th century was the era of the 'social engineer.' Few beliefs have been as unshakable in our times as the belief that man has it in his power to transform society in any manner that he desires. Political institutions, economic systems, social customs and even the human spirit itself have been conceived as merely so many parts of a child's erector set that can be taken apart and reassembled in any manner seen fit by those who possess the will and the power to do so.

The totalitarian states of the 20th century, of course, offered the most dramatic examples of this mentality. Marxism was imposed on the Russian people as the result of a 'grand vision' which claimed that man's nature was only a product of social and economic forces. Change the property relationships in society, eradicate certain 'undesirable' human types manifesting a 'bourgeois' mode of thought, 're-educate' the masses into a proper 'class consciousness' and a 'new man' and a 'new society' would be born. The human being was just so much 'materialistic' putty to be refashioned by those who had the insight and foresight to know what kind of culture and society the realization of this 'brave new world' required.

National Socialism in Germany merely changed the ingredients in this social chemistry; the formula for preparing the final solution, however, was the same as that in Lenin's and Stalin's Soviet Union. Men were products of their race and the blood in their veins. Eradicate the racial impurities; re-educate the German people into a correct understanding of eugenic 'science'; reorder the social and property relationships so that individual interests were controlled and made subordinate to the supposed needs of the 'Volk', and a master race, a superior breed of men, could be made to master and rule the world.

While neither as extreme nor as ruthless as in the totalitarian states, the economic policies of the Western democracies have not differed in their implicit premises about either the possibility or the desirability of remaking

34

society into some preferred pattern. If income seems unfairly distributed, taxing policies can correct the 'injustices'. If the choices and buying habits of the public are conceived as 'immoral' or misdirected, laws and regulations can be passed to eradicate or modify them. If employers do not pay workers enough to correspond to some abstract view of a 'living wage' or the 'real worth' of a human being, legislation can see to it that no one is to be hired for less than the 'fair' amount. If the industrial structure of the economy appears too 'concentrated' in a handful of firms, regulations can divide the industries up into the 'optimal' size production units; or if the production units appear too small, or located in the 'wrong' place, or managed in an 'inefficient' or undesired manner, laws and regulations can be passed to consolidate them, or relocate them or supervise their organization and decision-making process in the preferred way. If resources appear too scarce, or misused by those who privately own them, wealth can be created from nothing by turning on the printing press and creating newly engraved pieces of paper money, embossed with an official stamp and the face of some honoured person of the past.

In the eyes of the social engineer, the economic order has been viewed as a mechanism, the workings and results of which can be changed, modified and restructured according to practically any desired design. Knowledge of the correct engineering techniques, they believe, enables mastery and control of the 'economic machine' of society.

Many of the 20th century's social engineering fantasies had their origin in socialist delusions. Unwilling to accept the perennial reality of scarcity, and the limits that scarcity imposes on our ability to fulfil all our wants and desires, socialists escaped into a dream world in which everything viewed as bad and undesirable was caused by private property ownership and the supposed exploitation of some men by others. They were willing to accept anything but the reality that it is the scarcity of means in relation to men's ends that places limits and constraints on what is possible at any time. It is so much easier to believe that if only the 'property relationships' of society were to be changed, man could finally have in his grasp the cornucopia of his dreams.[1]

In the 20th century, the belief that social engineering was not only desirable but possible greatly influenced the way many economists have looked at the workings of markets and the processes of production. Their conceptions of the economic order created strong ideas about what is possible: these conceptions have been part of the intellectual glue with which the rationale and the principles of the interventionist and welfare states have been constructed. Some of these economists have served as advisors to the social engineers, offering and explaining methods to manipulate the system to produce the desired results.[2]

Such a claim will arouse bewilderment in some and anger in others. After all, many of the leading proponents of the view of economics with which I shall be contrasting Austrian economics have been uncompromising opponents of social engineering. In the early part of the 20th century, two leading figures in economics, Gustav Cassel of Sweden[3] and Vilfredo Pareto of Italy,[4] were forceful advocates of the market economy. And in later decades the members of the Chicago School of Economics, whose proponents have included such eminent spokesmen for competitive capitalism as Milton Friedman[5] and George Stigler,[6] have forcefully opposed the planning and interventionist mentality. And yet I suggest that, to a certain extent, the conclusions they reach are due to the introduction of elements into their reasoning that are not to be found in the 'economic models' with which they profess to construct a case for the market order.

I am not suggesting that they surreptitiously introduce 'value judgments' into what is otherwise a scientific and 'value-free' argument, and therefore mix up positive statements about 'what is' with normative statements about 'what ought to be'. Rather, I am suggesting that they often introduce implicit assumptions into their analysis that are not part of the economic models they use, or they 'stretch' the meaning of certain parts of the models to incorporate aspects of economic reality that do not fit comfortably in their analytical framework.

THE LOGIC OF CHOICE: MAN AS PASSIVE RESPONDER TO ECONOMIC CONSTRAINTS

The problem that I am describing revolves around the question, 'What is economics?' Since the 1930s, most economists have replied to this question by saying that economics is the science of the Logic of Choice. Individuals have ends that they wish to achieve but find that the means available to attain them are too limited for their complete satisfaction. Trade-offs have to be made; achieving some of the ends desired with the means available requires forgoing the achievement of others. Individuals, therefore, have to choose; they must decide what is more important to them and what, under the circumstances, is less important to them.

Given that scarcity imposes choice, how does the individual decide what he is to do? The standard answer is that the individual compares the alternatives he desires (and the degrees of relative importance these alternatives have for him) with the terms under which they are offered to him on the market. In other words, prices determine the terms under which these alternatives may be obtained; and the individual responds to the prices he finds in the market by buying various amounts of the goods he is interested in, until he has purchased that combination of goods that, under the price trade-off terms, seems to him the most 'optimal', given the limited means at his disposal to purchase them.

Change the relative prices at which these alternatives are offered on the market, and the individual will most likely select a different combination; he will tend to buy greater amounts of the goods that have gone down in price and smaller quantities of those that have gone up in price by comparison. He will *respond* to the trade-off constraints within which he finds himself by economizing in an 'efficient' manner.

The Logic of Choice that the consumer follows has its counterpart in the decision making that occurs on the production side, as well. There are various technological ways of combining physical resources (land, labour, capital) for the production of various commodities. Like the consumer, the business firm faces alternatives and constraints in making production decisions. There are different commodities that can be produced; the choice as to which one to invest in is determined by a comparison of the market prices at which the products could be sold in comparison to the market prices of the resources that would have to be purchased or hired to do the actual producing. What product to produce and with what combination of resources to do the producing, as well as how much to produce, are determined by the production alternatives which offer the largest expected net profit for the firm.

Market prices are the trade-off constraints in terms of which both the consumers and producers make their decisions. They tell market traders the relative scarcities of commodities and resources, and the choice-paths to follow, given consumer preferences and producer profit goals. But if prices are so important for both the efficient use of resources and the maximum satisfaction of people's wants or ends, where do these prices in the market come from? And what ensures that the prices are the 'correct' prices, by which is meant prices that bring about an equilibrium, between the various demands in the economy with their respective supplies?

Generally, prices are assumed to be 'given'; that is, people find prices already present in the market and they react to the price constraints they find in the market. 'Equilibrium prices' are determined by a 'mental experiment'. Economists imagine that individuals are offered commodities at alternative hypothetical prices and they register their willingness to buy various amounts at those prices; individual suppliers are offered alternative prices and they register their willingness to sell alternative amounts. A comparison of the alternative supplies and demands by all the potential traders enables a determination of which price in each market will ensure equilibrium. This is usually followed by another 'mental experiment', a 'general equilibrium' analysis, in which, realizing that each market is interdependent with all the others, a similar type of exercise must be undertaken to ensure that *all* markets are simultaneously in equilibrium; that is, that the equilibrium in one market does not have a 'spill-over' effect that would leave another market out of equilibrium.

Finally, all market activity occurs against a background of legal, political and social institutions. These institutions specify property rights, legal procedures for adjudication of disputes, and the rules under which various forms of market activity are considered legitimate by both law and unwritten custom. These are usually treated in economic analysis as 'given'; that is, as already existing. Or it will be assumed that the institutions are different from what they are, and a comparison is made between the responses and economizing acts of individuals in one set of such institutions with their responses and economizing acts in an alternative set.

In one sense, this summary of the theoretical framework used by most economists is a sweeping generalization. New and interesting work is constantly going on in the economics profession and many of the assumptions and tools of analysis are being modified and revised in various ways all the time.[7] And yet this summary of the way economists in general tend to view the world is not unrealistic. The framework they use, and practically all variations of it, have one particular thing in common: a view of man and the nature of his conduct in the social and economic environment.

In the late 19th century, economists came under the spell of the methods of the natural sciences. The successes of the 'experimental method' in the natural sciences convinced many in the social sciences that the methods that had worked so well in one area of study should be applicable with equal success in other fields as well.[8] Economists began to emphasize the 'quantitative' dimension discernible in market phenomena. It was argued that, after all, every part of the economic landscape had its quantitative aspect: quantities of supply and quantities of demand, ratios of exchange and rates of change, both at a moment in time and over a period of time. Reduction of human activity to its purely quantitative dimensions meant, as well, that in principle all economic relationships could be reduced to and expressed in terms of mathematical functions and interrelationships.

But this also meant that *man was now reduced to a mathematical function*. He became one of the variables of the 'economic system', along with the quantities of inputs and the physical transformation functions with which those resources could be converted into outputs. Man became merely one of the 'data' of the system: his wants and desires became a set of mathematical 'preference orderings'; his judgment concerning the usefulness of commodities for ends he wished to pursue became 'price elasticities of demand'; his evaluations of opportunities from which he could select became amounts of 'alternative product' that could have been produced if he had not employed quantities of resources for the manufacturing of something else.

And, finally, this meant that man himself was now a 'dependent variable'. That is, the human agents in the economic model became *passive responders* to the given constraints and trade-offs with which they were confronted in the 'choice situation'. Their role became one of *reaction* to changed circumstances that were given to them in the model for the purpose of precise 'determinate solutions', which are meant to portray inherently necessary new 'equilibrium states' and changed 'optimal' choice combinations of inputs or outputs.

Such a view of both man and the workings of an economic system clearly leaves unanswered – and indeed unasked – some essential and obvious questions. What is the process through which an ends–means relationship emerges in men's minds, and which makes the realization of scarcity and the necessity of choice an inescapable part of human reality? From where come the trade-offs in terms of which men must select? And how do these trade-offs change over time? How do prices actually arise in the exchange processes of the market? And if the prices are not equilibrium prices, what is the process by which they change, and who changes them? Resources do not spontaneously or automatically come together to make finished products; so who brings them together, decides how they shall be used, creatively imagines new products to produce and devises new cost-saving ways to apply resources over time to supply more and better products? How do the institutions through which and the institutional order within which choices are made come into being and change and evolve over time?

In an economic model in which human actors are conceived as passive elements, who merely respond and react to the changing circumstances given to them, it is easy to start thinking of actual human beings as if they were *only* dependent variables. Concepts influence thought and thoughts often guide our view of reality. As dependent variables, men come to be thought of as objects to be manipulated and controlled in the directions we desire them to move, and to take on the values and characteristics we desire them to possess. It is a view of man that makes social engineering seem not only possible but almost required.

The nature of the social engineering mentality and the dangers that it posed were clearly understood by Adam Smith in the middle of the 18th century. It was expressed in his famous analysis of what he called 'the man of system' in his first book, *The Theory of Moral Sentiments*:

> The man of system ... is apt to be very wise in his own conceit, and is often so enamored with the supposed beauty of his own plan of government, that he cannot suffer the smallest deviation from any part of it. He goes on to establish it completely and in all its parts, without regard to the great interests or to the strong prejudices which may oppose it; he seems to imagine that he can arrange the different members of the great society with as much ease as the hand arranges the different pieces upon a chess-board; he does not consider that the pieces upon the chess-board have no other principle of motion besides that which the hand impresses upon them; but that, in the great chessboard of human society, every

single piece has a principle of motion of its own, altogether different from that which the legislature might choose to impress upon it.[9]

Economists have built up a conception of man that makes him seem nothing more than a chessboard piece that passively waits and who will faithfully respond, as expected, according to his 'preference function', as the social engineer moves him to a new place on the economic chessboard, or confronts him with a new situation of modified constraints and trade-offs to which he is supposedly to react.

THE AUSTRIAN SCHOOL OF ECONOMICS: ITS HISTORY AND SIGNIFICANCE

In the late 19th century there emerged another group of economists who also saw man as a decision maker, a chooser among alternatives in the face of scarcity and trade-offs. Yet the conception of man that slowly developed in their writings, and their approach to understanding the nature and workings of the economic order, were dramatically different from those of the economists who tended to dominate economic thinking in the 20th century.

They became known as the members of the Austrian School of Economics. The Austrian School was begun in 1871 with the publication of a book by Carl Menger entitled *Grundsätze der Volkswirtschaftslehre*.[10] He soon attracted two young economists, Eugen von Böhm-Bawerk[11] and Friedrich von Wieser,[12] who saw the potential in his analysis of man and the market process. In the 1880s, they developed Menger's ideas in books of their own. And they soon attracted such attention among economists that their approach to economic theory became internationally known as the 'Austrian' approach, in recognition of the national origin of these first contributors of what was rapidly becoming a distinct school of thought. By the time of World War I, in 1914, the 'Austrian School' designated a group of economists of many nationalities with a common view of man and the market economy.[13]

In the period between the two world wars, in the 1920s and 1930s, the Austrian School brought forth a new group of members, many of whom rose through this century to international stature. Among them were Ludwig von Mises, Hans Mayer, Friedrich von Hayek, Fritz Machlup, Gottfried Haberler, Oskar Morgenstern, Lionel Robbins, Ewald Schams, Paul Rosenstein-Rodan, Richard Strigl and Leo Schönfeld-Illy. Their contributions during this period covered practically every facet of economic theory and policy.

The Austrian School fell into eclipse in the 1940s and the 1950s as Keynesian economics rose to power and prominence in both the universities and the halls of political power. But in the 1960s, and particularly in the 1970s, there emerged renewed interest in the Austrian approach as both Keynesian theory and policy fell into disrepute. A new generation of Austrian economists began to write and influence the economics profession. Among the most prominent members of this new Austrian School were Israel M. Kirzner[14] and Murry N. Rothbard.[15] They and many others have restated the Austrian perspective and applied it in new and original ways.

The importance of their contributions arises from the fact that their view of man is not of a passive reactor, but rather a purposeful actor and creator. They have attempted to use this starting point to explain the logic of human activity and to trace how markets arise, prices are formed and production decisions are made; how competitive processes in the market bring about changes and adjustments that tend towards a coordination of human plans involving a multitude of demanders and suppliers. And they have tried to explain the process by which market institutions emerge and evolve over time.

The leading figure among the Austrian economists in developing this approach in the 20th century was Ludwig von Mises,[16] and it is primarily in terms of an outline of his formulation of Austrian economics that I will attempt to summarize the Austrian perspective.[17]

THE LOGIC OF ACTION: MAN AS DOER AND CREATOR OF MARKET OPPORTUNITIES

In the Austrian view, man is, above all else, the being who acts. Man has intentionality and he pursues purposes; he applies means to satisfy his ends and he designs plans to succeed in this endeavour. But those ends and means are not given to him. In a real and fundamental sense, man creates them himself. Possessing consciousness, man mentally projects himself into the future and imagines conditions and states of affairs that he would prefer to his actual conditions, or which might prevail if he did not try to influence future events. He attempts to discern causal relationships in the world in which he lives and, thereby, to discover paths of action that, if successful, would enable him to attain his desired ends.[18]

In this process *man himself creates the trade-offs and evaluates their significance to him*. He decides on the ends that may compete for the use of the means that are believed by him to be too scarce for fulfilment of all he would like to attain. He must decide what is worth giving up – the 'price' paid – to gain something else instead. The opportunity costs of his decisions, in other words, are ultimately, and in a fundamental sense, ones of his own making. He makes judgments as to the possibilities of how the means may be used and therefore what goals are in his reach and which are not. And these judgments, evaluations and decisions are the elements within which choices will finally be made.

Looking at man in this way is what the Austrians call the *subjectivist method*, that is, looking at the world from the perspective of the actor. What people view as 'ends' to pursue, 'means' to use for different tasks, the 'costs' and the 'benefits' from different choices which are contemplated, are only meaningful and intelligible when understood from the individual actor's point of view. It is always a human mind considering possibilities that classifies, orders and arranges the physical things of the world into categories of meanings and purposes; it is how the human actors assign meanings to things that determines what they are (in the context of the purposes and plans they have constructed) and which then guides their conduct towards those things in their environment.[19]

Furthermore, the human actor's imaginings about the desirable, and his actions to bring certain desired ends to fruition, always occur in a condition of uncertainty and imperfect knowledge. If choice means selection from among alternatives, this must imply that the chooser believes that his actions can influence the future and thus the future, from his perspective, is not 'pre-ordained'. This also means that, while he undertakes various actions today with the intention of bringing about a desired state of affairs tomorrow, he can never be certain that events and circumstances may not eventually differ to various degrees from his expectations. Thus, matching every action that is undertaken with its hope of a 'profitable' outcome, there is the possibility of disappointment and 'loss'.[20]

All human action, therefore, contains an entrepreneurial element. That is, all human action is *speculative action* focusing on an uncertain future, with the hope and the expectation that the actions planned and initiated will bring forth a profit, from the individual actor's point of view; but there always exists the possibility of a loss.

Exchange arises when individuals perceive possibilities for profit through the trading of various things they possess or could produce. But the potential for trade is made by the actors themselves, it is not given to them. Trade is ultimately a *meeting of minds*. Each individual must first make a trade in his own mind, asking himself what he values more and what he values less and on what terms he might be willing to give up what he has for what he desires more. At least one of them must convey a willingness to trade to the other and inform the other of possibilities that exist between them for mutual gains from trade. At least one must tender an offer or make a bid to initiate the 'haggling' that may ultimately result in an exchange. The terms of exchange – the prices on the market – therefore emerge out of the meeting of human minds, who *create their own opportunities* for improving their respective conditions.[21]

Thus what is often taken as the 'given' data in neoclassical economics – the ordered preferences of the agents, the endowments and characteristics of means, and the prices at which the agents may enter into trade with each other – are what the Austrians attempt to explain: their origin in and emergence from the mental acts of conception and perception of the actors themselves. The most elementary of market phenomena, the Austrians argue, are not things that men are confronted or endowed with by some external source. *Rather, they arise out of the activities of the participants of the market. This is the reason for Austrians, such as Mises, having long argued that realistic theorizing about and understanding of market phenomena cannot be separated from a theory of human action, and why the 'Logic of Choice' must be grounded in the wider context of a 'Logic of Action,' out of which choices emerge.*

THE MARKET PROCESS, ENTREPRENEURSHIP AND THE ROLE OF PRICES

The market is the arena in which the plans of a multitude of human actors converge. Sellers meet buyers, resource owners meet potential employers. The market economy is a complex web of human activity, a vast and diverse social system of division of labour. Men specialize their tasks and trade what they have produced for what others have for sale. It is an arena in which the plans and desires of each individual are interdependent with and dependent upon the actions of all the others who participate in the community of exchange. Each can attain the ends he desires only if he succeeds in anticipating what others in the economy may wish to acquire and the terms at which there might be a sale. A market economy is founded on the idea of voluntary exchange and, thus, each individual's own self-interest requires him to serve his fellow men if he is to obtain from them that which he desires. Each competes in the market-place with others who, in turn, are also attempting to attain their ends through exchange; and each finds his place in the division of labour through a discovery of his comparative advantage, that is, a discovery of his relative productive advantage in comparison to those others.

But at the heart of the market, in the Austrian perspective, is the entrepreneur. Among the comparative advantages in the market is the capacity for vision and discovery, the ability to discern possibilities and conceive of plans to bring those possibilities into existence. It is always a human mind that discovers opportunities and discrepancies between market supplies and demands, from which profits may be captured through a more effective meeting of consumer wishes in society; creates a plan; brings resources together; and imagines ways of using those resources in new and innovative ways that change the economic landscape from what it was before. And it is the competitive process, the active rivalry among entrepreneurs attempting to gain the profits that may exist in the market, which serves as the test of entrepreneurial imaginings in relation to market realities. Those who have seen the future more clearly reap the profits that flow from a successful satisfying of consumer demands; those whose anticipatory judgments lag too far behind reality suffer losses and are finally weeded out of their entrepreneurial role in the division of labour. It is a contest that never ends; new entrepreneurs emerge and others pass away. Each day brings new opportunities and new entrepreneurial imaginings of the possible and the profitable.[22]

If knowledge were perfect, the task of market competition, in the sense of active rivalry among entrepreneurs, would be redundant. If all possibilities and capacities inherent in various resources and production possibilities were already known, if all the existing or possible patterns of consumer preferences for alternative goods were, in fact, 'given' (as much of neoclassical economics often assumes they are for purposes of analysis), then a competitive process would have no purpose.

The crucial importance of market competition, the Austrians have argued, is precisely that we *do not know* all possibilities or where they might lead. If, for example, we knew from the start who ran fastest, and the finishing order of all those who might run a race with him, then a race would not have to be run. With the results of any race that could be run already known, the actual running of any such race(s) would be unnecessary, and indeed a waste of time and resources. We hold the race among the competitors precisely because we do not know who may win or the relative position of the others on the track. Competition – to use Friedrich von Hayek's phrase – serves as a 'discovery procedure' for finding out the relative capacities and capabilities of the runners who wish to try. Nor is our knowledge made perfect by having once held a race. Knowing the success of a runner in one contest does not grant us knowledge about the outcome of the next trial. Each of the runners has his 'good' and 'bad' days; between races the runners train, try out new techniques and improve their practice times; some runners find age catching up with them, while new runners appear and enter the competition; not all races are run on the same track or in the same weather conditions. All these factors, and others, carry the potential for new outcomes.

For similar reasons, competition serves as a 'discovery procedure' in the economic arena. It is through competition that we discover the comparative advantages of all the participants in the social division of labour, that is, where they can best fit in the wide nexus of exchange and the processes of production, and how they should modify their activities and their positions in the division of labour over time in the face of never-ending change.[23]

Within each line of production it is the pressure of rival entrepreneurs that serves as the stimulus for each to try to discover exactly how best they can produce, to find out just how inexpensively (in terms of use of resources) they can market a product, and to discern the avenues and paths of improvement. The production functions and the monetary-cost curves that neoclassical economists tend to treat as 'given' must, in fact, be 'discovered': what are the possibilities and possible ways of combining the factors of production, and how might the known methods be improved upon or radically changed? Each change on the production side, in turn, modifies the supply and price circumstances that others now face in the market, which further challenges each of them to discover even newer possibilities in the changed market conditions.

The creative quality of competition starts to show itself once we see this side and meaning to market activities. Each, in his corner of the market, is put in the position of creatively imagining improvements on all that has gone before so as to keep up with, and if possible to move ahead of, his rivals. Competition is, therefore, a never-ending 'testing' process, an arena of trial and error with each estimating the profitable possibilities, and acting upon their respective judgments, in the context of their individual and particular knowledge of the time, place, circumstances and interpretive evaluations concerning the meanings of and potential in the various market conditions.

But it is not only on the production side that the creative discovery process is at work. It is pervasively present on the demand side as well. Indeed, it is the judgments concerning demand that guide the decisions on what to produce, how to produce, where to produce and when to produce. It is the *expected patterns* of consumption that guide production in various directions. The expectational element in judgments concerning future demand refers to more than just the position and shape of demand curves for various given, or presently marketed, products. It relates also to the creative discovery of possible improvements in the qualities and varieties of the products consumers might desire. The most dramatic of these discoveries concerns the marketing of new products, for here the creative act involves the imagining of things never produced, marketed or sold before. The entrepreneur must project himself into the minds and possible situations of others (possible consumers) and ask himself, 'Would they find this product desirable, what features would be attractive and in what price ranges, to different age groups in different income groups, in, perhaps, different geographical locations?'

Profits are won by those whose expectations and projections of future possibilities come closer to reflecting the actual shape of future market conditions.[24] Losses, on the other hand, are borne by those entrepreneurs whose imaginings of the future fail in various degrees to capture the eventual shape of supply and demand conditions. The competitive process, as a consequence, serves as a weeding-out mechanism. Those entrepreneurs who earn profits have their financial positions enhanced in the market and, thus, acquire the wherewithal to expand their activities; those entrepreneurs who consistently suffer losses see their financial position diminished and, therefore, experience a contraction in their capacity to control and decide on the use and applications of resources. As a consequence, financial capacity to manage and direct the production activities of the economy are always tending to be shifted into the hands of those entrepreneurs who demonstrate the greatest capability for successful anticipation of future market conditions.

It is in the context of appreciating the significance of the entrepreneur that the Austrian theory of market prices can best be understood. In neoclassical economics, as we saw, prices are primarily seen as constraints within which consumers and producers economize, either for utility or for profit maximization. While the Austrians have neither denied nor belittled this conception of the role of prices in the market economy, their focus has been in a different direction, in analysing what prices assist in bringing about a competitive order.

In a social division of labour in which face-to-face knowledge of all the other traders in the market became increasingly impossible (as there occurred a spatial and temporal development of market activities), market prices emerged as the informational coordinator of a multitude of individual plans of people dispersed, first around a local area, then across a nation and, finally, in the 19th and 20th centuries, around the world. How prices perform this coordinating activity was explained with great force by Hayek in his 1945 essay, 'The Use of Knowledge in Society', and it has served as one of the starting points for Austrian analysis of market price phenomena ever since:

> The price system is just one of those formations which man has learned to use (though he is still very far from having learned to make the best use of it) after he had stumbled upon it without understanding it. Through it not only a division of labor but also a coordinated utilization of resources based on an equally divided knowledge has become possible. We must look at the price system as such a mechanism for communicating information if we want to understand its real function.
>
> Assume that somewhere in the world a new opportunity for the use of some raw material, say, tin, has arisen, or that one of the sources of supply of tin has been eliminated. It does not matter for our purpose – and it is significant that it does not matter – which of these two causes has made tin more scarce. All that the users of tin need to know is that some of the tin they used to consume is now more profitably employed elsewhere and that, in consequence, they must economize tin. There is no need for the great majority of them even to know where the more urgent need has arisen, or in favor of what other needs they ought to husband the supply ... The whole acts as one market, not because any of its members survey the whole field, but because their limited individual fields of vision sufficiently overlap . . .
>
> The most significant fact about this system is the economy of knowledge with which it operates, or how little the individual participants need to know in order to be able to take the right action. In abbreviated form, by a kind of symbol, only the most essential information is passed on and passed on only to those concerned. It is

more than a metaphor to describe the price system as a kind of machinery for registering change, or a system of telecommunications which enables individual producers to watch merely the movement of a few pointers, as an engineer might watch the hands of a few dials, in order to adjust their activities to changes of which they may never know more than is reflected in the price movement.[25]

Market prices integrate the actions of a vast number of individuals, without the intercession or command of a central coordinating authority. A fascinating mutual interdependency arises that leaves each and every individual free to use his particular knowledge of his own circumstances, yet enables each to adjust to the changing conditions of the overall market.

Every person's decisions influence the use of resources and commodities and become reflected in price changes for both inputs and goods for final sale. These price changes in the market then become 'new data' for others in the market who now, in turn, modify their decisions in their corners of the market. Their actions, likewise, then affect the market in the form of new changes in supply and demand that are, again, captured in the form of modifications in market prices. There results a mutual feedback as all traders learn about the actions of others through the medium of prices and mutually adjust their activities to be consistent with the decisions of others.

It is this spontaneous order of emerging patterns of coordination through the communication device of prices that Adam Smith was partly groping to express when he spoke of an 'invisible hand' in the market, and which is the heart of the Austrian conception of a dynamic market process and market order. Furthermore, this Austrian manner of thinking about market prices and the process by which they convey information to the various corners of the social system of division of labour also highlights an essential way in which the Austrian theory differs from neoclassical economics. Neoclassical economics tends to think of the market as a set of supply and demand functions with which the economist searches mathematically for a simultaneous solution that is viewed as the defining characteristic of general market equilibrium. *Austrian economics conceives of the market as a coordinating process of sequential change through time in which actors, each guided by their own particular knowledge, expectations and creative judgments, discover information and discern opportunities in a setting of rivalrous competition.*

MONEY PRICES, RELATIVE PRICES AND 'MACROECONOMICS'

All the complexities and intricacies of the market would be impossible if all trade and exchange had to occur through barter. Every exchange ratio between two goods represents a price that must be weighed in making decisions in the market. In barter, every commodity that enters the circle of exchange now possesses as many prices as goods against which it can exchange. Every commodity joining the circle of exchange multiplies the number of prices that any chooser may have to evaluate and compare to make his purchases effectively and apply his efforts for the ends that he chooses to pursue. The problem of calculating the relative values of all the exchange opportunities in the market soon exceeds any reasonable capability of the human mind in a condition of barter.

But the use of a medium of exchange, a commodity that comes to be used as an intermediary between all exchanges, now makes the mentally impossible quite intellectually feasible. With money on one side of every exchange – with commodities and resources traded for money and money traded for commodities and resources – all goods in the market have one price, their money price. Money now can serve as the common denominator through which and on the basis of which the relative values of both finished goods ready for sale and the factors of production, whose use enables the production of all those finished goods, can be compared against one another. The diverse and heterogeneous is convertible to the comparable and homogeneous. Rationality in the use of means to satisfy ends is thus introduced into the market economy.

All economists would tend to agree with this statement of money's 'functions', that is, as a medium of exchange and as a unit of account. The particular Austrian twist to the theory of money in the market economy is the manner in which money and monetary exchange serve as the link that integrates macroeconomics with microeconomics. Indeed, the Austrians have argued that macroeconomics is inseparable from a properly developed microeconomics.[26]

Money relationships in an economy simultaneously reflect the relative price relationships between goods in the market and the general purchasing power of the monetary unit. With money on one side of every exchange in a monetary economy, a comparison of the number of units of money that must be paid for the respective resources and commodities offered on the market provides the means for economic calculation: estimations of the trade-offs between goods in the market, and evaluations concerning the comparative profitability of alternative lines of production. At the same time, the array of exchange ratios between money and those individual goods offered on the market specifies the general value of money.

Furthermore, any change in relative prices among goods potentially modifies the purchasing power of money, and any change in the value of money has its influence on the structure of relative prices prevailing on the market. Every change in the pattern of demand for or supply of goods and services tends to bring with it a change in the relative amounts of money offered or asked for those goods and services on the market, which in turn tends to change the relative prices between those goods and services. But all such changes simultaneously mean a change in the array of exchange ratios between money and the goods traded on the market, since it is through changes in the pattern of money spending for those goods that the relative price changes emerge in that market; thus the value of money against goods is changed as well, and at the same time.

Likewise, any change in either the supply of or demand for money modifies the exchange ratios between money and the goods and services sold on the market, and thus changes the purchasing power of the monetary unit. But any change in the willingness or ability to spend or demand sums of money in the market, that will bring about a change in the value of the monetary unit, can only manifest itself through a change in the demands for or supply of the various goods on the market, which invariably results in a change in the relative prices between those commodities and resources.

Hence, in Austrian monetary theory there logically exists no analytical dichotomy between the 'real' economy (concerning relative supply, demand and price relationships) and the 'monetary' economy (concerning the nominal or absolute value of goods). But this also means that in the Austrian conception of the workings of a money economy there is no place for a separate realm known as 'macroeconomics'.

Monetary economics, in the Austrian framework, traces the consequences that follow from any change in the demand for or supply of money on the value of money – the exchange ratios between money and other marketed commodities. But this also means, at the same time, that monetary economics is an analysis of the impact of changes in the demand for or supply of money on *the structure of relative prices*, modifications of which constitute the process through which any change in *the scale of prices* is brought about on the market.

It is through these changes in the structure of relative prices, an integral element of which is cost–price relationships, that the Austrians discover the origin of those fluctuations in 'total output', 'total employment' and so on that for 70 years has been labelled 'macro' phenomena. These fluctuations, from the Austrian point of view, are the result of misinformation fed into the market price structure, usually by changes in the supply of money.[27]

By deflecting relative prices from the pattern that they otherwise would have taken on if a change in the supply of money had not occurred, entrepreneurial judgments concerning 'real' or 'underlying' market conditions can be distorted. And these monetary-induced changes in relative prices can bring about misallocations of labour and malinvestments of capital that will have to be corrected for when the monetary disturbances are no longer working their influence on the structure of relative prices. This is the basis for the Austrian insistence that inflation and unemployment are not trade-offs between which 'society' can choose. *Rather, in the Austrian framework, inflationary forces, by distorting the structure of relative prices in the very process of changing the general value of money, generate the conditions for future unemployment when the allocational and investment errors caused by monetary forces are discovered, once the monetary expansion is either stopped or slowed down.*

TIME, PRODUCTION AND INTERTEMPORAL EXCHANGE

To speak of a use of means to attain desired ends is to speak of a cause leading to an effect, a 'before' and an 'after', a 'becoming' and a 'became'. Time is inseparable from the very idea of human action. Action implies causality and causality implies the passage of time. Time, therefore, pervades the human condition in two ways. First, means are always used in the present and the ends desired through their use will only come to fruition in the future. Hence a temporal horizon always pervades every human plan. Second, the passage of time has a meaning and a significance for the participants in the market; 'sooner or later' and 'now or in the future' are not matters between which human beings are indifferent. When something can be used, or when it may be available for use, are matters for evaluation and choice and they pervade practically every decision the human actor makes. Hence every choice contains within it the element of a *time preference*.[28]

Resources can be applied in different ways, with different results over different time horizons. Human evaluations and estimates concerning the future determine the uses and over what periods of time economic means will be applied for the attainment of various ends. Individuals must evaluate the importance of that which can be obtained closer to the present in comparison to the significance of that which can only be obtained through a greater investment of time, but which lies further in the future.

Individual evaluations of the importance of time opens up new opportunities for gains from trade. People whose time preferences differ concerning their desire for satisfaction in the present, versus a willingness to wait until later in the future, may discover profitable exchange opportunities. Those who are willing to defer consumption and the uses of resources in the present may find individuals who desire access to a larger quantity of resources in the present and are willing to pay a price in the future for the present use of those resources. An intertemporal price emerges in the market as participants evaluate and 'haggle' over the value of time; *the rate of interest is that intertemporal price*. The rate of interest reflects the time preferences of the market actors concerning the value of resources and commodities in the present in comparison to their value in the future.

But time also pervades the relationship between the employer and those employed in the processes of production. The entrepreneur undertakes production activities 'today' and over a series of 'tomorrows' until that point is reached in the future at which a product is ready for sale to consumers. In purchasing resources and hiring the services of labour over those days leading to that 'future', he forgoes the alternative uses and opportunities for which the means at his disposal might have otherwise been applied in the present. Those he hires, on the other hand, are paid incomes in the present for services rendered; they are given the financial capacity to purchase desired consumer and other goods in the present and over the days leading up to the completion of the product that will only be available for possible sale to some group of consumers at a point in the future. The employees, therefore, are saved the necessity to defer their own consumption or use of resources until that product is ready for sale. The entrepreneur trades income in the present (salaries paid to workers for services rendered during the production process) in exchange for a possible income in the future (a product that labour has assisted in producing which might be saleable for a price that compensates the entrepreneur for the expenditures he has incurred). As a result, if the market was in equilibrium, a positive discrepancy would exist between what the entrepreneur earns from the sale of a product and the monetary outlays he has incurred in hiring labour and resources for its manufacture; and that discrepancy represents the implicit interest return to him for having forgone the use of a portion of his wealth during the period of production, during which he has hired various factors of production.[29]

Nothing in the production process occurs 'automatically' or is guaranteed in terms of its outcome. The use of resources, the time horizons over which they are applied and the purposes for which they are applied – all these decisions and many more are the result of time preference evaluations and entrepreneurial visions of the possible and the profitable. They are caused by those who act in the market-place, they are guided by those actors, they are maintained by those actors and they are changed by those actors.

The intertemporal price – the market rate of interest – that connects those whose time preferences differ and from which an exchange across time emerges, is only the most visible element in the structure of intertemporal relationships that interconnects the intricate processes of production that permeate an economy. An appreciation of this aspect of the social division of labour is a hallmark of the Austrian emphasis on the idea of 'capital' as a structure of intermediary steps leading to the completion of a commodity serviceable for use and consumption.

The division of tasks in the processes of production results in production being divided into 'stages' that requires coordination of complementary actions in and through time. This 'vertical structure of production', that represents the various production steps leading to a finished consumer good, is as dependent on the relative price relationships that connect them as is the 'horizontal structure of production', that reflects the demands for *different* finished products, for the production of which labour and resources may be applied through time. The vertical structure of production, therefore, is linked by a set of intertemporal prices reflecting the (discounted) value of the outputs and the resources devoted to their production at each of the production stages.[30]

The Austrian theory of the business cycle, developed by Ludwig von Mises in the 1920s and Friedrich von Hayek and others in the 1930s, is an application of Austrian monetary theory to a particular problem: how do changes in the money supply, introduced through financial markets (predominantly applied for investment purposes), distort the intertemporal price (the interest rate) with which the present value of investments are evaluated in terms of prospective profitability? Furthermore, how does this distort the structure of relative prices in and between the stages of production? How does this influence the initiation or extension of investments with time horizons different from the ones that would have been undertaken if the money supply had not been changed in the manner it was? By modifying these relative price relationships, the intertemporal coordination that market forces normally tend to keep in proper order is disrupted, generating the phenomena usually labelled as 'macroeconomic instability' – inflation, unemployment, the 'business cycle' – but which the Austrians see as having been introduced by an external force (monetary expansion or contraction via central bank management of the money supply) and which is not inherent in the market economy.[31]

The Austrians, therefore, consider an understanding of the intertemporal relationships that permeate both the loan market and the relative price structure connecting the processes and stages of production to be paramount in economic analysis. These relationships are not only the market links that connect savings and investment decisions, but, when combined with the Austrian theory of the non-neutrality of money, offer a fruitful avenue for comprehending essential characteristics and patterns in the 'business cycle'.

INSTITUTIONS THAT ARE THE RESULT OF HUMAN ACTION, BUT NOT OF HUMAN DESIGN

Among the Austrian Economists, Carl Menger (the founder of the Austrian School) and Friedrich von Hayek (the member of the school who received the

Nobel Prize in economics in 1974) were particularly interested in the issue of the emergence of social institutions that are often essential to the smooth working of social and economic orders, but which are neither designed nor planned into existence.[32]

All of the Austrians have emphasized as an essential methodological premise that *all* social and market phenomena must be explained in terms of individual human action. It is only individuals who think, evaluate, choose and act. Man as an individual is the elementary building block from which all the events in the market-place ultimately arise.[33]

Yet, while all actions are ultimately the product of human purposes set into motion, not all the results of such human action are part of the original intentions of those social and market participants. *Indeed, the Austrian emphasis on the fact that all choice and action is undertaken with imperfect knowledge and under conditions of uncertainty means that outcomes will always contain elements not expected or planned for by the actors themselves. Many of the most basic institutions of the society, the Austrians have argued, are the unintended outcomes of individual action: language and law, social customs and etiquette, cultural rules of conduct and manners all represent such instances.*

The origin of money has been the most dramatic example that the Austrians have used to exemplify the unintended outcomes of human action in the market-place.[34] As men search out opportunities for gains for trade, as they discover potential trading partners from whom they might buy or to whom they might sell, they often find that barriers stand in the way of mutual benefit. The individual with whom one wishes to exchange does not desire the commodity that one has for sale; or the indivisibility of the goods precludes a mutually satisfactory ratio of exchange. Rather than leave the market-place frustrated, a market actor may attempt to find some alternative good that is desired by the other, or that is more easily divisible into mutually acceptable portions. Hence he trades away what he possesses for something he does not desire, because he can use this other thing as a medium of exchange with which he can purchase that which he, in fact, wishes to obtain.

The discovery in the market that some individuals have successfully attained their goals by this indirect, but no less effective, route attracts similar behaviour in others who have felt similar frustrations under barter exchange. Slowly, over time, through repetition and continual success with the use of a particular commodity as a medium of exchange, that commodity may become 'institutionalized' through habit, experience and custom. It comes to be 'taken-for-granted' by a widening circle of transactors as the commodity that everyone readily and always accepts in exchange; it finally becomes the money-good.

But the importance that the Austrians assign to the theory of institutions that are the result of human action, but not of human design, goes beyond an analytically pleasing solution to many of the phenomena of society. It brings to the forefront an essential quality that is characteristic of a market order: its ability to utilize more knowledge than any one mind or group of minds can ever hope to comprehend and successfully integrate for purposes of economic coordination. By following certain rules and by acting in accordance with them, individuals are able to integrate themselves into a vast system of social division of labour for attainment of their particular ends and goals in a manner that is far more productive than if they were self-sufficient or participating in only a small community of fellow human beings.

And, as Hayek has emphasized, many of these rules of conduct and procedure are learned 'tacitly' by being born into and participating in the various realms of social interaction. Language and manners are merely two of the most general and obvious. Being guided by the price signals of the market in one's corner of the market is another. A further one is the method(s) of interpersonal interpretation of market agents that we all use to anticipate and coordinate our plans with the actions of our fellow market participants; it is a method that grows out of the institutionalization of certain roles and activities in the market, that enables people to form more or less correct expectations concerning the 'typical' actions and responses that are likely from various individuals when they are undertaking particular tasks in the market-place.[35]

The Austrians argue that many of the institutions that retrospectively are seen as essential for the existence and coordination of the social and economic order have emerged 'spontaneously' from market and societal interactions. Often it may be impossible to fully appreciate what has occurred and what significance it has for the social and market orders until long after such institutions have come into existence. *Furthermore, it is only through the emergence and existence of such unplanned or 'spontaneous' institutions that a society of great economic and cultural complexity can be maintained, because only such institutions are able to integrate and use more knowledge than any social engineer could ever hope either to master or to apply successfully.*

AUSTRIAN ECONOMICS AND THE LIMITS OF ECONOMIC POLICY

For the Austrians, man is not a dependent variable moving along a preference function, pushed from one quantitative value to another with every shift in the 'given' constraints. He is far more than a passive responder to the social engineer's fine-tuning of the economic system. Man is an actor, a doer, a creator. He is the centre of the system, not an element merely in it, waiting to be manipulated.

But more is involved here than just a moral judgment about the indignities involved in treating human beings as if they were just pieces on the great chessboard of society. How one conceives of man and, therefore, his place and significance in society, can have immense consequences as to whether, to use Adam Smith's words, 'the game of society will go on, easily and happily' or 'miserably'.

The social engineer's conception of man, which unfortunately is reinforced and rationalized by the model of man used by too many economists, easily falls into the trap of what Hayek referred to as 'the pretense of knowledge'.[36] If man is conceived purely (or primarily) as a responder, a reactor to the circumstances given to him, it is a short step to thinking that all economic and technological change, all improvements in the structure and institutions of the system, should, and perhaps must, come from outside the system. The system, given this view of man, would seem to have no self-generating sources of change or improvement. New knowledge, new information all come from the outside and must be provided to the individual choosers.

If the prices for some commodities or resources appear to be 'wrong' in terms of the supply and demand conditions, a change in those prices to correct the imbalances requires some authority to do the changing. If capital formation and investment are considered 'too slow' or 'too fast', the relative prices to which the market agents obediently respond must be modified to ensure the 'optimal' rate of growth. Socialism is merely the most extreme form of this mentality. The social planner comes to believe that he has the capacity to accumulate and interpret all the pertinent information in the market and then successfully plan an entire economy from 'the centre'.

The Austrian critique of socialism focused on the fact that the planner could never know all the relevant information needed to plan a society effectively. If the Austrian emphasis on 'subjectivism' is fully appreciated, the reason that socialism cannot and has not worked is easily understood. Knowledge and information are divided and dispersed among all the individuals of society. Everyone possesses some of the knowledge of society, but no one possesses all or even a large fraction of it. Each market actor imagines goals and designs plans based upon the knowledge he possesses, and the interpretations and meanings he gives to those possibilities. In the market economy, individuals use the price system to communicate information through the process of competitive bidding for commodities and resources, and they are able, through this method, to find out whether their plans and expectations are consistent with actual market conditions.

Socialism prevents all of this. Those who possess the knowledge and have the capacity to use it creatively in various ways are prohibited from doing so.

Not allowed to own private property or the means of production, individuals have no personal avenue through which to express their entrepreneurial judgments about the possibilities of the future. As a consequence, there is no way that they can convey their judgments to others as to the relative values that they are willing to place on the resources of the society as means to achieving their entrepreneurial goals. The planner lacks the very information to make the intelligent decisions that he claims his central planning perspective offers him. Either the market actors, guided by their own purposes and plans, are free to use their own knowledge within the system, or else the 'game of society' goes on 'miserably' as the 'man of system' tries to arrange the pieces on the chessboard of society.[37]

Interventionism and the welfare state are merely less ambitious applications of the same social engineering mentality. Rather than presume to remake society from top to bottom, the interventionists merely wish to alter its features and some of its outcomes. The results are no less disastrous than under socialism; they have just taken on a different form and developed in different ways over time.[38]

The failure of socialism around the world and the increasing disappointment with the results of the interventionist state as well may mean that the era of the social engineer may finally be passing from the social scene. But the social engineer's mentality will always continue to exist for as long as economists and others continue to conceive of man and the market as so much raw material to redesign or modify at the margin.

We need to think of man and his place in society in a better and more realistic manner. We must see man as actor, doer and initiator. We need to think about the market as a dynamic and creative entrepreneurial process. We need to see prices as the ever-changing reflection of shifting market conditions, and we need to appreciate how those prices are used by social actors for acquiring information about exchange and production opportunities. We need to keep in mind our limited and imperfect knowledge that precludes any of us from having the ability to plan or regulate an economy for an outcome superior to that which the market can produce on its own.

It is the Austrian School of Economics that offers just such an alternative approach for understanding and appreciating men, markets and the social order. And that is its lasting significance for 20th-century economic thought.

NOTES

1. For an analysis of the psychology of the socialist and social engineering type, see Ludwig von Mises, *The Anti-Capitalistic Mentality* (Princeton: D. Van Nostrand, 1956); for historical examples of this mentality, see Igor Shafarovich, *The Socialist Phenomenon* (New

York: Harper & Row, 1972); also Gustave Le Bon, *The Psychology of Socialism* [1899] (New Brunswick, NJ: Transactions Books, 1982); and Bertrand de Jouvenel, 'The Attitude of Intellectuals to the Market Economy', *The Owl* (January 1951) 19–27.

2. Cf. Wilhelm Röpke, *Civitas Humana: A Humane Order of Society* [1944] (London: William Hodge & Co. Ltd., 1948) pp. 17–18.

3. Gustav Cassel, *Recent Monopolistic Tendencies in Industry and Trade: Being an Analysis of the Nature and Causes of the Poverty of Nations* (Geneva: League of Nations, 1927); 'From Protectionism Through Planned Economy to Dictatorship' (Richard Cobden Lecture, 1934), reprinted in *Planned Society: Yesterday, Today and Tomorrow*, Findley MacKenzie (ed.) (New York: Prentice-Hall, 1937) pp. 775–98.

4. Vilfredo Pareto, 'Les Systèmes Socialistes' [1902], translated in excerpts in *Vilfredo Pareto, Sociological Writings*, selected by S.E. Finer (Totowa, NJ: Rowman and Littlefield, 1966) pp. 103–5 and 123–42.

5. Milton Friedman, *Capitalism and Freedom* (Chicago: University of Chicago Press, 1962); *Free to Choose* (New York: Harcourt Brace Jovanovich, 1980).

6. George J. Stigler, *The Citizen and the State: Essays in Regulation* (Chicago: University of Chicago Press, 1975); *The Economist as Preacher and Other Essays* (Chicago: University of Chicago Press, 1982); George J. Stigler (ed.), *Chicago Studies in Political Economy* (Chicago: University of Chicago Press, 1988).

7. For example, Louis Makowski and Joseph M. Ostroy, 'Perfect Competition and the Creativity of the Market', *Journal of Economic Literature* (June 2001) 479–535, attempt to revise and restore the usefulness of the perfect competition model by modifying it to incorporate many of the Austrian and related criticisms of the model's assumptions, especially the notion of the economic actor as a passive price taker; another instance is the development of a 'new institutionalism' that emphasizes the role of property rights, transaction costs and contract theory; see Eirik G. Furubotn and Rudolf Richter, *Institutions and Economic Theory: The Contribution of the New Institutional Economics* (Ann Arbor, MI: University of Michigan Press, 2000). And there have been attempts to bring together Austrian views on the nature of the market process and a 'spontaneous order' with the recent developments in what has come to be called 'complexity theory'; see Edgar Peters, *Patterns in the Dark: Understanding Risk and Financial Crisis with Complexity Theory* (New York: John Wiley, 1999) and David Simpson, *Rethinking Economic Behaviour: How the Economy Really Works* (New York: St Martin's Press, 2000).

8. See Friedrich von Hayek, *The Counter-Revolution of Science* [1952] (Indianapolis, IN: Liberty Press, 1979); Ludwig von Mises, 'Natural Science and Social Science' [1942], in Richard M. Ebeling (ed.), *Money, Method and the Market Process, Essays by Ludwig von Mises* (Boston: Kluwer Press, 1990) pp. 5–18; Mises, *Theory and History* (New Haven: Yale University Press, 1957) pp. 240–63.

9. Adam Smith, *The Theory of Moral Sentiments* [1759] (New Rochelle: Arlington House, 1967), pp. 342–3.

10. Carl Menger, *Principles of Economics* [1871] (New York: New York University Press, 1981); *Investigations into the Method of the Social Sciences, with Special Reference to Economics* [1883] (New York: New York University Press, 1985); Ludwig von Mises, 'Carl Menger and the Austrian School of Economics' [1929], in Richard M. Ebeling (ed.), *The Clash of Group Interests and Other Essays by Ludwig von Mises* (New York: Center for Libertarian Studies, 1978) pp. 28–38.

11. Eugen von Böhm-Bawerk, *Capital and Interest*, 3 vols [1884–1889; 1914] (South Holland, IL: Libertarian Press, 1959); *Shorter Classics of Eugen von Böhm-Bawerk* (South Holland, IL: Libertarian Press, 1962). On Böhm-Bawerk, see Richard M. Ebeling, 'Eugen von Böhm-Bawerk: A Sesquicentennial Appreciation', *Ideas on Liberty* (Feb. 2001) 36–41.

12. Friedrich von Wieser, *Natural Value* [1889] (New York: Augustus M. Kelly, 1971); *Social Economics* [1914] (New York: Augustus M. Kelley, 1967).

13. Ludwig von Mises, 'The Historical Setting of the Austrian School of Economics', in Bettina Bien Greaves (ed.), *Austrian Economics: An Anthology* (Irvington-on-Hudson, NY: The Foundation for Economic Education, 1996) pp. 53–76; Lawrence H. White, *Methodology of the Austrian School Economists* (Burlingame, CA: Ludwig von Mises Institute, 1986);

Richard M. Ebeling, 'Austrian Economics – An Annotated Bibliography: The Austrian Economists' and Ludwig M. Lachmann, 'The Significance of the Austrian School of Economics in the History of Ideas', in Richard M. Ebeling (ed.), *Austrian Economics: A Reader* (Hillsdale, MI: Hillsdale College Press, 1991) pp.3–16 and 17–39.

14. Israel M. Kirzner, *The Economic Point of View* [1960] (Kansas City, KS: Sheed Andrews and McMeel, 1976); *Competition and Entrepreneurship* (Chicago: University of Chicago Press, 1973); *Perception, Opportunity and Profit* (Chicago: University of Chicago Press, 1979); *Discovery and the Capitalist Process* (Chicago: University of Chicago Press, 1985); *The Meaning of Market Process* (New York/London: Routledge, 1992); *The Driving Force of the Market: Essays in Austrian Economics* (New York/London: Routledge, 2000); on Kirzner's contributions, see Richard M. Ebeling, 'Israel M. Kirzner and the Austrian Theory of Competition and Entrepreneurship', *Freedom Daily* (August 2001) pp.8–14.

15. Murray N. Rothbard, *Man, Economy and State: A Treatise on Economic Principles*, 2 vols (Princeton: D. Van Nostrand Co. Inc., 1962); *America's Great Depression* (Princeton: D. Van Nostrand Co. Inc., 1963); *Power and Market: Government and the Economy* (Menlo Park, CA: Institute for Humane Studies, 1971); *The Logic of Action*, 2 vols (Lyme, NH and Cheltenham, UK: Edward Elgar, 1997).

16. Among Ludwig von Mises' most important works are *Human Action: A Treatise on Economics* [1949] (New York: Foundation for Economic Education, 4th edn, 1996); *The Theory of Money and Credit* [1912] (Indianapolis, IN: Liberty Classics [1953] 1981); *Socialism: An Economic and Sociological Analysis* [1932] (Indianapolis, IN: Liberty Classics [1951] 1981); *Epistemological Problems of Economics* [1933] (New York: New York University Press (1981); and *The Ultimate Foundations of Economic Science* [1962] (Kansas City, KS: Sheed Andrews and McMeel, 1976).

17. On Mises' life and contributions, see Murray N. Rothbard, *Ludwig von Mises: Scholar, Creator, Hero* (Burlingame, CA: Ludwig von Mises Institute, 1988) and Chapter 3 of the present volume; in addition see Richard M. Ebeling, 'Planning for Freedom: Ludwig von Mises as Political Economist and Policy Analyst', in Richard M. Ebeling (ed.), *Competition or Compulsion: The Market Economy versus the New Social Engineering* (Hillsdale, MI: Hillsdale College Press, 2001) pp.1–85, and Richard M. Ebeling, 'The Economist as the Historian of Decline: Ludwig von Mises and Austria Between the Two World Wars', in Richard M. Ebeling (ed.), *Globalization: Will Freedom or World Government Dominate the International Marketplace?* (Hillsdale, MI: Hillsdale College Press, 2002) pp.1–68. Also see Ludwig von Mises, 'My Contributions To Economic Theory,' *Planning for Freedom*, 4th edn (South Holland, IL: Libertarian Press, 1980) pp.224–33.

18. Mises, *Epistemological Problems of Economics* pp.12–17; *Human Action* pp.11–36.

19. Mises, *Human Action* pp.41–3; Murray N. Rothbard, *Individualism and the Philosophy of the Social Sciences* (San Francisco: Cato Institute, 1979); also Richard M. Ebeling, 'Austrian Subjectivism and Phenomenological Foundations', in Peter J. Boettke and Mario J. Rizzo (eds), *Advances in Austrian Economics*, Vol. 2, Pt A (1995) pp.39–53.

20. Mises, *Human Action*, pp.92–118; *The Ultimate Foundations of Economic Science*, pp.62–72.

21. Cf. R.G. Collingwood, 'Economics as a Philosophical Science', *Ethics* 36 (1926); see also Richard M. Ebeling. 'Human Action, Ideal Types and the Market Process: Alfred Schutz and the Austrian Economists', in Lester Embree (ed.), *Schutzian Social Science* (Netherlands: Kluwer Academic Press, 1999) pp.115–34.

22. Mises, *Human Action*, pp.257–326; Kirzner, *Competition and Entrepreneurship*.

23. Friedrich von Hayek, 'Competition as a Discovery Procedure', in *New Studies in Philosophy, Politics, Economics and the History of Ideas* (Chicago: University of Chicago Press, 1978) pp.179–90; Israel M. Kirzner, *Discovery, Capitalism and Distributive Justice* (New York: Basil Blackwell, 1989) pp.72–96.

24. Mises, 'Profit and Loss', in *Planning for Freedom*, pp.108–50; also Richard M. Ebeling, 'Expectation and Expectations-Formation in Mises's Theory of the Market Process', in Peter J. Boettke and David L. Prychitko (eds), *The Market Process: Essays in Contemporary Austrian Economics* (Aldershot, UK and Brookfield, VT: Edward Elgar Publishing Co., 1994) pp.83–95.

25. Friedrich von Hayek, 'The Use of Knowledge in Society' [1945], in *Individualism and Economic Order* (Chicago: University of Chicago Press, 1948), pp. 85-6.
26. See Pascal Salin, 'Macro-Stabilization Policies and the Market Process', in K. Groenveld, J.A.H. Maks and J. Muysken (eds), *Economic Policy and the Market Process: Austrian and Mainstream Economics* (Amsterdam/New York: North-Holland, 1990) pp. 201-21; David Simpson, *The End of Macro-Economics?* (London: Institute of Economic Affairs, 1994); Steven Horwitz, *Microfoundations and Macroeconomics: An Austrian Perspective* (London/New York: Routledge, 2000).
27. Mises, *Theory of Money and Credit* pp. 146-68; *Human Action* pp. 398-432; 'The Non-Neutrality of Money', in *Money, Method and the Market Process*, pp. 69-77; Hayek, *Prices and Production* [1935] (New York: Augustus M. Kelley, 1967), pp. 1-31; Gerald P. O'Driscoll, Jr, *Economics as a Coordination Problem* (Kansas City, KS: Sheed Andrews and McMeel, 1977) pp. 35-91; Roger W. Garrison, *Time and Money: The Macroeconomics of Capital Structure* (New York/London: Routledge, 2001); Steven Horwitz, *Microfoundations and Macroeconomics: An Austrian Prespective*; and Chapter 5 of the present volume.
28. Mises, *Human Action* pp. 479-90; Frank A. Fetter, *Economic Principles* (New York: The Century Co., 1915), pp. 235-61; Fetter, 'Interest Theories, Old and New' [1914], in Murray N. Rothbard (ed.), *Capital Interest and Rent* (Kansas City, KS: Sheed Andrews and McMeel, 1977) pp. 226-55; Rothbard, *Man, Economy and State*, pp. 313-86.
29. Böhm-Bawerk, *Capital and Interest*, Vol. 1, pp. 263-71.
30. Böhm-Bawerk, *Capital and Interest*, Vol. 2, pp. 79-118; Hayek, *Prices and Production*, pp. 32-68; Richard Strigl, *Capital and Production* [1934] (Auburn, AL: Mises Institute, 2000); Mises, *Human Action*, pp. 490-505; Ludwig M. Lachmann, *Capital and Its Structure* [1956] (Kansas City, KS: Sheed Andrews and McMeel, 1978); Rothbard, *Man, Economy and State*, pp. 273-301; Israel M. Kirzner, 'An Essay on Capital' [1966], in *Essays on Capital and Interest: An Austrian Perspective* (Cheltenham, UK and Brookfield VT: Edward Elgar, 1996) pp. 13-123); Mark Skousen, *The Structure of Production* (New York: New York University Press, 1990); Peter Lewin, *Capital in Disequilibrium: The Role of Capital in a Changing World* (London/New York: Routledge, 1999); and Roger Garrison, *Time and Money: The Macroeconomics of Capital Structure*.
31. Mises, *The Theory of Money and Credit*, pp. 377-404; 'Monetary Stabilization and Cyclical Policy' [1928], in Israel M. Kirzner (ed.), *Classics in Austrian Economics: A Sampling in the History of a Tradition*, Vol. 3 (London: William Pickering, 1994) pp. 33-111; *Human Action*, pp. 538-86; Hayek, *Prices and Production*; *Monetary Theory and the Trade Cycle* [1933] (New York: Augustus M. Kelley, 1966); see also Ludwig von Mises, Friedrich von Hayek, Gottfried Haberler and Murray N. Rothbard in Richard M. Ebeling (ed.), *The Austrian Theory of the Trade Cycle and Other Essays* [1978] (Auburn: Ludwig von Mises Institute, 1983); Roger W. Garrison, 'Intertemporal Coordination and the Invisible Hand: An Austrian Perspective on the Keynesian Vision', in Richard M. Ebeling (ed.), *Austrian Economics: A Reader* pp. 531-50.
32. Carl Menger, *Investigations into the Method of the Social Sciences, with Particular Reference to Economics* [1883], pp. 139-59; the works by Friedrich von Hayek that focus most intensely on this subject are: *The Counter-Revolution of Science*; *The Constitution of Liberty* (Chicago: University of Chicago Press, 1960) pp. 22-130; 'The Results of Human Action, but not of Human Design', in *Studies in Philosophy, Politics and Economics* (Chicago: University of Chicago Press, 1967); *Law, Legislation and Liberty*, vols 1 and 2 (Chicago: University of Chicago Press, 1973, 1976).
33. See Murray N. Rothbard, *Individualism and the Philosophy of the Social Sciences* (San Francisco: Cato Institute, 1979).
34. Menger, *Principles of Economics*, pp. 257-71; 'On the Origin of Money', in Richard M. Ebeling (ed.), *Austrian Economics: A Reader*, pp. 483-504.
35. Friedrich von Hayek, *Order - With or Without design? Selections from F.A. Hayek's Contribution to the Theory and Application of Spontaneous Order*, comp. Naomi Moldofsky (London: The Centre for Research into Communist Economies, 1989); also Antony Flew, *Thinking About Social Thinking: The Philosophy of the Social Sciences* (New York: Basil Blackwell, 1985) pp. 54-80.

36. Friedrich von Hayek, 'The Pretense of Knowledge' [1974] in *New Studies*, pp.23–34; this essay was Hayek's Nobel lecture. See also Hayek, *The Fatal Conceit: The Errors of Socialism* (Chicago: University of Chicago Press, 1989).

37. Mises, *Socialism: An Economic and Sociological Analysis: Bureaucracy* [1944] (Cedar Falls, IA: Center for Futures Education, 1983); *Human Action* pp.689–715; *Collectivist Economic Planning*, Friedrich von Hayek (ed.) (London: George Routledge & Sons, 1935); Hayek, *Individualism and Economic Order* pp.119–208; Trygve J.B. Hoff, *Economic Calculation in the Socialist Society* [1949] (Indianapolis, IN: Liberty Classics, 1981); Murray N. Rothbard, 'Ludwig von Mises and Economic Calculation Under Socialism', in Lawrence S. Moss (ed.), *The Economics of Ludwig von Mises: Toward a Critical Reappraisal* (Kansas City, KS: Sheed Andrews and McMeel, 1976) pp.67–77; Karen Vaughan, 'Economic Calculation Under Socialism: The Austrian Contribution', *Economic Inquiry* (October 1980), pp.535–44; Don Lavoie, *Rivalry and Central Planning: The Socialist Calculation Debate Reconsidered* (New York: Cambridge University Press, 1985); and see Chapter 4 of the present volume.

38. Mises, *Planning for Freedom*, pp.1–35; *Critique of Interventionism* [1929] (New Rochelle, NY: Arlington House, 1977); *Liberalism: A Socio-Economic Exposition* [1927] (Kansas City, KS: Sheed Andrews and McMeel, 1978) pp.75–95; *Human Action* pp.716–79; Rothbard, *Power and Market*; Don Lavoie, 'The Development of the Misesian Theory of Interventionism', in Israel M. Kirzner (ed.), *Method, Process and Austrian Economics* (Lexington, MA: Lexington Books, 1982) pp.169–89; Israel M. Kirzner, 'The Perils of Regulation: A Market-Process Approach', in Richard M. Ebeling (ed.), *Austrian Economics; A Reader* pp.618–54; Alexander H. Shand, *Free Market Morality: The Political Economy of the Austrian School* (New York: Routledge, 1990); Sanford Ikeda, *Dynamics of the Mixed Economy: Toward a Theory of Interventionism* (New York/London: Routledge, 1997), and see Chapter 8 of the present volume.

3. A rational economist in an irrational age: Ludwig von Mises

Every period of history is indelibly stamped with the impression of the dominant ideas of its time. It is for this reason that students of history sometimes claim that the 19th century began in 1815 with the downfall of Napoleon and ended with the advent of the Great War in August 1914. The dominant ideas of this century (ideas that owed their origins to 18th-century ideas about the natural order, the rights of man and representative government) were the ideas of classical liberalism. Moreover, it was owing to these ideas that the 19th century saw the rise of great political and economic reform movements that liberated man from autocracy and mercantilism, and that gave many people in Europe and North America more limited government, more free enterprise, more peace and tranquillity than had ever been known before.

The 20th century, which had its dawn with the opening shots of World War I, really ended in 1991 with the collapse of the Soviet Union. It was dominated by ideas of a radically different sort. It can legitimately be claimed that the 20th century was a counter-revolution against the classical liberalism of the previous century. Wherever we looked, the state grew in power. Constitutionally limited government was perverted into a process of interest group plundering through the mechanisms of seemingly unlimited democracy or totalitarian dictatorships. The free market economy was either strangled in a web of controls and regulations or extinguished under the blows of various forms of socialist central planning. Free trade and international peace were replaced by war, conflict, genocide and mass terror.

The totalitarian variants of the counter-revolution against classical liberalism symbolically came to an end with the collapse of the Soviet Union in 1991. Thus the demise of the most radical and extreme form of collectivism can be said to have marked the intellectual end of the 20th century. Less than a year after the end of World War I, in 1919, Austrian School economist Ludwig von Mises anticipated what these collectivist demons held in store for mankind. In a much neglected, but profoundly insightful, book titled *Nation, State and Economy*, Mises analysed the causes and consequences of World War I. Toward the end of the book, he warned,

With the World War mankind got into a crisis with which nothing that happened before in history can be compared. There were great wars before; flourishing states were annihilated, whole peoples exterminated. All that can in no way be compared with what is now occurring before our eyes. ... War has become more fearful and destructive than ever before because it is now waged with all the means of the highly developed technique that the free economy has created. Bourgeois civilization has built railroads and electric power plants, has invented explosives and airplanes, in order to create wealth. [Statism] has placed the tools of peace in the service of destruction. With modern means it would be easy to wipe out humanity at one blow. In horrible madness Caligula wished that the entire Roman people had *one* head so that he could strike it off. The civilization of the twentieth century has made it possible for the raving madness of the modern [statists] to realize similar bloody dreams. By pressing a button one can expose thousands to destruction.[1]

Mises' audience was the German-speaking people of Central Europe who had suffered great losses of life and wealth during the war and were now facing the burden of the Treaty of Versailles, with its imposition of heavy reparations payments to the victors and its significant transfers of German territory to surrounding countries. He told his German readers that, in facing their future, they had two alternatives. One was to plot revenge, plan for a World War II, and make each individual subservient to the political goals of conquest and domination. If Germany followed this path, Mises said, 'A new war that Germany might wage could easily ... end with the complete annihilation of the German people.' The other path was to renounce war, conquest and collectivism. He reminded them:

The second course that the German people can take is that of completely turning away from imperialism. To strive for reconstruction only through productive labor, to make possible the development of all powers of the individual and of the nation as a whole by full freedom at home – that is the way that leads back to life. ... The Germans ... will better serve their [interests] if they strive for democracy and self-government. ... Never has the German people sunk so low as today. If it is now to rise again, then it can no longer strive to make the whole great at the expense of individuals but rather must strive for a durable foundation of the well being of the whole on the basis of the well being of individuals. It must switch from the collectivistic policy that it has followed so far to an individualistic one.[2]

In the 20th century, Germany and many other countries around the world chose to follow the collectivist path. Whether in the extreme forms of the Nazi and Soviet regimes or the more moderate forms of the interventionist-welfare state, governments have dominated man and society in our times. They have chosen domestic and foreign plunder as avenues to wealth and power. The consequences have been all around us our entire lives: fascist and communist totalitarianism, the Great Depression, World War II, disastrous experiments in socialist planning and control, the growth of the taxing and spending state, the regulated economy and the welfare state.

MISES' LIFE AND CONTRIBUTIONS

From before World War I until his death in 1973, Ludwig von Mises spoke for reason and rationality in a world that was caught in the grip of irrational dreams – dreams of wealth through the destruction of war, freedom through the mechanisms of oppression and terror, human harmony through group conflicts and mass murder, and greater prosperity through confiscation of property and control over people's lives.

In place of these irrationalities, Mises developed what he called a theory of 'human action' and social cooperation through the peaceful relationships of the market economy. He based his theory on the intellectual foundations laid by the economists who had come before him. He placed great emphasis, for example, on the lasting contributions of the classical economists of the 18th and 19th centuries, especially on their discovery of the workings of a 'spontaneous market order', independent of and superior to any system of government design, control or command. He also believed that several of the classical economists had pointed in the right direction toward an understanding of the epistemological and methodological foundations of economic science.[3]

An equally important influence on Mises was the contributions of the Austrian School economists who preceded him, especially those of Carl Menger, Eugen von Böhm-Bawerk, and Friedrich von Wieser. From these men Mises adopted and developed the theories of 'subjective value and marginal utility', the theory of 'production and interest' and the theory of 'costs as opportunities forgone'.[4]

Born in 1881 in Lemberg, Austria-Hungary,[5] Mises studied at the University of Vienna and graduated in 1906 with a doctorate in jurisprudence. He began working for the Austrian Chamber of Commerce and Industry as an economic analyst in 1909, a full-time position he retained until 1934. Beginning in 1913, he taught at the University of Vienna as a *privatdozent* (an unsalaried lecturer), through which he influenced an entire generation of young Austrian economists. He also formed a *privatseminar* (a private seminar) beginning in 1920, which met twice a month from October to June at his Chamber of Commerce office; the members included economists, sociologists, political scientists, philosophers and historians, many of whom became leading figures in their respective disciplines.[6]

In 1926, Mises organized the founding of the Austrian Institute for Business Cycle Research. Friedrich A. Hayek served as the first director,[7] and Oskar

Morgenstern soon joined the staff as a researcher. The Institute rapidly acquired international recognition for its analytical and statistical studies on Austrian and Central European economic trends, often preparing reports for the League of Nations. Until 1934, Mises served as Acting (Executive) Vice-President of the Institute.

Mises also was a prominent participant in the Austrian Economic Society, the German-based Association for Social Policy, the European Free Trade Association and the International Rotary Club. He was frequently invited to deliver lectures before various industrial associations and at universities throughout Central and Western Europe. He also often wrote articles for the Austrian press, analysing the events and trends in economic policy.[8]

In 1934, Mises accepted a position as Professor of International Economic Relations at the Graduate Institute of International Studies in Geneva, Switzerland, a position he held until July 1940, when, as an exile from the hostile environment of Nazi-occupied Europe, he left for the United States.[9] For several years he had difficulty in finding a teaching position at an American university. Finally, in 1945, he was appointed as a visiting professor in the Graduate School of Business Administration at New York University. He retained this 'visiting' status at NYU until he retired at the age of 89 in 1969. At NYU, Mises attracted a new generation of students who helped bring about a revival of the Austrian School of economics in the USA, beginning in the 1960s and 1970s. He died on 10 October 1973, at the age of 92.

What gained Mises an international reputation was a series of brilliant books that not merely broke new ground in various areas of economic theory and policy, but also challenged the collectivist and interventionist biases of his time. The most important among his many writings are *The Theory of Money and Credit* (1912; 2nd edn, 1924); *Socialism, An Economic and Sociological Analysis* (1922; 2nd edn, 1932); *Liberalism* (1927); *Critique of Interventionism* (1929); *Epistemological Problems of Economics* (1933); *Nationalökonomie* (1940); *Bureaucracy* (1944); *Omnipotent Government* (1944); *Human Action: A Treatise on Economics* (1949);[10] *Planning for Freedom* (1952); *The Anti-Capitalistic Mentality* (1956); *Theory and History* (1957); *The Ultimate Foundations of Economic Science* (1962); and *The Historical Setting of the Austrian School of Economics* (1969). There appeared, posthumously, his memoirs written in 1940, *Notes and Recollections* (1978), and most recently another previously unpublished work originally written in 1940, *Interventionism: An Economic Analysis* (1998). Collections of some of his essays have been published under the titles *Money, Method and the Market Process* (1990), *Economic Freedom and Interventionism* (1990) and *Selected Writings of Ludwig von Mises*, Vol. 3: *The Political Economy of International Reform and Reconstruction* (2000) and Vol. 2: *Between the Two World Wars: Monetary Disorder, Interventionism, Socialism and the Great Depression* (2002).

THE RATIONALITY AND LOGIC OF HUMAN ACTION

To fully appreciate a writer and his work, it is important to recall the historical and intellectual context in which he developed and argued his ideas. This is especially true for a fair interpretation of Mises' conception of human action and the premises on which it was based. From the perspective of the modern philosophy of science – with its insistence on never assuming anything, except the tentativeness and uncertainty of human knowledge – some of Mises' phrases seem misplaced or anachronistic. Nowadays, methodologists and philosophers of science wince when they read Mises' statements that our knowledge in economics is *a priori*, or prior to any empirical experience, and has the status of 'apodictic certainty'.[11]

From the 1920s to the 1940s, a strange set of ideas had gained hold of the minds of intellectuals, especially on the European continent. Particularly in the German-speaking world in which Mises lived and worked there had occurred what he referred to as a 'revolt against reason'.[12] The Nazi type of philosophy of man and science rejected the existence of a universal reason to guide man's understanding of the physical world and of man himself. It also assumed that German science and the reasoning upon which it was based were different from Jewish, Hungarian, Czech or Polish science, because German reason was guided by the special racial group characteristics unique to the German people. German logic was different from Jewish, Hungarian, Czech or Polish logic and, therefore, German thought and reality were distinct from Jewish, Hungarian, Czech or Polish thought and reality. Logic, reason and reality were 'in the blood' and stored as the racial heritage of the group to which the individual belonged.[13] Only the *Führer*, the embodiment of the spirit and soul of the racial group, through the power of his will, could envision and guide the destiny of the German people.

Marxism offered merely a different version of the same idea. The consciousness and therefore the reasoning of the individual were defined by the class to which he belonged. The material methods of production determined the property relationships of the society (the 'superstructure' of the society); and the relationships that men had to property ownership defined them as belonging to one class or another. This, in turn, determined the logic appropriate for each individual in the context of the requirements and 'interests' of his class. Only the select few who were part of the leadership of the revolutionary cadre had the capacity to understand what the 'laws of history' required of each individual, as a member of a class, in that irreconcilable conflict between classes that would eventually generate the inevitable triumph of the socialist future to come.

A third strain of thought during these decades was that of 'positivism', which argued that the only reality was that of the physical and quantitatively measurable objects and relationships of the world. This applied to man himself; our understanding of ourselves was to be reduced and confined only to those qualities and characteristics that were open to 'objective' measurement and quantification. Mind was to be thought of purely as matter – which responded, in principle, in determinate ways to external stimuli. Through this 'scientific method', matter and man would be both predictable and open to manipulation for various social engineering purposes.

Mises' own views about the nature of reason and reality were direct responses to these intellectual currents in the Europe of his time. In reply to these alternative conceptions of man and man's place in the world, he argued that reality was the same for all men. The external world and its natural scientific laws and relationships were not different for different racial groups. Regardless of the rhetoric used, German scientists were confronted with the same reality as Jewish, Hungarian, Czech or Polish scientists. They operated on the basis of the same hypotheses, they performed similar experiments, and they worked with the same laws of physics, chemistry and biology. And they reasoned about laws, relationships and hypotheses according to the same logic as that used by scientists of all nationalities.

Mises argued that our experience of interacting with other human beings demonstrates that all men, regardless of their race or class, possess the same logic of thought. They can and do draw the same inferences from the reasoning process. In other words, all men clearly possess a similar logical structure of thought.[14] If this was not the case, it would be impossible for men of the 20th century to read the writings that have been passed down to them from the ancient Greeks, Egyptians and Chinese. They simply could not comprehend what men of an earlier age were saying.[15] Furthermore, it would be both meaningless and a waste of time for men to attempt to persuade, argue with, or reach common conclusions with other human beings. They could not 'reason together'. The fact that men in all times and in all places *do* reason with each other implies that in all human interactions men work from the assumption that others can understand (and then either concur or disagree with) the logic they have employed in order to get others to see their point of view.

Mises noted that, if the National Socialists and the Marxists were correct concerning the existence of different logic among racial groups or classes, there would be no solution to differences in ideas and opinions among men. Racial wars and class conflicts would be the inevitable result, and would threaten the destruction of civilization.[16] He expressed this at a September

1932 meeting of professional economists and social scientists in Dresden, Germany, only four months before Hitler came to power:

> We must take it for granted that the logical structure of thought is immutable throughout the whole course of time and is the same for all races, nations and classes. We know very well that the majority of the German people – and even most educated Germans – do not share this point of view. ... A Marxist ... who condescends to discuss a scientific problem with people who are not comrades of his own class has given up the first and most important principle of his theory. If thought is conditioned by the thinker's social existence, how can he understand me and how can I understand him? If there is a 'bourgeois' logic and a 'proletarian' logic, how can I, the 'bourgeois' come to an understanding of him, the 'proletarian'? Whoever takes the Marxist point of view seriously must advocate a complete division between 'bourgeois' and 'proletarian' science; and the same is true, *mutatis mutandis*, of the view of those who regard thought as determined by the race or the nationality of the thinker. ... In my opinion, the position of dogmatic Marxism is wrong, but that of the Marxist who engages in discussions with representative of what he calls 'bourgeois science' is confused. The consistent Marxist does not seek to refute opponents whom he calls 'bourgeois'. He seeks to destroy them physically and morally.[17]

If we do not assume that there is a common logic and logical way of thinking that all men share, there is no way for men to agree about the nature and properties of the physical world around them. Nor can men have any hope of coming to conclusions concerning the most appropriate means to attain their mutual social ends. Applying our reason to the problems of understanding the natural and social world neither ensures certainty of results nor provides protection from fallibility nor removes the likelihood that other minds in the future will discover things that will supersede the knowledge of the present. Nonetheless, reason remains man's only distinctive tool to comprehend the world and devise ways for improving his existence.[18]

Obviously, other minds and their workings are not open to direct observation and study; the only mind to which we have any such direct access is our own, through self-reflection and introspection. And thus we can never claim conclusive proof that other minds are logically structured exactly like our own. But it is a 'working hypothesis' that has so clearly shown its validity throughout human experience that its certainty cannot reasonably be denied.[19] (Even the 'madman' follows a similar logic in his actions that, if we but place ourselves in his world and assume his points of reference, are understandable and even 'rational'. It does not matter if we disagree with the premises upon which he has drawn certain conclusions – it is enough that he presumes they are true.)[20]

Let us agree, for the moment, that all men's minds do have a common logical structure and that they do understand and can communicate with one another. On what basis can it be assumed that the way their minds work is consistent with an ability to master correctly the workings of the physical laws of the natural world? This is an important question, since comprehension of the world is essential if men are to discover the causalities upon which their survival and improvement are dependent. Mises' answer was delivered in the form of a hypothesis. He suggested that it might well have been the case that, in the long evolution of man, there have been branches of the human family that did not possess logical structures of thought consistent with, and therefore able to successfully adapt to, the laws through which the natural world operates. As a result, these branches died out. Only the branch that developed the logical structures of thought compatible with physical reality prospered. The human race, as we know it from recorded history, is the branch that had developed those ways of thought most compatible with discovering the laws and causal relationships of the natural world.[21]

While man lives and acts in a world of physical objects and causalities, the laws of human action, Mises argued, reside within himself. Action is none other than *reason applied to purpose*. Therefore everything there is to know about the essence and meaning of human action is discoverable through introspective reflection – through that which allows our own minds to tell us what it means 'to act'.[22] This is all that Mises meant when he said that *praxeology* (the name he used for what he called the 'science of human action') begins with a self-evident and *a priori* truth, and that all of the logic of economics is then a deductive spinning out of all the implications from the concept of 'action'. Why is the concept of 'action' an axiom rather than a postulate? Perhaps in this case it is better to answer a question with another question: who cannot look within himself, reflect on the nature of his own conscious conduct and see that all his conscious actions (regardless of their many concrete forms) have a unifying general characteristic, which is the purposeful and intentional pursuit of chosen ends?[23] Mises first clearly expressed his views on this subject in 1933:

> In our view the concept of man is, above all else ... the concept of the being who acts. Our consciousness is that of an ego which is capable of acting and does act. The fact that our deeds are intentional makes them actions. Our thinking about men and their conduct, and our conduct toward men and toward our surroundings, in general, presuppose the category of action.[24]

You are reading these words I have written; you turn the page to read the next passage in which I am trying to explain more of Mises' ideas and arguments; you stop, perhaps, to think about the reasonableness of what I am trying to argue; perhaps you pick up a glass or cup that may be sitting on a table next to the chair in which you are sitting; you notice that it is getting dark, so you reach over and turn on a lamp; you hear the telephone ring, and you put down this book to pick up the receiver; after the call, you decide that there is something else you would rather do than finish reading my essay right now (or ever!). Everything you do in your conscious life is a manifestation of man as an acting being. You cannot deny this self-evident truth, because to deny it would be to deny what you are and what you do every waking moment of your life.

You are the being who acts and, in interacting with others, you assume the same about them. If this is not true, then why do you act towards others – your family, your friends, your associates, or even strangers – in a way that is different from the way that you act towards inanimate objects? Even a madman who talks to his pencil does so because he believes (however erroneously) that the pencil has consciousness, that it can understand what he is saying and will therefore behave differently towards him than those other objects in his imaginary world to which he does not assign such humanlike characteristics.

If it is now asked, what does it mean to act and to be able to act, Mises asserted that three prerequisites must be and always are present:

1. *Causality* The actor must believe that there exist discoverable causal relationships in the world that, if applied in some appropriate way, can bring about a desired effect. In other words, if 'B' is a desired goal or change of circumstance, the actor must believe that there exists a causal factor 'A' that can be brought into play to bring 'B' into existence. If he does not believe in the existence and usability of 'A', then any action to try to bring about 'B' is pointless and impossible.[25]
2. *Uncertainty* The actor must believe that he can influence the course of events in such a way as to change his circumstances from what they are or will be if he does not intervene. From his point of view, the actor must believe that the future can be made different through his action. From his perspective, there is a range of uncertainty about how the future may develop and which he can try to influence.[26]
3. *Temporality* The existence of causality incorporates the concept of time. Every action contains within it distinctions between 'before', 'during' and 'after'. Every action, therefore, occurs through time and in time. And as a result, every action contains within it a conception of a 'period of production' that leads to the desired outcome, regardless of whether that period of time is a matter of a few minutes or many years.[27]

While these three elements – causality, uncertainty and time – are inseparable from the very notion of the 'doing' of action, they remain necessary, but not sufficient, conditions. For an action to be undertaken, that is, for the actor to want and to be able to undertake some action, three other conditions must be present:[28]

1. *Felt uneasiness* The actor must be dissatisfied in some way with existing circumstances, or the circumstances that he believes are likely to develop if he does not act in some manner to change them.
2. *Imagined and preferred state of affairs* The actor must be able to imagine a situation that would be more desirable than the present one, or the one that is likely to arise if he does not try to do something to change it. No matter how unsatisfactory the existing or expected state of affairs may be, if he could not imagine one that would be an improvement, then any action on his part would be to substitute a less preferred state of affairs for a more preferred one.
3. *Beliefs or expectations about the availability of means and methods to bring a preferred state of affairs into existence* The actor must believe that he has or can have access to and disposal over appropriate means to bring his preferred state of affairs into existence when and how he expects he will need to do so. If he does not have such beliefs and expectations, then he will regard action as futile.

From these fundamental concepts of and preconditions to all conscious human action, Mises argued, all the core principles and relationships of economics can be derived. To say that man is purposeful is to say that he pursues *ends*; to pursue ends, he must believe that there are *means available* to attain them. The reality of the world in which man finds himself is one in which *useful means are found to be insufficient to attain simultaneously all his desired ends* (if nothing else were scarce, the time at man's disposal is insufficient to achieve all his desired ends simultaneously). That man must choose among the ends for which the means at his disposal shall be applied implies that *the means have degrees of multiple use* so that a decision has to be made as to whether they should be used in one way or another. And *having to choose among the ends for which the scarce means shall be applied requires man to rank or arrange his ends in order of importance to him.*

But ranking ends in order of importance also implies that man weighs the *costs* and *benefits* from making one choice rather than another. What must be forgone or given up as the price for possibly attaining some other goal ranked as more important is the cost of the individual's decision. And that which he pursues or possibly achieves by paying that price is the benefit he may receive from the choice he has made. Thus he chooses that end to pursue that he believes will be more profitable (the one that, on net balance, will make him better off) and he tries to avoid selecting some alternative that would in comparison generate a loss (the one that, on net balance, would make him worse off). Furthermore, most choices are not categorical (either/or decisions), but instead marginal ones (choices concerning incremental trade-offs of a little more of one desired end at the expense of a little bit less of some other desired end).[29]

Now, all of these concepts and relationships – ends and means, costs and benefits, profits and losses, prices to be paid and trade-offs to be made at the margin of decision making – are the stock and trade of practically all modern economists. They provide the analytical schema within which economists arrange and order the human events of the world for theoretical understanding and application. But Mises' point was to emphasize that these are not merely useful categories and concepts, not just good working hypotheses that economists may adopt or not, depending upon how they wish to organize the 'data' or 'facts' of the human world. Instead, they are the only way the data and facts can be organized so as to present the general and universal properties necessary for comprehending and understanding the reality of the human world. Why? Because these are the concepts, categories and relationships through which real men act and choose; there are no others from which to select. They represent the way our minds actually work and that comprises the *Logic of Action*. We cannot separate ourselves from them, since they represent the mental framework within which our minds operate.[30]

HUMAN COOPERATION AND THE RATIONALITY OF THE MARKET ECONOMY

Since the time of the ancient Greeks, the benefits of human cooperation through a social system of division of labour have been understood in Western thought.[31] But it was in the 18th-century writings of the French physiocrats and the Scottish moral philosophers that its significance and importance for social theory was fully appreciated. Through a division of labour, productivity is increased far above what men in isolation can ever hope to attain. It also acts as a stimulus for industry, since now the variety and the quantity of goods that may be obtained through the exchange of specialized productions work as incentives for each to increase his own output of tradable wares as the means of acquiring what others may have for sale. And the more extensive the market becomes on which goods can be sold, the greater now the potential benefits from a more intensive development of the division of labour.[32]

From this insight, these 18th-century thinkers were able to undermine much of the mercantilist ideology of their time. They demonstrated that trade among nations is mutually beneficial and in no way harmful to any nation's 'interest'. Indeed, as other nations become more developed and more prosperous, the market expands for one's own nation's specialized productions.[33] But the advantage from international trade comes not from the ability to export but from the opportunity to import. Exports are only the means through which a nation can acquire from other countries products that it cannot produce at home, or cannot produce at a cost less than the price offered by another country. Trade among nations offers the consumers of each participating country more goods, different goods and cheaper goods than if the demanders of desired commodities were limited to the production possibilities of domestic producers.[34]

The final demonstration of the mutual benefit from international trade came with the development of the theory of 'comparative advantage' in the early 19th century. That trade would be beneficial can be seen clearly enough if each nation can produce some product that its trading partners cannot produce at all, or if each nation can produce some product at a lower cost that none of its trading partners can match. But the English classical economists, especially David Ricardo, showed that trade can still be beneficial for a nation even if it is absolutely more cost-efficient in producing every product in comparison to its potential trading partners.

Suppose that Englishmen could produce one yard of cloth in four hours and harvest a bushel of potatoes in one hour, while Irishmen took 12 hours and two hours, respectively. Clearly, England is a lower-cost producer than Ireland in both cloth and potatoes. England is three times more productive at cloth manufacturing and twice as productive in potato harvesting. But equally clear is the fact that England is comparatively more cost-efficient in cloth manufacturing. That is, when England forgoes the manufacture of a yard of cloth, it can harvest four bushels of potatoes. But when Ireland forgoes the manufacture of a yard of cloth, it can harvest six bushels of potatoes. If England and Ireland were to trade cloth for potatoes at the price ratio of, say, one yard of cloth for five bushels of potatoes, both nations could be better off, with England specializing in cloth manufacturing and Ireland in potato harvesting. England would now receive five bushels of potatoes for a yard of its cloth, rather than the four bushels if it harvested at home all the potatoes it consumed. And Ireland would receive a yard of cloth for only giving up five bushels of potatoes, rather than the six bushels if it manufactured at home all of the cloth it used.[35]

In these ideas, Mises saw the basis for a comprehensive theory of society, the social order and the market economy. Ricardo's theory of comparative advantage, he said, should more rightly be called the 'Ricardian Law of Association':[36]

> Ricardo expounded the law of association in order to demonstrate what the consequences of the division of labor are when an individual or a group, more efficient in every regard, cooperates with an individual or a group less efficient in every regard. ... The law of association makes us comprehend the tendencies which resulted in the progressive intensification of human cooperation. We conceive what incentive induced people not to consider themselves as rivals in a struggle for the

appropriation of the limited supply of means of subsistence made available by nature. We realize what has impelled them and permanently impels them to consort with one another for the sake of cooperation. Every step forward on the way to a more developed mode of division of labor serves the interests of all participants. ... The factor that brought about primitive society and daily works toward progressive intensification is human action that is animated by the insight into the higher productivity of labor achieved under the division of labor.[37]

What are the origins of the advantages from a division of labour? Mises argued that division of labour arose from two conditions found in the human circumstance: the inherent inequality among men to perform various tasks and the unequal distribution of natural resources and raw materials with which men are able to manufacture the goods that service their ends. There is also the frequent situation that the strength necessary to perform various physical tasks is beyond the capacity of one man. While this would create occasional instances in which men would need each other's assistance, this alone would not generate the incentive for permanent human bonds of association and collaborative effort. Only those two inequalities in the human condition create the lasting benefit from mutual assistance through specialization of activities.[38]

Herein lies the origin of society, the mutual and permanent cooperative endeavour of men to improve their circumstances and expand the possibilities before them:

Society is cooperation; it is community in action. ... Once labor had been divided, the division itself exercises a differentiating influence. The fact that labor is divided makes possible further cultivation of individual talent and thus cooperation becomes more and more productive. Through cooperation men are able to achieve what would have been beyond them as individuals, and even work which individuals are capable of doing alone is made more productive ... The greater productivity of work under the division of labor is a unifying influence. It leads men to regard each other as comrades in the joint struggle for welfare, rather than as competitors in a struggle for existence. It makes friends out of enemies, peace out of war, society out of individuals. ... Society exists only where willing becomes co-willing and action co-action. To strive jointly towards aims which lone individuals could not reach at all, or not with equal effectiveness - that is society. Therefore, society is not an end but a means, the means by which each individual member seeks to attain his own end. That society is possible at all is due to the fact that the will of one person and the will of another find themselves linked in a joint endeavor. Community of work springs from community of will. Because I can get what I want only if my fellow citizen gets what he wants, his will and action become the means by which I can attain my own end. ... The division of labor is what first makes social ties: it is the social element pure and simple.[39]

However, Mises pointed out that there were, in general terms, two forms in which cooperation could be established and maintained in society: *hegemonic* and *contractual* relationships. The hegemonic relationship is based on command and subjugation. One group of individuals imposes its will upon another group through the use or threat of force, making the subjugated group serve and obey the interests and orders of the ruling or commanding group. Cooperation by some is made compulsory. The contractual relationship is based on voluntary agreement and mutual consent of the participants of the association. This distinction between systems of social cooperation, he said, has long been understood in social theory as the distinctions between the society of status or contract, military nations or industrial nations, collectivist economies or market economies. But the advancement of civilization has arisen from the slow replacement of the hegemonic relationship by the society of contract.[40] Individual freedom, voluntary association and market-based cooperation have served as the basis for the material and cultural advancement of mankind.[41]

But the potential for cooperation through contractual association in a market economy depends upon the emergence and maintenance of certain crucial institutions, Mises explained:[42]

1. *Private property*, that is, the private ownership of the means of production. Individuals have the right of possession and use of not only goods ready for consumption, but the factors of production out of which goods and services can be manufactured for sale and use.[43]
2. *Freedom*, that is, the liberty of each and every individual to be guided by his own purposes and plans, on the basis of which he voluntarily integrates himself into the social system of division of labour through contract and mutual agreement.[44]
3. *Peace,* that is, the removal and abolition of violence from human relationships, because it is only in a climate of tranquil association that each individual can feel secure to apply his mind and efforts to creative improvements to the human condition.[45]
4. *Equality*, that is, equal personal and political freedom before the law so each individual may have the liberty to integrate himself into the system of division of labour as he thinks more profitable, without legal barrier or restriction.
5. *Inequality of wealth and income*, that is, each individual's material position in society is dependent upon his success in serving others in the system of division of labour, with the relative income and wealth positions of each individual reflecting his inevitably unequal accomplishment in this endeavour.[46]
6. *Limited government*, that is, the political authority is restricted in its powers and responsibilities to those tasks required for the securing of the peace under which each individual's freedom and property is protected from violence and aggression.[47]

Mises stressed that the foundation of society was the first item on the list, the institution of private property. It is the basis on which individuals have had the incentives and the capabilities to apply themselves to improve their own circumstances and that of others, through their participation in the division of labour.[48] And, finally, it is the basis on which a rational use of the resources at people's disposal in society can be most efficiently applied to serve various ends.

In a market economy, Mises explained, it is not necessary for each individual to have possession and direct control over the particular resources, raw materials, land or labour skills upon which the satisfaction of each of his individual wants and ends are dependent. In a system of division of labour, these means of production are set to work for him, even though they are owned and controlled by others with whom he has no immediate or personal association. The owners of these things can only attain their own particular purposes if they successfully put them to work manufacturing and providing what others desire, so they in turn can obtain in exchange what they desire for the satisfaction of their own ends.[49]

But how do those owners of the means of production know what others in the society desire to purchase and how do they know if they are utilizing in a cost-efficient manner the resources they either own or can acquire on the market in manufacturing goods that they can sell to those others? The solution to this dilemma is provided by economic calculation. The fact that resources are privately owned and may be bought and sold on the market along with finished consumer goods enables the emergence of ratios of exchange, or prices, which reflect the appraised value of the means of production in alternative uses. These market-generated prices then serve as the basis for evaluating their use in alternative productive activities in the society. Mises explained the nature of economic calculation in the following manner:

> Money calculation ... provides a guide amid the bewildering throng of economic possibilities. It enables us to extend judgments of value which apply directly only to consumption goods – or at best to production goods of the lowest order [those closest to the finished consumer goods stage] – to all goods of higher order [factors of production applied at more indirect stages of production processes]. Without it, all production by lengthy and roundabout processes would be so many steps in the dark. Two things are necessary if computations of value in terms of money are to take place. First, not only goods ready for consumption but also goods of higher orders must be exchangeable. If this were not so, a system of exchange relationships could not emerge. ... No single man, be he the greatest genius ever born, has an intellect capable of deciding the relative importance of each one of the infinite number of goods of higher order. No individual could so discriminate between the infinite number of alternative methods of production that he could make direct judgments of their relative value without auxiliary calculations. In societies based on division of labor, the distribution of property rights effects a kind of mental division of labor, without which neither economy nor systematic production would

be possible. In the second place, there must be a general medium of exchange, a money, in use. And this must serve as an intermediary in the exchange of production goods equally with the rest. If this were not so, it would be impossible to reduce all exchange relationships to a common denominator. ... Without such assistance, in the bewildering chaos of alternative materials and processes, the human mind would be at a complete loss.[50]

Mises continued in the same vein,

Capitalist economic calculation, which alone makes rational production possible, is based on monetary calculation. Only because prices of all goods and services in the market can be expressed in terms of money is it possible for them, in spite of their heterogeneity, to enter into a calculation involving homogeneous units of measurement. ... In the market, where all goods and services can be traded, exchange ratios, expressed in money prices, can be determined for everything bought and sold. In a social order based on private property, it thus becomes possible to resort to monetary calculation in checking on the results of all economic activities. The social productivity of every economic transaction may be tested by the methods of bookkeeping and cost accounting. ... This is the decisive objection that economics raises against the possibility of a socialist society. It must forgo the intellectual division of labor that consists in the cooperation of all entrepreneurs, landowners, and workers as producers and consumers in the formation of market prices. But without it, rationality, i.e., the possibility of economic calculation, is unthinkable.[51]

In Mises' view, economic calculation is the mental tool that enables the development and evolution of the complex system of division of labour upon which the modern market economy is dependent. It is what gives rationality to the economic order and its market processes.[52] Given the scarcity of the means to serve human ends, we see that men must weigh their competing ends, rank them in order of importance, and proceed to assign the means at their disposal in a manner that applies them in way that reflects the relative significance of the ends they can serve. But the more intricate and indirect the production processes utilized to satisfy those numerous ends, the more there is a need for a way to reduce physically heterogeneous means to some type of common denominator to determine whether or not, in value terms, they are being employed for the satisfaction of some end less important than some other for which they might be applied. The prices competitively formed on the market provide this device. Once more, we may refer to Mises' own words:

We may view the whole market of material factors of production and of labor as a public auction. The bidders are the entrepreneurs. Their highest bids are limited by their expectations of the prices consumers will be ready to pay for the products. The co-bidders competing with them, whom they must outbid if they are not to go away empty-handed, are in the same situation. All these bidders are, as it were, mandatories of the consumers. But each of them represents a different aspect of the consumers' wants, either another commodity or another way of producing the same commodity. The competition among the various entrepreneurs is essentially a competition among the various possibilities open to individuals to remove as far as possible their state of uneasiness by the acquisition of consumer goods. ... The competition between the entrepreneurs reflects these prices of consumer goods in the formation of the prices of the factors of production. The fact that the various wants of the individual, which conflict because of the inexorable scarcity of the factors of production, are represented on the market by the various competing entrepreneurs results in prices for those factors that make economic calculation not only feasible but imperative. ... To the entrepreneur of capitalist society a factor of production through its price sends out a warning: Don't touch me, I am earmarked for the satisfaction of another, more important need. ... An entrepreneur who does not calculate, or disregards the result of calculation, would very soon go bankrupt and be removed from his managerial function.[53]

Economic calculation serves two functions in the market economy, Mises concluded. It enables the entrepreneurial decision maker to evaluate after a production process has been undertaken and goods have been sold to consumers whether his economic plans had been successful or not, that is, whether, *ex post*, a profit or a loss has resulted from his activities. It also serves as the anticipatory framework enabling the entrepreneur to make decisions concerning the future. The entrepreneur, on the basis of the prices of the immediate past, forms his judgments, *ex ante*, concerning the direction and intensity of consumer demand for various products in the future. This then serves as the limit for appraising the usefulness and value of bidding for and utilizing various factors of production in different combinations, given the prices those factors of production are found to cost in the markets for resources. The rivalrous bids of competing entrepreneurs ensures that the prices that emerge on the market for the factors of production tend to reflect the relative values of the consumer goods they can assist in manufacturing. Market prices and competition ensure that the value of the means of production represents the value of the consumer ends that they can serve.[54]

Mises observed that the competition of the market does not just enable the formation of the prices that serve as the tool for economic calculation; it also serves as the method by which each participant in the division of labour discovers his most advantageous employment. 'Competition is an element of social collaboration, the ruling principle within the social body,' he explained.[55] Rather than implying conflict, competition is a method for peaceful cooperation. Each man estimates what his most highly valued use might be in the social system of division of labour, as a source of potential income for himself. Through the process of competition, he discovers whether his judgment has been correct. If someone else can perform a task more successfully and profitably in the competition for a particular consumer business, then the lower than expected income or profits he earns serves as a signal that his contribution to the social process of production should be found elsewhere. Through this process each finds his most socially valuable function – as entrepreneur, landowner, capitalist or labourer – in the division of labour.[56]

At the same time, the competitive process of social cooperation reduces the capricious element from human relations. Precisely because of the near universal reduction of human relationships in the market economy to an 'exchange nexus' of dollars and cents, arbitrary or discourteous behaviour towards others carries a price that makes each think twice before he acts thoughtlessly or rudely in the consumer–producer or employer–employee relationships of the market. Explained Mises:

> It is customary to complain that, nowadays, personal considerations are banished from business life and that money rules everything. But what really is here complained of is simply that, in that department of activity which we call purely economic, whims and favors are banished and only those considerations are valid which social cooperation demands. ... There is no place for the arbitrary, where exact money reckoning enables us completely to calculate action. If we allow ourselves to be carried away by the current laments over the stony-heartedness of an age which reckons everything in terms of shillings and pence, we overlook that it is precisely this linking up of action with considerations of money profit which is society's more effective means of limiting arbitrary action. It is precisely arrangements of this kind which make the consumer, on the one hand, the employer, the capitalist, the landowner and the worker, on the other – in short, all concerned in producing for demands other than their own – dependent upon social cooperation. ... The conduct of the employer to the employee is part of a social process. If he does not deal with the employee in a manner appropriate to the social valuation of the employee's service, then there arise consequences which he himself has to bear. He can, indeed, deal badly with the employee but he himself must pay the costs of his arbitrary behavior [in losing a valuable employee to a rival employer]. ... This, then is freedom in the external life of man – that is, he is independent of the arbitrary power of his fellows. ... Capitalism ... no longer divides society into despotic rulers and rightless serfs. All relations are material and impersonal, calculable and capable of substitution. With capitalistic money calculations freedom descends from the sphere of dreams to reality.[57]

Through the emergence of a social system of division of labour, men learned how to increase their ability to improve materially and culturally their earthly circumstances from primitive subsistence to one of humane comfort and ease.[58] Instead of a struggle for existence not only against the niggardliness of nature but in conflict with their fellow human beings, they devised a civil society for peaceful cooperation and collaboration for mutual improvement and betterment. The institutions of the market economy offered the methods for a rational economic calculation and allocation of the scarce resources of the earth for the satisfaction of their ends. It also offered a reasonable and non-arbitrary way of determining what the relative income and wealth of each man should be as an indicator of his reward for serving others in the pursuit of the fulfilment of his own ends in the system of division of labour. And it enabled even the weak and the less efficient to find a niche for earning the means for life through the logic of comparative advantage.[59]

The insights and analysis of the classical economists had created the basis for the political and legal reforms of the 19th century that resulted in the freeing of men and markets from the regulatory and controlling hands of governments. The philosophy of classical liberalism had created the foundation for an appreciation of the importance and value of individual liberty, private property and free markets. The results were rising standards of living, growing populations, improved quantity and quality of the amenities of life, more leisure time and more resources for science, art, literature and all the other signifiers of a great and good society.

Using their reason, Mises argued, men had not only been able to comprehend the nature and laws of the physical world; they had also begun to comprehend the logical character of human action and the potential for a rational social order. Facing an inescapable scarcity of insufficient means to serve their various ends, men must order their affairs to go logically about the satisfaction of the things they consider, in their own minds, as the most important goals to fulfil. But two problems face them in this endeavour: their own strength and abilities are limited, and they know others are facing the same perennial problem. They can either try to satisfy their desires through self-sufficient efforts while at the same time initiating or warding off the plundering attacks of others, or they can devise ways of drawing others into cooperative activities for improving their circumstances.

Through much of human history, cooperation was imposed by compulsion or hegemonic bonds, as Mises calls them. Slowly, men came to see that cooperation could be extended and made more productive when consent and voluntary agreement served as the basis of collaboration for mutual rather than unilateral benefit. The society of contract began to replace the society of status, caste and command. The market economy started to supersede the regulated economy. The classical economists had shown that there could be order without design, that market competition could both integrate and coordinate multitudes of people in a great society of 'natural liberty', as Adam Smith had called it.

The coordination and rationality in the social system of division of labour was dependent, as Mises made clear, on the institutions of private property and market competition that enabled the formation of money prices on the basis of which economic calculation became possible. All the goods and resources that might enter the orbit of human use and exchange could now be valued and appraised to determine what their most highly valued uses and most cost-effective applications might be in the interdependent and intricate network of production and trade. The nexus of market prices that emerged out of the interactions of all the participants in the market-place ensured a rational allocation of the scarce means of production for the satisfaction of consumers' ends and at the same time determined the relative income share that each participant earned as a reflection of the market's judgment of the value of his contribution to the social process of production. At the same time, competition served as the peaceful means through which each member of this collaborative process found his appropriate niche in the division of labour, through which he served his fellow men and they in turn served him.

But before a completely free market capitalism could be established and achieve even greater heights in improving and civilizing mankind, opposing forces arose in the late 19th and 20th centuries. Socialism and interventionism emerged as the two challengers to and enemies of the rationality of the free market economy.[60]

THE IRRATIONALITY OF SOCIALIST PLANNING AND INTERVENTIONIST REGULATION

Before Ludwig von Mises published his article on 'Economic Calculation in the Socialist Commonwealth' in 1920,[61] most criticisms of socialism and a planned economy focused on the weakening of work incentives with the abolition of private property and the threat to human freedom if the state became the monopoly producer and employer under nationalization of the means of production. Though a few writers before World War I had criticized the possibility of successful central planning, Mises' analysis was the first thorough challenge to the socialists' claim that central planning could economically outperform private, competitive market capitalism.[62]

The economic problem, Mises argued, concerns the efficient use of the scarce means of production to serve our various ends. If all means of production, regardless of their physical characteristics, were, for production purposes, perfectly interchangeable (or substitutable) for one another there would be little difficulty in deciding how to apportion them among competing production uses. They could, in random fashion, be distributed among chosen production purposes, with the only criterion being that they would be applied for those activities that reflected in descending order the preferred consumer ends for which they could be used until no further production plan could be undertaken because the means had been completely exhausted.

There would also be no difficulty in deciding how to utilize available means of production if each and every such physical factor of production was usable for one and only one production activity: in other words, if there were no substitutability among them at all. Means 'X' would be used for production purpose 'X' and means 'Y' would be used for production purpose 'Y', or they could not be used at all. In other words, there would be no problem in having to decide whether some amount of means 'X' should be used for production purpose 'Y' instead of production purpose 'X'.

Now, for some purposes, some physical means of production can be almost perfectly substituted for each other, and there may be some physical means of production that are almost uniquely use-specific. But in a wide variety of cases the various physical means of production have degrees of substitutability among themselves for desired production activities. The economic problem, Mises said, is precisely to have some way of determining which use, in value terms, is the most efficient application for such means of production.[63]

For example, Mises suggested, suppose that it was being decided whether it would be economically advantageous to build a railway line between two cities separated by a mountain. The rail line could be built over, around or through the mountain. How would it be decided whether or not it would be worth the cost in resources, raw materials and labour that would have to be expended in its construction by one of these possible routes, in terms of the alternative production uses in the society for which those factors of production could be utilized?

In the market economy, Mises replied, the solution to this problem is fairly simple. The decision maker would make an estimate whether or not the prospective revenue to be earned by selling passenger tickets and charging cargo fees to potential users would be greater than the expenditures necessary for the construction and maintenance of the rail line along one of those routes. Suppose that the over-the-mountain route would involve a greater cost than the expected monetary return, but that either the around-the-mountain or through-the-mountain routes would cost less than the expected revenue. Which of these two routes should be chosen? Suppose that the around-the-mountain route could be built and maintained at less cost than the through-the-mountain route, if the tunnel through the mountain were to be constructed with the technologically very durable material, say, of platinum. If the tunnel were to be constructed with concrete rather than platinum it would be less durable and would require more frequent maintenance. On the other hand, the concrete-lined tunnel would then result in the through-the-mountain route coming in at a lower cost (even with the higher maintenance expenses) than the around-the-mountain route. The through-the-mountain route with a concrete-lined tunnel would clearly be the most cost-efficient project for the decision maker to undertake.

It would only be the existence of market-based prices for both the finished good (passenger and cargo transportation) and the factors of production in their alternative uses that would enable this decision to be made on the basis of economic calculation. But how would the socialist central planner be able to make this decision, Mises asked. How would he know which of the technologically feasible methods of production was most economical and most efficient? Having nationalized all the means of production, abolished market competition, and eliminated the ability of people openly to express their valuations and appraisals in the form of market-based prices for both finished goods and the factors of production, how would the central planner know the real opportunity costs – the forgone benefits – from applying and using goods and resources in any number of alternative ways? He would not.[64] Socialist central planning, therefore, meant the end of economic rationality. As Mises wrote,

> In any social order, even under Socialism, it can very easily be decided which kind and what number of consumption goods should be produced. No one has ever denied that. But once this decision has been made, there still remains the problem of ascertaining how the existing means of production can be used most effectively to produce these goods in question. In order to solve this problem it is necessary that there should be economic calculation. And economic calculation can only take place by means of money prices established in the market for production goods in a society resting on private property in the means of production. That is to say, there must exist money prices of land, raw materials, semi-manufactures; that is to say, there must be money wages and interest rates. … Where there is no market there is no price system, and where there is no price system there can be no economic calculation.[65]

Mises readily admitted that one could imagine a socialist world in which the preceding capitalist methods of production were taken over with no modifications or changes. One could also imagine that no further changes would ever again affect this socialist society. And one could imagine that this economy, which was in equilibrium before the 'socialist triumph', now remained frozen in time. Then the socialist central planners would not have to worry about the problem of economic calculation. They would merely, year-in and year-out, reproduce the methods of production found when the private owners of the means of production were expropriated.

But this is not, and would never be, the world in which a socialist regime would find itself. If nothing else, income and wealth would be redistributed according to socialist conceptions of 'social justice' following the great transformation and, therefore, the patterns of demand for various goods would be different. This would in itself require a redirection of production and the reallocation of the factors of production, meaning a set of new decisions concerning the most rational use of the resources at the central planners' disposal. And apart from this, in the real world technological possibilities do change, available resources do become greater or smaller for various reasons, and the demands of the public (even the socialist proletarian public) do change over time. All these changes, whether occurring in sequence or simultaneously, would require readjustments in the forms and types of production. But the socialist central planners would lack the ability to know rationally how to respond and adjust to a world of inevitable change. 'Thus,' judged Mises, 'in the socialist commonwealth every economic change becomes an undertaking whose success can be neither appraised in advance nor later retrospectively determined. There is only groping in the dark. Socialism is the abolition of rational economy.'[66]

Mises' 1920 challenge to the advocates of socialist central planning created a firestorm of controversy that did not completely come to an end until the final collapse of the Soviet Union in 1991. But it can be said that, by the 1930s, Mises had won the great debate of capitalism versus socialism, because beginning in the late 1920s the more astute advocates of socialism realized that Mises had made a devastating criticism in his analysis of the role of market-based prices for the rational use of resources in any complex economic order. They attempted to construct alternative theories of 'market socialism',[67] but Mises and his Austrian colleague Friedrich A. Hayek were able to demonstrate the limits and unworkability even in this strange contortion of attempting to combine markets with central planning.[68]

If socialist central planning represented a reversion to economic irrationality, did this then mean that a free market economy was the only rational system of economic order? Not in the eyes of many in the 20th century. Instead, the ideal in most Western countries became a 'middle way' or 'mixed economy' of regulated markets, politically redistributed income and partially controlled prices and production. Mises argued that this form of state interventionism was, in the long run, no more workable and sustainable than socialism. Indeed, he insisted that the distorting effects of government intervention in the workings of the market economy necessarily leads to a situation in which those introducing such interventions must either reverse themselves and allow a freer market to be re-established or extend the interventions and controls until a form of socialist-type command economy is imposed through the accumulation of government rules and regulations over the market system.

What is a state intervention in the market economy? Mises defined it in the following way:

Interventionism is a limited order by a social authority forcing the owners of the means of production and entrepreneurs to employ their means in a different manner than they otherwise would. ...

The authority interferes with the operation of the market economy, but it does not want to eliminate the market altogether. It wants production and consumption to develop along lines different from those prescribed by an unhampered market, and wants to achieve its aim by injecting into the working of the market orders, commands, and prohibitions for whose enforcement the police power and its apparatus of violent compulsion and coercion stand ready. But these are *isolated* acts of intervention. It is not the aim of the government to combine them into an integrated system which determines all prices, wages, and interest rates and thus places full control of production and consumption into the hands of the authorities. ... What characterizes it as such is the fact that the government does not limit its activities to the preservation of private ownership of the means of production and its protection against violent or fraudulent encroachments. The government interferes with the operation of business by means of orders and prohibitions. ... The intervention ... forces the entrepreneurs and capitalists to employ some of the factors of production in a way different from what they would have resorted to if they were only obeying the dictates of the market. Such a decree can be either an order to do something or an order not to do something.[70]

Mises also emphasized the nature of such intervention by pointing out what stands behind the government's regulations:

It is important to remember that government interference always means either violent action or the threat of such action. ... Government is in the last resort the employment of armed men, of policemen, gendarmes, soldiers, prison guards, and hangmen. The essential feature of government is the enforcement of its decrees by beating, killing, and imprisoning. Those who are asking for more government interference are asking ultimately for more compulsion and less freedom.[71]

Mises did not deny an essential role for government in society. Indeed, if there were not an agency that had the ability to protect life and property, enforce contracts and guard against fraud, the social order of peaceful cooperation through division of labour would be impossible.[72] But he argued that the task of social and economic theory was to determine the limits beyond which extension of government coercion no longer serves the maintenance of the social order of mutual interdependency through specialization and market exchange and instead threatens to weaken or undermine its operation.

In a free market, the structure of competitively determined prices serves the function of coordinating the actions of multitudes of participants in the division of labour. Every change in supply or demand ultimately represents a change either in the preferences of consumers for various goods or the willingness and ability of producers to provide their services, resources and abilities in the processes of production. Entrepreneurs function as the actual decision makers in the market economy, who determine what shall be produced, employ the factors of production, and direct and coordinate those factors in the production processes. But entrepreneurs are guided in their decisions and activities by their anticipation concerning the goods and services consumers may desire to buy at various points in the future. Failure to anticipate correctly consumer demand means that the entrepreneur will suffer losses rather than earn the profits for which he had hoped.

The prices he offers and pays for employing those factors of production are determined by the prices he believes he will recoup from sales to those consumers in the future. The competition among rival entrepreneurs means that the prices and wages paid for the purchase or hire of the factors of production are tending to equal the market value of the products their employment assists in producing.

In the market, the ability of entrepreneurs successfully to offer consumers the products they want and to offer them on better terms than their closest rivals is tested constantly every day in the arena of exchange. Control over production decision making in the market, therefore, is always open to change and modification. Successful entrepreneurs earn profits that enable them to expand their production activities. Less successful entrepreneurs either earn small or no profits, or suffer actual losses; these entrepreneurs over time lose the financial wherewithal to maintain their control over the production processes in the market. Hence, in the market economy decision making and control over the production processes in society are tending to be maintained or transferred to those individuals who demonstrate their continuing ability to perform this specialized and important task better than others in the social system of division of labour.[73]

According to Mises, government interventions disturbed and redirected this market-based process from following the patterns and forms it would have taken if guided solely by the anticipated and actual demands of the general consuming public. State interventions, he said, can be understood under several broad headings: consumption prohibitions, taxation, production restrictions and regulations, and price controls.

Consumption prohibitions attempt to prevent directly individuals from consuming or using particular goods or services. The rationale for such prohibitions has to do with the desire of some members of the society to restrain or prevent other members of the society from satisfying their wants for particular types of commodities. Thus the government may make illegal the purchase, sale and consumption of narcotics or alcoholic beverages or the use of tobacco products. The goal is to eliminate the demand for certain goods by banning their acquisition and use under threat of governmental punishment.

Mises admitted that the issue of whether or not to prohibit certain consumer desires goes beyond the purely economic question of the direct and indirect market consequences that may follow such bans. But he pointed out that, once the government takes on the responsibility for determining which goods and services individuals may peacefully and voluntarily purchase and use, there is no logical limit to extending such prohibitions:

> But once the principle is admitted that it is the duty of government to protect the individual against his own foolishness, no serious objections can be advanced against further encroachments. A good case can be made out in favor of the prohibition of alcohol and nicotine. And why limit the government's benevolent providence to the protection of the individual's body only? Is not the harm a man can inflict on his mind and soul even more disastrous than any bodily evil? Why not

prevent him from reading bad books and seeing bad plays, from looking at bad paintings and statues and from hearing bad music. ... These fears are not merely imaginary specters terrifying secluded doctrinaires. It is a fact that no paternal government, whether ancient or modern, ever shrank from regimenting its subjects' minds, beliefs, and opinions. If one abolishes man's freedom to determine his own consumption, one takes all freedoms away.[74]

As Mises also perceived, 'A free man must be able to endure it when his fellow men act and live otherwise than he considers proper. He must free himself from the habit, just as soon as something does not please him, of calling for the police.'[75]

Taxation may be necessary for the funding of the limited, though essential, functions of a government devoted to the protection of individual liberty and property, but Mises said that, when it goes beyond the modest levels that would be required in a truly free market society, it threatens to become a vehicle for the distortion or destruction of the market economy. Thus an excise tax or an import tax may be imposed as a source of government revenue. But the same tax can be utilized as a device to repress or restrict the purchase or sale of a commodity or service. Thus a tax on tobacco products can be raised to a level sufficiently high for the government's tax revenue to be less than if it were set at a lower level. But it can be set at that higher level precisely to serve as a method for inducing a decrease in the quantity demanded by the smoking public, with the tax potentially high enough for it to suppress all legal purchases of tobacco products. In this case, the tax serves as a tool for the government's attempt to prohibit consumption.

Or an import tax or tariff can be raised to such a height that it also brings in less government revenue than if it were set at a more modest level. But, in this case, it serves as a method to make the importation and sale of a foreign commodity more costly for the consuming public than their purchasing of a domestic alternative to the foreign good. Its purpose is to act as a protectionist device to secure a larger portion of the domestic market to a domestic producer than would have been the situation under a regime of free trade. Protectionist import duties, however, reduce the benefits and potentials from an international division of labour, resulting in goods being more costly and the variety available to the consuming public being reduced. Resources and labour are misdirected into less efficient uses, lowering the standard of living of both the domestic and the foreign community of buyers and sellers.

Taxation can also serve as a method of partial expropriation of wealth and income. Thus a progressive income tax penalizes success and achievement on the part of some members of the society in better satisfying the consuming public. As such it reduces the incentives for savings, investment and work. The end result is a slowing down of the rate of capital formation, technological innovation and entrepreneurial creativity in improving the economic conditions of the society. The society is poorer and is kept poorer than might have been the case if taxation did not discriminate against excellence and ability.

Finally, total confiscatory taxation has as its purpose the actual destruction of the market economy by expropriating wealth and property with the implicit or explicit purpose of transferring the ability to produce from the hands of private individuals to the government.[76]

Production restrictions and regulations are designed to prevent production methods from taking the form they would have if guided purely by entrepreneurs' estimates concerning the types of goods consumers desire and their judgments concerning the most efficient way to produce them. Mises elucidated:

> Each authoritarian interference with business diverts production, of course, from the lines it would take if it were only directed by the demand of the consumers as manifested on the market. The characteristic mark of restrictive interference with production is that the diversion of production is not merely an unavoidable and unintentional secondary effect, but precisely what the authority wants to bring about. ... Restrictions of production means that the government either forbids or makes more difficult or more expensive the production, transportation, or distribution of definite articles, or the definite modes of production, transportation, or distribution. ... The effect of the interference is that people are prevented from using their knowledge and abilities, their labor and their material means of production in the way in which they would earn the highest returns and satisfy their needs as much as possible. Such interference makes people poorer and less satisfied.[77]

Production restrictions can take the form, for example, of licences to practise various professions or trades, tax benefits that favour certain types of enterprises and industries, labour laws that limit or prohibit employment of women or children, or the requirement of membership of a union to be employed.[78] They can also take the form of regulations on the size of enterprises, the form and type of marketing methods that firms may utilize, the technical methods that can be employed in production processes, or regulations on the ways enterprises in the market are permitted to compete for consumer business.

The price of such production restrictions and regulations, Mises emphasized, included higher costs of production, limitations on innovation and product development, rigidity in the adaptability of firms to market conditions, and barriers preventing various individuals and groups from taking advantage of market opportunities to improve their material and social circumstances. The cumulative result of such restrictions and regulations, he concluded, was a tendency to reduce or retard the development of the productive capacity of people in the society. The evolution of the division of labour is forced to take a less efficient path than the market, left to itself, would have taken. Society, again, is poorer than it would have been if only the market was left free and unencumbered by state interventionism.[79]

Finally, Mises wrote that price controls undermine the most fundamental functioning of the market economy. Prices, as we have seen, act as the central coordinating device in the market. Through them, production is directed toward the satisfaction of consumer demand, and the costs of the means of production (through entrepreneurial competition for their purchase, hire and use) tend to reflect the value of the goods that can be manufactured. Every change in prices, either for finished consumer goods or for the factors of production, serves as a signal of market change and as the data for revised economic calculations regarding new, more cost-efficient ways in which those factors should be utilized and combined to satisfy consumer demands.

A change in price is precisely meant to act as the information and the inducement for any needed changes concerning what should be produced and how. Government control or manipulation of a market price brings about distortions in market activity that are inconsistent with the actual supply and demand conditions prevailing in the overall economic order. Furthermore, the distortions and imbalances price controls induce create a situation in which such controls may end up being extended throughout more and more segments of the economy until the entire structure of market prices and the direction of production come under government command.

Mises' classic example to demonstrate this process was a government control on the price of some basic product such as milk. Suppose that the government wished to make milk more readily available at a more reasonable price by setting the price of milk below the free market price. Milk retailers would now find their selling price set by the government was at a level below their cost of buying that milk at the wholesale level. The supply of milk at the retail level would, as a result, decrease – the opposite of what was the intention behind the government price control. The government now finds itself in a dilemma: it can either repeal the price control and let the market determine the price, or it can extend the control to the wholesale milk market by imposing a maximum price at which wholesale dealers may sell milk to retail outlets. If it does extend the control, the government now creates the same type of imbalance, but at one stage further removed from the consumer. The wholesale dealer finds that his selling price is now set below the price he must pay for milk from the dairy farmer. The wholesaler now purchases less milk from his farming sources, once again reducing the amount of milk available at the retail level. The government, once again, faces the same dilemma, either to free prices from its controls or to extend the controls once more, this time to the price the dairy farmers can charge the wholesale purchasers.

If the government once more extends the range of its price controls, a milk shortage results from production cutbacks at the farming level, since the farmers, too, have costs of manufacturing that are now found to be higher than the maximum price the government lets them charge to the wholesalers. If the government insists upon enforcement of its price controls, they must now be extended to those sectors of the market that provide the resources and equipment upon which the farming industry is dependent.

The dynamics of this government-created series of price and production distortions must lead to the controls being extended to wider and wider segments of the economy, until finally the entire structure of market prices comes under government command. The necessary and essential connection and interdependency among the entire network of prices means that either they are left free to coordinate the interacting demands and supplies of the market or the government must replace the market with its own network of administratively imposed price and production controls. If the latter occurs, the market has been replaced by planning. As Mises frequently reminded his readers, the interventionist 'middle-of-the road' threatens to lead to socialism, if the interventions are taken to their logical end.[80]

ECONOMIC RATIONALITY AND IRRATIONAL ECONOMIC POLICY

Mises' conclusion from his investigation into the nature and workings of socialist and interventionist systems was that there was no viable alternative to a functioning free market economy.[81] Socialist central planning meant the end of all economic rationality through the abolition of private property, market competition and prices. Interventionism, while not so radical in its effects, nonetheless disrupted the functioning of the price system and undermined the activities of market-directed entrepreneurs and enterprise decision makers guided by the profit motive to attempt to serve best the consuming public.

Not only could the market economy be shown theoretically to be far superior to any other system of economic organization, but the history of the last three hundred years also demonstrated the market's liberating quality in providing a wide range of freedom, unsurpassed economic improvement, and potential for peace and cultural advancement. So why was the market economy opposed, resisted and condemned by so many in society? Mises offered several reasons for this strange and peculiar phenomenon.

First, he suggested that modern society still carried the cultural residue of the ancient world, with its hostility to work and money. Among the ancients, moneymaking, commerce and trade, middleman speculation and money lending were condemned as beneath and unseemly for a free man of culture and refinement. These were lower aspects of the daily affairs of life, often involving tasks and activities properly belonging to the slave or servant.

In the Middle Ages and the early modern period, the man of letters and the artist lived outside the arena of market transactions for their existence; instead, they had patrons among the nobility or the Church who subsidized and sheltered them from the uncertain winds of earning a living. With the dawn of the market economy, such patronage began to diminish in size and security. Intellectuals were now increasingly thrown upon the market to make their own way, and to do so by serving the tastes and fashions of an emerging middle class and the wider general public. They were unable to pursue a calling for its own sake, for a higher purpose above the cultural vulgarity of the presumably uneducated common man.

Resentment, Mises suggested, often grew into a matching envy and anger when friends, relatives and those of apparently lesser cultural sensitivity earned far greater incomes than the intellectual and artist, while at the same time these 'bourgeois' increasingly held a higher social status in society than this cultural elite. Intellectuals dreamed of better worlds, more cultured social arrangements, different human relationships than those fostered and rewarded in the market. They became social engineers conjuring up visions of planned societies more to their liking and within which they would be appreciated and have positions of power and recognition. The intellectuals became the designers and proselytizers of beautiful socialist futures to come.[82]

Second, Mises said, the market economy has been opposed because it not only ignores privilege and status, but it also undermines them. Each individual's social and economic position must be won and retained through one means: success in serving the other members of the society by offering a product or service in the social system of division of labour better than that of rivals. There are no guarantees in the market. As a result, those whose economic and social position is challenged by the competition of others attempt to use the government to restrict free competition. Special interest group politics resists the functioning of the market. And, in the process of successfully winning privileges and favours, special interests also succeed in creating conflicts among a growing number of segments of the society as groups vie for the fruits of state intervention.[83]

Third, said Mises, there is a significant lack of understanding on the part of most people about the nature and actual working of the market economy. Understanding the market order requires a certain degree of abstract reasoning in which the individual appreciates how his actions and those of multitudes of others are integrated into an interdependent system of cooperation connected through the incentives and valuation information provided by the price system. As a result, the arguments for socialism or interventionism have often seemed appealing to many.[84] If an individual does not hold the position he would like to have, or does not earn the income that he thinks he deserves, he is easily persuaded that his circumstance is not due to the reality of his ability and worth as estimated in the processes of market exchange. No, it is due to greedy employers, selfish businessmen and sinister speculators manipulating markets and prices. The 'solution' seems to be government-mandated minimum wages, government-guaranteed prices, government redistribution of 'unearned' wealth to the deserving and needing. 'Unfair' competition can be rectified through regulatory policies and business taxes.

Finally, Mises provided another reason for the resistance to the rationality of the market economy: a cultural lag. The market economy and its institutions have developed and incorporated an increasing number of people and generations who find themselves living and working in the capitalist society, but their everyday thinking about man and the social order are still based on older conceptions of man and society more appropriate to precapitalist existence. 'One cannot make a social philosophy one's own as easily as a new costume. It must be earned – earned with the effort of thought,' Mises said. 'More menacing than barbarians storming the walls from without are the seeming citizens within – those who are citizens in gesture but not in thought.'[85]

CONCLUSION

All these reasons for opposition to the market economy have helped create the philosophies and ideologies of socialism and interventionism that have dominated the 20th century. They have produced that 'revolt against reason' that Mises fought to oppose through his analysis of the logic of human action and the rationality of the market economy.

Both supporters and opponents of Ludwig von Mises and his ideas have called him dogmatic, uncompromising and intransigent, but if one actually reads his work, it is clear that Mises had only one dogma: the importance of using our reason. He had one uncompromising principle: the rule of rational argument. He had one intransigence: the courage and duty to accept and act upon what our logic dictates.

In spite of the trends prevailing during his lifetime, Mises chose to swim against the tide. He was confident that trends could change. They had in the past, and they would again.[86] He devoted his life and work to reasoning and writing both for those in his own time and for others who would follow. He said as much in the preface for the 1932 edition of *Socialism*:

> I know only too well how hopeless it seems to convince impassioned supporters of the Socialist Idea by logical demonstration that their views are preposterous and absurd. I know too well that they do not want to hear, to see, or above all to think,

and they are open to no argument. But new generations grow up with clear eyes and open minds. And they will approach things from a disinterested, unprejudiced standpoint, they will weigh and examine, will think and act with forethought. It is for them that this book is written.[87]

Mises believed that no man could stand apart as a passive observer of the great intellectual battles of the time. Each man was called upon to make his contribution:

> Everyone carries a part of society on his shoulders; no one is relieved of his share of responsibility by others. And no one can find a safe way out for himself if society is sweeping towards destruction. Therefore everyone, in his own interest, must thrust himself vigorously into the intellectual battle. None can stand aside with unconcern, the interests of everyone hangs on the result. Whether he chooses or not, every man is drawn into the great historical struggle, the decisive battle into which out epoch has plunged us. … Whether society shall continue to evolve or whether it shall decay lies … in the hand of man. Whether Society is good or bad may be a matter of individual judgment; but whoever prefers life to death, happiness to suffering, well-being to misery, must accept society. And whoever desires that society should exist and develop must also accept, without limitation or reserve, private ownership in the means of production.[88]

Ludwig von Mises' writings stand as one of the great contributions in this intellectual battle of ideas. And if the 21st century turns out to be freer and more prosperous than the 20th century, it will have been in some part due to his unrelenting defence of human freedom, economic liberty and the free market order.

NOTES

1. Ludwig von Mises, *Nation, State and Economy: Contributions to the Politics and History of Our Time* [1919] (New York: New York University Press, 1983) p. 216
2. Ibid., pp. 218–19. Twenty years before World War II began, Mises warned the Germans that militarism would lead to unprecedented disaster. Given the millions of German lives lost and the near-destruction of German industry, he was proved right. At the same time, he predicted that sticking to production and trade would lead to unprecedented peace and prosperity. In postwar Gerrnany, he was proved right once again.
3. Ludwig von Mises, *Epistemological Problems of Economics* [1933] (New York: New York University Press, 1981) pp. 17–22; also, Murray N. Rothbard, 'Praxeology as the Method of the Social Sciences' [1973], in *The Logic of Action*, Vol. I (Cheltenham, UK and Lyme, NH: Edward Elgar, 1997) pp. 40–52.
4. On the central ideas of the Austrian School of economics, see Ludwig von Mises, 'The Historical Setting of the Austrian School of Economics' [1969], in Bettina Bien Greaves (ed.), *Austrian Economics: An Anthology* (Irvington-on-Hudson, NY: Foundation for Economic Education, 1996), pp. 53–76; Ludwig M. Lachmann, 'The Significance of the Austrian School of Economics in the History of Ideas' [1966], in Richard M. Ebeling (ed.), *Austrian Economics: A Reader* (Hillsdale, MI: Hillsdale College Press, 1991) pp. 17–39; and Richard M. Ebeling, 'The Significance of Austrian Economics in Twentieth-Century Economic Thought', chapter 2 in the present volume.

5. Now known as Lvov, Ukraine.
6. For recollections of Mises' private seminar by some of its members, see Margit von Mises, *My Years with Ludwig von Mises* (Cedar Falls, IA: Center for Futures Education, 2nd edn, 1984), Appendix I: 'Impressions of the Mises Vienna Seminar', pp.199–21; and Ludwig von Mises, *Notes and Recollections* [1940] (South Holland, IL: Libertarian Press, 1978) pp.97–100.
7. See, Richard M. Ebeling, 'Friedrich A. Hayek: A Centenary Appreciation', *The Freeman* (May 1999) 28–32.
8. For a summary and interpretation of Mises' activities as a policy analyst and advocate in Austria in the years between the two world wars, see, Richard M. Ebeling, 'The Economist as the Historian of Decline: Ludwig von Mises and Austria Between the Two World Wars', in Richard M. Ebeling (ed.), *Globalization: The International Marketplace* (Hillsdale, MI: Hillsdale College Press, 2002) pp.1–69; a large number of Mises' writings on the problems of Austrian economic policy from 1918 to 1938 are collected in Richard M. Ebeling (ed.), *Selected Writings of Ludwig von Mises*, Vol. 2: *Monetary Disorder, Interventionism, Socialism and the Great Depression* (Indianapolis, IN: Liberty Fund, 2002). Also see Richard M. Ebeling, 'Planning for Freedom: Ludwig von Mises as Political Economist and Policy Analyst', in Richard M. Ebeling (ed.), *Competition or Compulsion? The Market Economy versus the New Social Engineering* (Hillsdale, MI: Hillsdale College Press, 2001) pp.1–85, for an exposition and analysis of Mises' conception of the social and economic order of a free society and his proposals for political economic reform in the post-World War II era; many of Mises' writings on postwar economic reconstruction are collected in Richard M. Ebeling (ed.), *Selected Writings of Ludwig von Mises*, Vol. 3: *The Political Economy of International Reform and Reconstruction* (Indianapolis, IN: Liberty Fund, 2000).
9. On the Graduate Institute of International Studies in Geneva and its intellectual environment in the years between the two world wars under its director William Rappard, see Richard M. Ebeling, 'William E. Rappard: An International Man in an Age of Nationalism', *Ideas on Liberty* (January 2000) pp.33–41.
10. See Richard M. Ebeling, 'Ludwig von Mises' Human Action: A 50th Anniversary Appreciation', *The Freeman* (September 1999) 32–7.
11. Ludwig von Mises, *Epistemological Problems of Economics* p.17: 'The theorems of economics are derived not from the observation of facts, but through deduction from the fundamental category of action. … They are of aprioristic derivation and therefore lay claim to the apodictic certainty that belongs to basic principles so derived.' Also *Human Action, A Treatise on Economics* (Irvington-on-Hudson, NY: Foundation for Economic Education, 4th edn, 1996) p.39: 'The theorems attained by correct praxeological [economic] reasoning are not only perfectly certain and incontestable, like the correct mathematical theorems. They refer, moreover, with the full rigidity of their apodictic certainty and incontestability to the reality of action as its appears in life and history. Praxeology conveys exact and precise knowledge of real things.'
12. Mises, *Human Action* pp.72–91.
13. As an example of this, see Johannes Stark, 'National Socialism and Science' [1934], in George L. Mosse (ed.), *Nazi Culture* (New York: Grosset & Dunlap, 1966) pp.205–7: 'The slogan has been coined, and has been spread particularly by the Jews, that science is international. … From the National Socialist side, in opposition to this view, it must be insisted upon with all possible emphasis that in the National Socialist state, even for the scientist, the duty to the nation stands above any and all other obligations. The scientist, too, must consider himself a member and a servant of the nation. Rather, in his work, he must serve the nation first and foremost. For these reasons, the leading scientific positions in the National Socialist state are to be occupied not by elements alien to the *Volk* but only by nationally conscious German men. But aside from this fundamental National Socialist demand, the slogan of the international character of science is based on an untruth, insofar as it asserts that the type and the success of scientific activity are independent of membership in a national group. … The spirit of the German enables him to observe things outside himself exactly as they are, without interpolation of his own ideas and wishes. … The German's love of nature and his aptitude for natural science is overwhelmingly a creation of

the Nordic–Germanic blood component of the Aryan peoples. ... The Jewish spirit is wholly different in its orientation: above everything else it is focused on its own ego, its own conception, and its own self-interest. In accordance with this natural orientation the Jewish spirit strives to heed facts only to the extent that they do not hamper his opinions and purposes.' See also Bruno Thüring, 'German Mathematics' [1936], ibid., pp. 208–15.

14. Mises, *Epistemological Problems of Economics* pp. 12–13; *Human Action* pp. 25 and 32–41; *The Ultimate Foundations of Economic Science* pp. 11–14 and 17–21.

15. Mises, *Epistemological Problems of Economics* p. 27: 'If thinking and action were really conditioned by place, time, race, nationality, climate, class, etc., then it would be impossible for a German of the twentieth century to understand anything of the logic and action of the Greek of the age of Pericles.' See also Ernst Cassirer, *The Myth of the State* (New Haven: Yale University Press, 1946) pp. 13–15: 'Language always shows us a definite and thorough-going logical structure, both in its sound system and in its morphological system. We have no evidence whatever for a "pre-logical" language. ... What holds for "primitive" language holds also for primitive thought. Its structure may seem to us to be strange and paradoxical; but it never lacks a definite logical structure. Even the uncivilized man cannot live in the world without a constant effort to understand that world. And for that purpose he had to develop and to use some general forms and categories of thought. The savage is no discursive thinker and dialectician. Nevertheless, we find in him, in an undeveloped and implicit state, the same capability of analysis and synthesis, of discernment and unification, that, according to Plato, constitute and characterize the dialectic art. When studying some very primitive forms of religious and mythical thought – for instance, the religion of totemistic societies – we are surprised to find to what a high degree the primitive mind feels the desire and the need to discern and divide, to order and classify the elements of its environment. There is hardly anything that escapes its constant urge for classification. ... The results of these first attempts to analyze and systematize the world of sense-experience are far different from ours. But the processes themselves are very similar; they express the same desire of human nature to come to terms with reality, to live in an ordered universe, and to overcome the chaotic state in which things and thoughts have not yet assumed a definite shape and structure.'

16. On Mises' critique of Marxian philosophy and class analysis, see *Theory and History* [1957] (Auburn, AL: Ludwig von Mises Institute, 1985) pp. 102–58; and *Socialism, An Economic and Sociological Analysis* (Indianapolis, IN: Liberty Classics, 1981), pp. 279–320; also 'The Clash of Group Interests' [1945], in Richard M. Ebeling (ed.), *Money, Method and the Market Process: Essays by Ludwig von Mises* (Norwell, MA: Kluwer Academic Press, 1990) pp. 202–14.

17. Mises, *Epistemological Problems of Economics*, pp. 204–6 and 186–94.

18. Mises, *Human Action*, pp. 21 and 89.

19. Ibid., p. 24. Mises readily conceded, 'It may be admitted that it is impossible to provide conclusive evidence for the proposition that my logic is the logic of all other people and by all means absolutely the only human logic and that the categories of my action are the categories of all other people's action and by all means absolutely the categories of all human action. ... But it is beyond doubt that the principle according to which an Ego deals with every human being as if the other were a thinking and acting being like himself has evidenced its usefulness both in mundane life and in scientific research ... the positivist must not overlook the fact that in addressing his fellow men he presupposes – tacitly and implicitly – the intersubjective validity of logic and thereby the reality of the realm of the alter Ego's thought and action, of his eminent human character.' And, *Theory and History* p. 248. See also Alfred Schutz, *The Phenomenology of the Social World* [1932] (Evanston, IL: Northwestern University Press, 1967) pp. 21–2.

20. On Mises' analysis of 'rationality' and its meaning, see *Epistemological Problems of Economics* pp. 31–5; *Human Action* pp. 19–22; and 'The Treatment of the "Irrational" in the Social Sciences' [1944], in Ebeling (ed.), *Money, Method and the Market Process*, pp. 16–36.

21. Ludwig von Mises, *The Ultimate Foundation of Economic Science* (Princeton: D. Van Nostrand, 1962) pp. 14–17.

22. Mises, *Epistemological Problems of Economics* pp.23-30; *Human Action* pp.32-41; *The Ultimate Foundations of Economic Science* pp.17-21. Also see Friedrich von Wieser, *Social Economics* [1914] (New York: Augustus M. Kelley, 1967) pp.8-9: 'The theoretical economist need never deplore a lack of the instruments which are employed in the exact natural sciences. Whatever advantages they may otherwise enjoy and great as are their achievements, they are none the less strangers to their object, nature. They may never scan the innermost recesses of nature. ... The group of practical sciences, of which economic theory is one, can accomplish more. The object of investigation is man in a condition of activity. Hence our mind ratifies every accurate description of the processes of his consciousness by the affirmative declaration that such is the case, and by the compelling feeling that it must be so necessarily. ... In these cases we, each of us, hear the law pronounced by an unmistakable inner voice. What unequaled advantage to the naturalist, could he, too, appeal to the voices of nature for their confirmation of the laws prevailing in the organic and inorganic world! Where the natural sciences can only offer proof, the theory of economics can persuade; it can enlist the unqualified inner consent of readers.' Also Fritz Machlup, 'If Matter Could Talk' [1969], in *Methodology of Economics and Other Social Sciences* (New York: Academic Press, 1978) pp.309-32.

23. Mises, *Epistemological Problems of Economics* p.13: '[Praxeology's] goal is the comprehension of the universal, and its procedure is formal and axiomatic. It views action and the conditions under which action takes place not in their concrete form, as we encounter them in everyday life, nor in their actual setting, as we view them in each of the sciences of nature and history, but as formal constructions that enable us to grasp the patterns of human action in their purity.' Also see *Human Action* p.39: 'The starting point of praxeology is not a choice of axioms and a decision about methods of procedure, but reflection about the essence of action'; *The Ultimate Foundations of Economic Science* pp.5-6: 'The starting point of praxeology is a self-evident truth, the cognition of action, that is, cognition of the fact that there is such a thing as consciously aiming at ends'; *Theory and History* pp.12-15 and 283-4.

24. Mises, *Epistemological Problems of Economics* p.14.

25. Mises, *Human Action* p.22: 'Man is in a position to act because he has the ability to discover causal relations which determine change and becoming in the universe. Acting requires and presupposes the category of causality. Only a man who sees the world in the light of causality is fitted to act. In this sense we may say that causality is a category of action. The category *means and ends* presupposes the category *cause and effect*.'

26. Ibid., p.105: 'The uncertainty of the future is already implied in the very notion of action. That man acts and that the future is uncertain are by no means independent matters. They are only two different modes of establishing one thing. ... If man knew the future, he would not have to choose and would not have to act.' See also *The Ultimate Foundations of Economic Science* pp.62-72.

27. Mises, *Human Action* p.99: 'The notion of change implies the notion of temporal sequence. ... The concepts of change and of time are inseparably linked together. Action aims at change and is therefore in the temporal order. Human reason is even incapable of conceiving the ideas of timeless existence and of timeless action. He who acts distinguishes between the time before the action, the time absorbed by the action, and the time after the action has been finished.'

28. Ibid., pp.13-14: 'Acting man is eager to substitute a more satisfactory state of affairs for a less satisfactory. His mind imagines conditions which suit him better, and his action aims at bringing about this desired state. The incentive that impels a man to act is always some uneasiness. A man perfectly content with the state of his affairs would have no incentive to change things. ... But to make a man act, uneasiness and the image of a more satisfactory state alone are not sufficient. A third condition is required: the expectation that purposeful behavior has the power to remove or at least to alleviate the felt uneasiness. In the absence of this condition no action is feasible. Man must yield to the inevitable. He must submit to destiny.'

29. Mises, *Epistemological Problems of Economics* p.24: 'As thinking and acting men, we grasp the concept of action. In grasping this concept we simultaneously grasp the closely

corresponding concepts of value, wealth, exchange, price, and cost. They are all necessarily implied in the concept of action, and together with them the concepts of valuing, scale of value and importance, scarcity and abundance, advantage and disadvantage success and failure, and profit and loss. The logical unfolding of all these concepts and categories in systematic derivation from the fundamental category of action and the demonstration of the necessary relations among them constitutes the first task of our science.' See also *The Ultimate Foundations of Economic Science* p.8. For a clear exposition of the logical unfolding of these basic and fundamental concepts of economics from the axiom of action, see Murray N. Rothbard, *Man, Economy and State: A Treatise on Economic Principles*, Vol. I [1962] (Los Angeles: Nash Publishing 1970) pp.1–66.

30.   Mises, *Human Action* p.198: 'Both in acting and in theorizing about acting, man can neither free himself from these categories nor go beyond them. A kind of acting categorically different from that determined by these categories is neither possible nor conceivable for man.' See also Mises, *Epistemological Problems of Economics* pp.95–6: 'Though the men of the Middle Ages would not have understood the law of marginal utility, they nevertheless did not and could not act otherwise than as the law of marginal utility describes. Even the man of the Middle Ages sought to apportion the means at his disposal in such a way that he attained the same level of satisfaction in every kind of want. ... Even in the Middle Ages no one voluntarily exchanged a horse for a cow unless he valued the cow more highly than the horse.' See also Eugen von Böhm-Bawerk, *Capital and Interest*, Vol. II: *The Positive Theory of Capital* [1914] (South Holland, IL: Libertarian Press, 1959), p.204: 'And for centuries long before science set up the doctrine of marginal utility, the common man was accustomed to seek things and abandon things, not in accordance with the highest utility that they are by nature capable of delivering, but in accordance with the increase or decrease in concrete utility that depends on each given good. In other words, he practiced the doctrine of marginal utility before economic theory discovered it'; also Eli F. Heckscher, 'A Plea for Theory in Economic History', *Economic History* (January 1929) pp.525–34.

31.   See Albert A. Trever, *A History of Greek Economic Thought* [1916] (Philadelphia, PA: Porcupine Press, 1978) pp.34–7, 70–71, 96, 146–7.

32.   See Edwin Cannan, *Collected Works of Edwin Cannan*, Vol. VIII: *A Review of Economic Theory* [1929] (London: Routledge/Thoemmes Press, 1997), pp.93–121; Frank Taussig, *Principles of Economics*, Vol. I (New York: Macmillan Co., 1913) pp.30–48; John Bates Clark, *Essentials of Economic Theory* [1907] (New York: Augustus M. Kelley, 1968) pp.59–73.

33.   David Hume, 'Of the Jealousy of Trade', in *Essays: Moral, Political and Literary* (Indianapolis, IN: Liberty Classics, 1987) p.331: 'Were our narrow and malignant policies to meet with success, we should reduce all our neighboring nations to the same state of sloth and ignorance that prevails in Morocco and the coast of Barbary. But what would be the consequence? They could send us no commodities: They could take none from us: Our domestic commerce itself would languish for want of emulation, example, and instruction: And we ourselves should soon fall into the same abject condition, to which we had reduced them. I shall therefore venture to acknowledge, that, not only as a man, but as a British subject, I pray for the flourishing commerce of Germany, Spain, Italy, and even France itself.'

34.   Adam Smith, *The Wealth of Nations* (New York: Modern Library, 1937), Bk I, Chs I–III and Bk IV, Ch. II.

35.   David Ricardo, *The Works and Correspondence of David Ricardo*, Vol. I: *On The Principles of Political Economy and Taxation* (Cambridge: Cambridge University Press, 1962) pp.128–49; see also Jacob Viner, *Studies in the Theory of International Trade* [1937] (New York: Augustus M. Kelley, 1965) pp.437–526; Gottfried Haberler, *The Theory of International Trade* (London: William Hodge, 1937) pp.125–44; on Haberler's contributions, see Richard M. Ebeling, 'Gottfried Haberler: A Centenary Appreciation', *Ideas on Liberty* (July 2000) 46–51.

36.   Mises, *Human Action* pp.159–64; *Nationalökonomie: Theorie des Handelns und Wirtwschaftens* [1940] (Munich: Philosophia Verlag, 1980), pp.126–33. *Nationalökonomie* was the original German language precursor to *Human Action*, published in Geneva,

Switzerland, shortly before Mises' immigration to the USA in the summer of 1940. See also Lionel Robbins, *The Evolution of Modern Economic Theory* (New York: Macmillan, 1970) pp. 32-3: 'It was realized too, although comparatively recently, that ... the famous theory of comparative costs ... is capable of providing, so to speak, an analytical stiffening of the traditional doctrine of the advantages of division of labor in general. Indeed, in our own time it has been represented with great cogency by von Mises as nothing less than the fundamental explanation of the spontaneous forces making for social cooperation in general - the *Ricardo'sche Vergesellschaftungsgesetz*, or Law of Association, as he calls it.'

37. Mises, *Human Action* pp. 159-60.
38. Mises, *Socialism* pp. 259-60; *Human Action* pp. 157-8.
39. Mises, *Socialism* pp. 259-61, 263-4, 275-6; *Human Action* p. 273: 'In nature there prevail irreconcilable conflicts of interests. The means of subsistence are scarce. Proliferation tends to outrun subsistence. Only the fittest plants and animals survive. ... Social cooperation under division of labor removes such antagonisms. It substitutes partnership and mutuality for hostility. The members of society are united in a common venture.' F.A. Hayek, 'The Confusion of Language in Political Thought' [1968], in *New Studies in Philosophy, Politics, Economics and the History of Ideas* (Chicago: University of Chicago Press, 1978) p. 90, points out that 'the term "catallactics", which has often been proposed as a replacement for the term "economics" as the name for the theory of the market order [is] derived from the Greek verb *katallatein* (or *katallasseiu*), which significantly means not only "to exchange" but also "to receive into the community" and "to turn from enemy into friend"'.
40. Mises, *Human Action* pp. 195-8.
41. Mises, *Socialism* pp. 268-9.
42. Mises, *Liberalism: The Classical Tradition* [1927] (Irvington-on-Hudson, NY: Foundation for Economic Education, 1996) pp. 18-38.
43. Mises, *Socialism* p. 277: 'The social function of private ownership in the means of production is to put the goods into the hands of those who know best how to use them, into the hands, that is, of the most expert managers. Nothing is more foreign to the essence of property than special privileges for special property and protection for special producers. Any kind of restraint such as exclusive rights and other privileges of producers are apt to obstruct the working of the social function of property.'
44. Ludwig von Mises, 'Liberty and Property' [1958], in *Two Essays by Ludwig von Mises* (Auburn, AL: Ludwig von Mises Institute, 1991) p. 34: 'In the market economy the individuals are free to choose the way in which they want to integrate themselves into the frame of social cooperation.'
45. Mises, *Socialism* p. 34: 'Economic action demands stable conditions. The extensive and lengthy process of production is the more successful the greater the periods of time to which it is adapted. It demands continuity, and this continuity cannot be disturbed without the most serious disadvantages. This means that economic action requires peace, the exclusion of violence.'
46. Mises, *Human Action* pp. 287-8: 'The inequality of individuals with regard to wealth and income is an essential feature of the market economy. ... What pressure is needed to impel an individual to contribute his share to the cooperative effort of production is exercised by the price structure of the market. This pressure is indirect. It puts on each individual's contribution a premium graduated according to the value which the consumers attach to this contribution. In rewarding the individual's effort according to its value, it leaves to everybody the choice between a more or less complete utilization of his own faculties and abilities.' See also Ludwig von Mises, 'On Equality and Inequality,' [1961], in Ebeling (ed.), *Money, Method and the Market Process* pp. 190-201.
47. Mises, *Human Action* p. 285: 'Government is a guarantor of liberty and is compatible with liberty only if its range is adequately restricted to the preservation of what is called economic freedom. Where there is no market economy, the best-intentioned provisions of constitutions and laws remain a dead letter.'
48. Ibid., pp. 264-5: 'All civilizations have up to now been based on private ownership of the means of production. In the past civilization and private property have been linked

together. ... If historical experience could teach us anything, it would be that private property is inextricably linked with civilization. ... The system of market economy has never been fully and purely tried. But there prevailed in the orbit of Western civilization since the Middle Ages by and large a general tendency toward the abolition of institutions hindering the operation of the market economy. With the successive progress of this tendency, population figures multiplied and the masses' standard of living was raised to an unprecedented and hitherto undreamed of level.'

49. Mises, *Socialism* p. 31: 'To have production goods in the economic sense, i.e., to make them serve one's own economic purposes, it is not necessary to have them physically in the way one must have consumption goods if one is to use them up or to use them lastingly. To drink coffee I do not need to own a coffee plantation in Brazil, an ocean liner, and a coffee roasting plant, though all these means of production must be used to bring a cup of coffee to my table. Sufficient that others own these means of production and employ them for me. In the society which divides labor no one is exclusive owner of the means of production, either of the material things or of the personal element, capacity to work. All means of production render services to everyone who buys and sells on the market.'

50. Ibid., pp. 101 and 103.

51. Mises, *Liberalism* pp. 71-2 and 74-5.

52. Mises, *Human Action* p. 199.

53. Ludwig von Mises, *Bureaucracy* (New Haven: Yale University Press, 1944) p. 29.

54. Mises, *Human Action* 212-14; *Epistemological Problems of Economics* pp. 156-9.

55. Mises, *Socialism* pp. 285-6.

56. Mises, *Human Action* pp. 117 and 338: 'Competitors aim at excellence and preeminence in accomplishments within a system of mutual cooperation. The function of competition is to assign to every member of a social system that position in which he can best serve the whole of society and all its members. It is a method for selecting the most able man for each performance. ... Competing in cooperation and cooperating in competition all people are instrumental is bring about the result, viz., the price structure of the market, the allocation of the factors of production to the various lines of want-satisfaction, and the determination of the share of each individual.'

57. Mises, *Socialism* pp. 170-71; *Human Action* p. 283: 'Now it is true that the employer has the right to fire the employee. But if he makes use of this right in order to indulge his whims, he hurts his own interests. It is to his own disadvantage if he discharges a better man in order to hire a less efficient one. The market does not directly prevent anybody from arbitrarily inflicting harm on his fellow citizens; it only puts a penalty upon such conduct. The shopkeeper is free to be rude to his customers provided he is ready to bear the consequences. The consumers are free to boycott a purveyor provided they are ready to pay the costs. What impels every man to the utmost exertion in the service of his fellow men and curbs innate tendencies toward arbitrariness and malice is, in the market, not compulsion and coercion on the part of gendarmes, hangmen, and penal courts; it is self-interest.' See also *Bureaucracy* pp. 36-9.

58. Mises, *Socialism* p. 271: 'Civilization is a product of leisure and the peace of mind that only the division of labor can make possible.'

59. Ibid., pp. 281 and 285-6: 'Society is the union of human beings for the better exploitation of the natural conditions of existence; in its very conception it abolishes the struggle between human beings and substitutes the mutual aid which provides the essential motive of all members united in an organism. Within the limits of society there is no struggle, only peace. ... People say that, in the competitive struggle, economic lives are destroyed. This, however, merely means that those who succumb are forced to seek in the structure of the social system of division of labor a position other than the one they would like to occupy. It does not by any means signify that they are to starve. In the capitalist society there is a place and bread for all. Its ability to expand provides sustenance for every worker.'

60. Ibid., p. 276; also *Human Action* p. 192-3.

61. Ludwig von Mises, 'Economic Calculation in the Socialist Commonwealth' [1920], in F.A. Hayek (ed.), *Collectivist Economic Planning* (London: George Routledge & Sons, 1935) pp. 87-130, or Israel M. Kirzner (ed.), *Classics of Austrian Economics*, Vol. III (London:

William Pickering, 1994), pp.3-30; Mises' critique of central planning was integrated into his wider 1922 treatise, *Socialism* pp.95-194.

62. See Chapter 4 of the present volume for an analysis of those writers before World War I who demonstrated the limits and impossibilities of socialist central planning, and a contrast of their views with Mises' critique of planning.

63. Mises, *Human Action* pp.206-9.

64. Mises, 'Economic Calculation in the Socialist Commonwealth' pp.108-9; Kirzner, *Classics of Austrian Economics* pp.15-16; Mises, *Liberalism* pp.71-2.

65. Mises, *Socialism* pp.123 and 113.

66. Mises, 'Economic Calculation in the Socialist Commonwealth' pp.109-10; Kirzner, *Classics of Austrian Economics* p.16; Mises, *Socialism* pp.121 and 187-8.

67. See, in particular, the most famous theory of market socialism by Oskar Lange, in *On the Economic Theory of Socialism* [1936-7] (New York: McGraw-Hill, 1964) pp.57-143.

68. Mises, *Socialism* pp.119-23; *Human Action* pp.698-715; Friedrich A. Hayek, 'Socialist Calculation: The Competitive "Solution"' [1940], in Bruce Caldwell (ed.), *The Collected Works of F.A. Hayek, Vol. X: Socialism and War* (Chicago: University of Chicago Press, 1997) pp.117-40, and 'Two Pages of Fiction: The Impossibility of Socialist Calculation' [1982], in Chiaki Nishiyama and Kurt R. Leube (eds), *The Essence of Hayek* (Stanford: Hoover Institution Press, 1984) pp.53-61.

69. Ludwig von Mises, *Critique of Interventionism* [1929] (Irvington-on-Hudson, NY: Foundation for Economic Education, 1996) p.4.

70. Mises, *Human Action* pp.718-19; also *Socialism* pp.485-6.

71. Mises, *Human Action* p.719; also *Socialism* p.491: 'What the interventionist aims at is the substitution of police pressure for the choice of the consumers. All this talk: the state should do this or that, ultimately means: The police should force the consumers to behave otherwise than they would behave spontaneously. In such proposals as: let *us* raise farm prices, let *us* raise wage rates, let *us* lower profits, let *us* curtail the salaries of executives, the *us* ultimately refers to the police.'

72. Mises, *Socialism* pp.45-6; *Liberalism* pp.34-8; *Human Action* pp.719-24; *The Ultimate Foundation of Economic Science*, pp.94-101.

73. Mises, *Human Action* pp.257-397; and 'Profit and Loss' [1951], in *Planning for Freedom* (South Holland, IL: Libertarian Press, 1980), pp.108-50.

74. Mises, *Human Action* pp.733-4.

75. Mises, *Liberalism* p.55.

76. Mises, *Human Action* pp.737-42 and 806-11; and *Interventionism: An Economic Analysis* [1940] (Irvington-on-Hudson, NY: Foundation for Economic Education, 1998) pp.51-5.

77. Mises, *Human Action* p.743.

78. Mises, *Critique of Interventionism*, pp.5-6.

79. Mises, *Human Action* pp.743-8; *Critique of Interventionism* pp.5-7; *Interventionism: An Economic Analysis* pp.17-21.

80. Mises, *Critique of Interventionism* pp.7-11 and 97-106; *Interventionism: An Economic Analysis* pp.23-34; *Human Action* pp.758-79; *Socialism* pp.488-90; *Planning for Freedom* pp.18-35 and 72-82.

81. Space does not permit a discussion of Mises' analysis of monopoly and cartels and his demonstration that, except when government intervention establishes and maintains them through legal privilege to select producers, they are, in the long run, unsustainable on a free market. The only exception, conceptually possible but historically rare, was cases in which a single producer (or a small group of cooperating producers) acquired control of an essential resource or raw material, without which a product could not be produced. Even in this case, the monopoly resource owner would be able to charge a 'monopoly price' only if consumer demand was sufficiently inelastic (that is, unresponsive to an increase in the price of the good) so that, at the higher monopoly price, the monopolist was able to earn a greater total revenue than if he sold the good at the lower price that would have prevailed on the market in a more competitive market environment. See *Liberalism* pp.90-95; *Socialism* pp.344-51; *Human Action* pp.357-79; and 'Monopoly Prices' [1944], in *Quarterly Journal of Austrian Economics* (Summer 1998) 1-28.

82. Mises, *Socialism* pp.419–23; *Epistemological Problems of Economics* pp.194–7; and *The Anti-Capitalistic Mentality* (Princeton: D. Van Nostrand, 1956). On the anti-market ideas of the ancient Greeks and Romans, see Lewis H. Haney, *History of Economic Thought* (New York: Macmillan, 1936) pp.56–85; and on the resentments of the intellectual against the market economy, see Bertrand de Jouvenel, 'The Attitude of the Intellectuals to the Market Economy', *The Owl* (January 1951) 19–27.

83. Mises, *Liberalism* pp.155–87; *Human Action* pp.315–19 and 748–55; also 'The Clash of Group Interests' [1945] in Ebeling (ed.), *Money, Method and the Market Process* pp.202–14.

84. Mises, *Socialism* pp.319–20.

85. Ibid., p.38

86. Mises, 'Trends Can Change' [1951], in *Planning for Freedom* pp.173–9.

87. Mises, *Socialism* p.13.

88. Ibid., pp.468–9.

4. Economic calculation under socialism: Ludwig von Mises and his predecessors

THE AUSTRIAN SCHOOL OF ECONOMICS IN THE YEARS BETWEEN THE WORLD WARS

The era between the world wars was a high watermark in the history of the Austrian School of Economics. Politically, World War I had been a catastrophe for Austria. The dual monarchy of Austria–Hungary, that had given the ruling House of Hapsburg reign over a vast central European empire, splintered into seven different pieces: a new Czechoslovakia, a separate Hungary, an enlarged Romania, a reborn Poland, an expanded Italy, a Serbian-led Yugoslavia and a small, land-locked 'Republic of Austria'. The new Austria was financially bankrupt and economically ruined. An English journalist described the situation in 1920: 'Vienna, instead of being the vital centre of fifty millions of people, finds itself a derelict city with a province of six millions. It is cut off from its coal supplies, from its food supplies, from its factories, from everything that means existence. It is enveloped by tariff walls.'[1] And the economic hardships of trade restrictions were soon joined by a devastating inflation that wreaked even more havoc on the crippled and weak new nation.[2]

But in spite of the political instability and economic hardships that plagued little Austria through most of the inter-war years, in the 1920s and early 1930s Vienna once again became one of Europe's cultural and intellectual centres. Vienna was home to Freud and the psychoanalytic movement, to Carnap and Schlick and the school of logical positivism, to Karl Popper and Ludwig Wittgenstein, to Hans Kelsen and the school of the 'pure theory of law' and to the Austrian School of Economics.[3]

At the University of Vienna, Hans Mayer held the senior chair vacated by Friedrich von Wieser's retirement in the mid-1920s.[4] Ludwig von Mises was senior economic consultant at the Austrian Chamber of Commerce, taught a seminar at the university, and led a 'private seminar' at his Chamber offices twice a month.[5] Around Mayer and Mises there developed an entire new generation of 'Austrian Economists', many of whom would gain international recognition in the decades to come: Friedrich A. Hayek, Fritz Machlup, Gottfried Haberler, Oskar Morgenstern, Paul Rosenstein-Rodan, Leo Schönfeld, Erich Schiff and Richard Strigl.[6] Indeed, by 1931, Lionel Robbins (a young enthusiast of the 'Austrians' at the University of London) could write: 'The School of Vienna, which in recent years, under the leadership of Professor Mayer and Professor Mises, has experienced such a marvelous renaissance, has laid the scientific world under yet another lasting obligation.'[7]

The 'lasting obligation' to which Robbins referred was the Austrian theory of the trade cycle, as first developed in the 1920s by Ludwig von Mises and then elaborated upon by Friedrich A. Hayek. Beginning with the choice processes underlying the individual demands for money, the Austrians explained the emergence of the value of money in the general market; how changes in the value of money originated either in the demand for or supply of money; how the structure of relative prices was distorted during the sequence of events culminating in a change in the value of money; and how such a process could have the characteristics of the 'business cycle' when changes in the supply of money originated in the loan market and distorted market rates of interest.[8]

In the 1920s, the Austrians had also formalized the concept of choice. Two variations on the choice theme were developed. One, found in the works of Hans Mayer and Rosenstein-Rodan, had emphasized the 'economizing' quality of choice: that choice was the relationship between a set of given ends ranked in terms of importance and a set of given means usable for alternative purposes which were to be allocated in the service of those ends. The other variation on the choice theme was developed by Ludwig von Mises, in which choice, and the resulting logic of the ends–means relationship, was an outgrowth of the wider concept of 'meaningful action'; action was 'meaningful' when the behaviour in question was guided by a purpose in mind, with the purpose defining the action in question as one of a certain kind.[9]

Another set of themes characteristic of practically all the Austrian economists of the period was that of change, time and uncertainty. Since Menger, the analytical 'twist' unique to the Austrians, in comparison to other schools of economic thought, has been an interest in problems of 'process' and adjustment to change in markets, rather than only a description and analysis of 'equilibrium states' that were the hallmark of the mathematical economists. In the 1920s and 1930s, the Austrians focused on an array of problems. How were prices dynamically formed on markets? What were the relationships between market changes in time and market adjustment for coordination through time? What did 'equilibrium' mean and how did it relate to different assumptions about the knowledge possessed by market actors? How did market participants form expectations for mutual coordination of plans in the social division of labour?[10]

The growing output of these Austrians soon began to have an expanding influence on economists far beyond the frontiers of the new Austrian Republic. Its impact was particularly felt in England, with the London School of Economics the centre of this interest. Arnold Plant relates that, when visiting an economics institute in Kiel, Germany, in early 1933, a German economist looking for a teaching position outside the domain of the new Nazi Reich, despondently commented, 'I suppose that the LSE will have no vacancy for me, now that you have become "ein Vorort von Wien" – a suburb of Vienna.'[11]

LUDWIG VON MISES AND THE DEBATE OVER SOCIALIST ECONOMIC CALCULATION IN THE HISTORY OF ECONOMIC THOUGHT

The leading figure in the post-World War I 'renaissance' of the Austrian School was Ludwig von Mises. It is hardly an exaggeration to say that almost all of the contributions for which the Austrians are credited in this period either began in one of Mises's works or were given additional insight and impetus to further development in his writings.[12] Already before World War I he had made a major and original contribution with the publication of the first edition of *The Theory of Money and Credit* in 1912.[13] But what drew Mises international attention and an impact that is still felt today (not only in the realm of 'pure theory', but also in the course of economic policy around the world) was his 1920 essay, 'Economic Calculation in the Socialist Commonwealth',[14] which became the centrepiece of his 1922 treatise, *Socialism: An Economic and Sociological Analysis*.[15] Hayek has told that, 'To none of us ... who read the book [*Socialism*] when it appeared was the world ever the same again ... [Wilhelm] Röpke ... [Lionel] Robbins or [Bertil] Ohlin ... would tell the same story.'[16]

First in his essay and then in his book, Mises challenged the socialists to explain how they would solve the fundamental problem that would confront them if they were to gain power and follow through with their stated programme of nationalization of all the society's means of production, the problem being how the socialist central planners would rationally allocate the scarce means of production among all their alternative uses, so as efficiently to provide a more plentiful supply of goods and services than under the 'anarchy' of capitalist, competitive production.

Mises had argued that the market economy was able to place calculable relative valuations on the means of production through the competitive pricing of those who wished to use them in alternative lines of production. But under socialism, with the elimination of private property and market transactions through a monetary medium of exchange, the socialist planners would have no rational method for assigning scarce resources among competing tasks for which they could be applied. As Mises curtly summarized the problem: 'Where there is no market, there is no price system, and where there is no price system there can be no economic calculation.'[17]

In the history of economic thought this has come to be seen as the great opening challenge to a debate that then raged for almost seven decades. Both socialists and anti-socialists have bestowed homage on Mises for having raised the veil from an earlier reluctance on the part of socialist critics of capitalism to explain how a centrally directed economy would function once property, prices and markets had been abolished.[18]

The answer that the socialists developed in the 1930s was that socialism did not have to mean the abolition of either markets or prices. In the most popular of these 'market socialist' formulations, that of the Polish economist Oskar Lange, it was proposed that the central planning agency would be assigned the task of setting 'parametric prices'. Socialist managers of nationalized firms would use this centrally set structure of resource prices for planning their production activities; if, at these prices, shortages or surpluses materialized, this would 'signal' to the central planners that relative resource prices were 'wrong', and through a process of trial and error the planners would move those prices until they were 'correct' and supplies and demands were matched. Lange was obviously so pleased that he was able to show that socialism could work, in spite of Mises' charge, that he flippantly suggested that, 'Both as an expression of recognition for the great service rendered by him and as a memento of the prime importance of sound economic accounting, a statue of Professor Mises ought to occupy an honorable place in the great hall of the Ministry of Socialization or the Central Planning Board of the socialist state.'[19]

But even as the socialists were hailing their 'solution' to the problem of economic calculation under socialism, it was pointed out that, in fact, the entire exercise had been a tempest in a teapot, because Mises had been proved wrong even before he wrote it. It appeared that before World War I two Italian economists, Enrico Barone and Vilfredo Pareto, had demonstrated that the system of mathematical equations that would be necessary to solve the problem of competitive general equilibrium under private ownership of the means of production were the same equations that would be necessary for equilibrium under socialism. As Schumpeter expressed it, 'The essential result of Barone's or any similar investigation is that there exists for any centrally controlled socialism a system of equations that possess a uniquely determined set of solutions, in the same sense and with the same qualifications as does perfectly competitive capitalism.' As a consequence, 'this means that so far as its pure logic is concerned the socialist plan makes sense and cannot be disposed of on the ground that it would necessarily spell chaos, waste, or irrationality.'[20]

Mises, therefore, seemed to be sandwiched between two sets of mathematical solutions (Barone's and Pareto's before him and Lange's after him) that appeared to make his entire argument redundant. Mises had failed to see, it was claimed, that 'the economic problem' was ultimately a mathematical one: what was required was the specifying of the shapes and positions of the respective supply and demand functions to find that solution that assured a simultaneous clearing of all markets, both for factors of production and for finished products. It appeared that Mises, who in a sense was accusing the socialists of not understanding economics, was not himself as good an economist as he thought. Mises' problem seemed to be the old one that Austrians have been accused of for almost a hundred years: he just did not understand mathematics or its applications to economics.[21]

The more recent contributions to the debate have put the issues involved on a different plane. Professor Donald C. Lavoie, in his exhaustive study, *Rivalry and Central Planning: The Socialist Calculation Debate Reconsidered*, cogently argued that, for all intents and purposes, the debate has been misunderstood. The historians of economic thought have failed to appreciate the tacitly different assumptions that Mises (and Hayek) were basing their argument upon, in contrast to those who saw a socialist solution to the calculation problem. As Lavoie expresses it: 'At the heart of the debate is a confusion between two fundamentally divergent views of "competition": (1) the rivalrous competitive process of the Austrians (similar to the classical notion), and (2) the neo-classical notion of a nonrivalrous, static, competitive equilibrium.'[22]

Mises and the Austrians, Lavoie explains, conceived of the market economy as a dynamic competitive process in which a complex system of division of labour was matched by an equally complex system of division of knowledge. Rivalry in the market was the means through which decentralized knowledge was conveyed to every corner of the economy via the price system to assist mutual coordination of production and consumption plans. At the same time, market rivalry was the means through which knowledge in the market was discovered and brought to bear for the satisfaction of consumer demands.

This 'Austrian' conception of the market process is in contrast to the neoclassical view of perfect competition, in which all the 'knowledge problems' of market coordination are assumed away, either by postulating the presence of 'perfect knowledge' on the part of all market participants or through the assumption that all relevant knowledge can be translated into quantitative and objective forms that are easily conveyable to planners for their use and application to the problem of resource allocation in a centrally organized economy.

This new interpretation of the calculation debate is reinforced when we take into consideration the brief overview of the Austrian School during the inter-war years that was given at the beginning of this chapter. The entire orientation of the Austrian 'approach' was precisely in terms of how markets worked under conditions of imperfect knowledge, constant change and the passage of time. Mises and the Austrians, therefore, were not defeated. Rather, the illusion of victory belonged to the 'anti-Misesians' because their conception of the market and the problem requiring a solution was different from Mises' conception of the market and the 'economic problem'. And since it is the neoclassical theory of perfect competition that is slowly falling further into disuse by economists, because of its unrealism, the economists' view of the market and economic processes is slowly coming around to Mises', as well.[23]

MISES' FORGOTTEN PREDECESSORS ON THE PROBLEMS OF CENTRAL PLANNING UNDER SOCIALISM

> The magnitude of the change [arising from the implementation of socialism] is perhaps best seen from the usual proposal to abolish the use of money. Let anyone try to imagine how the business of a great country is to be carried on without money and prices, how the value to society of various species of labor is to be estimated, and how the relative utilities of consumable commodities and transient services are to be calculated, and he will soon discover that the abolition of money would logically end in the abolition of the division of labor. (J. Shield Nicholson, *Principles of Political Economy*, 1893)[24]

But before the book can be closed on the history of the socialist calculation debate there is at least one more chapter that needs to be added. The 'standard' interpretation, as we saw, points out that Mises may have initiated the debate, but he was preceded by two economists – Barone and Pareto – who had tried to offer a solution through the avenue of mathematical general equilibrium analysis.

Earlier than that, it is said, neither socialists nor non-socialists confronted the issue. Socialists spoke either in generalizations about the coming paradise of an exploitation-free society, or condemned speculation on the socialist society of the future as 'unscientific'. Anti-socialists devoted their energies either to condemning a socialist society as the ultimate tyranny in which all would be slaves to a super-collectivist state that would own, produce and distribute everything, or to warning that the elimination of private property would be a threat to both production and progress because of the demise of the direct link between work and reward. The question of how the socialist planners would go about the mundane business of deciding what to produce or how to allocate scarce resources among industries in the economy was left untouched.

While generally true of most economists and popular writers on socialism before World War I, this is not the whole truth. There was a small minority of economists who attempted to deal precisely with this question, yet they seem to have been completely forgotten, with two exceptions, one of which was the 'forgotten' Herman Gossen who has over the years been given belated recognition on this point. But while Gossen's were passing comments in a book on marginal utility theory, other writers devoted *entire chapters* to the subject in larger studies on various aspects of socialism.[25]

There are five books in particular which deserve recognition for their work on this topic, and with which we shall be concerned in this section: Albert Schäffle's *The Quintessence of Socialism* (1874)[26]; Paul Leroy Beaulieu's *Collectivism* (1885)[27]; William Graham's *Socialism: New and Old* (1891)[28]; Victor Cathrein's *Socialism: Its Theoretical Basis and Practical Application* (1890)[29]; and Benedict Elder's *A Study of Socialism* (1915).[30] What is noteworthy about their contributions is the manner in which they anticipated some of the ideas later developed by Mises, Hayek and other Austrians about the essential insurmountable difficulties precluding the effective functioning of a centrally directed socialist economy. As we will see, their view of competition, their conception of the role of markets and prices and their view of the particular 'knowledge problems' confronting any attempt at central direction of economic affairs were similar to the arguments that the Austrians presented in the 1920s, 1930s and 1940s.

That their view of competition was similar to the Austrians' is not very surprising. As has been pointed out by previous writers, the 'Classical' conception of competition was exactly opposite that of modern micro-economic textbook theory.[31] Lionel Robbins has clearly described the classical notion:

> it is clear that the claims of the Classical Economists for competition and the market do not rest upon any very precise mathematical or semi-mathematical conception of statical equilibrium. Indeed, I cannot help suspecting that if they had been confronted with the systems of this sort which have been developed since their day, they would have had some hesitation in acknowledging a near family relationship. Their conception of the mechanism of the System of Economic Freedom was surely a conception of something more rough and ready, something much more dynamic and real than these exquisite laboratory models.[32]

And the economists we are to discuss were indeed 'Classical' in this sense.

Albert Schäffle

Albert Schäffle seems to have been the first to have systematically tried to conceive of what a centralized economy would look like by asking what the socialists said they wished to eliminate in the present (capitalist) economic system. This then led him to tease out the nature of the alternative socialist economy. Since Schäffle's contribution has been discussed already in some detail by T.W. Hutchison,[33] we need only emphasize the essential points. In *The Quintessence of Socialism*, Schäffle explains: 'Critically, dogmatically, and practically, the cardinal [socialist] thesis stands out – collective instead of private ownership of all instruments of production (land, factories, machines, tools, etc.); "organization" of labor by society, instead of distracting competition of private capitalists ... public organization of the labor of all on the basis of collective ownership of all the working materials of social labor; and, finally, distribution of the collective output of all kinds of manufacture in proportion to the value and amount of the work done by each worker.'[34] Over a series of brief chapters Schäffle explains the socialist criticisms of the existing capitalist system and why the establishment of socialism logically requires an end to private ownership of the means of production, the elimination of the 'wage system', the abolition of interest and rent, the prohibition of commodity trading and speculative markets, and the demise of a money system of exchange: 'if we suppose the production of private capitalists to be removed,' says Schäffle, 'and a unified, organized common-production in its place, buying, selling, competition and markets, prices and payment by money are at once superfluous. Within the socialist economic organization they are even impossible'.[35] And he asks us to visualize the resulting economic order:

> Imagine the control of all production vested in a single office of public economy, in a single central office, representing the bureaus of production and sale, it being insignificant whether this control was arranged in the spirit of federal or of centralistic socialism. In such a case no doubt an actual transport of products from one factory to the other, and a delivery to the consumers, would have to be organized from the central and intermediate stations in the economic organization; transportation, housing, and storage, in order to secure the distribution of each article of production over all the necessary districts in the right proportion and at the right time, and in proportion to the public returns stating the demand of each district, become unavoidable. Therefore, transport and storage, which accompany the trade of today, would be the necessary concomitants of the barter of the socialistic state, and would be conducted in accordance with the centralized filing of accounts, bookkeeping, and settlement between all the branches of business. But this barter could no longer be a private transaction or exchange, therefore no longer trade, nor purchase and sale in a continuous chain of private transactions. Trade would disappear, would really have become superfluous.[36]

Schäffle explains that, under divided decision making in a private property order, the coordination of the processes of production and the satisfaction of consumer demands are established through trading on markets, in which prices act as both checks and incentives on economic planning in various directions. But, under socialism, 'The bureaus of disposal ascertain the demand, distribute accordingly the national labour among the different classes of trade, and among the departments of production, transport, and storage, and their bureaus, and fix the value of the produce in proportion to the labour-time socially necessary to be spent upon it [Karl Marx]. The produce would be distributed in accordance with the thus regulated value, by way of liquidation of the labour-accounts of the entire body of producers.'[37]

In the market economy, Schäffle reminds the reader, money performs two functions, as a 'general standard of value', for the comparison of the relative value of things entering into exchange, and as a 'vehicle of value', that is, as a general medium of exchange through which all exchanges are facilitated.[38] Under socialism, the unit of account would be labour time invested in the production of commodities; and labour certificates representing the quantities of 'socially necessary' labour contributed by each member of the production process would serve as the medium by which labourers would present claims against various quantities of finished goods in the state's storehouses.[39]

Schäffle has two basic questions about the workability of a socialist economy along the lines presented: (1) is the premise correct that 'the social cost of labour is the standard of the value of commodities?' and (2) whether the socialist society, on the basis of its labour theory of value, could successfully have a principle for the allocation of labour among alternative uses in the economy?

On the first point, Schäffle declares that 'the "value" of commodities clearly does not depend solely on the cost, but also on the value in use, i.e., the urgency of demand. Without considering the varying use-value of different labour and different products, it is impossible to conceive a socialistic estimate of value, which could take the place of the present market value as contemplated by normal political economy'. If 'use-value' was disregarded, 'socialistic demand and supply would fall into a hopeless quantitative and qualitative discrepancy, which would be beyond control'.[40]

But quite separate from the necessity of the pricing of final goods at prices that equalize demand with existing supply (and, therefore, the avoidance of potential shortages and surpluses at 'wrong' labour-time determined prices), did the socialist society have a pricing method for the distribution of labour among employments? Since the direction of labour must reflect the uses for labour in different sectors of the economy, Schäffle saw the same problem as in the pricing of final output. Unless labour could be priced at rates that deviated from the value as measured in terms of labour time, no rational mechanism would exist for guiding labour into appropriate channels. 'Unless this use-value is comprised in the social estimate [that is, in the pricing of goods and labour services],' concluded Schäffle, 'that is, without a *corresponding imitation of all incidents which affect value in the present market*, it is not conceivable that any authoritative direction of the consolidated productive system could keep the demand for labor and for goods, as to quantity or kind, in harmony with the supply of labor and of goods – that is, could preserve that economical balance of work under consumption which is daily reestablished, though only by jerks, under the influence of market prices.'[41]

For our other authors, Schäffle's analysis often served as a signpost for their own criticisms of socialist central planning. But Schäffle's conclusions were seen by them as more of a rationale of how socialism could be made to work through the imitation of market-type pricing, rather than as a refutation of the socialist ideal. Hence they saw their task as demonstrating how there was no substitute for actual private, competitive markets.

Paul Leroy Beaulieu

Paul Leroy Beaulieu's *Collectivism* is a detailed critique of the socialist indictment of the private property order originally published in 1885. After challenging the socialist arguments against private property and an analysis of Marx's labour theory of value, he turns to an analysis of the socialist alternative.

A leading error in the socialist argument, insists Leroy Beaulieu, is the inability to appreciate the workings of the spontaneous order that emerges from the voluntary interactions of a multitude of men following their respective interests. 'A force is not necessarily unregulated because it acts automatically,' argues Leroy Beaulieu, 'on the contrary, it is most probably more regular, more uniform and more purposeful in its action, than a force which is entirely directed by volition – a fundamental truth which is quite disregarded by collectivists.' He reminds the reader that, without state intervention or the assistance of regulation, great cities like Paris and London are daily provisioned with all the necessities and conveniences of life. And all of this is brought about 'unconsciously'. 'Persons who are absolutely ignorant to the general welfare, are nevertheless completely successful in supplying these great cities with the required quantities of all the innumerable commodities demanded by their inhabitants.' 'This wonderful automatic adjustment of supply and demand is far from being an incoherent and anarchic force, as asserted by collectivists.'[42] What guides actors in the market is prices, 'the automatic regulators'. Yet it is prices that would disappear in a regime of state ownership; instead of the information currently supplied by prices for assisting production decisions, the planners will have to rely upon the collection of statistics about supply and demand conditions prepared by 'committees of inquiry'. Yet statistics, Leroy Beaulieu says, can never serve as an effective substitute for the fluctuations in prices that always are 'a more rapid and certain indication of the required amount of production than statistical abstracts'. Not only would the centralized statistical bookkeeping be a colossal task, it had to be remembered that

> they are defective in many respects, and when the subject to which they relate is complex, they are always liable to be affected by the idiosyncrasy of the compiler. Another cause which makes this source of information deceptive and not to be relied on, is the delay, often considerable between the occurrence of the events and the completion of the statistics relating to them.[43]

Furthermore, '*even the most perfect statistics can do no more than supply information, which has then to be interpreted, and interpretations are certain to vary widely.*' Only '"Price" is the sure guarantee of an adequate supply,' declared Leroy Beaulieu, 'and is thus the guardian of the subsistence of humanity.'[44]

> Deprived of this guidance, and without the incentive of personal interest, accounts and statistics, however complete, would be of very little use, and unless they were the mundane representatives of an omniscient providence, the directors of production would be quite unable to avoid occasional excess or deficiency of supply, which would cause terrible disorder and confusion, with effects infinitely more serious than mistakes made by private enterprise, which, as a whole, is never actuated by precisely similar motives; thus its errors correct each other, and being uninfluenced by prejudice, or *amour propre*, it shows a marvellous quickness of adoption; mistakes committed by the state would be not only far more serious, but far more difficult to remedy.[45]

Under the market system individuals possess free rein within the constraints of their income to choose and demand whichever products they desire. Since it was the provision of desired commodities that was the source of the seller's own income, self-interest was harnessed to the satisfaction of consumer demand. 'Today,' said Leroy Beaulieu, 'it is demand that determines supply, and private enterprise is always on the alert to meet it.' The producer is incessantly required to search out new and improved methods of production and capture profits by creating discrepancies between selling prices and the prices of factors of production by lowering costs. And this alertness to such profit opportunities is incessant because all profits are temporary in a competitive environment; as soon as one rival succeeds in such endeavours, the attention of his competitors is aroused and they soon attempt to match and exceed his accomplishments.[46]

Both incentive and price systems would be gone with the arrival of the socialist alternative, and with dire consequences:

We see then, that the momentous problem of the adjustment of supply and demand under a collectivist *regime*, in all localities and in all industries, remains unsolved. The play of prices would vanish with the disappearance of private trade, as also would that variation in profit which, although apparently unjust, is in reality the instrument by means of which harmonious interaction between production and requirements is maintained. In place of these potent and benign forces, the only safeguard against disaster would be infallibility on the part of the economic administration of the socialist state; but history and experience show that state administration, so far from being infallible, is, on the contrary, far inferior to private administration in respect of certainty and promptitude of conception and execution. On the one side is private interest, always alert and active; and on the other, officials hampered by rigid regulations imposed by a bureaucracy, slaves of red tape, capable of dealing with normal conditions only, and impotent when confronted with the exceptional difficulties and unexpected vicissitudes to which the economic world is always liable. Again, on the one side we have the energies of millions of men freely and actively engaged in work which they understand, on which their living depends, and which, therefore, they perform with the greatest keenness; and on the other, the cool indifference of administrators, who would be quite as much benumbed as stimulated by the responsibilities thrown upon them.[47]

Nor, Leroy Beaulieu points out, is it explained what procedure will be used to select the planners – the 'committees of control', as he calls them.[48] He also considers it illegitimate for the collectivists to point to industries currently administered by the state as examples of how an extended system of socialism would work. He reminds the socialists that these public sectors copy similar private administrations in organizing their affairs. And 'the present faults of public administration would increase because the privately managed industries which now serve more or less as models, and which maintain the spirit of emulation, would have disappeared'. Furthermore, the complexity of task and administration would multiply significantly under complete socialism, in comparison to isolated state industries in a sea of private enterprise.[49]

Finally, in a separate chapter, Leroy Beaulieu challenges the validity and practicability of the labour theory of value as a standard of remuneration or technique for directing labour into alternative lines of production. He points to three problems in this context. First, that the simple conception of 'socially necessary labour' as the basis for measured labour time falls into a quagmire once we take under consideration the differing physical conditions that will require differing amounts of labour to produce the same quality and quantity of output; and the insolubles of varying qualities and types of labour and the establishment of calculations of what multiples are skilled labour of 'simple labor'. Second, the pricing of labour in terms of some form of labour time standard of work performed would leave unanswered the question of what *non-compulsive* method would be available to attract labour into alternative occupations or industries, if wages could not fluctuate as remunerative price signals to guide the required changing distributions of labour among sectors in the economy over time. And, third, if commodities were priced at state retail shops on the basis of labour time invested in their production, this would result in the lack of a 'price mechanism' to limit demand to existing supply, and would lead to only slowly corrected surpluses and shortages.[50]

This latter difficulty, Leroy Beaulieu points out, would soon result in the re-emergence of private speculation and trading, that is, the black market:

> Although all purchases would legally have to be made in the national shops, and no person would be permitted to buy goods from his neighbour, it is certain that the more energetic members of society, with the connivance of the more inert, would in the long-run establish a complete system of illicit trade. How would it be possible to prevent an economical person who saved some labour-cheques [that is, the medium in which he was paid by the state for labour services rendered] and who foresaw that certain goods were likely to rise in price, from buying and storing them, and selling them when the expected rise occurred at a price somewhat lower than that charged in the national shops? ... However severe the regulations might be, it would be impossible to suppress this private commerce.

Leroy Beaulieu also anticipated the re-emergence of an illegal loan market, on which labour cheques (representing claims on goods at state stores) could be lent out at interest.[51]

William Graham

William Graham begins his analysis of socialism by explaining that a socialist system requires collective ownership of the means of production and distribution of collectively produced output on the basis of some measure of labour time performed. Products will be distributed at public warehouses and all industries will be directed by managers who would now be employees of the state. Like Leroy Beaulieu, he critically evaluates the meaning and complexities of devising a labour standard of value.[52] Graham explains: 'There will be no market in the socialist kingdom and no money. Markets and market prices are now useful to adjust supply and demand; this will be unnecessary under Collectivism, because the State will do it through labor bureaus and statistics.' Whereas, in the market economy, 'Money is now chiefly needed as a general medium of exchange; something with which you can buy anything, something for which you can sell anything ... In the Socialist State you will get for your work or your special services the desired things ... simply by presenting your labor cheques at the State stores.'[53]

Production decisions would reside ultimately in the hands of the state managers who would decide what was to be produced, in what quantities and of what qualities. An essential flexibility in the competitive market would be lacking in the socialist state: the capacity for innovation and improvement. In the market an individual needs only to convince a few to back his idea financially; but in the socialist state, it will be required to gain the approval of the entire planning agency to direct a portion of 'the society's' resources in a new manner.[54] This same reluctance to change and innovate would result in the demise of the market principle that it is demand that determines the allocation of resources.[55]

But the main thrust of Graham's argument is the dilemma of attempting to use the labour standard of value for purposes of economic calculation. With the elimination of markets and prices, Graham asks,

> How are we to know how much a worker produces in a cotton or linen factory where machines are working as well as he, and where the work of twenty different kinds of laborers is necessary as well as his to the final product? Where this is a common result from different kinds of human labor, from machine labor, and even from the gratuitous labor of natural forces, how are we to measure the amount of the product, thus due to such different cooperant agents, with which an individual is to be credited?[56]

The Marxian answer, says Graham, sounds easy enough: 'Labor-force is converted into labor-time, of which products are only a "congelation". Products are "congealed labor-time". Laborers in the factory who have worked the same number of hours are to get the same wages, the more skilled being reduced to the average by some, we know not what, rule of conversion.'[57] But, assuming that a conversion rule was available, the computational trail would be immense that would have to follow each and every product from its beginnings in its most unfinished state, through stages of production, through the various types of labour the product would have to pass through, including all the intermediate transporters: 'We must then add the number of hours' labor of unloading, the hours of the dockhands and wharfingers, the hours of the draymen who convey it to the railway station, of the railway porters, of the guards and engine-drivers. All these mere carriers have a claim on the ultimate product, or on products in general, measured by their number of hours or work, or labor-time – a very unequal measure indeed for the railway porter, and the railway guard or engine-drivers, the former of whom only bestowed a few minutes' hard work, and the latter not definitely measurable work on the goods at all, their time being spent in the general transport and care of both passengers and goods.' The intricacies of the computational detail would grow more and more complex as the production path of each and every product was followed through literally every physical step of its respective production processes. And, finally, Graham says, 'As to the bookkeepers' own labor I will only say that, however difficult it would be to measure it on the theory under consideration, it would be very real and responsible.'[58]

But the capacity for the entire computational process and the apportionment of 'labor-cheques' as payment for work preformed requires a rule for converting skilled into unskilled labour, and Graham explains that no such conversion table is objectively capable of being constructed, the types, qualities and characteristics of the multitude of labourers being too great and heterogeneous for the discovery of a physical common denominator.[59] And, hence, there collapses any hope for an objective law of distribution.

Graham, like Schäffle and Leroy Beaulieu, emphasizes the dilemma of labour-time priced commodities when the demand for the goods is greater or less than the supply at the labour-cheque redemption rate. The state manager must either raise or lower the labour-cheque redemption rate to bring supply into balance with demand, or see the accumulation of surpluses or frustrated consumers because of shortages. In the next planning period, output can be modified, but what would be the mechanism and incentives through which labour would be redirected, if wages could not fluctuate to reflect changing patterns of demand?[60]

The artificial labour 'prices' for commodities in the economy would merely lead to the re-emergence of markets and prices for the facilitating of illegal and speculative transactions. Yet Graham emphasizes that these illegal market transactions will be a distorted reflection of an open market and would be narrowly confined to those areas in which traders could evade the restrictions on private ownership of factors of production. The end result would be a set of perverse unintended consequences:

> On the whole we may say that the well-intentioned but ambitious attempt of the Socialists to suppress Money, the Investment list and the Stock Exchange, would lead to much greater visible evils than exist at present, not to speak of other evils certain from analogy, though, without trying the hazardous experience, we cannot describe them precisely ... To dispense with money ... in a great modern complicated society, especially on having a great foreign trade, would be fraught with disaster and chaos.[61]

Victor Cathrein

For Victor Cathrein, the inferiority of a socialist system of planning in comparison to the market economy is the latter's ability to take advantage of an intellectual division of knowledge in a manner that is not possible in the socialist society.

The central task of the socialist state is to 'regulate the national production', but regulation of production requires estimation of 'social demand' on a daily, weekly, monthly and yearly basis. Nor could one begin socialist planning from the existing pattern of demand, because the redistribution of property and wealth with the implementation of socialism would significantly modify those demand patterns. The socialist state would, therefore, have to acquire detailed and personal information from individuals and households about the demands of all the members of the society, to ensure that the right things are produced in the correct quantities at the desired times. Only by this procedure could the planners avoid the risk and waste of over- or under-production:

> But a census is mere child's play compared with a determination of social demand ... it would be necessary to inquire into the daily need of every man and every family in the most varied circumstances. Even the smallest details in the matter of clothing, underwear, toilet articles, traveling outfits, writing materials, amusements, and luxuries would have to be ascertained and tabulated. Add to all this the numerous articles of food which are required even in the humblest family, the supplying of the kitchen with fuel and cooking utensils, the fitting up of the drawing rooms and bedrooms with furniture and ornamentation, the lighting and heating, the stocking of the pantry ... The authorities will have to supply needle and thread to replace the missing shirt-button. All these items must be tabulated for the determination of the demand upon which the great system of production is to be based. And all of this would have to be done not for one family, but for the millions of families which constitute a modern state and for every one of their members.[62]

And Cathrein emphasizes that this is only a fraction of all the various private and public demands for which the central planners would be required to form detailed estimates.[63] The information required by the 'central bureau' concerning demand would have to be matched with equivalent information about the supplies of various types and quantities of factors of production, including the talents, inclinations, strengths and abilities of all the members of the potential labour force.[64]

Cathrein's question, after this enumeration of responsibilities to be assigned to the state, is 'Can any human wisdom be equal to this stupendous task?' The advantage of the market is precisely the decentralization of responsibilities, which includes the 'knowledge' responsibilities expected from any one participant in the market.

First, Cathrein argues, under the market individuals are required neither to anticipate each and every one of their wants in advance nor to commit themselves to advance purchases. 'At present everyone is at liberty to supply all his own wants at pleasure, either by his own labor or by purchase, when and where and from whomsoever he pleases, whether at home or abroad. Thus he is enabled to conceal the secrets of his household from the public gaze.'

Second, in the division of labour each commercial establishment is only required to concern itself with a comparatively small section of the overall market: 'the immense difference between a single comparatively small company, established for a limited purpose, and an entire commonwealth made up of several millions of human beings' makes it significantly easier for the former to manage successfully the collection and use of relevant knowledge.[65] At present, Cathrein says,

> Countless commercial travelers study the condition of the market; the most advantageous chances of buying and selling are ascertained. The transportation and distribution of commodities throughout the country is taken charge of by numerous business concerns. All this work and care, which at present is divided among thousands of different firms, would fall to the share of the socialist central government. In its hands would converge the millions of intricate threads of international relations. Can any human wisdom be equal to this stupendous task?[66]

The knowledge requirements for central direction of economic production and distribution make the market the only alternative: for in the market the division of tasks limits the amount of information each unit is to be responsible for and, thus, is manageable in a complex economy.

Benedict Elder

For Benedict Elder, the greatest weakness of the socialist economy is that it lacks a competitive process for market discovery of entrepreneurial talent. 'Direction is necessary to the simplest motion,' Elder states, and 'There is no human action that is not directed by the human brain.' This is no less true in the realm of the organization and direction of production. If the market does not select the entrepreneurs – the 'brains' behind the production process – how shall leadership in the socialist economy be selected?[67] Elder sees no reason to believe that the labourers in the firm would have the ability to pick from among themselves, or from outside, the decision maker for the organization.

If the managers for the firms are to be selected by 'the central authority in Socialismdom', what criteria shall they use? They might look for honesty and 'good intentions'; but what is really wanted is 'ability'. Ability cannot be bestowed and the 'known limitations of human capacity' forbid any likelihood that the central authorities would have the ability to discern ability in others; particularly since each individual finds it difficult to even interpret correctly his own abilities.[68]

There is no test of the 'fit' or 'unfit' for the directing of enterprise other than the market test itself:

> Capitalists, both large and small, fail; they fail singly and in groups; they fail not for lack of capital or of co-operation, but for lack of competent and reliable management in the business ... Competition unfailingly registers, in all their bearings, the mistakes and the shortcomings of each person within its domain, and with stern precision it assesses the penalty of financial loss for each delinquency

suffered to exist … the invariable law of competition is to eliminate the unfit from the industrial field and to yield to the fit exactly that measure of control they are fitted to sustain.[69]

Since under socialism there would be no market competition to test ability in satisfying consumer demand, there would be no method to sort out the competent from the incompetent entrepreneurs. Indeed, there would exist no method even to discover who they were. 'Directive ability must be determined automatically [that is, through market competition], or it must be left to the erring, weak, not always unbiased and sometimes vicious judgment of men to determine.'[70]

In an interesting way, Elder comes close to Hayek's argument that the market rewards 'service' and not 'merit'.[71] Just as there is no method to determine the assignment of this entrepreneurial function independently of success in market competition, Elder argues that there is no objective standard for the implementation of the socialist slogan 'From each according to his ability' independently of the market process that 'rewards' individuals for services rendered and therefore demonstrates each individual's comparative ability and place in the social division of labour. 'By its proposal to do away with competition and with profits, the reward flowing from, and, therefore, the incentive to, competition, the Socialist economic aim is reduced to an impossible and ridiculous economic absurdity.'[72] Also, for Elder, there is no valuation standard for the economic calculation of the relative value of labour and other resources, other than the prices on the market.

He justifies his rejection of any notion of a labour standard of value in an extremely 'Austrian' fashion. 'The Socialist conception of value is comprehended in the single idea that it is an exchange characteristic. It is peculiar to commodities,' says Elder. 'It is determined by labor, the only measurable thing that is common alike in all commodities.' But, continues Elder, 'The root fallacy of the teaching thus outlined is found in the assumption that equal values are received and demanded in the course of exchange … But in truth, exchange takes place only when values are unequal. Both parties to every exchange demand and believe they receive a greater value than they relinquish by the exchange.'[73] There is no standard of remuneration, therefore, other than the markets. And it is the market rates of remuneration that permit the calculation of profit so competition can function.

The Contribution of Mises' 'Forgotten' Predecessors

When looked at as a group, these 'forgotten' contributors to the debate over socialist planning present a set of criticisms of socialism and defences of the market that distinguish them from other anti-socialists of their period who emphasized the negative political or incentive consequences that would follow from the establishment of the socialist state. At the same time, they stand extremely close to the Austrian side of the debate.

Each of them clearly sees competition as a process rather than a state of affairs. Competition acts as an impetus to economic improvement, but it is also the mechanism through which markets are coordinated by actors discovering discrepancies in supply and demand and undertaking positive actions to correct for the discrepancies. Competition is also a discovery method for the disposition of talents to their comparative advantages. Indeed, for Elder, there is no method of discovering who are the competent entrepreneurs independent of the competitive process that tests, selects and sorts out the 'abilities' of each in the division of labour.

The discovery procedures would all be absent under socialism because the elimination of private ownership prohibits the rivalrous bidding and the use of resources that is the testing ground. The banishing of trading logically disposes of market prices. And as we saw with each of them, particularly Leroy Beaulieu, it is the price system that weaves together a spontaneous social order and gives direction to everything that occurs in the market. Prices are the binding threads of social coordination that socialism throws away, with nothing put in its place except intricate and incomprehensible statistical information that arrives late, is subject to poor organization and is susceptible to divergent interpretations that cloud the capacity for successful central planning.

Once the extent of the information and knowledge burdens that now fall on the shoulders of the central planners is appreciated, Cathrein asks us to appreciate even more the effective solution that the market provides through decentralized responsibility and decision making. Each participant in the productive division of labour is given a manageable task, with responsibility for only a portion of the entire knowledge required for general economic coordination.

And all of these men grasped the impossibility of the labour theory of value, for assigning either 'redemption' prices on final goods and services available in state warehouses, or 'labour-value' for time rendered in participation in the production process. Both involved the assignment of arbitrary values to inputs and outputs in a way that logically had no relationship to the underlying supply of and demand for either factors of production or final goods and services. Only the competitive market process has the capacity for discovering in an environment of change what relative prices should be assigned to both commodities and resources.

We find the essence of their message conveyed in the following passage from the 1908 volume by Robert Flint, *Socialism*:

> no council of the wisest men in London, although invested with absolute powers, could feed, clothe, lodge and employ the population of that city, were no man

allowed to act without having their authority, were no competition permitted in buying and selling, and were wages and prices prohibited, and some supposedly strictly rational determination of what labour was to receive and what commodities were to be exchanged for, adopted instead. The problem involved is of a kind which cannot be solved by the reasoning and calculation, the legislation and administration, even of the wisest and most uncontrolled rulers: it can only be solved, as it is actually solved, by leaving men free, each to seek his own interest and to attend to his own business, to carry his services or his goods where the rise of wages or of prices shows that they are most wanted, and to withhold them where the fall of wages or of prices warns him that the market is overstocked. Even when this method of freedom and of nature is followed numerous mistakes will occur, but they will be comparatively slight, and those of one man will counteract those of another ... But let the collectivist method be tried, and the risks of mistakes will be immensely increased, the provisions which nature has made for their correction will be prevented from operating, the amount of mischief produced by each error will be vastly multiplied, and the faculties and activities of the individuals composing society will be but feebly brought into exercise ... May we not safely conclude that what they [the Collectivists] dream of as organization would be ruinous disorganization?[74]

LUDWIG VON MISES ON ECONOMIC CALCULATION UNDER SOCIALISM IN THE 1920S

This is the decisive objection that economics raises against the possibility of a socialist society. It must forgo the intellectual division of labor that consists in the cooperation of all entrepreneurs, landowners, and workers as producers and consumers in the formation of market prices. But without it, rationality, i.e., the possibility of economic calculation, is unthinkable. (Ludwig von Mises, *Liberalism*, 1927)[75]

It is very likely that Mises was familiar with most or all of the critics of socialism discussed in the previous section. In *Human Action*, Mises refers to Gossen, Schäffle, Pareto, N.G. Pierson and Barone as earlier economists who had addressed the problem of socialist planning before 1920.[76] In *Socialism*, Mises refers to Victor Cathrein's book on socialism, but in the context of Cathrein's discussion of the relationships between Christianity and private property.[77] And Paul Leroy Beaulieu is quoted, but from another of his books on the collectivist conception of the state.[78]

When we turn to Mises' *Notes and Recollections* to discover possible influences on him in the evolution of his thinking on socialist planning and calculation, he offers few details. His earlier work on monetary theory had brought home to him the importance of money prices for market calculation and how changes in the value of money can distort such calculations.[79] 'When I set out to work further on the ideas in my book, *Socialism*, I felt compelled to develop especially the fundamentals of catallactics,' Mises explains. 'Any theory of socialism that does not have at its very foundation a consideration of the problem of economic calculation, is simply absurd.' In 1919, he presented his paper on 'Economic Calculation in the Socialist Commonwealth' at the *Nationalökonomische Gesellschaft* (the Austrian Economic Society), and it appeared the following year in *Archiv für Sozialwissenschaft und Sozialpolitik*.[80] This is all the information that Mises was willing to provide.

A starting point for an analysis of Mises's contribution is to ask in what ways his 1920 article and 1922 book were improvements upon the arguments that the earlier critics of socialist planning had developed. These earlier writers, as we saw, focused on two pricing problems. First, how would final goods offered for distribution by the state be priced to ensure balances between supplies and demands of each and every commodity offered for redemption? And second, how would labour of various types and qualities be priced so their distribution among alternative lines of production would ensure balances between their supplies and demands in various sectors of the economy? Having seen the inapplicability of a labour theory of value, they showed that only prices competitively formed on markets could fulfil the task.

Mises, too, critically evaluated the labour theory of value as a standard for economic calculation and also emphasized its inherent unworkability.[81] He also pointed out the potential for a discrepancy between the supply and demand for finished commodities at the centrally administered 'price' for those commodities.[82] But what clearly distinguishes Mises' analysis from the earlier commentators' is his clarity of exposition of what the problem of economic calculation under socialism is really about, and the particular use he makes of it to demonstrate the 'impossibility' of socialism.

All human action involves acts of exchange, Mises argued. In evaluating finished goods, 'calculation' is fairly easy in that the individual decides whether he prefers one alternative to the other. And, having made that choice, he may be able to evaluate the relative value to him of simple methods of production and the relative value of the resources which may be applied to them for the production of the finished goods in question. But once the alternative production methods develop degrees of complexity, in terms both of the types of different resources that could be utilized by those methods and of the temporal stages through which the resources would have to pass, direct and simple comparisons of the relative merits of the alternative production methods available are no longer possible. The variety of *technical* alternatives through which a finished product may be produced increases in number and the physical substitutions between various resources become so varied that the human mind, with its finite powers, becomes unable to make rational comparisons among them to make sure that the 'least cost' method has been chosen.[83]

The happy circumstance, Mises argued, was that in the market the plethora of heterogeneous physical commodities are reduced to a common denominator; that is, they all possess ratios of exchange with each other, expressed in terms of one commodity, the one that serves as the generally used medium of exchange – the money good. And this fortuitous circumstance contained a threefold advantage: 'In the first place we are able to take as the basis of calculation the valuation of all the individuals participating in trade ... Secondly, calculations of this sort provide a control upon the appropriate use of the means of production ... Finally, calculations based upon exchange values enable us to reduce values to a common unit.'[84] However, two things were required for such calculation to be feasible: 'First, not only goods ready for consumption but also goods of higher orders [that is, the factors of production] must be exchangeable ... In the second place, there must be a general medium of exchange, a money, in use.'[85]

Without a general medium of exchange through which all commodity prices are expressed, the goods on the market would not all share a common denominator for comparison and evaluation of the relative value of those goods in terms of each other. Without the inclusion of factors of production among the goods traded on the market there would not exist an array of money prices for them that could serve as the common denominator for evaluating the relative costs of using those resources in alternative combinations and the selection of the 'least cost' methods. And, finally, the inclusion of practically all members of the society in the exchange process means that the resulting market prices incorporate the valuations and preferences of the community as a whole, and therefore include the widest range of information about alternative uses for goods and resources, and their registered 'weight' as captured in those prices.

All these tools for economic calculation, Mises explained, would be lacking in the socialist society. Having nationalized the means of production, the state would have abolished any opportunity for individuals either to bid for or to offer those resources for alternative uses, for there would be nothing to buy or sell; with nothing to buy or sell, no prices for factors of production would come into existence; and without prices for factors of production (prices incorporating the judgments and valuations of a multitude of people having uses for those resources) the socialist planners would lack a rational method for assigning relative valuations to those goods. And as a result the socialist state would have deprived itself of the only avenue for efficient allocation of the resources now at its disposal. As Mises expressed it years later in his volume, *Bureaucracy*, 'A socialist manager would be like a man forced to spend his life blindfolded.'[86]

Mises' particular improvement *and originality* over the earlier critics of socialist planning was his attention to the special problems that arise in 'roundabout' capitalistic methods of production. The dilemma facing the decision maker in the planned economy does not refer merely to the allocation of labour among alternative employments. Rather, the problem refers to the task of selecting among all of the alternative combinations of many types of physical and human resources that are all technically capable of producing a particular product or set of products, and which involve different investment period time horizons. Which among the technical blueprints would represent the *least-cost* combination of resources (in terms of the relative values of those resources in competing uses) is the question the socialist planner could not answer.[87] Why? Because the planner would lack the price information that converges in the market as a composite statement of all the community members' conceptions, beliefs and valuations concerning the usefulness of those scarce resources for all the competing tasks they could serve. The socialist planner would lack the communications device through which the voice of 'the people' could be heard. In his 1927 volume, *Liberalism*, Mises concisely summarized this:[88]

> This is the decisive objection that economics raises against the possibility of a socialist society. It must forgo the intellectual division of labor that consists in the cooperation of all entrepreneurs, landowners, and workers as producers and consumers in the formation of market prices. But without it, rationality, i.e., the possibility of economic calculation, is unthinkable.

Developing the type of idea that we found in Cathrein, Mises also emphasized that economic calculation in the market facilitates an 'intellectual division of labour' not only among industries and firms, but within firms and organizations, as well. Authority and responsibility for tasks and uses of knowledge are divisible within units of firms because the monetary results of each can be compared and judged in terms of success against the calculable monetary alternatives outside the firm or organization. Responsibilities for uses of specialized knowledge can be given wide discretion, while being overseen through monetary accounting methods.[89]

But the real, critical importance that Mises saw in the capacity for economic calculation is that it serves as an evaluation compass in a never-ending sea of economic change. If we lived in a 'static' world in which both natural and social changes were absent and the economy had adjusted to the prevailing 'data' of the social and economic surroundings, economic calculation would be redundant, explains Mises. There would be nothing more to calculate, now that calculation had performed its task and economic relationships were in equilibrium. Repetition requires no compass.

It is change that requires a compass to guide movement through uncertain circumstances. Capital goods are consumed in production, similar ones replace them or new kinds are installed instead. But has the 'capital' been maintained? Has the production process that has consumed capital produced profit or loss? This can only be determined through monetary calculation, under which the market values of the physical goods can be added and evaluated to determine whether the 'capital' is intact.[90]

Mises' challenge to socialism is to explain how it will solve the inevitable calculation problems that will surround any planning minister who undertakes 'capitalistic' production processes to fulfil the socialist promise of creating a horn-of-plenty. Mises' challenge is still waiting for an answer.

ECONOMIC CALCULATION AND 'MEANINGFUL ACTION': MISES' SUBJECTIVIST CRITIQUE OF SOCIALISM

Monetary calculation is entirely inapplicable and useless for any consideration which does not look at things from the point of view of individuals. (Ludwig von Mises, *Human Action*, 1949)[91]

A full understanding of Ludwig von Mises' critique of socialism would be incomplete, however, if it concluded with his writings in the 1920s. And, in considering Mises's later formulation of his argument, we are only looking at it in the context in which he believed it should be evaluated.[92] Mises presented his restatement, first, in *Nationalökonomie: Theorie des Handelns und Wirtschaftens*[93] (published in 1940 while he was still Professor of International Economic Relations at the Graduate Institute for International Studies in Geneva) and, then, in *Human Action: A Treatise on Economics*[94] (published in 1949 after his moving to America and taking up a position as visiting professor in the School of Business Administration at New York University).

The nature and problems of economic calculation are at the heart of Mises's entire conception of the possibilities for and limitations of a functioning economic order: 'Economic calculation is the fundamental issue in the comprehension of all problems commonly called economic,' in his own words.[95] Indeed, it is clear from a reading of the arguments that run through all of *Human Action* that Mises was firmly convinced that all that is generally referred to as a prosperous civilization rests upon the capacity for market actors to utilize a form of economic calculation in their use of the scarce resources available to them. But Mises was equally insistent on emphasizing that economic calculation has been and is only possible because of the emergence and maintenance of a social order respectful of private property, and containing relatively free competition and a fairly stable medium of exchange.[96]

In this, the argument can be considered as an elaboration and refinement of the one found in his 1920 article and 1922 book on economic calculation. But it is the wider setting in which the argument is presented that needs to be appreciated. The hallmark of Mises' approach in *Human Action* is the insistence that all social and economic theory must be grounded in *methodological individualism* and *methodological subjectivism*. The first requires economic analysis to explain all the complex phenomena of the market as the result of the actions and interactions of individuals pursuing various purposes in mind with means available to them. The second draws attention to the fact that all human actions are 'meaningful', in the sense that the actions are guided by purposes in mind and therefore have a meaning for the actor as defined by him. This latter principle also carries the logical implication that understanding of the actions of men requires an analytical orientation that appreciates the way in which the actors order and interpret the objects and relationships that surround them and to which they assign significance for the achievement of their ends; these are the mental schemas on the basis of which human plans are constructed by actors and which guide their actions. The analyst, therefore, tries to understand the world as seen from the actor's point of view.[97]

'The market,' Mises said, 'is the focal point to which the activities of the individuals converge. It is the center from which the actions of the individuals radiate.'[98] The relationships of the market, he argued, were constituted through webs of meaningful actions of mutual orientation. The relationships that emerged, were maintained and which changed over time, always possessed two meanings for each of the actors participating in them: the meaning they see in their own conduct and the meaning they interpret in the actions of the other(s), and which guide their own response to those others.[99] The market is where the plans of a multitude of men meet, with those plans either fulfilled or frustrated in the arena of consummated exchanges. And it is in the market that prices arise for both finished goods and factors of production.

Prices can be conceived as a mirror that absorbs images and reflects them. The images absorbed are in the form of bids and offers that compositely form into the prices of commodities and resources; and these composite price images reflect back to each participant in the market as a guide for actions under consideration. Each provides his contribution to the resulting composite price on the basis of his circumstances subjectively conceived, in terms of both the ends they desire and their perception of the world in which their actions are being undertaken. And, in turn, each utilizes and assigns significance to the prices reflecting out of the market in terms of plans in mind and expectations held about the shape of things to come.

The crucial word here is *expectations*. The particular quality of relationships in the market web of mutual orientation is that they require anticipatory judgments on the part of the participants. This arises from the system of division of labour in which specializations in respective lines of production require each to anticipate likely trading opportunities in the future as a basis for various production and exchange decisions in the present. And the essential uncertainty of the future, towards which all human activity is directed, means that all actions are 'speculative' in nature.[100]

Mises also emphasized that every decision to buy or sell was based upon one of two purposes in the minds of the market actors: either a *valuation* of the prospective importance of a commodity for satisfaction of some end in mind by the chooser or an *appraisement* of the significance that a commodity or resource might have for others at a point in the future (and, therefore, the present significance of the commodity or resource as a means for future exchange opportunities for the achievement of desired ends).[101] The reality of price begins in and reflects the mental images of the traders' conceptions of the future and that future's relevancies and opportunities for fulfilment of respective ends in mind.

The creative quality of pricing judgments and, therefore, price formation in the market process is expressed most clearly in Mises' 1951 essay, 'Profit and Loss':

> The fact that in the frame of the market economy entrepreneurial profit and loss are determined by arithmetical operations has misled many people. They fail to see that essential items that enter into this calculation are estimates emanating from the entrepreneur's specific understanding of the future state of the market ... It is the entrepreneurial decision that creates either profit or loss. It is mental acts, the mind of the entrepreneur, from which profits ultimately originate. Profit is a product of the mind, of success in anticipating the future state of the market.[102]

Thus the formation of prices and the meaning of prices are always contextual from the respective actors' points of view. Prices have no meanings and no significance out of these contexts. The essence of prices, therefore, is not their quantitative ratios, because those ratios are derivatives and not primaries. It is the anticipatory images of future market configurations that determine what valuations and appraisements entrepreneurs place upon factors of production in terms of the prices they might be willing to pay to acquire their use, in relation to expected prices for the goods and services those resources can produce. Profit is the expected discrepancy between those two beliefs. But beliefs only exist in the minds of individuals contemplating alternative courses of action. And, therefore, what is 'meaningful' in terms of pricing and production possibilities for one individual may be 'meaningless' from the perspective of another. For the same reason, retrospective evaluation of either a 'profit' or a 'loss' only has full significance for the individual who is judging the outcome of a course of action from the context of his own estimation of 'success' or 'failure' in the circumstances in which he finds himself.

Mises lucidly expressed the subjectivist quality that permeates both the pricing and economic calculation processes in his discussion of cost accounting:

> Cost accounting is therefore not an arithmetical process which can be estimated and examined by an indifferent umpire. It does not operate with uniquely determined magnitudes which can be found out in an objective way. Its essential items are the result of an understanding of future conditions, necessarily always colored by the entrepreneur's opinion about the future state of the market. Calculating costs is a mental tool of action, the purposive design to make the best of the available means for an improvement of future conditions. It is necessarily volitional, not factual. In the hands of an indifferent umpire it changes its character entirely.[103]

This is why Mises said, 'Economics is not about things and tangible material objects; it is about men, their meanings, and actions. Goods, commodities, and wealth and all other notions of conduct are not elements of nature; they are elements of human meaning and conduct. He who wants to deal with them must not look at the external world; he must search for them in the meaning of acting men.'[104]

Economic calculation, therefore, only occurs in the context of a personal point of view, that is, the personal points of view of each trader entering the nexus of exchange, and is 'meaningful' only in that context. And this brings us to Mises' 'subjectivist' critique of socialism. In the midst of his discussion of economic calculation and its importance in providing a method for valuational orientation for owners and users of scarce resources, Mises adds a short subsection on 'The Theory of Value and Socialism'. Towards the end of it, he says that 'the illusion that a rational order of [socialist] economic management is possible owed its origin to the value theory of the classical economists and its tenacity to the failure of many modern economists to think through consistently to its ultimate conclusions the fundamental theorem of the subjectivist theory'.[105]

It is easy to read this only as an accusation that 20th-century economists have erred by forgetting that, since value is a 'subjective' phenomenon of rank ordered preferring, there cannot exist an objective standard of value from which to evaluate materials or men in the market; a reminder that tastes and preferences are 'personal' and not open to measurement. Thus a pillar of socialist theory necessarily falls to the ground.

But a careful reading of Mises' argument in the context of his general discussion of economic calculation suggests that, when he refers to thinking through the subjectivist theory to its 'ultimate conclusion', he is referring to something more than the foundation of utility theory alone. The subjectivist theory emphasizes that 'subjective preferences' about goods emerge out of the context of subjective (that is, personal) perspectives with which each interprets circumstances and opportunities. The 'illusion', therefore, that Mises refers to is really the failure to follow the analytical path back to the 'meanings of men' instead of stopping at the measurables of matter.

The wider subjectivist perspective suggests why Mises viewed the proposals of Oskar Lange for a type of market socialism ultimately as unworkable as rigid central planning.[106] First, Mises insists that Lange and others have confused the role and tasks of a manager within a firm with the function of the entrepreneurs and capital owners who guide the direction and allocation of resources into alternative market avenues in the face of changing profit opportunities in the market. The former attends to tasks assigned to him, given a prior capital investment decision that has placed resources at the disposal of the manager. The manager's horizon is necessarily a different one from that of the entrepreneur or capitalist, both in terms of incentives and ultimate responsibilities.

Another way of saying this is that the *meaning* of price and profit opportunities is necessarily different, given the subjective perspectives from which the actors evaluate market conditions. Their perspectives guide their actions and their perspectives are determined by the way they interpret the circumstances in which they find themselves. The permitted property rights relationships in an environment of even market socialism results in different forms of 'meaningful actions' than in an institutional setting in which capital may be privately owned and utilized in a corridor of wide discretion in market transactions. A socialist order cannot successfully 'play' at market relationships, because the external institutional order has its influence only in terms of how the actors functioning in them interpret the order's *meanings* as avenues for achieving the individual aims of the participants.[107] And the use and disposal of capital and resources have a different meaning for opportunities for profitable action under market socialism than under competitive, private capitalism.

Secondly, Mises rejected the idea of a central planning agency setting 'parametric' prices in the economy and periodically revising them if faced with either surpluses or shortages resulting from the buying and selling of competing socialist firms. 'Prices,' Mises says, 'are a market phenomena. They are generated by the market process and are the pith of the market economy. There is no such thing as prices outside the market ... It is the very essence of prices that they are the offshoot of the actions of individuals and groups of individuals acting on their own behalf.'[108]

If we understand prices to be an absorbing and reflecting mirror constructed out of a multitude of subjective meanings and orientations, then the setting of prices by government, even for the purpose that Lange suggests, is the setting of something that for Mises is not a price at all. Prices emerge out of the interaction of men pursuing purposes within their perspective contexts. Lange's central planners would be attempting to make prices synthetically on the basis of *their* interpretation of what they see as the quantitative, external manifestations (surpluses or shortages) resulting from the meaningful actions of others. It would be an attempt to draw a picture of a mirror image, on the basis of what the artist thinks the mirror image would look like if there was one.

Mises found it amusing enough that, after the incessant condemnation of the market economy in all its aspects, socialists were now assuring all concerned that, following the revolution, there would still be markets and prices, only they would operate under new management.[109] Imitation, after all, is the highest form of flattery, no matter how imperfect it may be.

THE SOCIALIST CALCULATION DEBATE IN CONTEXT

> The current mania for comprehensive economic planning by the State may appear, half a century hence, as just another of the red herrings which fate throws across the forward march of free peoples. (John Jewkes, *Ordeal by Planning*, 1948)[110]

In retrospect, the writings of the late 19th-century critics of socialism that were discussed earlier now appear extremely insightful and prophetic. In the 1890s and 1900s, socialism was still an ideal, advocated by many but implemented by none. These early critics anticipated many of the essential problems that have eventually brought central planning into disrepute. They were able to discern the weak spots in the socialist programme precisely because they were free of the mathematical formalism of 20th-century economics. They approached the problem commonsensically. Competition was what most people think of it as: a rivalrous process. Common sense also showed that knowledge is far from perfect and what the human mind can grasp is limited. Society had developed an institutional order that enabled these problems to be overcome. Informational responsibilities were decentralized through competition and division of labour. And all the multitude of actions were effectively connected one with the other through the price system that guided supply in the direction of demand and registered all changes in the market with great rapidity.

Mises' writings on socialism were a logical extension of this approach. Being a good Mengerian, it was not surprising that Mises should approach the problem of socialist planning in the context of wondering how the planners would plan in a world of change and uncertainty through time.[111] Socialism's elimination of private ownership of the means of production abolished the arena in which competitive bids could generate the prices that were essential for calculative evaluation of every step and aspect of the production process. And it was Mises' focus on this aspect of the socialist planning problem that made his an original and important contribution to the debate.

What inhibited acceptance of Mises' argument by most economists was their attempt to think about this argument in the emerging context of a formal general equilibrium theory. This new context seemed to make Mises' argument redundant because the assumptions supporting this framework either hid or assumed away the real-world market conditions that Mises believed had to be addressed if the socialists were to make their case successfully for a system of centralized planning.

The failure of central planning socialism during the last half-century has destroyed its legitimacy as a serious institutional alternative to market-based relationships. Practically all socialists, both inside and outside the socialist countries, came to accept and increasingly endorse some form of 'planning-through-markets'. As a leading advisor to Mikhail Gorbachev expressed it during the Soviet Perestroika period, what the Soviet Union needed was 'Socialism with cost accounting ... Prices must be raised to real cost.'[112] Cost prices are taken by the proponents of market socialism to mean something 'real', that is, real expenditure of inputs or monetary outlays. And prices in general are seen as something that balances the scale between quantitative amounts of demand and supply.

The way this is expressed, however, means that Mises' message is still not understood. Yet the arguments for market-formed socialism can only be criticized in terms of Mises' subjectivist approach. As Mises emphasized, 'Costs are a phenomenon of value. Costs are the value attached to the most valuable want-satisfaction which remains unsatisfied because the means required for its satisfaction are employed for the want-satisfaction the cost of which we are dealing with.'[113] Costs, in other words, are evaluative *states of mind*, and, therefore, can only be understood in terms of 'meaningful action': that is, in terms of the perspective from which and within which the actors undertake various activities. Economic calculation and the offering of a price and the weighing of a set of prices for production plans only occurs, and only has relevancy, in the context of the respective individual points of view. What a price means for calculative purposes, therefore, only has meaning in the subjective context of the purposes in mind that define and determine the significance of that price.

An appreciation of the 'subjectivist' perspective means that the Misesian message is still as relevant as ever. Unfortunately, it also means that it is a message still waiting to be fully understood.[114]

NOTES

1. Norman Angell, *The Fruits of Victory* (London: The Labour Publishing Co., 1921) p.27; see also Elizabeth Wiskerman, *Europe of the Dictators, 1919-1945* (New York: Harper & Row, 1966) pp.17-19.

2. For a summary and analysis of the political and economic situation in Austria in the period between the two world wars, and Ludwig von Mises' role as a policy analyst and advocate in Vienna during this period, see Richard M. Ebeling, 'The Economist as the Historian of Decline: Ludwig von Mises and Austria Between the Two World Wars', in Richard M. Ebeling (ed.), *Globalization: Will Freedom of World Government Dominate the International Marketplace?* (Hillsdale, MI: Hillsdale College Press, 2002) pp.1–69.

3. See William M. Johnston, *The Austrian Mind: An Intellectual and Social History, 1848–1938* (Berkeley, CA: University of California Press, 1972); Allan Jamik and Stephen Toulmin, *Wittgenstein's Vienna* (New York: Simon and Schuster, 1973).

4. On Hans Mayer and his contribution to the Austrian school, see Alexander Mahr, 'Hans Mayer-Leben und Werk', *Zeitschrift für Nationalökonomie*, Bd. 16 (March 1956) pp.3–16; and Wilhelm Weber, 'Hans Mayer', *Handwörterbuch der Sozialwissenschaft*, Bd. 7 (Stuttgart: Gustav Fischer, 1961) pp.364–5.

5. Gottfried Haberler, 'Mises' Private Seminar', *Wirtschftspolitische Blätter*, 28, no. 4 (1981) 121–6; a slightly shorter version of Haberler's essay may be found as an appendix to Ludwig von Mises, *Planning for Freedom* (Spring Mills, PA: Libertarian Press, 1980) pp.276–8; also a wide variety of reminiscences of Mises' *privatseminar* have been collected and added as an appendix to Margit von Mises, *My Years with Ludwig von Mises*, 2nd rev. edn (Spring Mills, PA: Libertarian Press, 1984) pp.199–210.

6. See Richard M. Ebeling, 'Austrian Economics – An Annotated Bibliography: The Austrian Economists', and 'Methodology of the Austrian Economists', in Richard M. Ebeling (ed.), *Austrian Economics: A Reader* (Hillsdale, MI: Hillsdale College Press, 1990) pp.3–16 and 43–54.

7. Lionel Robbins, 'Foreword' in Friedrich A. Hayek, *Prices and Production* (New York: Macmillan, 1930) p.ix.

8. See Chapter 5 of the present volume for a summary and explanation of the Austrian approach to monetary theory and policy.

9. See Jack Wiseman, 'Lionel Robbins, The Austrian School, and the LSE Tradition', in Warren J. Samuels (ed.), *Research in the History of Economic Thought and Methodology*, Vol. 3 (Greenwich, CT: JAI Press, 1985) pp.147–60, for a summary of some aspects of the development of the Austrian theory of the logic of choice.

10. Richard M. Ebeling, 'Expectations and Expectations-Formation in Mises' Theory of the Market Process', in Peter J. Boettke and David L. Prychitko, *The Market Process: Essays in Contemporary Austrian Economics* (Aldershot, UK and Brookfeld, VT: Edward Elgar Publishing 1994) pp.83–95.

11. Sir Arnold Plant, 'Homage to Hayek', *Selected Economic Essays and Addresses* (London: Routledge & Kegan Paul, 1974) p.170.

12. See Richard M. Ebeling, 'Mises' Influences on Modern Economic Thought', in Kurt R. Leube (ed.), *Die Österreichische Schule der Nationalökonomie*, Vol. 2 (Vienna: Manz Publisher, 1996) pp.263–76, for a general appreciation and interpretation of the impact of Mises' writings on 20th-century economic theory in a number of different areas. For a brief discussion by Mises on how he saw his own work in the history of economic ideas, see 'My Contributions to Economy Theory', in *Planning for Freedom*, pp.224–33, which was a lecture delivered at the Faculty Club of New York University in 1940. The evolution of his ideas is discussed in all too brief detail by Mises in his *Notes and Recollections* (Spring Mills, PA: Libertarian Press, 1978).

13. Ludwig von Mises, *The Theory of Money and Credit*, 3rd rev. edn (1912; 2nd rev. edn, 1924; Indianapolis, IN: Liberty Fund, 1981).

14. Ludwig von Mises, 'Economic Calculation in the Socialist Commonwealth', in F.A. von Hayek (ed.), *Collectivist Economic Planning* (London: George Routledge & Sons, 1935), pp.87–130. The essay originally appeared under the title, 'Die Wirtschaftsrechnung im sozialistischen Gemeinwesen', in the *Archiv für Sozialwissenschaften*, 47 (1920).

15. Ludwig von Mises, *Socialism: An Economic and Sociological Analysis*, 3rd rev. edn (1922; 2nd rev. edn, 1932; Indianapolis, IN: Liberty Fund, 1981). The book originally appeared under the title, *Die Gemeinwirtschaft: Untersuchungen über den Sozialismus* (Jena: Gustav Fischer, 1922).

16. F.A. Hayek's, 'Tribute to Ludwig von Mises', appendix three in Margit von Mises, *My Years with Ludwig von Mises*, p. 220.
17. Mises, *Socialism*, p. 131; 'Economic Calculation in the Socialist Commonwealth', p. 111.
18. Examples of crediting Mises for being the first (or primary influence) to raise the question as to whether economic calculation would be possible under socialism can be found in Hayek's introduction to *Collectivist Economic Planning*, p. 32; Trygve J.B. Hoff, *Economic Calculation in the Socialist Society* (1938; 1949; Indianapolis, IN: Liberty Press, 1981) p. 2, and Karen I. Vaughn's introduction to this edition, p. x; Dominick Armentano, 'Resource Allocation Problems Under Socialism', in William P. Snavely, *Theory of Economic Systems*, with contributions by Morris Singer and Dominick Armentano (Columbus, OH: Charles E. Merrill, 1969) pp. 127-8.
19. Oskar Lange, 'On the Economic Theory of Socialism', in Oskar Lange and Fred M. Taylor, *On the Economic Theory of Socialism* (1936; New York: McGraw-Hill, 1964) p. 57; Lange, too, said that, 'it was chiefly due to Professor Mises' challenge that many socialists became aware of the very existence of such a problem'.
20. Joseph A. Schumpeter, *History of Economic Analysis* (New York: Oxford University Press, 1954) p. 989.
21. That this charge of mathematical ignorance is least of all applicable to Ludwig von Mises has been assured by no less an authority than the noted mathematician Karl Menger, Jr, who referred to Mises' knowledge of mathematics and probability theory; see Karl Menger, *Selected Papers in Logic and Foundations, Didactics, Economics* (Dordrecht: D. Reidel, 1979) p. 259.
22. Don Lavoie, *Rivalry and Central Planning: The Socialist Calculation Debate Reconsidered* (New York: Cambridge University Press, 1985) p. 259.
23. It is worth pointing out that, while Hayek is usually credited with having drawn attention to the problem of market coordination under conditions of a division of knowledge, Mises had already referred to this circumstance and how the competitive market was the only method for utilizing that divided knowledge; see Mises, *Socialism* p. 101; 'Economic Calculation in the Socialist Commonwealth', p. 102; see also Richard M. Ebeling, 'Planning for Freedom: Ludwig von Mises as Political Economist and Policy Analyst', in Richard M. Ebeling (ed.), *Competition or Compulsion: The Market Economy versus the New Social Engineering* (Hillsdale, MI: Hillsdale College Press, 2001) pp. 1-85, especially pp. 24-9.
24. J. Shield Nicholson, *Principles of Political Economy*, Vol. 1 (New York: Macmillan, 1893) pp. 432-3.
25. I have made a search through all the major (and many of the minor) works on the socialist calculation debate. With one exception, none of these 19th-century and early 20th-century critics of socialist central planning are even mentioned in any of this literature. It is particularly strange that no Austrian economist has ever drawn attention to their works, because, as we shall see, they anticipated many of the salient points of the Austrian critique of both socialism and neoclassical competition theory.
26. Albert Schäffle, *The Quintessence of Socialism* [1874] (London: Swan Sonnenschein, 1892).
27. Paul Leroy Beaulieu, *Collectivism* [1885] (London: John Murray, English trans., 1908); Leroy Beaulieu was a professor at the College of France.
28. William Graham, *Socialism: New and Old* (New York: A. Appleton, 1891); Graham was professor of political economy and jurisprudence at Queen's College, Belfast, Ireland.
29. Victor Cathrein, *Socialism: Its Theoretical Basis and Practical Application* [1890] English trans., rev. and enl. by Victor F. Gellelmann (New York: Benziger Brothers, 1904); Father Cathrein was a Jesuit priest in Germany.
30. Benedict Elder, *A Study of Socialism* (St Louis, MO: B. Herder, 1915).
31. Paul J. McNulty, 'A Note on the History of Perfect Competition', *Journal of Political Economy* (August 1969) 395-9.
32. Lionel Robbins, *The Theory of Economic Policy in English Classical Political Economy* (London: Macmillan, 1952) p. 16.

33. T.W. Hutchison, *A Review of Economic Doctrines, 1870-1929* (Oxford: Clarendon Press, 1953) pp.294-6; Hutchison also points out some interesting remarks made about a socialist economy by Lejo Brentano and Erwin Nasse (ibid.), pp.296-7; see also Hutchison, *The Politics and Philosophy of Economics* (Oxford: Basil Blackwell, 1981) pp.171-2.
34. Schäffle, *The Quintessence of Socialism*, pp.7-8.
35. Ibid., p.70.
36. Ibid., pp.71-2.
37. Ibid., p.74.
38. Ibid., pp.78-9.
39. Ibid., pp.80-1; Schäffle explains that 'socially necessary labour' is 'labour of such a kind as must be *on the average* expended, according to the existing national standard of technique, for a unit of supply, in order to produce the commodity to the whole extent of the demand for it' (p.82).
40. Ibid., pp.86-7.
41. Ibid., p.93; my emphasis.
42. Paul Leroy Beaulieu, *Collectivism*, pp.157-8.
43. Ibid., pp.161-3.
44. Ibid., p.169; my emphasis.
45. Ibid., p.164.
46. Ibid., pp.133 and 165.
47. Ibid., p.174.
48. Ibid., p.160.
49. Ibid., pp.175-7.
50. Ibid., pp.186-201.
51. Ibid., pp.205-6.
52. William Graham, *Socialism: New and Old*, pp.152-9.
53. Ibid., pp.160-61.
54. Ibid., pp.165-6.
55. Ibid., p.176.
56. Ibid., p.187.
57. Ibid., p.188.
58. Ibid., pp.189-92.
59. Ibid., pp.193-8.
60. Ibid., pp.205-6.
61. Ibid., pp.224-5.
62. Cathrein, *Socialism: Its Theoretical Basis and Practical Application*, pp.269-70.
63. Ibid., pp.271-2.
64. Ibid., pp.274-5.
65. Ibid., p.169.
66. Ibid., p.273.
67. Elder, *A Study of Socialism*, pp.263-4.
68. Ibid., p.267.
69. Ibid., p.268.
70. Ibid., p.270.
71. Friedrich A. Hayek, 'The Mirage of Social Justice', in *Law, Legislation and Liberty*, Vol. 2 (Chicago: University of Chicago Press, 1976).
72. Elder, *A Study of Socialism*, p.276.
73. Ibid., pp.291, 294.
74. Robert Flint, *Socialism*, 2nd edn (London: Sir Isaac Pitman & Sons, 1908) p.164.
75. Ludwig von Mises, *Liberalism* [1927] (Kansas City, KS: Sheed Andrews and McMeel, 1978) p.75.
76. Ludwig von Mises, *Human Action: A Treatise on Economics*, 3rd rev. edn (Chicago: Henry Regnery, 1966) p.701.
77. Mises, *Socialism*, p.459.
78. Ibid., p.53.

79. In his 1919 volume, *Nation, State and Economy* (New York: New York University Press, 1983) pp.160-5, Mises had emphasized the falsification of capital accounting that an inflation can cause with a resulting consumption of capital under the illusion that capital is being maintained. Fritz Machlup, in his article, 'The Consumption of Capital in Austria', *The Review of Economics Statistics* 27, no. 1 (15 January 1935) 13, pointed out that 'Professor Ludwig v. Mises was the first, so far as I know, to point to the phenomenon of the consumption of capital' due to inflation. 'As a member of a committee appointed by the Austrian Government (including two other committeemen, Dr. Dollfuss and Dr. Pella) Mises also emphasized comprehensive factual information', in a report entitled *Bericht über die Ursachen der wirtschaftlichen Schwierigkeiten in Österreich* (Vienna, 1931). Cf., also, Nicholas Kaldor, 'The Economic Situation of Austria', *Harvard Business Review*, 10, no. 1 (October 1932) 23-34.

80. Ludwig von Mises, *Notes and Recollections* (1940; Spring Mills, PA: Libertarian Press, 1978), p.111.

81. Mises, *Socialism*, pp.113-16.

82. Ibid., pp.138-9.

83. Mises, 'Economic Calculation in the Socialist Commonwealth', pp.95-7, 102-3; *Socialism*, pp.97-9, 101-2.

84. Mises, *Socialism*, p.99; 'Economic Calculation in the Socialist Commonwealth', pp.97-8.

85. Mises, *Socialism*, p.101; 'Economic Calculation in the Socialist Commonwealth', pp.101-2.

86. Ludwig von Mises, *Bureaucracy* (1944; Spring Mills, PA: Libertarian Press, 1983) p.30.

87. Mises, *Socialism*, pp.123-4; in the terminology of microeconomic theory, the socialist planner is confronted with an *isoquant* depicting all the alternative physical combinations through which a given goal could be attained (for example, a desired level of output); but he possesses no *isocost*, the price ratio at which inputs can be obtained, with the price ratio representing the market-established opportunity costs of those resources in alternative uses.

88. Mises, *Liberalism*, p.75.

89. Mises, *Socialism*, pp.112-13.

90. Ibid., pp.104-5, 124-5, 177-8, 180-83; Mises, 'Economic Calculation in the Socialist Commonwealth', pp.109-10.

91. Mises, *Human Action*, p.229.

92. Mises, *Notes and Recollections*, p.112: 'My *Nationalökonomie* finally afforded me the opportunity to present the problems of economic calculation in their full significance.'

93. Ludwig von Mises, *Nationalökonomie: Theorie des Handelns und Wirtschaftens* (1940; Munich: Philosophia Verlag, 1980).

94. Mises, *Human Action*.

95. Ibid., p.199; Mises, *Nationalökonomie*, p.187.

96. Mises, *Human Action*, pp.264-5.

97. Ibid., pp.41-3; Mises, *Nationalökonomie*, pp.31-3.

98. Mises, *Human Action*, p.258.

99. Ibid., p.26: 'The question we have to deal with is whether it is possible to grasp human action intellectually if one refuses to comprehend it as meaningful and purposeful behavior aiming at the attainment of definite ends.' In analysing an exchange, 'what is essential in such an offer and distinguishes it from other offers cannot be described without entering into the meaning which the acting parties attribute to the situation'; and see p.194, where Mises refers to the exchange relationship as the 'fundamental social relation' involving 'intentional mutuality.' See also, *Nationalökonomie*, p.180, where Mises refers to 'Weschselwirkung wischen Menschen' - 'reciprocal actions between men'; and Max Weber, *Critique of Stammler* (1907; New York: The Free Press, 1977) pp.109, 112.

100. Mises, *Human Action*, p.290.

101. Ibid., pp.331-2.

102. Ludwig von Mises, 'Profit and Loss', in *Planning for Freedom* (Spring Mills, PA: Libertarian Press), pp.120, 126.

103. Mises, *Human Action*, pp.349-50.

104. Ibid., p.92.

105. Ibid., p.206.
106. Mises rejected the possibility of a mathematically derived general equilibrium 'solution' to the problem of socialist central planning because it totally ignored the influence of time and change on the outcome of economic events. An equilibrium state that an economy might hypothetically approach would not be independent of the path by which it was reached. It was impossible to know the actual path leading towards equilibrium because every step taken along the path would be influenced by and dependent upon the knowledge, preferences and expectations of the economic actors during the continuing process. But, argued Mises, it was impossible from the perspective of 'today' for the economic actors to know their future knowledge, preferences and expectations over the sequence of numerous 'tomorrows' that would culminate in a hypothetical equilibrium state. Hence computing a future equilibrium from the standpoint of present information concerning preferences, technological possibilities and resource availabilities could never solve 'the economic problem' under socialism. See Ludwig von Mises, 'The Equations of Mathematical Economics and the Problem of Economic Calculation in a Socialist State' [1938], in *The Quartery Journal of Austrian Economics* (Spring 2000) 27-32; and Mises, *Human Action*, pp.710-15.
107. Mises, *Human Action*, pp.705-10.
108. Ibid., pp.395-7.
109. Ibid., p.706.
110. John Jewkes, *Ordeal by Planning* (London: Macmillan, 1948) pp.1-2.
111. Cf. Arthur W. Marget, *The Theory of Prices*, Vol. 2 (1942; New York: Augustus M. Kelley, 1966) p.189, where Marget observes that Mises' 'discussion of the role of uncertainty and "estimate" in the calculations underlying the pricing process, like so many other elements in Mises's theoretical position, may be said to follow directly in the path traced out by Menger'.
112. 'Growing Pains of Reform', *Newsweek* (7 September 1987) p.56. This is an interview with Tatyana Zaslavskaya.
113. Mises, *Human Action*, p.396.
114. See Ludwig von Mises, 'Observations on the Russian Reform Movement' [1966], in Richard M. Ebeling (ed.), *Money, Method, and the Market Process: Essays by Ludwig von Mises* (Norwell, MA: Kluwer Academic Publishers, 1990), pp.232-7, for Mises' critical evaluation of the mid-1960s proposals.

5. Ludwig von Mises and the gold standard

In the 1930s, Oskar Morgenstern once gently criticized British economist Lionel Robbins for creating a false impression of the Austrian School of Economics to English-speaking readers. Morgenstern argued that, in *The Nature and Significance of Economic Science*, Robbins had represented 'the Viennese economists ... in certain important points as being much more of a school with uniform views than they really are'.[1] What Morgenstern was alluding to was the fact that, while those whom we now classify as the inter-war members of the Austrian School viewed themselves as sharing an intellectual heritage coming from the earlier writings of Carl Menger, Eugen von Böhm-Bawerk and Friedrich von Wieser, there was no unanimity among them concerning either the theoretical or policy implications of that heritage.[2] On the one hand, the Austrians stood as a cohesive group in their emphasis on methodological individualism, their focus on the subjectivist nature of the data of economic science and in their defence of a 'causal–genetic' or process analysis of economic phenomena in opposition to the 'functional' or equilibrium approach of the Lausanne school.[3] On the other hand, extensive and often heated debates were carried on within the school; among the questions in dispute were whether economics was an *a priori* or an empirical science, the role of psychological elements in the theory of value, the laws of imputation of value to factors of production, and the basis for the discounting of future goods against present goods.

In matters of policy, unanimity was just as rare. In general, the Austrian economists of the period had a common belief in the relative superiority of the market as an institutional framework for economic coordination. But the school was far from any agreement as to the superiority of unadulterated *laissez-faire*. Among the senior members of the Vienna group only Ludwig von Mises can be considered to have argued a consistent case for classical liberalism and economic freedom. And to the extent that some of the younger members of the school came to support a more or less free market position on most policy issues, it seems that it was mainly through Mises' influence.[4]

MONETARY THEORY AND THE AUSTRIAN ECONOMISTS

In monetary theory and policy there was also less than unanimous agreement among the Austrian economists, though here, again, the participants viewed themselves as beginning their discussions upon a common intellectual inheritance. In this instance the foundations were to be discovered, for the most part, in the earlier writings of Menger, Böhm-Bawerk and Knut Wicksell. A common element in each of their contributions was an emphasis on analysing economic and monetary processes in 'individualistic' or disaggregated terms.

In his lengthy essay on money, 'Geld', Menger criticized the mechanical transactions assumptions underlying the then prevailing concept of the velocity of circulation of money. Rather than beginning with the economy as a whole, Menger argued that the aggregate demand for money had to be constructed or built up from the individual demands for money, and the latter had to be understood in terms of choice-theoretic decisions concerning preferences for cash holdings in the face of uncertainty and speculation about the future.[5]

For the later Austrians, a crucial aspect in Böhm-Bawerk's capital theory was its focus on the various relationships and interdependencies in the production processes. Production not only took time but also involved a structure of complementary steps leading to the successful completion of finished goods. The temporal web of stages of production, within which decentralized production plans and activities were being undertaken, was held together and coordinated through the system of market prices and the rate of interest.[6]

Wicksell's importance was in his demonstration of how a cumulative rise or fall in prices could be brought about through changes in the money rate of interest. What was significant in his exposition was his explanation of the mechanism by which a cumulative process could be set in motion *and* its effects on the various prices in the structure of production.[7] The cumulative rise or fall in prices was brought about through the emergence of a discrepancy between the money rate of interest, at which loans could be secured, and the anticipated rate of profit as perceived by potential borrowers in the market. A money rate below (or above) the 'natural rate',[8] however, was not neutral in its effects on various prices in the economy. The role of the rate of interest as a capitalization factor meant that a lowering (or raising) of the money rate of interest would enhance (or reduce) to a greater extent the expected profitability of long-term, as opposed to short-term, investments. In the cumulative process, while all prices would be rising (or falling) the effect would be relatively more intensive in those production processes that would be considered more 'roundabout'.[9]

LUDWIG VON MISES' WRITINGS ON MONETARY THEORY AND THE BUSINESS CYCLE

These three strands of thought were brought together by Ludwig von Mises, first in *The Theory of Money and Credit* (originally published in 1912 and revised in 1924)[10] and in his monograph, 'Monetary Stabilization and Cyclical Policy' (1928).[11] Using Menger's theory of the origin of money[12] and cash balance approach, Mises constructed a theory of the value of money that successfully incorporated the concept of marginal utility and broke out of the dilemma of the Austrian circle.[13] However, the explanation of a given value of money was only a preliminary step (albeit a theoretically important one) to the construction of a dynamic analysis of the process by which *changes* in the purchasing power of money occur in the market, an analysis which he attempted to construct in purely methodological individualistic terms.[14]

In the Misesian schema, effects of changes in the demand for or supply of money never manifest themselves simultaneously or immediately in all segments of the market. Any changes, whether in the demand for money or in its supply, always have their origin with changes in the circumstances of individual decision makers, either with a change in the desire for cash balances with the nominal quantity of money in the economy unchanged, or a change in the nominal quantity of money available to individuals with preferences for cash holdings unchanged, or a combination of the two. While the end result of such changes in individual circumstances was, for the economy as a whole, a rise or fall in the general purchasing power of money, this end result only emerged as the culmination of a sequential process through which each market participant came to be affected by the initial change in the monetary position of some individual(s). During this 'transmission mechanism', Mises saw relative prices and incomes as being modified in ways that (potentially) had both temporary and permanent effects.

Money, therefore, was seen by Mises as necessarily and always non-neutral in its effects on the 'real' economy. This was due to the fact that monetary expansions and contractions could work their effects upon the economic system only through changes in the monetary demand and supply positions of the individual transactors, who then transmitted their changed circumstances to others through modifications in their buying and selling patterns. As the impact of a monetary expansion (or contraction) came to be diffused through the economy, each step of the process would see changes in the relative demands for various products, bringing about changes in relative prices, the relative profitabilities of alternative production activities and, therefore, the relative income positions of various individuals and groups in the economy. In Mises' eyes, it was only through this type of microeconomic 'step-by-step' analysis of the way monetary forces worked their effects upon the *structure* of relative prices that one could logically explain how a change in the demand or supply of money brought about a modification in the general *scale* of prices.[15]

It also highlighted the fact that money's 'real effects' on an economy were not just its influence upon the level of total employment and output. Even if an economy was at 'full employment', the process by which a monetary change was introduced into the system, and then sequentially came to be spread through the whole economy, could influence (at least for as long as the monetary change continued and had not worked its way through the entire system) the *real* pattern or allocation of production activities and the distribution of income. Any changes in total employment or output during a monetary expansion or contraction would themselves be one of the consequences of the (at least temporary) changes in the relative structure of prices and wages occurring as a result of the process by which changes in the general purchasing power of money emerged.[16]

Mises' theory of the business cycle is an application to a particular case of his more general theory of the non-neutrality of money. More specifically, it attempts to explain the process by which an expansion in the supply of credit (in excess of voluntary savings) through the loan market can bring about disproportional investment in the 'higher stages of production' that in the course of the cycle will be found to be unsustainable (given the savings available in the economy as a whole). Mises carried out the exercise by combining Böhm-Bawerk's capital theory and Wicksell's interest rate mechanism with his own sequence analysis of monetary forces.

How changes in the quantity of money and credit would influence the direction and pattern of economic activities depended upon the point at which and the form in which the additional (or subtracted) sums were introduced into (or withdrawn from) the system. In the case of the business cycle, Mises postulated that additional credits were in the form of producer loans. Assuming that prior to the credit expansion the rate of interest was one at which the loan market was in equilibrium,[17] additional demand for funds could be stimulated only by a lowering of the market rate which, in relation to the preceding equilibrium rate, would enhance the prospective profitability of various investment projects that earlier were viewed as too costly by potential borrowers. With savings decisions of ultimate income recipients assumed unchanged, borrowers who have taken up the additional credits would begin new 'roundabout' processes of production in excess of (in Böhm-Bawerkian terms) the subsistence fund available to sustain the factors of production during the production period.[18] The expenditures on new investment projects manifest themselves as increased demands for factors of production in the 'higher orders' of the production structure.[19] Factor prices in these sectors of the economy tend to rise, changing the opportunity cost of alternative employments. Labour and complementary resources are drawn into these activities, either from alternative production uses or from the ranks of the unemployed.[20] As 'higher order' expenditures are transformed into factor incomes, the consumption demand of those employed in the new occupations increases, tending over time to bring about a rise in the prices of finished goods. The rising prices for 'lower order' consumption goods now reverse the relative profitability of alternative employment opportunities in the economy, tending to draw resources away from the 'higher order' projects. If the credit expansion had been a single-injection phenomenon, Mises argued, the higher order projects begun would now either have to be abandoned because of the higher costs of their completion or the unavailability of complementary investments or, if completed, to operate at a rate of return less than initial expectations.[21]

However, if the credit expansion is continued and, particularly, continued at an increasing rate, an upward price-spiralling competitive race is set in motion between those who period after period receive the additional sums initially and attempt to maintain or draw additional factors of production into the more roundabout processes and those who later in the repeated sequential process experience increases in the demand for and prices of their products and attempt to retain or redirect resources back to less roundabout production activities. The process could only come to an end in one of two ways, Mises argued: either through a conscious decision on the part of the monetary authorities to halt the credit expansion or through a complete collapse of the monetary unit in a hyperinflation. But once the monetary expansion came to an end, an economic downturn was inevitable. The distortions in the structure of relative prices, the misdirections of resources among the higher orders of production and the relative income shares created by 'forced savings' would all be found to be unsustainable with the removal of the monetary prop that had established and maintained them during the upturn.[22] An adjustment of relative prices, a reallocation of the factors of production among alternative uses and a shift in relative income shares would all be part of the prerequisites for a return to an economic situation consistent with the underlying pattern of consumer demands and time preference for present and future goods as they would now show themselves in an environment free from monetary influences.[23]

MONETARY POLICY AND THE AUSTRIAN ECONOMISTS

Mises' theory of the business cycle became the centrepiece around which

Austrian discussions of monetary and cyclical phenomena revolved during most of the inter-war period. The most prominent expositor and elaborator of the theory was Friedrich A. von Hayek,[24] who, along with Lionel Robbins,[25] created an international recognition for the 'Austrian Theory of the Business Cycle'. Expositions and applications were also presented in the 1930s by Gottfried Haberler,[26] Fritz Machlup[27] and Erich Schiff.[28] Richard Strigl, in a restatement of Böhm-Bawerk's capital theory, incorporated a version of the theory in his analysis of monetary influences on the capital structure.[29] There were even right-wing and left-wing proponents of the theory in England. The former included, besides Robbins, Frederic Benham[30] and H.F. Fraser[31] and, partly, T.E. Gregory.[32] The latter group included M.A. Abrams,[33] E.F.M. Durbin[34] and Hugh Gaitskell (who later was a leader of the British Labour Party).[35] In the United States, C.A. Phillips, T.F. McManus, and R.W. Nelson used the Austrian theory as the analytical framework for their economic history of the Great Depression.[36] And the Austrian analysis was even integrated into a popular American economics textbook of the late 1930s.[37]

The policy conclusions to be drawn from the Austrian theory of the trade cycle, however, were far from uniform. On the left, Abrams and Durbin concluded that the theory demonstrated the instability of private banking and capitalism in general, and therefore the necessity for state central planning and nationalization of banking and credit institutions. On the right, Benham and Fraser argued for the British central bank to return to a gold standard with institutional reforms that would enhance wage flexibility and business competitiveness to lift the British economy out of the depression and be responsive to future changes in economic circumstances. Lionel Robbins, in the most lucid and eloquent of the Austrian analyses of the Great Depression, also called for a return to the gold standard under which the central banking authorities would play by the international rules of the game in expanding and contracting the domestic currency to reflect changes in the distribution of gold among the nations of the world; but no rigid straitjacket was proposed, Robbins believing at the same time that some discretionary authority should be left in the hands of the central bank 'to mitigate the instability of business'.[38]

Among the Austrians in the more narrow sense, discussions concerning the appropriate goals and methods for monetary policy centred upon the question of 'neutral money'. Wicksell had given different definitions for the term, the 'natural rate' of interest.[39] In some places he used the term to mean that rate at which saving equalled investment. In other places it was defined as the rate of interest at which a stable 'price level' was maintained. In the late 1920s and early 1930s, some of the Austrian school economists attempting to use and extend the Wicksellian framework for purposes of business cycle analysis came to see a contradiction between these two definitions.[40] Friedrich von

Hayek, in particular, emphasized that, in an economy experiencing increases in productivity that, *ceteris paribus*, would result in a declining price level due to the increasing output, a rate of interest sufficiently low to bring about an increase in the supply of money in circulation to keep the price level stable would be below that rate at which the demand for capital would be equal to the supply of savings in the economy. Hence a policy of price level stabilization through the use of the interest rate mechanism could generate a discrepancy between saving and investment that might set in motion a cyclical process of the type described by Mises.[41]

If money had the potential for such destabilizing influences on the structure of production because of the non-neutral manner in which monetary injections could impinge upon the structure of intertemporal prices, then, Hayek concluded, the scientific question confronting monetary policy was how to 'neutralize' money's effects on the relative prices of the economy. It was evident to Hayek that increases in the supply of money to compensate for productivity increases were both unnecessary and, in fact, inherently disruptive. However, circumstances did exist, Hayek said, in which changes in the money supply were justified to maintain monetary neutrality. These involved changes in the demand for money, specifically, changes either in the payment 'habits' of the community or in the number of monetary transactions between the stages of production. Hayek, though, was extremely cautious in his prescriptions: the practical difficulty of instituting such a monetary policy arose from the microeconomic problem the central banking authority would have in seeing to it that the changes in the quantity of money were distributed to (or withdrawn from) those specific individuals experiencing changes in their demand for money. He concluded that possibly the only realistic system for the minimization of cyclical fluctuations was a 100 per cent reserve gold standard under central bank supervision.[42]

Both Gottfried Haberler and Fritz Machlup drew similar conclusions about the rules for a policy of neutral money. A change in the price level, Haberler argued, could have its origins from either the money side or the goods side. In the former category, there was general agreement, he said, concerning the undesirable consequences of monetary expansions or contractions that brought about an absolute rise or fall in the price level. Absolute inflation was injurious, he stated, because by falsifying interest rate signals it set in motion capital investments in excess of savings, with an eventual economic crisis due to the disequilibrium relationships created by the credit expansion. Absolute deflation merely brought about a depression without a boom, a depression from which the economy would recover only when prices and wages had adjusted downward sufficiently to be consistent with the smaller quantity of money in the economy.

There still remained the question, Haberler said, of a relative inflation. By this he meant an increase in the quantity of money that just counterbalanced changes on the goods side that in the absence of the monetary expansion would have resulted in a lower price level. He distinguished between three types of changes from the goods side: changes in the techniques of production, a lengthening of the processes of production and an increase in population. In the first case, which represented an increase in productivity or output per head, a fall in prices was not detrimental, in that the greater outputs produced at lower costs and sold at lower prices were planned for by the respective producers; while the producers might err in failing to anticipate correctly the shape and position of the respective demand curves they faced, this was a matter of relative prices and not absolute prices. A monetary expansion to compensate for productivity increases would, as in the case of an absolute inflation, distort the rate of interest and market prices with a resultant misdirection of resources and an eventual depression. However, in the latter two cases, Haberler argued, both a lengthening of the production structure in which there occurred an increase in the number of times the unfinished products changed hands before reaching the consumption stage, and an increase in population with only a proportional increase in the volume of production (output per head remaining constant) would put unnecessary downward pressure on nominal wages and prices simply because of an insufficiency of means of exchange to service the larger number of transactions. Thus a monetary accommodation to compensate for the latter two cases was justified. While the various index numbers that could serve as a guide for a policy of neutral money might be difficult to construct in terms of scientific precision, Haberler believed it was possible to use less exact ones, if this was done with caution.[43] He did point out, however, that the institution of a national monetary policy to neutralize money's influences on the 'real' economy might be inconsistent with the maintenance and operation of an international gold standard.[44]

Fritz Machlup made similar arguments: falling prices due to productivity increases were not inherently destabilizing and any monetary compensation, because of its influence on the rate of interest and the structure of production, could only generate cyclical distortions. The 'proper limits' for monetary adjustment on the part of the central banking authorities were, he said: counteracting deflation resulting from spontaneous hoarding, an increase in the number of households desiring to hold cash balances and increases in the number of transactions steps in the stages of production. However, like Hayek, Machlup was extremely doubtful about the ability of the monetary authorities to introduce the compensations in a manner that would not, in fact, bring about new distortions in the economy.[45]

Not all of the Austrian economists shared this view concerning the limits of compensatory monetary policy. Alexander Mahr insisted that a policy of neutral money could retard economic growth. Firms experiencing increases in productivity, and for whose products market demand was highly elastic, would absorb an increasing share of the purchasing power of the buying public; revenues would decline in competing industries, slowing capital investment in those sectors, and any resistance to wage reductions by workers in these latter industries could generate increasing unemployment. Mahr concluded, therefore, that stabilization of the price level was preferable to a falling price level.[46]

Many of the Austrians in the inter-war period, as we have seen, accepted Mises' reformulation and refinement of Wicksell's theory of the cumulative process as a logically satisfactory framework for understanding the emergence and phases of the business cycle. The problem of trying to neutralize monetary influences on the real economy led almost all of them to accept and endorse, *in theory*, an activist role for the central monetary authority. Their hesitation to advocate its implementation was due to the *practical* difficulties that were seen as insurmountable for the foreseeable future. The gold standard – albeit a cautiously managed one – was a second best to minimize the undesirable consequences from monetary disturbances. An unmanaged, privatized gold standard never seriously entered into their discussions.

MISES' VIEWS ON GOLD, MONETARY MANIPULATION AND SOUND MONEY

While Mises' writings were the basis for many of the subsequent Austrian analyses of cyclical fluctuation, his own policy conclusions diverged radically from theirs. Unlike most of the other Austrian economists, Mises wholeheartedly and enthusiastically endorsed the gold standard as the most desirable monetary framework for a market economy. His reasons for doing so were both practical and theoretical, and both need to be understood to appreciate his grave doubts about government management of the monetary system and his forceful defence of a gold standard.

As a political economist, Mises viewed the gold standard as the only monetary system that could free the determination of the purchasing power of money from the influence of government intervention.[47] Looking over the broad sweep of history, it was absolutely clear to him that the history of money was nothing less than one long tragic account of incessant state debasement of the monetary unit and an accompanying disruption of economic progress and social development. From the coin clipping of ancient kings and princes through the tidal waves of paper money inflations to the manipulative subterfuge of modern central banking, political influence or control over money and banking had brought in its train nothing but economic havoc and social conflict.[48]

Deceptions and delusions were behind this sorry course of events, Mises argued. From the first time a ruler debased the gold or silver content of the coinage that was either left in his custody or ordered into his vaults, inflation has been a deceptive method by which the political authority could garnish an additional portion of the citizenry's wealth without the blatant seizure of property or taxation of income. Inflation became a means for the imposition of a hidden tax that both enhanced the economic position of the state in the society and enabled the government to cultivate the impression among the populace that it, compared to all others in the community, possessed the magical powers to turn stones into bread. The state could produce benefits for all at a cost to none. But the truth behind the fantasy, Mises insisted, was that what government gave to some it could only provide by taking from others. The state could *redistribute* wealth; it could not *create* it. It was precisely because of money's non-neutrality, that its full influences were only felt through time and not simultaneously in all segments of the market, that money creation could enhance the real incomes of some at the expense of others – those closest to the point of monetary injection being the early recipients of the additional sums of money.[49]

The second delusion, Mises said, was the confusion between money and capital. The arena in which savings was lent and borrowed had colloquially become known as the 'money market'. There arose from this the mistaken belief that interest rates were high because money was scarce and that the solution to high rates of interest was an expansion in the supply of money available for loans. But interest rates were what they were, Mises argued, not because of a lack of money but, rather, because of a scarcity of capital. The insufficiency of means in relation to desired ends imposed the requirement of choice upon human agents. Just as individuals had to allocate their scarce means among alternative uses in the present, they likewise constantly had to make decisions on how to allocate those means available now among uses in the present and the future. The rate of interest was nothing more than the intertemporal price established by the higgling of the market between those who wished to use those present means here and now and those desiring to utilize them for purposes not coming to fruition until later. Monetary injections entering the money markets might have the capacity *temporarily* to lower the rate of interest and redistribute the available resources among different agents in the economy, but it could not necessarily create new capital. It was the very conclusion of Mises' theory of the trade cycle that misdirections of capital through such interest distortions could only lay the seeds for a future recession when the distribution of capital and labour among various types of investment projects came to be seen to be incompatible with the savings base upon which the society's production structure rested.[50]

Finally, the third delusion that Mises saw was the belief that the source of employment was the level of 'effective demand' and that lapses from full employment could be corrected through sufficient increases in the total purchasing power in the economy. The first principle from which all economic reasoning begins is the existence of an insufficiency of means to achieve all the purposes agents would desire to attain. A denial of scarcity would be a denial of the need for either choice or economizing. It would imply a world in which the available means *exceeded* the ends they could serve. In such an environment no one would have to work, for there would be no work needing to be done, and the only dilemma facing *everyone* would be how to allocate leisure time among alternative entertainments. But in a world of scarcity there is always work to be done because there remain ends for which the means are still insufficient. Mises concluded, therefore, that the fundamental truth of Say's law remained intact: in a world of constant change, in which production today was guided by expectation about consumers' demands tomorrow, too much of some things and too little of others might be produced. But an overabundance of all things such that employment for all those desiring employment could not find it at some market-established structure of wages was logically impossible as long as there still remained unfulfilled human wants.[51]

If an economy was suffering from prolonged high unemployment, the source lay not with deficient 'aggregate demand' but rather with a pervasive disequilibrium in the structure of relative prices and wages that precluded the necessary adjustment in product and factor markets for a return to 'full employment'. The attempt to overcome such cost–price rigidities, Mises insisted, through the device of monetary expansion could succeed only for as long as prices rose while money wages remained constant or increased to a lesser degree. Only through 'money illusion' could inflation succeed in bringing about a decline in the real cost of labour sufficient to bring about a return to full employment. As early as 1931, however, Mises argued that, in fact, trade unions were quite conscious of changes in real wages due to changes in the purchasing power of money, and the likelihood of their long-term passivity at the bargaining table in an inflationary environment was not to be expected.[52] The pursuit of full employment via the printing press could only set in motion an upward spiral of wage demands on the part of the unions and an ever increasing monetary expansion to compensate for the unemployment caused by the capture of real wages in excess of potential market-clearing rates.[53]

As long as the reins of power over the money supply remained in or near the hands of the government, Mises was convinced that the temptation for its use and abuse in the pursuit of short-run, political objectives was inevitable. Only the removal of the government's hand from the crank of the printing press could eliminate the historical pattern of booms and busts, inflations and depressions, induced misdirections of labour and capital with the resulting squandering of scarce resources, and general monetary debauchery.

But besides political economic grounds, Mises believed there were theoretical reasons for doubting the ability of a monetary authority to succeed in neutralizing money's impact on the real economy, reasons that separated him from most of the other Austrian economists of the inter-war era. The implicit assumption among those Austrians who were attracted to the theoretical possibility of a neutral money policy was that one could disentangle those influences on the structure of relative prices that were due solely to real causes in the economy from those having their origin purely from the side of money. Their hesitations centred on the practical ability to undertake such a policy with the existing state of knowledge and institutional arrangements. The problems, as we saw, concerned the construction of the appropriate price indexes and the difficulty of directing the monetary changes to those points in the economy at which changes in the quantity of money in circulation were called for.

The heart of Mises' disagreement with the arguments for a neutral money was that it appeared to him as a will-o'-the-wisp just as illusive as the search for a 'stable' money. It implicitly viewed money as an element *in* the economic system yet somehow *apart* and *separable* from it. In the 1920s, Mises used much ink in arguing against those who at the time were advocating a policy of price level stabilization. He saw them as drawing a dichotomy between money and the real economy that was fundamentally flawed. On the one side was the real sector driven by and kept in order through a system of relative prices. On the other side was the quantity of money and the velocity at which that money turned over in facilitating the exchanges of the real sector. Changes in the supply of money or in its rate of turnover could influence the 'level' of prices, but except during transition periods following a change in money or its velocity, the real economy was independent of the monetary lubricant that kept the parts in motion. Stabilization of the price level, it was claimed, would ensure that disturbances from the money side would be neutralized. Any changes that then occurred would have their origin in and be limited to real changes on the sides of supply and demand.[54]

In contrast to this view of money's role in the economy, Mises insisted that money was not only *in* the economy, it was what *bound* the market process together into a single web of exchange. 'Nothing can happen in the orbit of vendible goods without affecting the orbit of money,' he argued, 'and all that happens in the orbit of money affects the orbit of commodities.'[55] In the nexus of exchange, money could be considered as the hub of a wheel holding together and connecting the spokes that represented the individual commodities of trade. Whatever occurred in the individual branches of industry was communicated to the rest of the system through the hub of money and any changes on the side of money were conveyed to the entire market through changes in the spectrum of individual exchange ratios between money and all of the goods of trade.[56] Everything that occurred on the side of the supply and demand for money, therefore, influenced and changed the relative prices of goods and everything that happened on the side of the individual supplies and demands for goods influenced and changed the general purchasing power of money.[57] The mirage of stable money dissolved away before the analyst's eyes as soon as money was seen as the one commodity always present on one side of every exchange, and every change in the relative prices between money and the individual goods against which it traded necessarily modified the value of money. As Mises starkly expressed it, the establishment of a stable money would require the freezing of all the relative prices among goods and between all the goods and money.[58]

The proposals for a neutral money were just as much a mirage, for here what was confused were conceptual tools of thought with the reality of the market process. When some of the other members of the Austrian School investigated the logical relationships between and the causal significance of various influences at work in the complex arena of goods and money, they utilized the basic device of all mental experiments: *ceteris paribus*.[59] Various factors were held constant, some elements were assumed away and others were treated as having properties different from how they were actually found in the empirical world of experience. All such techniques were legitimate methods of theoretical analysis for the purpose of comprehending a world of complex phenomena in which all of these factors and elements were simultaneously at work and enmeshed in an intricate web of incessant change and adjustment.[60] But theoretical comprehension and empirical differentiation were worlds apart. It was precisely because of the difficulty or impossibility of the latter that the analyst had to have recourse to the former. To assume as differentiable in practice that which was only intelligible in theory was to confuse the domain of reality with the realm of ideas.

The fundamental flaw in the proposals for a neutral money was that a theoretical conception used for purposes of understanding the real price and production relationships in the economy – money (in substance, if not in form) treated as a *numéraire*, an element *in* the economy, but *not of it* – was considered of practical applicability. This confused an abstract concept of money with the reality of money in the *real* economy, a real economy in which money was inseparable from and integral to the continuing market process. Money, in Mises' eyes, could be nothing but *non-neutral*, for it was the unique commodity that entered into one side of every act of exchange. Any change on the side of goods had its influence on the side of money by generating changes in incomes, demands and, therefore, the relative preferences for cash balance holdings; and every change in the individual demands for cash balances sent out new ripples of change throughout the economy resulting in a new configuration of relative demands for goods.[61]

What, then, was the desirable end of monetary policy if neither stable nor neutral money were attainable goals? For Mises the answer was 'sound' money. Sound money was a commodity money neither stable in value (because money's value, like all other goods' value, was a matter of relative prices) nor neutral in its effects on the economy (because of the pervasive presence of money in the nexus of exchange, which meant it was always a dynamic element for change). What sound money connoted was a monetary system fully integrated into and a part of the very market process which the use of money facilitated in growing, developing and enhancing. What sound money was to be free of was the intervention of the political authorities, intervention that only succeeded, as Mises saw it, in producing economic disruption, social upheaval, deceptive taxation and squandered capital – all through the false signals of manipulations of the money supply. And why gold as the basis for a sound money system? Argued Mises:

> Because, as conditions are today and for the time that can be foreseen today, the gold standard alone makes the determination of money's purchasing power independent of the ambitions and machinations of governments, of dictators, of political parties, and of pressure groups. The gold standard alone is what the nineteenth-century freedom-loving leaders (who championed representative government, civil liberties and prosperity for all) called 'sound money'.[62]

GOLD, MONETARY REFORM AND FREE BANKING

In Mises' view, the gold standard as a monetary system had not been fully integrated into the market economy. Through most of its modern history it had functioned in a twilight zone, partly in the market and partly under the influence of the state. The result was that it evolved in an extremely bastardized form, with government control increasing as the 19th century passed into the 20th. Finally, with the outbreak of World War I, the international gold standard – which had facilitated a hundred years of world economic growth and trade, and which had slowly integrated a set of national economies into a world economy – was first circumvented and then overthrown in the flood of national paper monies that financed the war efforts of both sides in the War to End All War.[63]

During the years following both world wars, Mises participated in the discussions and debates on how a 'sound money' gold standard could be established. Read in isolation, his contributions on the subject could suggest that at various times his views on monetary reform changed significantly. When studied in conjunction with each other, however, the various arguments and proposals not only show themselves to be consistent with each other, but represent what Mises saw as, ideally, a step-by-step programme for reform with the final goal being complete liberation of money from the political arena.

The first step on the road to monetary reform, Mises argued, had to be an immediate and complete end to all increases in the quantity of money by the central monetary authority.[64] Mises' rejection of what has come to be referred to as a 'gradualist' policy of inflationary deceleration was argued for two reasons. First, he believed that only such a radical shift in policy could succeed in breaking inflationary expectations; second, there was no way to diminish the side-effects of an inflation coming to an end. The argument frequently made in defence of gradualism is that it would enable participants in the economy to adjust their prices and wage contracts in such a fashion that nominal values could more easily conform to the lower rates of monetary change and, therefore, diminish any 'real' effects on the economy that might arise from an end to inflation. However, the real effects from inflation in Mises' framework were not caused by a failure of the rates of change in prices and wages *in general* to conform to rates of monetary increase. Rather, the real effects of inflation were caused by money's differential and sequential effects on demands and prices during the inflationary process that gave a 'wrong twist' to the distribution of labour and capital among alternative uses in the economy. Further inflation, even at a lower rate, offered no solution to the malinvestments already generated in the economy; all that continued monetary expansion could succeed in doing would be to delay the necessary corrections in the structure of production or, in fact, to distort the economic process further with even more adjustments called for at the end of the day.

Mises' own proposal for the next phase of monetary reform involved several stages.[65] The *first stage* would involve three simultaneous steps: a total prohibition on the issuance of any additional money and credit by the Central Monetary Authority; a 100 per cent reserve requirement on all future deposits in the banking system; and complete freedom for all citizens to own, buy and sell gold, either domestically or in foreign markets, without any interference or intervention on the part of the government or the Federal Reserve.

The *second stage* would be undertaken after a period of time had elapsed. After the gold markets had settled down and a free market price had emerged between gold and dollars (free from any monetary manipulations on the part of the Monetary Authority) the government would declare a new parity at which dollars would be legally redeemed for gold.

The *third stage* would then involve the establishment of a Conversion

Agency with the legal responsibility to convert dollars into gold (with the use of a gold fund 'lent' by the Treasury, interest-free and for an indefinite period. The Treasury would be required afterwards to buy all dollars offered for sale by the Conversion Agency and extinguish, in cooperation with the Federal Reserve, all notes thus acquired. The Conversion Agency also would be required over time to mint and offer in exchange to dollar holders gold coins for small denomination notes (that is, five, 10 and 20-dollar bills).

Mises' proposal for the establishment of a new parity rather than a re-establishment of a previous one followed from his analysis of the influence of money on the economy. Legal redemption at an older parity would require a contraction in the money supply until, in theory, all outstanding dollars could be exchanged for gold. However, just as a monetary expansion was non-neutral in its effects, so too was a monetary contraction. Employment, output and the direction of production would all be adversely affected for as long as the contraction continued and had not completely worked its influence through the economy, with a fall in prices and wages.[66] In response to the argument that a monetary contraction following a monetary expansion merely compensated and corrected for the distortions caused during the inflation, Mises replied: 'If a man has been hurt by being run over by an automobile, it is no remedy to let the car go back over him in the opposite direction.'[67]

With the implementation of these reforms, the monetary system would have moved close to what Mises considered the positive aspects of the Currency School programme as expressed in Peel's Bank Act of 1844.[68] While establishment of this much of a reform programme would be considered a major step towards sound money, it was not the final step in Mises' mind. Total and complete removal of state control, influence and power over the supply of money could be established and guaranteed only through the demise of central banking, *in any form*, and its replacement by a system of free banking.[69]

What inhibitions would exist under free banking to prevent the same type of monetary consequences as under central banking? To Mises the answer was clear: the forces of the market. Any bank that attempted to expand its note and credit issues in excess of rather conservative bounds would suffer the consequences of the reflux mechanism. In other words, the principles that the classical economists had so lucidly explained under the heading of the specie-flow mechanism in trade between nations would operate in the same manner between competing, private banks doing business in the same political territory. A bank that expanded its note issue in excess of the demand to hold on the part of its clients would have those notes returned to it through the clearing house as those notes were presented for redemption by other banks on behalf of their clients. If the bank's liabilities exceeded its possession of the note liabilities of the other banks, it would experience a reserve drain that would require a note contraction on its part to ensure its solvency. Thus the market process contained its own system of checks and balances to limit the expansion of money substitutes on the basis of gold reserves.

And what determined the availability of gold? The profitability of gold production as determined, on the one hand, by gold's purchasing power as money and its price for industrial uses and, on the other hand, the costs of mining as reflected in the relative market values of factors of production in alternative uses. Freed from the discretion of political authority, money, like every other commodity in the circle of trade, would be under the sway of supply and demand. Money would now be fully integrated into the market process and totally subject, in the final analysis, to the preferences of consumers as demonstrated in voluntary acts of exchange.[70]

While Mises considered the establishment of a system of sound money a prerequisite for the operation of a free market, it was impossible to establish such a monetary system in isolation from other trends in the society and in the social fabric. The conquest of money by the state was indicative of an ideological conquest in society that saw prosperity through planning, equality through egalitarianism, freedom through force and autonomy through autarky. A free money could only prevail, ultimately, in a free society. As Mises clearly expressed it at the height of the Great German Inflation:[71]

> The belief that a sound monetary system can once again be attained without making substantial changes in economic policy is a serious error. What is needed first and foremost is to renounce all inflationist fallacies. This renunciation cannot last, however, if it is not firmly grounded on a full and complete divorce of ideology from all imperialist, militarist, protectionist, statist, and socialist ideas.

That is a task that falls upon all of us who desire to take up the Austrian heritage as exemplified in the writings of Ludwig von Mises.

NOTES

1. Oskar Morgenstern, *The Limits of Economics* [1934] (London: William Hodge, 1937) p. 155. The English title is deceptive; the original German, *Die Grenzen der Wirtschaftspolitik* (*The Limits of Economic Policy*), more correctly captures the purpose of the book.
2. Cf. Alan R. Sweezy, 'The Interpretation of Subjectivist Value Theory in the Writings of the Austrian Economists', *Review of Economic Studies*, 1 (1933–34) p. 176: 'In spite of a common tradition and far-reaching agreement on many points, the present group harbors deep-rooted differences of opinion in its midst.'
3. Cf. Ludwig M. Lachmann, 'The Significance of the Austrian School of Economics in the History of Ideas' [1966], in *Capital, Expectations and the Market Process* (Kansas City, KS: Sheed, Andrews and McMeel, 1977) pp. 55–62.
4. Cf. F.A. Hayek, 'The Transmission of the Ideals of Economic Freedom' [1951], in *Studies in Philosophy, Politics and Economics* (Chicago: University of Chicago Press, 1967) pp. 197–8; also Hayek, 'Appendix I: Tribute to Ludwig von Mises' [1956] in Margit von Mises, *My Years with Ludwig von Mises* (New Rochelle, NY: Arlington House, 1976) pp. 189–90.

5. Carl Menger, 'Geld' [1909], reprinted in *Grundsätze der Volkswirtschaftslehre* (Vienna: Holder-Pichler-Tempsky A.G., Zweite Auflage, 1923) pp.325–31. This, of course, was consistent with Menger's general doubts about the construction and use of economic aggregates and his emphasis on always relating them back to the purposes of the individual agents whose actions brought them into existence; cf. his criticisms of the concept of 'national wealth' in Carl Menger, *Principles of Economics* [1871] (New York: New York University Press [1950], reprinted 1981) pp.111–13. On Menger's cash balance approach, see Arthur W. Marget, *The Theory of Prices*, Vol. 1 [1938] (New York: Augustus M. Kelley, 1966) p.418.

6. Eugen von Böhm-Bawerk, *Capital and Interest*, Vol. 2, *The Positive Theory of Capital* (South Holland, IL: Libertarian Press, 1959) pp.77–118; also cf. Ludwig M. Lachmann, 'Böhm-Bawerk und die Kapitalstruktur', *Zeitschrift für Nationalökonomie* (August 1959) pp.235–45.

7. Knut Wicksell, *Interest and Prices* [1898] (New York: Augustus M. Kelley [1936], reprinted 1965) pp.81–101.

8. The exact meaning of the term 'natural rate' in Wicksell is not unambiguous; Marget, *The Theory of Prices*, Vol. 1, pp.201–4, was able to distinguish at least eight different senses of the natural rate in Wicksell's writings. The four most common ones were the natural rate as (1) the anticipated rate of profit; (2) the rate at which savings equals investment; (3) the rate at which real capital would be lent without the intermediation of money, that is *in natura*; (4) the rate at which the price level remained stable. The first, the natural rate as the anticipated rate of profit, seems to be the meaning Wicksell has in mind in the chapter titled 'The Rate of Interest as Regulator of Commodity Prices', in *Interest and Prices*.

9. This skewing effect of changes in the rate of interest on production decisions was later emphasized by Fritz Machlup in 'The Rate of Interest as Cost Factor and as Capitalization Factor', *American Economic Review* (September 1935) 459–65; see also his earlier article, 'The Liquidity of Short-term Capital', *Economica* (August 1932) 271–84.

10. Ludwig von Mises, *The Theory of Money and Credit* [1924] (Indianapolis, IN: Liberty Classics [1952], reprinted 1981).

11. Ludwig von Mises, 'Monetary Stabilization and Cyclical Policy' [1928] in Israel M. Kirzner (ed.), *Classics in Austrian Economics: A Sampling from a Tradition*, Vol. 3 (London: William Pickering, 1994) pp.33–111.

12. Carl Menger, *Principles of Economics*, pp.257–71; *Investigations into the Method of the Social Sciences with Special Reference to Economics* [1883] (New York: New York University Press, 1985) pp.152–5; and 'On the Origin of Money' [1892], reprinted in Richard M. Ebeling (ed.), *Austrian Economics: A Reader* (Hillsdale, MI: Hillsdale College Press, 1990) pp.483–504.

13. An early criticism of marginal utility theory was that it claimed to explain the emergence of prices on the basis of the marginal evaluation of goods, but, the critics said, for a marginal evaluation of goods to occur, it was first necessary for there to exist ratios of exchange at which commodities could be traded and towards which evaluations could be directed; hence the marginal utility theorists were accused of having to assume the existence of the very thing (prices) the theory was meant to explain, thus moving in a logical circle. On how the Austrians proposed to escape from the circle through the introduction of *expectations* and the distinction between *expected* prices and *realized* prices, see Böhm-Bawerk, *Capital and Interest*, Vol. 2, pp.240–43; Leo Schönfeld-Illy, *Das Gesetz des Grenznutzen* (Vienna: 1948) pp.183–238; and Israel M. Kirzner, *Market Theory and the Price System* (Princeton, NJ: D. Van Nostrand, 1963) pp.105–41.

   Similar criticisms were levelled against the application of marginal utility theory to explain the value of money. Mises argued that it was true that the evaluation of the marginal utility of money was dependent upon the pre-existence of the monetary unit having a specific purchasing power. Since money was directly serviceable neither for consumption nor for production but, rather, acquired its utility as a good on the basis that it could be held in the form of cash balances to facilitate future acts of exchange, any present demand for the money good presupposed its having an existing purchasing power. But logically no circular reasoning was involved, Mises argued. Money's present purchasing power could be 'regressed' back to that point at which the money good was used for the first time as a medium of exchange, before which the commodity's exchange value would have been based purely upon its utility as a consumption and/or production good; see Mises, *The Theory of Money and Credit*, pp.129–46; also Mises, *Human Action, A Treatise on Economics*, 3rd edn (Chicago: Henry Regnery, 1966) pp.408–16; also Murray N. Rothbard, *Man, Economy and State: A Treatise on Economic Principles*, Vol. I [1962] (Los Angeles: Nash Publishing, 1970) pp.231–7.

14.   Like Menger, Mises rejected the analytical usefulness of the concept of the velocity of circulation of money. He argued that both the velocity concept and the equation of exchange, of which the concept was a component, were methodologically inappropriate as theoretical devices in the service of economic reasoning, both being carry-overs of an earlier methodological holism; see Mises, 'The Position of Money among Economic Goods' [1932], in Richard M. Ebeling (ed.), *Money, Method and the Market Process: Essays by Ludwig von Mises* (Norwell, MA: Kluwer Academic Press, 1990) p.61:

> The attempts to solve the problem of the value of money with reference to the economy as a whole, rather than through market factors, culminated in a tautological equation without any epistemological value. Only a theory which shows how subjective value judgments of buyers and sellers are influenced by changes in the different elements of the equation of exchange can legitimately be called a theory of the value of money.
>
> Buyers and sellers on the market never concern themselves with the elements in the equation of exchange of which two – velocity of circulation and the price level – do not even exist before market parties act and the other two – the quantity of money (in the economy as a whole) and the sum of transactions – could not possibly be known to the parties in the market. The importance which the various actors in the market attach, on the one hand, to the maintenance of a cash balance of a certain magnitude and, on the other hand, to the ownership of the various goods in question determines the formation of the exchange relationships between money and goods.

Cf. also *Human Action*, pp.399–400; on Mises' theory of the demand for money in comparison to some alternative approaches, see Richard M. Ebeling, 'Variations on the Demand for Money Theme: Ludwig von Mises and Some Twentieth-Century Views', in John W. Robbins and Mark Spangler (eds), *A Man of Principle: Essays in Honor of Hans Sennholz* (Grove City, PA: Grove City College Press, 1992) pp.127–38.

15.   Mises, *The Theory of Money and Credit*, pp.160–68 and 237–43; *Nation, State and Economy* [1919] (New York: New York University Press, 1983) pp.155–8; 'Monetary Stabilization and Cyclical Policy', pp.95–6; *Human Action*, pp.412–16; and 'The Non-Neutrality of Money' [1938], in Richard M. Ebeling (ed.), *Money, Method and the Market Process: Essays by Ludwig von Mises*, pp.69–77.

16.   The different meanings of the 'real effects' of monetary expansion or contraction in the writings of quantity theorists have not always been explicitly brought out.

17.   In some places Mises uses the 'natural rate' to signify that rate at which intertemporal loans would be made *in natura*; see *The Theory of Money and Credit*, pp.393–4 and 'Monetary Stabilization and Cyclical Policy', p.122. In other places the 'natural rate' is defined as the loan market rate at which investment would be equal to savings; see *The Theory of Money and Credit*, pp.399–400, and 'Monetary Stabilization and Cyclical Policy', p.124; for Mises' more sophisticated explanation of the meaning of the equilibrium loan market rate(s) – one that incorporates time preference, the risk factor in the evaluation of individual loans and any 'premiums' for changes anticipated in the purchasing power of money – see *Human Action*, pp.538–48.

18.   Mises' expositions of his theory of the trade cycle can be found in *The Theory of Money and Credit*, pp.396–404; 'Monetary Stabilization and Cyclical Policy', pp.118–30; and *Human Action*, pp.550–75. For an exposition of the Austrian theory in the context of the Great Depression and in contrast to the Keynesian view, see Richard M. Ebeling, 'The Austrian Economists and the Keynesian Revolution: The Great Depression and the Economics of the

Short-Run' and, for a comparison of Mises' monetary and business cycle theory with that of Joseph A. Schumpeter, 'Two Variations on the Austrian Monetary Theme: Ludwig von Mises and Joseph A. Schumpeter on the Business Cycle', both in Richard M. Ebeling (ed.), *Human Action: A 50-Year Tribute* (Hillsdale, MI: Hillsdale College Press, 2000) pp. 15–110 and 149–187, respectively.

19. In *The Theory of Money and Credit*, pp. 399–401, Mises refers to the effects of credit expansion as involving a 'lengthening of the average period of production'. In *Human Action*, pp. 556–8, the questionable Böhm-Bawerkian terminology is left behind and the focus is rather on the fact that the lowered money rate of interest and additional credit set off the undertaking of investment activities of varying types, shapes and forms (not just a 'lengthening') that will be found to be unsustainable in view of the savings available to maintain the capital structure of the economy.

20. On the effect of unemployed resources in the initial stages of the upturn, see Mises, 'Monetary Stabilization and Cyclical Policy', p. 125; and *Human Action*, pp. 578–80; and *Interventionism: An Economic Analysis* [1940] (Irvington-on-Hudson, NY: Foundation for Economic Education, 1998) pp. 42–3.

21. Ludwig von Mises, 'Inconvertible Capital' [1931], in *Epistemological Problems of Economics* [1933] (New York: New York University Press [1960] reprinted 1981) pp. 225–31.

22. Mises argued that the changes in relative income shares during the monetary expansion could, in theory, bring about a permanent change in the rate of interest if the modifications in wealth positions among social groups were from those with higher time preference to those with lower time preference. But whether this occurred would depend upon the circumstances of the historical case, no *a priori* argument on the matter could be made. On the possibility of 'forced saving', see *The Theory of Money and Credit*, pp. 238–9 and 'Monetary Stabilization and Cyclical Policy', pp. 121 and 126–7. For an account of the development of the 'forced saving' concept in the 19th century, see Friedrich A. Hayek, *Prices and Production* (New York: Augustus M. Kelley [1935], reprinted 1967), pp. 101–4; and Hayek, 'A Note on the Development of the Doctrine of "Forced Saving"' [1932], reprinted in *Profits, Interest, and Investment* [1939] (New York: Augustus M. Kelley, 1969) pp. 183–97; also, Fritz Machlup, 'Forced or Induced Saving: An Exploration into its Synonyms and Homonyms', in *Economic Semantics* (New Brunswick, NJ: Transaction Books [1963] 1991) pp. 213–40.

23. It is perhaps of interest to note that C. Bresciani-Turroni, in a review of Hayek's *Monetary Theory and the Trade Cycle* (*Economica*, August, 1934) 347, believed that the Austrian theory was very instructive in explaining the course of the Great German Inflation of the early 1920s:

> The changes in the structure of production, brought about by inflation, and later by currency stabilization, were most apparent in Germany. During the inflation period the substantial fall in real wages, which meant a 'forced saving' on a large scale, allowed the productive resources of the country to be deflected from the production of consumer goods to that of fixed capital. This continued as long as the new issues of paper money exerted a pressure upon real wages. But the situation changed when the value of money was stabilized. Then an adjustment of real wages began, which showed the insufficiency of the 'fund for the maintenance of labor'. The demand for consumers' goods increased, that of producers' goods on the whole declined, and the prices of the latter diminished relatively to those of the former. This resulted in a redistribution of productive resources. A shift to the production of consumers' goods was distinctively observed in 1924. The so-called 'stabilization crisis' with its most striking feature, the 'scarcity of capital', was nothing else than a readjustment of the whole structure of production, which had been distorted during the inflation period.

Cf. Bresciani-Turroni's *The Economics of Inflation* [1931] (New York: Augustus M. Kelley [1937], reprinted 1968) pp. 183–223 and 359–97.

24. Friedrich A. von Hayek, *Monetary Theory and the Trade Cycle* [1929] (New York: Augustus M. Kelley [1933], reprinted 1966); *Prices and Production* [1st edn, 1931] (New

York: Augustus M. Kelley [2nd rev. edn, 1935], reprinted 1967); *Profits, Interest and Investment* (New York: Augustus M. Kelley [1939], reprinted 1969).

25. Lionel Robbins, 'Consumption and the Trade Cycle' [1932] reprinted in Susan Howson (ed.), *Economic Science and Political Economy: Selected Articles by Lionel Robbins* (London: Macmillan, 1997) pp.117–32; *The Great Depression* (New York: Macmillan 1934); 'The Two-fold Roots of The Great Depression: Inflationism and Interventionism', in Graham Hutton (ed.), *The Burden of Plenty* (London: George Allen and Unwin, 1935), pp.103–14.

26. Gottfried Haberler, 'Money and the Business Cycle' [1932] reprinted in Richard M. Ebeling (ed.), *The Austrian Theory of the Trade Cycle and Other Essays*, by Ludwig von Mises, Gottfried Haberler, Murray Rothbard and Friedrich A. Hayek (Auburn, AL: The Ludwig von Mises Institute [1978], reprinted 1996) pp.37–64; and in Anthony Y.C. Koo (ed.), *The Liberal Economic Order*, Vol. II (Aldershot, UK and Brookfield, VT: Edward Elgar, 1993) pp.160–74.

27. Fritz Machlup, *The Stock Market, Credit and Capital Formation* [1931] (London: William Hodge, rev. edn, 1940); *Führer durch die Krisenpolitik* (Vienna: Julius Springer, 1934); 'Can We Control the Boom?, a Conference at the University of Minnesota, May 11, 1937', *The Day and Hour Series*, no. 20 (The University of Minnesota Press, October 1937) pp.11–18.

28. Erich Schiff, *Kapitalbildung und Kapitalaufzehrung im Konjunkturlauf* (Vienna: Julius Springer, 1933).

29. Richard von Strigl, *Capital and Production* [1934] (Auburn, AL: Mises Institute, 2000); 'Der Wicksellsche Prozess', *Weltwirtschaftliches Archiv*, bd. 60 (1942) pp.443–64.

30. Frederic Benham, *British Monetary Policy* (London: P.S. King and Son, 1932).

31. H.F. Fraser, *Great Britain and the Gold Standard* (London: Macmillan, 1933).

32. T.E. Gregory, *Gold, Unemployment and Capitalism* (London: P.S. King and Son, 1933) p.xiii: 'Whilst I am by no means an adherent of the terminology or even of some of the tenets of the Viennese School, I do believe that they are right in thinking that in the course of upward movement of the trade cycle profound modifications in the structure of production take place and that monetary policy or theory cannot be negligent of this aspect in putting forward remedial measures.'

33. M.A. Abrams, *Money and a Changing Civilization* (London: John Lane, The Bodley Head, 1934).

34. E.F.M. Durbin, *Purchasing Power and Trade Depression* (London: Jonathan Cape, 1934); *The Problem of Credit Policy* (London: Chapman and Hall, 1935); 'Money and Prices', in G.D.H. Cole (ed.), *What Everybody Wants to Know about Money* (New York: Alfred A. Knopf, 1933) pp.253–79.

35. H.T.N. Gaitskell, 'Four Monetary Heretics', in Cole (ed.), *What Everybody Wants to Know about Money* pp.280–335.

36. C.A. Phillips, T.F. McManus and R.W. Nelson, *Banking and the Business Cycle* [1937] (New York: Arno Press and *The New York Times*, 1972).

37. Albert L. Meyers, *Elements of Modern Economics* (New York: Prentice-Hall, 1937) pp.278–93 and 336–49.

38. Robbins, *The Great Depression*, pp.164–72.

39. See note 8, *supra*.

40. Members of the 'Stockholm School', also working in the Wicksellian tradition, came to similar conclusions; see Erik Lindahl, 'The Rate of Interest and the Price Level' [1930], in *Studies in the Theory of Money and Capital* [1939] (New York: Augustus M. Kelley, 1970) pp.139–268; Gunnar Myrdal, *Monetary Equilibrium* [1933] (New York: Augustus M. Kelley, 1965). On the similarities and differences in the 'Austrian' and 'Swedish' analyses, see Richard M. Ebeling, 'Money, Economic Fluctuations, Expectations and Period Analysis: The Austrian and Swedish Economists in the Interwar Period', in Bert Tieben (ed.), *The Austrians in Debate* (London: Routledge, 1997) pp.42–72.

41. Hayek, *Monetary Theory and the Trade Cycle*, pp.113–14; *Prices and Production*, pp.23–8.

42. Hayek, *Prices and Production*, pp.105–28; *Monetary Nationalism and International*

Stability [1937] (New York: Augustus M. Kelley, 1971) pp.73-94. As late as 1960, Hayek still believed in the necessity for a government monopoly over the money supply; see *The Constitution of Liberty* (Chicago: University of Chicago Press, 1960) pp.324-39. Only in *Choice in Currency* [1976], reprinted in *New Studies in Philosophy, Politics, Economics and the History of Ideas* (Chicago: University of Chicago Press, 1978) pp.218-31 and, more fully, in *Denationalization of Money* (London: Institute of Economic Affairs [1976], rev. edn, 1978) did Hayek conclude that monetary stability could only be approached through a divorce of money from state control, through a system of competitive currencies issued by private banks; however, his proposal for private moneys was one based, not on the gold standard, but rather on fiat currencies whose values would be stabilized by the banks on the basis of an index of commodity prices. For a critical analysis of Hayek's proposal, see Richard Ebeling, 'Decontrolling Money', *Libertarian Review* (March-April 1977). Hayek's suggestion in *Choice in Currency* that a way to curb governmental inflationary policies was to eliminate legal tender laws and allow citizens of each country domestically to use any national currency that they found preferable was, in fact (though Hayek does not mention it), proposed much earlier by Richard Strigl, 'Gibt es eine Sicherung gegen Inflation?', *Mitteilungen des Verbandes österreichischer Banken und Bankiers* (1932) N. 15/6.

43. Gottfried Haberler, *The Different Meanings Attached to the Term 'Fluctuations in the Purchasing Power of Gold' and the Best Instrument or Instruments for Measuring Such Fluctuations*, Official No. F/Gold/74 (Geneva: League of Nations, March 9, 1931).

44. Gottfried Haberler, *The Theory of International Trade* [1933] (London: William Hodges, 1936) p.47.

45. Fritz Machlup, *The Stock Market, Credit and Capital Formation*, pp.174-201; also cf. Machlup, 'Inflation and Decreasing Costs of Production', in H. Parker Willis and John M. Chapman (eds), *Economics of Inflation* (New York: Columbia University Press, 1935) pp.280-87.

46. Alexander Mahr, *Monetary Stability, and How to Achieve It*, Public Policy Pamphlets, no. 9 (Chicago: University of Chicago Press, 1933); and Mahr, 'Technological Progress and Monetary Policy', in *Guest Lectures in Economics*, Twenty Lectures Delivered in English at Professor G.U. Papi's Seminar, Institute of Economics and Public Finance, Faculty of Law, University of Rome, 1956-1961, edited by Elizabeth Henderson and Luigi Spaventa (Milan: Dott. A. Giuffrè, 1962) pp.144-53.

47. Mises, 'Monetary Stabilization and Cyclical Policy', p.78; *The Theory of Money and Credit*, p.416; *Human Action*, p.474.

48. Mises, *Human Action*, p.781.

49. Mises, *The Theory of Money and Credit*, pp.222-3; *Nation, State and Economy*, pp.151-65; 'Stabilization of the Monetary Unit - from the Viewpoint of Theory' [1923], in *On the Manipulation of Money and Credit*, pp.36-8.

50. Mises, *Human Action*, p.403; 'The Gold Problem', in *Planning for Freedom*, 4th edn (South Holland, IL: Libertarian Press, 1980) pp.187-90.

51. Mises, 'Lord Keynes and Say's Law', in *Planning for Freedom*, pp.64-71.

52. Mises, 'The Causes of the Economic Crisis: An Address' [1931], in *On the Manipulation of Money and Credit*, pp.199-200.

53. Mises, 'Gold versus Paper' [1953] and 'Full Employment and Monetary Policy' [1957], in Bettina Bien Greaves (ed.), *Economic Freedom and Interventionism* (Irvington-on-Hudson, NY: The Foundation for Economic Education, 1990) pp.76-86.

54. Mises, *The Theory of Money and Credit*, pp.236-8 and 399-406; 'Monetary Stabilization and Cyclical Policy', pp.90-98; and 'The Suitability of Methods of Ascertaining Changes in Purchasing Power for the Guidance of International Currency and Banking Policy' [1930], in Richard M. Ebeling (ed.), *Money, Method and the Market Process, Essays by Ludwig von Mises*, pp.78-95.

55. Mises, *Human Action*, p.418.

56. Mises followed some of the classical economists (cf. Jacob Viner, *Studies in the Theory of International Trade* [1937] [New York: Augustus M. Kelley, 1965] pp.311-14) in defining the purchasing power of money as the spectrum of individual exchange ratios between money and the goods against which it traded. See *The Theory of Money and Credit*, p.188;

Human Action, p.402. Also cf. Murray N. Rothbard, *Man, Economy and State*, Vol. I, p.205.

57. The dynamics of money's influence on the structure of relative prices as well as the ever-changing character of supply and demand in general resulted in Mises declaring all attempts to measure scientifically changes in the purchasing power of money as insolvable. All the methods and techniques for the construction of index numbers were considered both static in quality and arbitrary in nature; cf. *The Theory of Money and Credit*, pp.187-94; 'Monetary Stabilization and Cyclical Policy', pp.83-9; 'The Suitability of Methods of Ascertaining Changes in Purchasing Power for the Guidance of International Currency and Banking Policy', pp.86-90; *Human Action*, pp.220-3. A similar conclusion had been reached by the well-known Dutch economist, N.G. Pierson in the late 19th century, 'Further Considerations on Index Numbers', *Economic Journal* (March 1896) 131: 'the only possible conclusion seems to be that all attempts to calculate and represent average movements of prices, either by index numbers or otherwise, ought to be abandoned'. On the problems with index numbers as a measure for changes in purchasing power, see the excellent and entertaining book by Bassett Jones, *Horses and Apples, A Study in Index Numbers* (New York: John Day, 1934); also Michael A. Heilperin, *International Monetary Economics* (London: Longmans, Green, 1939), the appendix on 'Note on the Use of Statistical Constructions', pp.259-70; and John W. Robbins, *The Case Against Indexation*, Monetary Tract no. 16 (Greenwich, CT: Committee for Monetary Research and Education, July 1976); for a statistician's objections, see M.J. Moroney, *Facts from Figures* (London: Penguin Books, 1953) pp.48-55.

It is perhaps of interest to note that, on the question of measuring changes in the purchasing power of money and the assumptions that money confronts a selection of goods whose relative prices among one another are either constant or uninfluenced from the side of money, Mises and Keynes held similar views; cf. John Maynard Keynes, *A Treatise on Money*, Vol. 1 (New York: Harcourt Brace, 1930) pp.79-88; and on money's influence on the structure of relative prices, the very 'Austrian'-type passages on pp.92-4.

58. Mises, 'Monetary Stabilization and Cyclical Policy', p.84; see the similar conclusion by Menger, 'Geld', p.299; and on Menger's views on the insolubility of stabilizing the value of money, see Charles Rist, *History of Monetary and Credit Theory* [1938] (New York: Augustus M. Kelley [1940], reprinted 1966) pp.372-3.

59. Mises, 'Monetary Stabilization and Cyclical Policy', pp.85-6.

60. Mises, *Human Action*, pp. 236-7, on the use of imaginary constructions.

61. Mises, 'The Non-Neutrality of Money'.

62. Mises, 'The Gold Problem', p.185.

63. Mises, *The Theory of Money and Credit*, pp.368-90; *Human Action*, pp.471-6.

64. Mises, 'Stabilization of the Monetary Unit - from the Viewpoint of Theory', p.17; *The Theory of Money and Credit*, p.448.

65. Mises, *The Theory of Money and Credit*, pp.448-52.

66. Ibid., pp.452-6.

67. Mises, 'The Non-Neutrality of Money', p.76.

68. Mises, 'Monetary Stabilization and Cyclical Policy', p.168.

69. Mises, *Human Action*, p.443.

70. Mises, *The Theory of Money and Credit*, pp.395-9; 'Monetary Stabilization and Cyclical Policy', pp.138-40; *Human Action*, pp.434-48.

71. Mises, 'Stabilization of the Monetary Unit - from the Viewpoint of Theory', p.49.

6. Classical liberalism and collectivism in the 20th century

THE EPOCH OF CLASSICAL LIBERALISM

Several times during the 20th century, the Western world passed through 'watershed' periods of crisis. The first occurred as a result of World War I. It brought the classical liberal epoch to an end in August 1914. How far away that liberal era now seems to us. Governments hardly fleeced their citizens: total tax burdens in Great Britain and the United States were only in the range of 10 or 15 per cent of national income; and the United States had had an income tax for only one year when the war began. The British government ran its world-encompassing empire as a vast free trade zone, open to all comers for trade and investment regardless of their nationality or citizenship. The United States, it is true, fluctuated between higher and lower tariffs, but within its three thousand mile span, the country contained few barriers to production, trade and exchange. And across the European continent, the tariff barriers were miniscule compared to what the rest of the 20th century experienced.

Matching the free movement of goods was the free movement of people. Emigration restrictions and immigration barriers were in their infancy. It was still a world with neither passports nor visa requirements. For the price of a railway ticket or passage in steerage across the Atlantic, even the poorest could pick up and move wherever personal inclination or economic opportunity led them to take up residence – and millions of people did so. Nor were there any barriers to the free movement of money and capital. Exchange controls, restrictions and limits on the transfer of investment capital between countries, and fluctuations in the exchange rates among currencies, were unknown. The Western world was bound together by one monetary system – the gold standard. Each national currency was redeemable on demand for a fixed amount of gold, gold coins circulated as actual media of exchange and these gold coins jingled in most people's pockets.

The welfare state was unheard of. Help for the unfortunate and those in temporary financial need was considered primarily to be a matter of community charity, individual philanthropy and church-related assistance. The degree to which voluntarism had succeeded was demonstrated by the comments of English economist William Stanley Jevons (who was not an advocate of *laissez-faire*), in his 1870 presidential address to the British Association for the Advancement of Science, that 'Could we sum up the amount of aid which is, in one way or another, extended by the upper to the lower classes, it would be almost of incredible amount, and would probably far exceed the cost of poor law relief.' But Jevons believed that voluntary charity, in this period of supposed Victorian stoneheartedness, had become excessively generous: 'It is well known that those towns where charitable institutions and charitable people abound, are precisely those where the helpless poor are most numerous. ... the casual paupers have their London season and their country season, following the movements of those on whom they feed. Mr. Goschen and the poor law authorities have of late begun to perceive that all their care in the administration of relief is frustrated by the over-abundant charity of private persons, or religious societies.' (It is worth recalling that this was before the charitable deduction could be made from one's income tax.)[1]

The Western nations were in their stated principles, if admittedly not always in their actual practice, committed to the ideal of individual liberty in practically all areas of life – social, economic and political.[2] This ideal has been explained by Wilhelm Röpke: 'It is the [classical] liberal principle that economic affairs should be free from political direction, the principle of a thorough separation between the spheres of the government and the economy. ... The economic process was thereby removed from the sphere of officialdom, of public and penal law, in short from the sphere of the "state" to that of the "market", of private law, of property, in short to the sphere of "society".'[3]

Collectivist clouds, it is true, had already started to form over the classical liberal terrain, even before the war. In 1913, German historian Hermann Levy pointed out that 'The Manchester School of *laissez-faire* has of recent years been brought face to face with two very momentous phenomena – Socialism and Neo-Mercantilism. These two very different tendencies have a common element in their opposition to the individualist doctrines of political economy. Socialism is concerned with the division of the product according to certain principles of 'justice', rather than with the development of potential production. Mercantilism is the most complete expression of an all-embracing regulation of industrial conditions by political wisdom and administrative practice. But both agree that industry should be organized by the State. Manchester Liberalism has been undermined bit by bit by the union of these two forces.'[4] But while the foundations of the old classical liberal order were being slowly chipped away in the years preceding World War I, in the daily affairs of ordinary men, the political and economic environment in which people went about their business of living and earning a living was still one of widely respected civil liberty and economic freedom.

WORLD WAR I AND THE RISE OF COLLECTIVISM

All of this changed with World War I. The German economist Gustav Stolper described the transformation that the war produced:

> Just as the war for the first time in history established the principle of universal military service, so for the first time in history it brought national economic life in all its branches and activities to the support and service of state politics – made it effectively subordinate to the state. ... Not supply and demand, but the dictatorial fiat of the state determined economic relationships – production, consumption, wages, cost of living. ... at the same time, and for the first time, the state made itself responsible for the physical welfare of its citizens; it guaranteed food and clothing not only to the army in the field but to the civilian population as well. ... Here is a fact pregnant with meaning; the state became for a time the absolute ruler of our economic life, and while subordinating the entire economic organization to its military purposes, also made itself responsible for the welfare of the humblest of its citizens, guaranteeing him a minimum of food, clothing, heating and housing.

And Professor Stolper pointed out that, even after the war came to an end, 'The free movement of capital has ceased. So has the free movement of emigration. Men and money both lie shackled under the might of the state ... The choking of free movement in manpower and capital is being intensified by the choking of free movement of commodities.'[5] The classical liberal world of individual rights, private property and civil liberty died on the battlefields of the war. Many of the cherished and hard-won freedoms of the 19th century were sacrificed on the altar of winning the war. And when the war was over, liberty, as it turned out, was the ultimate victim. Behind the war-time slogans of 'making the world safe for democracy', 'the right of national self-determination' and 'a league of nations for the securing of world peace', nation states had grown strong with power. Wartime controls had replaced free enterprise; exchange controls and import–export regulations had replaced free trade; confiscatory taxation and inflation had undermined the sanctity of private property and eaten up the accumulated wealth of millions. The individual and his freedom had shrunk ... and the state and its power were now gigantic.

And the collectivist demons had been set loose on the world. By the 1930s, there was not one major country devoted to the principles of liberalism. Regardless of the particular variation on the collectivist theme, practically every government in the world had or was implementing some form of economic planning and restricting the personal and commercial freedoms of its own citizenry. In the Soviet Union, the state owned and controlled all of the resources and means of production. The central planning agencies in Moscow directed production and distribution. In Fascist Italy and Nazi Germany, property and resources remained nominally in private hands, but the use and disposal of that property and those resources were controlled and directed according to the dictates of the state. In Great Britain, free trade and the gold standard had been abandoned in the early 1930s during the depths of the Great Depression. Protectionism, interventionism, welfare statism and monetary manipulation were the active policy tools of the British government.

Throughout Europe and the rest of the world, the various nation states had erected tariff barriers, regulated industry and agriculture, limited the free movement of their people and restricted civil liberties. The USA followed the same course. Franklin Roosevelt's New Deal was a conscious and active attempt to impose a fascist-type economic order on America, through the National Recovery Administration (NRA) and the Agricultural Adjustment Act (AAA). As Stuart Chase, one of the intellectual developers of the New Deal ideology, said, 'We propose then a national Planning Board [be] set up under the auspices of the Federal government ... and manned by engineers, physical scientists, statisticians, economists, accountants and lawyers ... Why should Russians have all the fun of remaking a world?'[6] And even after much of the New Deal had been declared unconstitutional in 1935, the Roosevelt administration continued on the collectivist road with economic regulation, deficit spending, public works projects, welfare statism, and monetary central planning through a paper currency no longer backed by or bound to gold.[7]

World War II only re-enforced the collectivist tendency. When the economists and political scientists in the West looked forward to the brave new world that would follow the destruction of Hitler, they all repeated in chorus that planning was inevitable in the postwar era. The only question open to dispute was whether it would be 'democratic' or 'totalitarian'.[8] But either way planning was coming. And plan they did. There was Sweden's attempt at a democratic 'middle way'.[9] There was the British Labour Party, which implemented nationalization of industry and tried to introduce forms of state planning.[10] There was French indicative planning.[11] And the planning fever soon spread to the emerging countries of the Third World, which fell under the sway of the Soviet planning model. New political elites in Asia and Africa seized the reins of power as the flags of the colonial rulers were lowered. They saw themselves as 'nation-builders' and building a nation required an economic foundation. The battle cry became 'from national liberation to national socialism'. There was 'African Socialism', 'Indian Socialism', 'Islamic Socialism', 'Zionist Socialism' and even the 'Burmese Road to Socialism'.[12]

It is often forgotten the appeal that the Soviet planning model had for the Third World in the late 1950s and the 1960s. This appeal was re-enforced by the economists in the West. Soviet statistics were often accepted at more or less face value – statistics that were frequently extrapolated out into the future and which suggested that the Soviet Union might surpass the Western world in industrial production and standards of living as early as the 1980s and 1990s.[13] Maybe history *was* on the side of the communists? From the perspective of the early 21st century, this seems like pure fantasy, but in the 1960s many intellectuals in the West were not sure.

THE END OF COLLECTIVISM AND THE PERSISTENCE OF THE INTERVENTIONIST WELFARE STATE

And now, in the wake of the collapse of Soviet socialism, with the last of the totalitarian demons set loose by events of World War I buried in the rubble of its own contradictions and impossibilities, Europe, the USA and indeed the world face another watershed of crisis. The crisis concerns whether the West will finally turn its back on the collectivist experience and attempt to retrace its steps to the liberal path that was left in 1914 – whether the Western world will return to the ideal of liberty over statism. For some the answer is already obvious. Has not the market economy shown its superiority over government planning, has not capitalism triumphed over economic collectivism? Is it not just a matter of the eastern European countries transforming themselves into economic and political systems similar to the ones in place in western Europe and the USA?

This view demonstrates just how successful the triumphs of collectivism and socialism have been over the ideal of liberalism and free market capitalism. The vast majority of people in the West believe that what they have is liberalism and the market economy. This is as true for Americans as it is for the people of western Europe. What exactly is anti-liberal and anti-capitalist in the USA?

In the new world of politically correct newspeak, Americans are free to say whatever they want – as long as it does not offend any ethnic, gender or racial group. They can pursue any career they choose – as long as they have been certified and licensed and have successfully passed inspection by an army of state regulators. They may come and go as they please – as long as they have been approved for a government-issued international passport, declared whether they are carrying more than $10 000 in currency, reported all taxable or forbidden items they wish to bring into the country, and not attempted to visit any foreign lands declared off-limits by the state. They may buy whatever satisfies their fancy – as long as it has been manufactured, packaged and priced according to government standards of safety, quality and fairness, and as long as it has not been produced by a foreign supplier who exceeds his import quota or who offers to sell it below the state-mandated 'fair-market price'.

Americans are free to go about their own affairs – as long as they send their children to government schools or private schools approved by the state; as long as they do not attempt to employ in a business too many of a particular ethnic, gender or racial group; as long as they do not attempt to plan fully for their own old age rather than pay into a mandatory government social security system; as long as they do not pay an employee less than the governmentally imposed minimum wage; as long as they do not attempt to construct on their own property a home or a business in violation of zoning and building ordinances; that is, as long as they do not try to live their lives outside the permissible edicts of the state.

And Americans freely take responsibility for their own actions and pay their own way – except when they want the state to guarantee them a job or a 'living wage'; except when they want the state to protect their industry or profession from competition either at home or from abroad; except when they want the state to subsidize their children's education or their favourite art or the preservation of some wildlife area or the medical research into the cure of some hated disease or illness; or except when they want the state to ban some books, movies or peaceful acts between consenting adults rather than trying to change the behaviour of their fellow men through peaceful persuasion or by personal example.[14]

That most who have just read this list of lost freedoms in the USA will be shocked that anyone should suggest that the state should not be concerned with these matters shows more than anything else how far we have come and are continuing to go down the collectivist road to serfdom. Whether the proponents of the collectivist path called their programme socialism, social democracy, 'liberalism', progressivism, the Swedish 'third way' or the welfare state, during the past three-quarters of a century the end result has been the same: an increasing undermining of the sanctity of private property, an expanding compulsory redistribution of wealth, a growing spider's web of government regulations over private enterprise, and state direction of economic activity through either nationalized industries, government-business 'partnerships' or subsidies and tax incentives to induce private business into those activities and locations desired by the state.

And regardless of the political label under which this gradual transformation of Western economic and social life has been brought about, the journey has led to one end. As economist Melchior Palyi expressed it in his book, *Compulsory Medical Care and the Welfare State*, 'In democracies the Welfare State is the beginning and the Police State the end. The two merge sooner or later.'[15] Why? Because, and inevitably, wherever the state superimposes itself on the affairs of men, compulsion and command replace the peaceful and voluntary relationships that are the hallmark of the truly free society. For if men do not obey, the state applies its police power to insist. If the reader considers the last statement an exaggeration, let him try to open and operate a business without proper government licences; or publicly announce and undertake the hiring of people below the state-mandated minimum wage; or try to replace a trade union member with a non-union worker in his business where union membership is required by law for employment; or try to not pay his social security taxes; or try to construct a building outside the state-mandated building codes or zoning ordinances; or try to enter or leave his country without a valid passport; or try to buy or sell openly chemical substances that the state has deemed the use of as 'socially undesirable'.

The French social philosopher Alexis de Tocqueville already understood in the first half of the 19th century the dangers from the incrementally imposed form of the collectivist ideal: the state, he explained in *Democracy in America*, 'covers the surface of society with a network of small complicated rules, minute and uniform, through which the most original minds and energetic characters cannot penetrate ... [government] provides for [people's] security, foresees and supplies their necessities, facilitates their pleasures, manages their principle concerns, directs their industry, regulates the descent of property, and subdivides their inheritances ... people ... [are] reduced to nothing better than a flock of timid and industrious sheep, of which the government is the shepherd. I have always thought that servitude of the regular, quiet, and gentle kind which I have just described might be combined more easily than is commonly believed with some of the outward forms of freedom, and it might even establish itself under the wing of the sovereignty of the people'.[16]

The extent to which the state now dominates, supervises, regulates, controls, manages and directs the social and economic order of the Western world frees classical liberalism and the market economy from any of the responsibility for society's ills for which the collectivists still attempt to blame capitalism. The market economy cannot be blamed for unemployment, when it is the state that long ago began the process of undermining a free, competitive labour market by imposing minimum wage laws, legalizing trade union monopolies and organized labour's strike threat, establishing unemployment benefits that subsidize the preferred choice of receiving income without the necessity of working, and imposing increasingly burdensome taxes connected with the private employer's hiring of workers in his firm or enterprise.[17]

The market economy cannot be blamed for pollution and environmental damage, when it is the state that has failed to fully specify or enforce private property rights, and therefore has prevented the market from 'internalizing' negative externalities connected with production and exchange.[18] The market economy cannot be blamed for inflations and recessions, when for practically the entire 20th century it was the state's monetary and fiscal policies that were responsible for causing macroeconomic fluctuations in employment, output and prices through the government's use of purely paper monies, central banking and deficit spending.[19]

The market economy cannot be blamed for international trade conflicts, when it has been the state that has prevented the freedom of trade, investment and exchange between the citizens of various countries through the introduction of tariff walls, import quotas, domestic content requirements, central bank intervention and manipulation of foreign exchange rates, and restrictions on the free movement of people from one part of the world to another.[20]

The market economy cannot be blamed for poverty, homelessness or the breakdown of the family, when it has been the state that has imposed tax and regulatory disincentives to capital formation, investment and job creation; when it has been the state that has retained rent controls in some urban areas and destroyed the profitability of low-income housing construction, and imposed zoning ordinances and building codes that raise the costs of apartment construction and maintenance; when it is the state that has undermined the nuclear family through its welfare rules for eligibility, created intergenerational welfare dependency among the poor, and weakened family values by the introduction of collectivist indoctrination and cultural social engineering in the curriculum of public schools.[21]

Nor can the market economy be blamed for continuing and even worsening race relations in the society, when it has been the state that has imposed a new tribal collectivism in both the public and private sectors, in which ethnic, racial and gender quota rules increasingly determine an individual's fate in terms of opportunities for higher education, employment and income earning; the politicizing of an individual's life opportunities on the basis of the accident of birth has resulted in people increasingly viewing those of other ethnic, racial and gender groups as threats to their own advancement, and therefore enemies in the battle for political power and the financial disbursements from the state.[22]

CONTINUING RATIONALES FOR THE REDISTRIBUTIVE STATE

The crisis of the late 20th century, therefore, is the crisis of the failure of collectivism in all of its forms, both its totalitarian type in the East and its democratic varieties in the West. But one would think that the experiences of the last half-century had never occurred when listening to some of the intellectuals on the left. Philosopher Richard Rorty has told his fellow intellectuals that 'the word "socialism" has been drained of force' and that after the experience of 'our Eastern European friends ... Marxist rhetoric is no

more respectable than Nazi rhetoric'. But did this mean that he now accepted
the fact that the belief in and the desire for social engineering should be given
up, that there is no alternative to a truly free, unregulated market economy?
No. 'Even now,' Rorty said, 'I am unwilling to grant that Friedrich von Hayek
was right in saying that you cannot have democracy without capitalism. All I
will concede is that you need capitalism to ensure a reliable supply of goods
and services, and to ensure that there will be enough taxable surplus left over
to finance social welfare.'

Indeed, for Rorty, the only lesson learned from the Soviet experience is that
comprehensive planning cannot work and that other less radical means must
be pursued to attain the same end, that is, social outcomes that he prefers to
the ones that emerge spontaneously out of the choices and interactions of free
men in the market economy. He is still searching for a 'kinder and gentler'
socialism. 'American leftist intellectuals stand in need of a new political
vocabulary,' Rorty explained, '[and] I suggest that we start talking about greed
and selfishness rather than about bourgeois ideology, about starvation wages
and layoffs rather than about the commodification of labor, about differential
per-pupil expenditure on schools and about differential access to health care
rather than about the division of labor into classes.'[23] Rorty may be trying to
change his vocabulary, but the ideological concepts behind the words remain
the same. He may admit that the attempt to make a 'new socialist man' is
impossible, but he still desires to manipulate men's lives and socially engineer
the distribution of the fruits of their labour. He still wants to impose his own
conception of egalitarian justice on society.

Professor Rorty is joined in this crusade to save some of the premises and
foundations of the socialist critique of the market economy by others, such as
Professor David Marquand. In a recent essay about what comes 'After
Socialism' Professor Marquand asks for some second thoughts before an
unreserved conclusion that market liberalism has triumphed over the socialist
ideal. While admitting that some of socialism's premises have been proved
wrong with the passage of time – the belief that socialism was historically
inevitable, that central planning by the state was more efficient than
decentralized private enterprise, and that socialism was the vehicle for the
progress of the working class in society – he believes that the ethics of
socialism continue to stand the test of time. 'Central to almost all [of the
socialist] gropings, however, were words like "co-operation", "commonwealth" and "fellowship" ... the term that encapsulated the essence of the
socialist ideal was fraternity.' The market economy, Professor Marquand
argues, has always represented a 'relentless pressure to commodify all social
goods', that is, to reduce all social relationships to a cold and calculating nexus
of exchange in which the warmth of human intercourse and the sense of
community were smothered by the 'bottom line' of profit and loss.[24]

But it may be asked, with the advantage of historical perspective, whether it was the market economy or socialism and the welfare state that destroyed many of the networks of human relationships that have traditionally been among the defining characteristics of civil society. As University of Chicago sociologist Edward Shils has reminded us, 'The idea of civil society is the idea of a part of society which has a life of its own, which is distinctly different from the state, which is largely in autonomy from it. ... The hallmark of a civil society is the autonomy of private associations and institutions as well that of private business firms. ... A market economy is the appropriate pattern of life of a civil society.'[25]

In civil society there is no longer a single focal point in the social order, as in the politicized society in which the state designs, directs and imposes an agenda to which all must conform and within which all are confined. Rather, in civil society there are as many focal points as individuals, who all design, shape and direct their own lives guided by their own interests, ideals and passions.

But the society of free individuals is not a society of unconnected, isolated individuals – 'atomistic man', as the critics of liberty will sometimes refer to him. As 18th and 19th-century French classical liberal, Count Destutt de Tracy, concisely expressed it, 'the social state ... is our natural state ... Society is ... a continual series of exchanges ... in which the two contrasting parties always both gain, consequently society is an uninterrupted succession of advantages, unceasingly renewed for all its members'.[26]

The 'exchange' relationships that emerge among free men in civil society, however, should not be viewed as meaning merely or only those involving the trading of what is narrowly thought of as 'goods and services', within the institutions of the market place. The network of exchange relationships includes community endeavours, religious and church activities, cultural associations and clubs, professional organizations and charitable callings. Indeed, any relationship in which men find that they have common interests, goals or shared beliefs becomes the foundation for the emergence of 'exchange', involving agreed-upon terms for association and collaboration for mutual benefit, and the enhancement of the quality, character and meaning of life for each and every participant.

Every free man belongs to numerous voluntary associations and institutions in the civil society. He forms or joins new ones as new interests and ideals develop during his life, and withdraws from others as his inclinations and circumstances change; and the associations and institutions to which individuals belong modify their goals and structures over time as the members revise their purposes and discover new rules more effective in achieving the ends of the organization.

Each individual, therefore, simultaneously participates in a variety of 'social worlds' with different people, with each of these social relationships representing different purposes and needs in his life. And cumulatively these various social worlds of civil society, with all the relationships within each of them and between them, create what the Austrian economist Friedrich Hayek called the spontaneous social order. He called it a 'spontaneous order' because the institutions, associations and activities among men that are the elements of this order are not the result of any prior central plan or regulated design; instead, they arise, evolve and maintain themselves as a result of the independent actions and interactions of the members of society.[27]

But, in the welfare state, all of these relationships of civil society are weakened and threatened with extinction as the state pre-empts the duties, responsibilities and obligations that traditionally have belonged to the family and the voluntary efforts of community members. And as David G. Green has shown in his monograph, *Reinventing Civil Society: The Rediscovery of Welfare without Politics*, throughout the 19th century, during the heyday of 'unbridled' capitalism and in an environment of 'rugged individualism', voluntarism and community effort were the free society's *successful* answer and natural method for 'cooperation' and 'fellowship'.[28]

The dehumanizing and anti-social consequences of the welfare state were understood even before the modern version was implemented in the 20th century. The older British welfare state – the poor laws system – came under heavy criticism by the classical liberals of the 19th century. Dr Thomas Chalmers, Professor of Moral Philosophy at St Andrews University in Scotland, in the 1820s and 1830s, for example, pointed out many of the unintended consequences that always seem to follow in the wake of dependency upon the state.[29]

Criticizing the British poor laws system, under which the status of 'pauperism' was legalized and on the basis of which individuals and families could draw their financial support from the state, Dr Chalmers saw four serious consequences. First, he said, it reduced the incentive for people to manifest the industriousness and frugality to care for themselves and their families, since now they knew that whether they worked and saved or not, the state could be relied upon to provide them with all the minimal necessities of life.

Second, he feared, it reduced if not eliminated the sense of family responsibility, knowing that the state would care for the old and the infirm, 'there is a cruel abandonment of parents, by their offspring, to the cold and reluctant hand of public charity', as children develop the attitude that since they have paid their taxes it is now the government's duty to do what relatives have traditionally done for each other.

Third, it threatened to harden the hearts of men towards their fellows, and diminish the spirit of voluntary giving to others in the community. When assistance to others in society is voluntary, there usually is aroused in us 'the compassion of our nature ... [which] inclines us to the free and willing movement of generosity'. But when charity is made compulsory by the state, Dr Chalmers argued, there is aroused in us, instead, 'the jealousy of our nature ... [which] puts us upon the attitude of surly and determined resistance'.

Fourth, it weakened the spirit of community and assistance among those who were less well off. Dr Chalmers noted that those who live in simple or poor conditions often show a support and sympathy for those around them who fall into even worse circumstances, and which creates a network of mutual help within those poorer portions of the wider community. But when each is made a ward of the state, the ties and connections between people in similar circumstances are weakened, with each now connected by one thread: their own individual dependency upon the state for all they need and desire.

And it should be added that Dr Chalmers, in the early decades of the 19th century, had already been confronted by all the types of arguments heard in the 20th century as to why the welfare state could not be repealed. He was confronted, for example, by the counter-argument that, without the mandatory provision of the state, the poor would fall into even worse conditions. And an even more forceful impediment to the denationalization of the welfare state, he said, came from the resistance of those who administered the system; that is, when the proponent of voluntarism 'comes into collision with the prejudices or partialities of those who at present have the right or power of management' of the welfare programmes.

The negative effects of the welfare state were also pointed out by Henry Fawcett, one of the last great classical economists. In his book, *Pauperism: Its Causes and Cures*, published in 1871, he explained that pockets of severe poverty existed in England at the very time of a growing and expanding British economy in which many in the society were obtaining rising standards of living that had never been known before. A primary culprit for this poverty amongst plenty, Fawcett argued, was the poor laws. The incentives of the poor laws system and the consequences that followed from them were no different from what we have seen in, for example, the USA in our own times. In Fawcett's words of 1871:

> Men were virtually told that no amount of recklessness, self-indulgence, or improvidence would in the slightest degree affect their claim to be maintained at other people's expense. If they married when they had no reasonable chance of being able to maintain a family, they were treated as if they had performed a meritorious act, for the more children they had the greater was the amount of relief obtained. All the most evident teachings of commonsense were completely set to nought. ... An artificial stimulus was then given to population. ... Population was also fostered by a still more immoral stimulus. A woman obtained from the parish [the local agency for the distribution of welfare] a larger allowance for an illegitimate than for a legitimate child. From one end of the kingdom to the other

people were in fact told not only to marry with utter recklessness and let others bear the consequences, but it was also said, especially to the women of the country, the greater is your immorality, the greater will be your pecuniary reward. Can it excite surprise that from such a system we have had handed down to us a vast inheritance of vice and poverty?[30]

And Fawcett pointed out to his readers that the welfare programmes of his day had created dependency 'by successive generations of the same family'. He reported that a government commission investigating the effects of the poor laws found 'three generations of the same family simultaneously receiving relief'. And, he also pointed out, that after a time it was common for those on welfare to begin to believe that they were entitled to it: 'the feeling soon became general that pauperism was no disgrace, and the allowance which was obtained from the parish was just as much the rightful property of those who receive it, as the wages of ordinary industry'.

Can anyone deny that the problems and concerns raised by people like Dr Chalmers and Professor Fawcett were intensified many times over during the 20th century, when socialist ethics were put into action by the modern welfare state? Can anyone, with a straight face, say that the politicization of social life has made that life more human or more humane? That it has produced that greater sense of community and fraternity that socialists have longed for for almost two hundred years? Or that it has raised public spiritedness among the general population?

To the contrary, it can be argued that socialist ethics have destroyed the source for such communitarian endeavours. The welfare state has weakened man's sense of societal responsibility because it has stolen from him, through redistribution of income, much of the financial means of practising it. What socialists never understood, and still do not understand, is that accumulated wealth is not merely a means for physical maintenance of oneself and one's family, plus additional sums of money for selfish leisure activities, but an expression of ourselves and what we wish and hope to be. And the way we use our wealth enables us to teach our children about those things that are considered worthwhile in life, as well. Accumulated wealth also enables individuals to perform many activities 'for free' that are considered the foundation of a free and good society – from community and church work to support for the arts and the humanities.

Deny an individual the honest income and wealth he has earned and you deny him the ability to formulate, and give expression to, his own purposes as a human being. And you deny him the capacity to make his voluntary contribution to the civilization and society in which he lives, as he sees best. Instead, these decisions and actions of responsible individuals are more and more concentrated in the hands of the state because, through taxation, the state denies individuals the capacity to do these things themselves and as they see fit. The state, thus, increasingly plans our lives, takes care of our children, and decides what 'socially desirable' projects and activities should be given support, and to what extent. And as the state grows stronger, the individual grows weaker. Individuals become weaker, not only in relation to the state, but as human beings because they no longer exercise those qualities and habits of mind that only self-responsibility and a sense of voluntary social interaction teach and make possible.[31]

In spite of Professor Marquand's beliefs and deepest desires, socialist ethics have been shown to be as bankrupt as all the other premises of the socialist system. There is neither ethical behaviour nor moral choice when the freedom to make both good and bad decisions is pre-empted by state monopolization of the way resources and income are allocated along alternatives in the name of some higher societal good. And to the extent that the state taxes incomes earned and wealth accumulated for redistributive purposes, to that degree the range of moral decision making is narrowed for the citizens of the country. It is a measure of the amount of anti-ethics introduced into the society by the state in the name of a mythical collectivist social good.[32]

Only in the free society can the spirit of charity, community and social responsibility be fostered and developed in an ever-increasing number of men. Only in an environment in which individuals are required to learn to exercise such behaviour, precisely because the state does not pre-empt or substitute itself for such conduct, can the ethical fibre of human beings be strengthened. And until we fully and completely give up the ethics of socialism, we will not have created the circumstances in which that desired voluntaristic and social ethic can mature and become habituated through intergenerational tradition.

NEW RATIONALES FOR THE NEOMERCANTILIST STATE

But if the socialist variety of collectivism remains alive under the cover of a new vocabulary of word manipulation and under the continuing rationale for a 'socialist ethics', so too is neomercantilism. Herbert A. Henzler (Professor of International Management at Munich University) defended 'The New Era of Eurocapitalism': 'The competitive battle senior [corporate] managers now face,' Henzler says, 'is a deeper struggle among different capitalist systems, each with its own distinctive set of values, priorities, institutions, and goals.' Corporate managers in the USA 'are most deeply committed to free markets and the effectiveness of individual action'. While 'capitalism in Japan is far less individualistic than its U.S. counterpart ... Japanese managers are expected to use profits to fund high, sustained levels of corporate investment, not to distribute them to shareholders'.

On the other hand, in Europe, he says, under 'our form of capitalism', corporate managers 'are expected to balance the need for corporate growth with the health of the physical environment and with the broader social welfare of the countries in which they operate'. Thus 'Eurocapitalism supports a social compact' between business, labour and government, because 'most Europeans would sacrifice the possibility of an unrestricted business environment that rewards a few with extreme wealth for the reality of many people with comfortable income'. Indeed, 'because of our mercantilist tradition, Europeans know that the interests of private companies and the state can run together in comfortable harness', with government serving as a 'potential source of managerial ideas and approaches'.[33]

At the same time, Thomas K. McCraw (Straus Professor of Business History at Harvard University) said what he sees as, 'The Trouble with Adam Smith'. McCraw admits that 'the battle between Adam Smith and Karl Marx is over … Smith and capitalism have won. But a second championship is under way, a contest between different kinds of capitalism. In one corner stands a relatively *laissez-faire* consumer variety represented by the United States. In the other corner is a more nationalistic, producer-oriented capitalism epitomized by Germany, Japan and the "Little Dragons" of East Asia'.

McCraw believes that, in our corporate industrial world of mass and giant production, long-term investments crucial to a nation's well-being cannot be left 'to the whims of individuals, who usually act in their own short-run interest … It must be done through organizations, and it is best done with the positive assistance of wise public policy'. If the USA is to match its Japanese and German rivals, America must follow their lead and 'act from a premise that the key unit of analysis is not the individual but the nation-state'. There must be a concerted action by 'firms, industrial groups, and elite public-sector ministries … to deploy resources so as to achieve stronger economic performance'. The keys to America's future, in McCraw's prevision, are 'nationalism, technology, organization, and power'.[34]

Finally, Clyde V. Prestowitz, Jr (president of the Economic Strategy Institute and general director of the Pacific Basin Economic Council) told us that we must go 'beyond *laissez-faire*'. Like our two other authors, Prestowitz argues that 'the truth is that there are different forms of capitalism, each deeply rooted and in competition with the others'. America's traditional policy of fostering global free trade and a borderless world must be set aside if America is not to merely survive in the world economy, but continue to be industrially and technologically pre-eminent. America's trading partners, particularly the Europeans and the Japanese, 'pursue policies designed to foster a favorable mix of industries. … All of them … have a producer rather than a consumer mentality'. Where industries are located 'can be influenced by policy, so that a clever country could raise its living standards by capturing a preponderance of [high-tech, high profits] industries'.

Prestowitz believes that agencies in the government should be assigned the task of selecting high-tech, high-wage industrial winners; transportation and communications infrastructures should be invested in by the government; a national health-care programme should be sponsored by the government; only those foreign investments should be allowed in the USA that benefit America's 'national interest'; and in trade negotiations with America's world partners, Americans must be ready to fight economic wars to protect their industries from foreign competition. 'Americans must reconcile themselves to a certain amount of trade management with Japan,' he says. And 'to break old structures and overcome the effects of industrial policies [of other nations] it may be necessary to negotiate affirmative action for imports and foreign investment'.[35]

In the post-Soviet era, both 'socialism' and 'central planning' have lost their respectability as language used in polite (and intelligent) society. And 'fascism' has been a word banished from serious public-policy discussions for more than half a century. This has left advocates of economic collectivism without a vocabulary – a legitimized set of terms with which to categorize and defend their case for government control and management of economic activity. The economic collectivists, therefore, have resorted to the same tricks they have used in the past: adopt the labels of their opponents and then subvert and pervert their meaning. At the beginning of the 20th century, this was the method that the socialists and neomercantilists used when they stole the word 'liberalism'. They argued that they – the newer liberals – wanted to complete the work the older liberals had begun. Their new liberalism wanted to add to the 'negative' protections of the older liberalism a set of 'positive' protections to enhance human freedom in the form of government welfare guarantees and a regulated or nationalized economy for a better serving of the common good.

Now a similar process is at work with the terms 'capitalism' and 'market economy'. To manage trade between nations is no longer mercantilism; to foster government–business partnerships for selected and directed industrial development is no longer economic fascism; to regulate and tax business for purposes of income redistribution is no longer the welfare state; to assign to governmental agencies the task of guiding the investment decisions of private enterprises is no longer state planning. Rather, all such policies are now nothing more than different forms of 'competing capitalism'. Through this linguistic subversion, the economic collectivists have hoped to legitimize their statist agendas by making it appear that arguing for socialism, planning, interventionism, state welfarism and neomercantilism is merely a dispute over which kind of capitalism we want.

It also enables them to avoid all the questions that would have to be answered if things were called by their right names. For example, after the disaster of central planning, how do they propose to know how to allocate resources and labour efficiently to alternative investment paths better than a price-guided, profit-driven system of decentralized decision making in a competitive market? Once they seriously start down the road of systematic national industrial policy to win against international competitors, what will be the outcome in terms of international relations, when several national governments try at the same time to establish their respective economy's pre-eminence in the same 'high-tech' industries and supposed 'high-wage' occupations? With a further politicization of the allocation of resources, with intensified government–business 'partnerships' for selecting of investments, and with even more conscious 'producer-oriented' policies in the form of various tax breaks and subsidies for business, how do the neomercantilist social engineers propose to prevent the increased incentives for 'producer-oriented' special interests to lobby and manipulate the political process for their own benefit at the expense of the general taxpaying and consuming public? As the ethnic and gender collectivism of education, employment and income quotas and group privileges are extended even further, what will happen to the foundations of civil society as people view their neighbours less and less as individuals with whom they interact for peaceful, mutual benefit, and instead come to view each other more and more as members of antagonistic groups in political competition for power and control?

In the 19th century, the classical liberals had offered solutions that not merely defused and minimized, but did away with many of these problems. Their method was to depoliticize and privatize social and economic relationships, to make the interactions among people in society the private affairs of voluntary, mutual agreement and peaceful persuasion. But in spite of the failure of Italian fascism, German National Socialism and Soviet socialism, even in the face of the political corruption and societal and economic failure of the welfare state, with total disregard for the contradictions and impossibilities inherent in all attempts to plan and direct the economic activities of millions, the political and economic collectivists seem determined to continue their resistance to the only rational political–economic alternative: the classical liberal society and the free market economy.

In 1932, the Austrian economist, Ludwig von Mises, admitted, 'I know only too well how hopeless it seems to convince impassioned supporters of the Socialist Idea by logical demonstration that their views are preposterous and absurd. I know too well that they do not want to hear, to see, or above all to think, and they are open to no argument. But new generations grow up with clear eyes and open minds. And they will approach things from a disinterested, unprejudiced standpoint, they will weigh and examine, will think and act with forethought.'[36] At the beginning of the 21st century, we can only hope that such a new generation may finally arise and triumph. Another century of various experiments in attempting to apply variations on the collectivist theme is too high a price for society to pay just so some can indulge their fantasies in trying to remake the political and economic orders in their preferred images.

NOTES

1. William Stanley Jevons, *Methods of Social Reform* [1883] (New York: Augustus M. Kelley, 1965) p. 197.
2. On the economic and political era before World War I, see John Maynard Keynes, *The Economic Consequences of the Peace* (New York: Harcourt, Brace and Howe, 1920) pp. 10–12; and Gustav Stolper, *This Age of Fable: The Political and Economic World We Live In* (New York: Reynal & Hitchcock, 1942) pp. 1, 7–8.
3. Wilhelm Röpke, *International Order and Economic Integration* (Dordrecht: Reidel, 1959) p. 75.
4. Hermann Levy, *Economic Liberalism* (London: Macmillan, 1913) p. 1.
5. Gustav Stolper, 'Lessons of the World Depression', *Foreign Affairs*, 9, no. 2 (1931) 244–5; and 'Politics versus Economics', *Foreign Affairs*, 12, no. 3 (1934) 365–6.
6. Stuart Chase, *A New Deal* (New York: Macmillan, 1932) pp. 219, 252.
7. Cf., Francis Neilson, *Control from the Top* (New York: Putnams, 1933); Lewis W. Douglas, *The Liberal Tradition* (New York: Van Nostrand, 1935); and A.S.J. Baster, *The Twilight of American Capitalism: An Economic Interpretation of the New Deal* (London: King, 1937).
8. Charles E. Merriam, 'The Place of Planning', in Seymour E. Harris (ed.), *Saving American Capitalism: A Liberal Economic Program* (New York: Alfred A. Knopf, 1948) p. 161: 'The alternative is not between planning and no planning, but between democratic planning and autocratic planning, between planning in a free society and planning under a dictatorship, whether Fascist or Communist ... Planning is coming. Of this there can be no doubt. The only question is whether it will be democratic planning of a free society, or totalitarian in character.'
9. Roland Huntford, *The New Totalitarians* (New York: Stein and Day, 1972).
10. Cf. John Jewkes, *Ordeal by Planning* (London: Macmillan, 1948); Bertrand de Jouvenel, *Problems of Socialist England* (London: Batchworth, 1949); Ivor Thomas, *The Socialist Tragedy* (New York, Macmillan, 1949); R. Kelf-Cohen, *Nationalization in Britain: The End of a Dogma* (London: Macmillan, 1959).
11. Cf. Vera Lutz, *Central Planning for the Market Economy: An Analysis of the French Theory and Experience* (London: Longmans, Green, 1969).
12. Cf. Arnold Rivkin, *Nations by Design: Institution-Building in Africa* (New York: Anchor Books, 1968); P.T. Bauer, *Indian Economic Policy and Development* (Bombay: Popular Prakashan, 1961); B.R. Shenoy, *Indian Planning and Economic Development* (Bombay: Asia Publishing House, 1963); Roger A. Freeman, *Socialism and Private Enterprise in Equatorial Asia: The Case of Malaysia and Indonesia* (Stanford: Hoover Institute, 1968); Alex Rubner, *The Economy of Israel* (London: Frank Cass, 1960); Deepak Lal, *The Poverty of 'Development Economics'* (Cambridge, MA: Harvard University Press, 1985).
13. Paul Samuelson, *Economics*, 7th edn (New York: MacGraw-Hill, 1967) pp. 790–92.
14. Cf. David Boaz and Edward H. Crane (eds), *Market Liberalism: A Paradigm for the 21st Century* (Washington, DC: Cato Institute, 1993) p. 6.
15. Melchior Palyi, *Compulsory Medical Care and the Welfare State* (Chicago: National Committee of Professional Services, 1949) pp. 13–14.
16. Alexis de Tocqueville, *Democracy in America*, Vol. II [1840] (New York: Vintage Books, 1945) pp. 336–7.
17. See W.H. Hutt, *The Theory of Collective Bargaining, 1930–1975* (London: Institute of Economic Affairs, 1975); *The Strike Threat System: The Economic Consequences of Collective Bargaining* (New Rochelle, NY: Arlington House, 1973); Emerson P. Schmidt, *Union Power and the Public Interest* (Los Angeles: Nash Publishing, 1973); F.A. Hayek, *1980s Unemployment and the Unions* (London: Institute of Economic Affairs, 1980); Morgan O. Reynolds, *Power and Privilege: Labor Unions in America* (New York: Universe

Books, 1984); Hans F. Sennholz, *The Politics of Unemployment* (Spring Mills, PA: Libertarian Press, 1987); Richard K. Vedder and Lowell E. Gallaway, *Out of Work: Unemployment and the Government in Twentieth-Century America* (New York/London: Holmes & Meier, 1993).

18. See John Baden and Richard L. Stroup (eds), *Bureaucracy vs. Environment* (Ann Arbor: University of Michigan Press, 1981); Bernard J. Frieden, *The Environmental Protection Hustle* (Cambridge, MA: MIT Press, 1979); Richard L. Stroup and John A. Baden, *Natural Resources: Bureaucratic Myths and Environmental Management* (San Francisco: Pacific Institute for Public Policy Research, 1983); Walter E. Block, *Economics and the Environment: A Reconciliation* (Vancouver, BC: Fraser Institute, 1990); Terry L. Anderson and Donald R. Leal, *Free Market Environmentalism* (San Francisco: Pacific Research Institute for Public Policy, 1991); Roy E. Cordato, *Welfare Economics and Externalities in an Open Ended Universe: A Modern Austrian Approach* (Boston: Kluwer, 1992).

19. See Melchior Palyi, *The Twilight of Gold, 1914-1936: Myths and Realities* (Chicago: Henry Regnery, 1972); *Managed Money at the Crossroads* (Notre Dame: University of Notre Dame Press, 1958); Jacques Rueff, *The Age of Inflation* (Chicago: Henry Regnery, 1964); *The Monetary Sin of the West* (New York: Macmillan, 1972); Henry Hazlitt, *The Inflation Crisis, and How to Resolve it* (New Rochelle, NY: Arlington House, 1978); F.A. Hayek, *Denationalization of Money* (London: Institute of Economic Affairs, 1976); H. Geoffrey Brennan and James Buchanan, *Monopoly in Money and Inflation* (London: Institute of Economic Affairs, 1981); Llewellyn H. Rockwell, Jr (ed.), *The Gold Standard: An Austrian Perspective* (Lexington, MA: Lexington Books, 1983); Barry Siegel (ed.), *Money in Crisis: The Federal Reserve, The Economy and Monetary Reform* (San Francisco: Pacific Institute for Public Policy, 1984); Hans F. Sennholz, *Money and Freedom* (Cedar Falls, IA: Center for Futures Education, 1985); Catherine England, *Banking and Monetary Reform* (Washington, DC: The Heritage Foundation, 1985); Kevin Dowd, *The State and the Monetary System* (New York: St Martin's Press, 1989).

20. See W.M. Curtiss, *The Tariff Idea* (Irvington-on-Hudson, NY: Foundation for Economic Education, 1953); Ryan C. Amacher, Gottfried Haberler and Thomas D. Willett, *Challenges to a Liberal International Economic Order* (Washington, DC: American Enterprise Institute, 1979); Melvyn B. Krauss, *The New Protectionism: The Welfare State and International Trade* (New York: New York University Press, 1978); Jan Tumlir, *Protectionism: Trade Policy in Democratic Societies* (Washington, DC: American Enterprise Institute, 1985); Jagdish Bhagwati, *The World Trading System at Risk* (Princeton: Princeton University Press, 1991); James Bovard, *The Fair Trade Fraud* (New York: St Martin's Press, 1991); Julian L. Simon, *The Economic Consequences of Immigration* (Cambridge: Basil Blackwell, 1989); Richard M. Ebeling, 'Economic Freedom and a New Liberal International Economic Order', in Richard M. Ebeling (ed.), *Global Free Trade: Rhetoric or Reality?* (Hillsdale, MI: Hillsdale College Press, 1993); Tomas Larsson, *The Race to the Top: The Real Story of Globalization* (Washington, DC: Cato Institute, 2001); Brink Lindsey, *Against the Dead Hand: The Uncertain Struggle for Global Capitalism* (New York: John Wiley, 2001); Douglas A. Irwin, *Free Trade Under Fire* (Princeton, NJ: Princeton University Press, 2002); and Chapter 10 of the present volume.

21. See Cecil Palmer, *The British Socialist Ill-Fare State* (Caldwell, ID: Caxton Press, 1952); Henry Hazlitt, *Man vs. The Welfare State* (New Rochelle, NY: Arlington House, 1969); *The Conquest of Poverty* (New Rochelle, NY: Arlington House, 1973); Martin Anderson, *Welfare: The Political Economy of Welfare Reform in the United States* (Stanford: Hoover Press, 1978); Terry L. Anderson and Peter J. Hill, *The Birth of the Transfer Society* (Stanford: Hoover Press, 1980); Roger A. Freeman, *The Wayward Welfare State* (Stanford: Hoover Press, 1981); Charles Murray, *Losing Ground: American Social Policy, 1950-1980* (New York: Basic Books, 1984); Ralph Harris and Arthur Seldon, *Welfare without the State* (London: Institute of Economic Affairs, 1987); Richard E. Wagner, *To Promote the General Welfare: Market Processes vs Political Transfers* (San Francisco: Pacific Research Institute for Public Policy, 1989); Jack D. Douglas, *The Myth of the Welfare State* (New Brunswick, NJ: Transactions Books, 1989); William Tucker, *The Excluded Americans: Homelessness and Housing Policies* (Washington, DC: Regnery Gateway, 1990).

22. See Thomas Sowell, *Race and Economics* (New York: David McKay, 1975); *Civil Rights: Rhetoric or Reality?* (New York: William Morrow, 1984); *Preferential Policies: An International Perspective* (New York: William Morrow, 1990); Walter Williams, *The State Against Blacks* (New York: McGraw-Hill, 1982); Nathan Glazner, *Affirmative Discrimination* (New York: Basic Books, 1975); W.E. Block and M.A. Walker (eds), *Discrimination, Affirmative Action, and Equal Opportunity* (Vancouver, BC: The Fraser Institute, 1981); Anne Worthham, *The Other Side of Race* (Ohio State University Press, 1981); Herman Belz, *Equality Transformed: A Quarter-Century of Affirmative Action* (New Brunswick, NJ: Transactions Books, 1991); Jarad Taylor, *Paved With Good Intentions: The Failure of Race Relations in Contemporary America* (New York: Carroll & Graf, 1992); Richard A. Epstein, *Forbidden Grounds: The Case Against Employment Discrimination Laws* (Cambridge, MA: Harvard University Press, 1992); Paul Craig Roberts and Lawrence M. Stratton, *The New Color Line: How Quotas and Privilege Destroy Democracy* (Washington, DC: Regnery Publishing, 1995); and Ellen Frankel Paul, *Equity and Gender: The Comparable Worth Debate* (New Brunswick, NJ: Transactions Books, 1989) pp.1–16.
23. Richard Rorty, 'The Intellectuals at the End of Socialism', *Yale Review* (Spring 1992).
24. David Marquand, 'After Socialism', in Alexsandras Shtromas (ed.), *The End of 'Ism'? Reflections on the Fate of Ideological Politics after Communism's Collapse* (Cambridge, MA: Blackwell Publishers, 1994) pp.45–58.
25. Edward Shils, 'The Virtue of Civil Society', *Government and Opposition* [Winter, 1991] 3–20.
26. Count Destutt de Tracy, 'Treatise on the Will and Its Effects', in *A Treatise on Political Economy* [1817] (New York: Augustus M. Kelley, 1970) p.6.
27. Friedrich A. Hayek, *Order - With or Without Design? Selections from F.A. Hayek's Contribution to the Theory and Application of Spontaneous Order* (London: The Centre for Research into Communist Economies, 1989).
28. David G. Green, *Reinventing Civil Society: The Rediscovery of Welfare without Politics* (London: Institute of Economic Affairs, 1993); also Robert Whelan, *The Corrosion of Charity* (London: Institute of Economic Affairs, 1996); Robert Sugden, *Who Cares? An Economic and Ethical Analysis of Private Charity and the Welfare State* (London: Institute of Economics Affairs, 1983); Stephen Macedo, *Liberal Virtues: Citizenship, Virtue, and Community in Liberal Constitutionalism* (Oxford: Clarendon Press, 1990); and Marvin Olasky, *The Tragedy of American Compassion* (Washington, DC: Regnery Gateway, 1992).
29. Thomas Chalmers, *Problems of Poverty* (London: Thomas Nelson & Sons, 1912) pp.213–20.
30. Henry Fawcett, *Pauperism: Its Causes and Cures* [1871] (Clifton, NJ: Augustus M. Kelley, 1975) pp.16–22.
31. See Bertrand de Jouvenel, *The Ethics of Redistribution* [1952] (Indianapolis, IN: Liberty Press, 1990); also David G. Green, *Equalizing People: Why Social Justice Threatens Liberty* (London: Institute of Economics Affairs, 1990); and Wilhelm Röpke, *Welfare, Freedom and Inflation* (Auburn, AL: University of Alabama Press, 1964).
32. See Ludwig von Mises, 'The Economic Foundations of Freedom', in *Economics Freedom and Interventionism* (Irvington-on-Hudson, NY: The Foundation for Economic Education, 1990) pp.3–4.
33. Herbert A. Henzler, 'The New Era of Eurocapitalism', *Harvard Business Review*, July–August (1992) 57–68.
34. Thomas K. McCraw, 'The Trouble with Adam Smith', *The American Scholar*, Summer (1992) 352–73.
35. Clyde V. Prestowitz, 'Beyond *Laissez-faire*', *Foreign Policy*, Summer (1992), 67–87.
36. Ludwig von Mises, *Socialism, An Economic and Sociological Analysis* [1932] (New Haven: Yale University Press, 1951) p.24.

7. The political myths and economic realities of the welfare state

THE ORIGIN OF THE MODERN WELFARE STATE

Austrian economist Ludwig von Mises began his 1922 treatise on *Socialism* with the observation that 'Socialism is the watchword and the catchword of the day. The socialist idea dominates the modern spirit. The masses approve of it, it expresses the thoughts and the feelings of all; it has set its seal upon our time. When history comes to tell our story it will write above the chapter, "The Epoch of Socialism".'[1]

It may seem that the socialist epoch has now come to a close. Nothing is in greater disrepute at the present time than the idea of government ownership of the means of production and the theory of comprehensive central planning. The material and spiritual destructiveness of the socialist ideal is too visible in Eastern Europe and the former Soviet Union for anyone seriously to propose a return to the total state as it was experienced in the 20th century, either in its fascist or its communist variation. Maybe the 21st century will see the renewal of its appeal under some new ideological garb. The appeal of Utopia, unfortunately, seems indestructible.[2] But for now, utopian collectivism is in hiatus.

However, the ghost of socialism past still haunts the present. That ghost of socialism past is the modern welfare state. Even in the face of the failure of Soviet-style socialism, the ideas that were the foundations upon which the Marxian scourge came to plague the globe still dominate and guide the thinking of social and economic policy in practically every country in the world. The reason for this is simple. The modern welfare state emerged as an attempt to meet the challenge of socialism's critique of the market economy, without the necessity for socialism's radical medicine for revolutionary transformation of society.

The birthplace of modern welfare statism was Imperial Germany during the last decades of the 19th century, in the reign of Wilhelm II and the administration of Chancellor Otto von Bismarck.[3] In the 1870s, the German Social Democratic Party had acquired increasing support among the German electorate and threatened to obtain a majority in the Reichstag, the German Parliament.[4] The electoral triumph of Germany's socialist party seemed likely in the near future. The German monarchy and the conservative parties realized that something had to be done to deflect popular support away from the socialists and back to the established order.

In the early 1880s, Kaiser Wilhelm agreed to sponsor the first welfare statist legislation that was enacted by the Reichstag. In the 1890s, Bismarck explained his tactical goal to William H. Dawson, an American historian and Bismarckian sympathizer: 'My idea was to bribe the working classes, or shall I say, to win them over, to regard the state as a social institution existing for their sake and interested in their welfare. It is not moral to make profits out of human misfortunes and suffering,' he concluded. 'Life-insurance, accident insurance, sickness insurance should not be subjects of private speculation. They should be carried out by the state or at least insurance should be on the mutual principle and no dividends or profits should be derived by private persons.'[5]

But it would be a mistake to interpret the birth of the modern welfare state as purely a cynical political pragmatism. It was also argued on the basis of a supposed higher 'social good' and a higher conception of human liberty than a 'mere' protection of life, liberty and property by the state. The proponents of this view were known as the German Historical School, leading members of which were Gustav von Schmoller, Adolph Wagner and Lujo Brentano, with a host of others who are now long forgotten, but who were extremely influential at the time in developing the political, economic and ethical rationales for the welfare state.[6] They rejected radical or Marxian socialism and advocated, instead, what they called state socialism.[7] William H. Dawson explained the difference:

> While Individualism restricts the functions of the state as much as possible, Socialism enlarges them; the Individualist would do everything without the state, the socialist would do everything with it. State socialism is the mean between these directions of thought; in it the two extremes meet. ... Socialism would abolish the existing political order altogether, while State Socialism would use the state for the accomplishment of great economic and social purposes, especially restoring to it the function, which Frederick the Great held to be the principal business of the state, of 'holding the balance' between classes and parties ... The nonintervention principle must be abandoned, since it has only led to greater and ever greater class and personal inequalities, and therefore to growing social disorganization and discontent ... Social interests can only be properly safeguarded when the state directly concerns itself with them. The aim must, therefore, be to widen the economic jurisdiction of the state.[8]

State socialism was meant to save the established order from revolutionary upheaval and societal disintegration by admitting many of the criticisms that socialists made against a market economy – exploitation of the workers by the employers, self-interested behaviour that failed to serve the general welfare, poverty of the many in the midst of material riches enjoyed by a few – and introducing a series of interventionist and welfarist policies that were to improve the economic lot of 'the masses'.[9]

The comprehensiveness of the German welfare state was emphasized in 1915 by another American admirer, Frederic C. Howe (a prominent intellectual who played a leading role in the Progressive movement and later served in Franklin Roosevelt's New Deal):

> The [German] state has its finger on the pulse of the worker from the cradle to the grave. His education, his health, and his working efficiency are matters of constant concern. He is carefully protected from accident by laws and regulations governing factories. He is trained in his hand and his brain to be a good workman and is insured against accident, sickness, and old age. While idle through no fault of his own, work is frequently found for him. When homeless, a lodging is offered so that he will not easily pass to the vagrant class. When sick, he is cared for in wonderful convalescent homes, tuberculosis hospitals, and farm colonies. When old age removes him from the mill or factory, a pension awaits him, a slight mark of appreciation from society, which has taken in labor all that his life had to give and left him with nothing more than a bare subsistence wage.[10]

Frederic Howe admitted that, under this system, with its pervasive controls and regulations, 'The individual exists for the state, not the state for the individual.' But he went on to explain that, in this German welfare paradise, the people did not lose freedom, rather they had a different kind of freedom than in America. 'This paternalism does not necessarily mean less freedom to the individual than that which prevails in America or England. It is rather a different kind of freedom,' Howe said. 'The German enjoys a freedom far greater than that which prevails in America or England. This freedom is of an economic sort. ... Social legislation directed against the exploitation of the worker and the consumer insures freedom in many other ways. It protects the defenseless classes from exploitation and abuse. It safeguards the weak. Universal education offers opportunities to even the poorest to advance whether it be in the service of the state or in the fields of individual effort. Germany protects industrial and social equality.'[11]

Furthermore, Howe explained that the principle guiding the policies of the welfare state was *expediency*. 'In the mind of the Germans, the functions of the state are not susceptible to abstract, a priori deductions. Each proposal must be decided by the time and the conditions,' he said. 'If it seems advisable for the state to own an industry it should proceed to own it; if it is wise to curb any class or interest it should be curbed. Expediency or opportunism is the rule of statesmanship, not abstraction as to the philosophical nature of the state.'[12]

To promulgate and diffuse these ideas, members of the German Historical School founded in 1872 a professional association called the *Verein für*

Sozialpolitik (Society for Social Policy). The opening address was given by Gustav von Schmoller, who emphasized that their purpose as a group was to see that 'a constantly increasing portion of our people shall share in the great possessions of civilization, in culture and material welfare. ... But such an end cannot be attained by the uncontrolled struggle of class against class and individual against individual, nor by the power of an all-embracing and all-controlling state. The state must be the regulator and moderator of the contending industrial classes, "the greatest moral institution for the education of human kind". Therefore, the state must have strength and power. Standing above the selfish interests of classes, it must enact laws, direct the community with a just hand, and protect the weak, raise the humble'.[13]

The idea and the ideology of the modern welfare state began to reach across the Atlantic to the shores of America in those last decades of the 19th century. From the 1870s to the turn of the century, a significant number of American social scientists – political scientists, sociologists, historians and economists – enrolled in German universities to acquire their PhDs and to complete post-doctoral studies. Germany was viewed not only as the land of poets and philosophers, but as the most advanced and progressive nation in the world in terms of social thinking and enlightened public policy. The German university became the Mecca of all dedicated and 'forward-looking' young scholars.[14]

By the beginning of the 20th century, almost a hundred American economists who were considered prominent in the economics profession at the time had studied at German universities during their younger years.[15] In 1885, some of these German-trained economists decided to follow the lead of their teachers, and they founded their own professional economic society: The American Economic Association. Wesley C. Mitchell has explained:

> The organizers were personally eager that the association should take the general attitude toward economics which was dominant in the Germany of their time, an attitude that was commonly characterized as 'Socialism of the Chair'. At that time the historical school was growing rapidly in Germany. It laid great stress upon the state as an institution, upon the role that it was destined to play in human life. ... These people took a bold attitude regarding the duties of the economists to participate in the great tasks of the state of shaping culture into forms that were worthy of man's high destiny. Ideas of this sort cropped up in the third article in the Constitution [of the American Economic Association] called 'Statement of Principles'. It begins as follows: 'We regard the state as an agency whose positive assistance is one of the indispensable conditions of human progress.' ... The statement went on: 'We believe that political economy as a science is still in an early stage of development ... While we appreciate the work of former economists, we look not so much to speculation as to the historical and statistical study of actual conditions of economic life for the satisfactory accomplishment of that development.' ... The next point was: 'We hold that the conflict of labor and capital has brought into prominence a vast number of

social problems, whose solution requires the united efforts, each in its own sphere, of the church, of the state and of science.' ... The last point read: 'In the study of the industrial and commercial policy of governments we take no partisan attitude. We believe in a progressive development of economic conditions, which must be met by a corresponding development of legislative policy.'[16]

The ideas of these economists, and those of their colleagues in the neighbouring fields of political science and sociology, soon served as the foundation for the welfare statist ideas that came to predominate in American public policy discussions in the period known as the Progressive Era.[17] Indeed, the entire assumptions from which economists thought about human welfare and public policy experienced a sea-change in a matter of a couple of decades. For example, in 1887, J. Laurence Laughlin, who founded the economics department at the University of Chicago, could still say in his textbook, *The Elements of Political Economy*:

> Socialism, or the reliance on the state for help, stands in antagonism to *self-help*, or the activity of the individual. That body of people certainly is the strongest and the happiest in which each person is thinking for himself, is independent, self-respecting, self-confident, self-controlled, self-mastered. Whenever a man does a thing for himself he values it infinitely more than if it is done for him, and he a better man for having done it. ... The man who hews out his own path gains power by so doing, and becomes self-reliant, sagacious, foresighted, and ready for further advance. ... If, on the other hand, men constantly hear it said that they are oppressed and downtrodden, deprived of their own, ground down by the rich, and that the state will set all things right for them in time, what other effect can that teaching have on the character and energy of the ignorant than the complete destruction of all self-help? They begin to think that they can have commodities which they have not helped to produce. They begin to believe that two and two make five. It is for this reason that *socialistic teaching strikes at the root of individuality and independent character*, and lowers the self-respect of men who ought to be taught self-reliance. ... The danger of enervating results flowing from dependence on the state for help should cause us to *restrict the interference of legislation as far as is possible*, it should be permitted only when there is an absolute necessity, and even then it should be undertaken with hesitation. ... The right policy is a matter of supreme importance, and we should not like to see in our country the system of interference as exhibited in the paternal theory of government existing in France and Germany.[18]

But in the years just before World War I, this was no longer the dominant view among economists. Any number of prominent economists from this period could be quoted to give a flavour of the 'new thinking'. I choose Henry Seager of Columbia University, who had gone to Europe in 1892 and spent a term at the University of Berlin studying with Gustav von Schmoller, and then spent a term at the University of Vienna studying with the Austrian economists, Carl Menger and Eugen von Böhm-Bawerk, but who came back to America primarily influenced on matters of public policy by the German Historical School.[19]

The closing chapters of his popular and widely used 1913 textbook, *Principles of Economics*, were devoted to a detailed analysis and justification for government intervention in the areas of labour unions, limitations on women's and children's labour, minimum wage laws and compulsory accident, sickness and unemployment insurance, in which the 'progressive' state programmes in Imperial Germany were presented as models for America to emulate.[20] Consistent with his German mentors, Seager explained the unrealistic utopianism and societal danger embedded in the arguments for radical socialism. What was needed was a moderate social-welfare reformism that would ameliorate the class and social conflicts that the socialists were right to cite:

> Although as regards the ultimate goal of economic progress there is a wide difference between socialists and nonsocialists, as regards the next steps in social advance all progressive thinkers on economic problems can make common cause. That progress must be away from the present gross inequalities in opportunity and wealth toward greater equality is the view of not only socialists, but of all economists and social reformers. That a chief means of effecting such progress must be a widening of the functions of the state in the direction of further limitations on the rights of property and the more rigid regulation of industries is also a conviction commonly shared. In fact, there is so little difference as regards their attitude toward the practical problems of the day between evolutionary socialists and progressive social reformers that it is often difficult to tell one from the other. ... Nonsocialists can see no reason to assign such an all-embracing role to the state in the industrial society of the future, but agree that there is urgent need of social reform in the present and that all should work together to secure it.[21]

By the time of World War I, socialism was triumphant over the minds of intellectuals and an increasing number of policy makers throughout Europe and North America. Even for those who had rejected the notion of radical, revolutionary upheaval to overturn the prevailing social order, the socialist idea had captured their soul.[22] Why? Because they had accepted the premises upon which the socialist ideal was constructed. The market economy was accepted as the source of unjustifiable inequality of income and status in society. The institution of private property was viewed as the source of social conflict and the exploitation of those luckless enough to be without legal title to any of the means of production. The market economy failed to reward the 'working class' with a sufficient remuneration to secure their own requirements for the vicissitudes of injury, old-age and periodic episodes of unemployment.

And, most importantly, the state was viewed as the institution of society that could and would harmonize the interests of a multitude of conflicting social and economic interests for a higher common societal welfare. The classical economists of the early 19th century had been critical of state intervention in market relationships. They doubted that the political authority had either the knowledge or the wisdom to manage the complex and changing currents of market activity effectively. And they were suspicious of governments having the power to bestow privileges on some and penalties on others, because, though the arguments for such bounties and prohibitions were couched in the language of serving the 'public interest', they understood that the actual purpose behind it was usually to serve some special interest at the expense of the society as a whole.[23]

Now the state was to be the great saviour of society, the cure for all its ills. All we needed to do was work together for the greater good. Is this an exaggeration? Here are the words of Richard Ely, professor of economics at the University of Wisconsin, co-founder of the American Economic Association and a leader of the welfare statist reform movement in the USA. He concluded his 1895 book on socialism and reform with the following hope and vision:

> Looking into the future we may contemplate a society with real, not merely nominal, freedom, to pursue the best; a society in which men shall work together for the common purposes, and in which the wholesale cooperation shall take place largely through government, but through a government which has become less repressive and has developed its positive side. We have reason to believe that we shall yet see great national undertakings with the property of the nation, and managed by the nation, through agents who appreciate the glory of true public service, and feel that it is God's work which they are doing, because church and state are as one. We may look forward to a society in which education, art, and literature shall be fostered by the nation, and in which the federal government, commonwealth, local community, and individual citizens shall heartily cooperate for the advancement of civilization. ... We may anticipate an approximation of state and society as men improve, and we may hope that men outside of government will freely and voluntarily act with trained officers and experts in the service of government for the advancement of common interests.[24]

In the society of the future, men would rise to a higher level of consciousness and employ themselves in government, seeing themselves doing God's work, and not for anything as narrow as their own self-interest. The distinction between civil society and the political authority would be obliterated, with private affairs and matters of state being indistinguishable and indeed practically interchangeable. Not only would the material concerns of old age, sickness and unemployment be secured from the cradle to the grave but so, too, would be the concerns of the spirit and the mind – education, art, literature. Here was the alternative offered by the welfare statists in place of the radical upheaval preached by their more extreme socialist cousins: moderate Utopia by political increment and democratic consensus.

THE POLITICAL-ECONOMIC REALITY OF THE WELFARE STATE

The West, including the USA, has been in the grip of the welfare state for more than a century. Wages and prices in many industries are either controlled, regulated or influenced by government. Methods of production and rules for the marketing and sale of goods and services are prescribed by governmental laws and decrees. The income earned by many is seized through taxation by the state and distributed to numerous privileged groups and special interests. A vast bureaucracy oversees and manages the affairs of millions in practically every aspect of personal, social and economic life. The state is everywhere. And the state intrudes into everything. There is hardly a corner of life in which the state does not penetrate and take a hand.[25]

The ideal of welfare statists like Richard Ely and Henry Seager has become reality. The distinction between society and the state has not become non-existent, but has become significantly diminished. Are you poor and unskilled? Don't try to work for less than the minimum wage; the government will come down on the employer with all its might. Want to work for an employer who would be glad to hire you? If it is a unionized industry, state and federal authorities will do everything in their power to stop you, unless you join the union and pay dues for union services that you may neither want nor agree with. Want to work at home on contract for some employer? The federal government has banned many forms of 'cottage industries' as 'exploitation', no matter how convenient and profitable it may be for both you and your employer.

Forget about being self-employed in many cities if you have in mind driving your own taxi cab. This is a monopoly privilege for those lucky or wealthy enough to obtain the necessary government licence. If you want to pursue one of dozens of various careers, you will find the same licensing restrictions; for the privileged few in these and similar professions, licensing ensures smaller supplies and higher prices than a more open market would provide.

You think you own your property and that it is constitutionally protected from unreasonable search or seizure? In the name of fighting organized crime and the drug cartels, the state has imposed forfeiture laws that enable government at practically every level to seize any of your property under any vague suspicion in the mind of a government agent that your property was acquired illegally; and the burden of proof falls on you – the accused victim – to prove that you are not guilty; and even if you succeed, do not expect an easy time getting your property back.

You consider that your home is your castle? Just try to remodel or modify it or add any structures to it without appropriate zoning ordinance approval; and, even if the approval is acquired, it may be revoked after the construction work has been done. You can also be stopped from doing anything with your property if it is declared to be a historical landmark.[26]

Affirmative-action laws and the Americans with Disabilities Act have become swamps of political privilege and plunder with which, in the name of equal opportunity and equal treatment, the state has the power to treat people unequally. And the power to make decisions is held by bureaucrats possessing their own prejudices, biases, political pressures and imperfections of knowledge.[27]

Find yourself on welfare assistance? If you are a man, the state may drive you from the household. If you are a woman, it may encourage you to have children born out of wedlock. And it may create disincentives for getting off the welfare assistance, and manipulate where and how you live.[28]

The examples that I have enumerated go beyond the narrow conception that many people have of the welfare state, under which government welfare is usually thought of as meaning those unemployed and in a low-income category who receive various forms of cash and in-kind assistance from the state. The welfare statists in the late 19th and early 20th century had no such narrow or limited conception.[29] As we saw, they desired every facet of life to be 'reformed' and integrated into a structure of 'social policy'. The rights to property were to be weakened to make the use of property conform to some conception of the 'public interest'. They viewed the free, unregulated market as an arena of exploitation, abuse and injustice; as a consequence every aspect of market activity would have to be open to intervention and regulation by the state for the benefit of the 'good of society' as a whole. And there were no rough and ready rules for the types or degrees of intervention; these were matters of ever-changing expediency, which they viewed as the mark of true 'statesmanship'. Pragmatism and 'opportunism' were the principles that were to be lived by in the New Era of the welfare state. We have been living in that New Era and those have been the principles that have guided the political process. The characteristics of the modern welfare state can be looked at under three headings: 'Bourgeois Socialism', the 'Welfare State Nomenklatura' and the 'Hubris of the Intellectuals'.

Bourgeois Socialism

Since the welfare state in all its modern complexity only developed in pragmatic increments over several generations, we now have a generation of people in both Western Europe and North America who cannot even conceive of a world without the welfare state. It seems 'natural', the normal state of affairs to which any reasonable person should take no exception. Indeed, most people, while they may complain or even disapprove of some particular programme financed by the state, think that the institutional order of the welfare state *is* the free society and *is* a free market economy. What people cannot see clearly is what the Italian economist and sociologist Vilfredo Pareto tried to explain over a hundred years ago, in 1891, as his native Italy was already setting out on the road to the modern welfare state: 'The actual condition of civil society, as it is today, is based not on free competition and respect for private property, but on the intervention of the state. So the governments of civilized peoples can be defined as bourgeois socialist.' If the use of the word 'socialist' in this manner shocked his readers at the time, he suggested, 'A looser definition could be that socialism wants the intervention of the state to change the distribution of wealth', with socialists 'divided into two types: socialists, who through intervention of the state, wish to change the distribution of income in favor of the less rich; and the others, who, even if they are sometimes not completely conscious of what they are doing, favor the rich'.[30]

The particular and peculiar characteristics of the modern bourgeois socialist welfare state can be best understood if it is contrasted with the system of redistributive welfare statism that existed before the 19th century, a system that was known as mercantilism.[31] In the 18th century, political privileges and favours were primarily bestowed upon a few select members of the society: landowners who were given agricultural protection from the competition of less expensive food suppliers in other countries; and particular merchants and manufacturers who were given the monopoly privileges to buy, sell and trade various goods and services. The vast majority of the society paid for the protections and privileges given to the few. They paid in the form of higher prices, inferior products and fewer consumer choices in the market. And their meagre income and wealth were severely taxed, not only to pay for the state subsidies of selected industries and exports, but also to finance the governmental bureaucracy that supervised it all.

The success of the 19th-century free trade movement, especially in England, was partly due to the fact that the advocates of economic liberty could point to the injustice of a system that gave privileges to a few, while making the majority of the people bear the burden. Mercantilism went against the grain of the new beliefs in political democracy and equal treatment before the law.

With the spread of the democratic ideal and the enlargement of the voting franchise, people increasingly came to view government as no longer the master, but rather as the servant. But a servant for what? For equal protection before the law, certainly. For equality in civil liberties, increasingly. But, unfortunately, *with the spread of socialist ideas in the late 19th and early 20th centuries, government also came to be viewed as an agency that should do things for the people, rather than only protecting them from the violence or fraud of others.*

And what people were told they should want government to do for them was guarantee their jobs and income; protect them from foreign competition and limit the entry of new competitors at home; ensure 'living wages' for their labour and 'fair' and 'reasonable' prices for their products; protect them from the common mistakes and misfortunes of everyday life; and relieve them of any responsibility for the community efforts that would otherwise demand of them charity and the giving of their own free time. *And all of these guarantees, protections and securities were to be provided at someone else's expense.*

As the ideal of a welfare-providing government for the people spread, those who hoped to gain some privileges from the government formed themselves into groups of common economic interest. In this way, they aimed to pool the costs of the lobbying and politicking that was required to obtain what they increasingly came to view as their 'right', that is, those things to which they were told they were 'entitled'.

No longer were redistributive privileges to be limited to the few, as under the old mercantilism. Now privileges and favours were to be available for all. Bourgeois socialism, therefore, heralded a new age, an *Age of Democratized Privilege*, and it now permeates the Western world. More and more people are dependent upon governmental spending of one form or another for significant portions of their income. And what the government does not redistribute directly, it furnishes indirectly through industrial regulations, price and production controls, and occupational licensing procedures.

As dependency upon the state has expanded, the incentives to resist any diminution in either governmental spending or intervention has increased. All cuts in government spending and repeals of interventions threaten an immediate and significant reduction in the incomes of the affected, privileged groups. And since all of the benefits to society which accrue from greater market competition and self-responsibility are not immediate but rather are spread over a period of time, there are few present-day advocates of a comprehensive reversal of all that makes up the modern welfare state.

Instead, practically every group in society continuously does battle for the maintenance of, or an increase in, their piece of the economic pie – not through open competition for consumer business, but through the political process, to gain a larger share through direct wealth redistribution or manipulation of the market.

This is not the process or the result that the proponents of the welfare state saw or promised, when they were first making the case for their form of moderate utopianism more than a hundred years ago. Why have democratic societies all around the world become battlegrounds for political privilege and economic plunder?

The answer is to be found in one of the ideas that Adam Smith did so much to popularize: the division of labour. 'The division of labor,' Smith explained, 'so far as it can be introduced, occasions in every art, a proportionate increase of the productive powers of labor.'[32] By specializing in various lines of production, the members of society are able to improve and increase their skills and efficiency to do various things. Out of these productive specializations comes an increased supply of all kinds of goods and services. The members of society trade away the larger quantities of each commodity they respectively can now produce for all the other goods offered by their fellows in the market arena. Society's members give up the independence of economic self-sufficiency for the interdependence of a social system of division of labour. But the gain is a much higher standard of living than any one of them could ever hope to attain just by using his own capabilities to fulfil all his wants and desires through his own labour.[33]

Each individual is now dependent upon others in the society for the vast majority of the goods and services he wishes to use and consume. But in a competitive market setting, this works to his advantage. Sellers vie with one another for his consumer business. They underbid each other and offer him attractively lower prices; they devise ways to produce and market new and improved products. As a consumer, the individual is the master of the market, whom all sellers must serve if they are to obtain his business. Viewed from the perspective of the consumer, the competitive market serves the public interest. The resources of society are effectively applied and put to work to satisfy the various wants and desires of the individuals of that society. The products which are manufactured are determined by the free choices of all the demanders in the market-place. Production serves consumption.

But the market looks totally different from the perspective of the individual producers. They, too, are dependent upon the market; they are dependent upon buyers being willing to purchase what they have for sale. While the market serves everyone as a consumer, no one can be a consumer unless he has been successful as a producer. And his success as a producer depends upon his ability to market and sell his products, or to find willing employers for his particular labour skills and abilities. As a consequence, for each producer the price of his own product or labour service tends to be more important to him than the prices of all the multitude of consumer goods he might purchase. Unless he earns the necessary financial wherewithal in his producer role, he cannot be a consumer of what others have for sale.

Being a consumer of many things, but the producer of usually one thing, each seller tends to view competition as a financial threat to his position in the market, as well as his specific share of the market. The incentive for each producer, therefore, is to want to limit entry into his corner of the market, or to reduce the amount of competition currently existing in his industry or profession. The only avenue for limiting competition, however, is the government. Only the government has the ultimate authority to prohibit permanently those who think they could do better in the market and who desire to try. Producers, therefore, have incentives to apply portions of the resources and wealth at their disposal for use in the political arena to gain or protect the market position they feel themselves unable to obtain or protect in an open field of competition. And as long as the costs of acquiring political privileges, protections and redistributions from the government are less than those of acquiring desired wealth through the voluntary transactions and associations on the market, producers have incentives to lobby and politick to achieve their ends.[34]

Welfare State Nomenklatura

In the political process of the welfare state, bourgeois socialism has both an accomplice and a rival. This accomplice and rival can be called the welfare state nomenklatura. 'Nomenklatura' is a Soviet term. It referred to those who wielded power and authority in the bureaucracy that oversaw and controlled the Soviet economy.[35] If the state is to regulate and control the market, supervise the condition and improvement of the poor, redistribute wealth, oversee the education of our children, plan the arrangement of cities and the preservation of the environment, subsidize the arts and prohibit or restrict access to 'socially harmful' substances, then there must be a group of 'trained officers and experts in the service of government for the advancement of common interests', whom Richard Ely expected to be agents motivated by 'the glory of true public service'.

It was typical of the socialist illusion that underlies the welfare statist rationale that it was presumed that the motives for human behaviour were determined by the cultural and social environment. In the beautiful future of social reform, men would no longer think only or even predominantly of their own interests. No, the 'experts' employed in the state agencies and bureaus, who were to be responsible for the remaking of society, would have but one purpose: the common interest. And 'men outside of government will freely and voluntarily act' with these selfless agents of the public interest for a greater common good than their own private gain and improvement.[36]

Yet the performance of the functions of the state are actually one of the specializations in the social system of division of labour. It is a source of income and power for those who occupy these positions of political authority and responsibility. Advancement, increased income and expanded jurisdiction as means for personal improvement all require the ever-renewed justification for their bureau or agency. Their relative income and relative power in the political arena depend upon the proof that their activity needs to be continued or expanded.

The private entrepreneur in the free market searches out unsatisfied consumer wants that he tries to fulfil better than any rival. The 'product' the members of the welfare state nomenklatura must sell is their competency to rectify or prevent the supposed 'failures' of the market. Indeed, they must constantly be on the lookout for new market failures. They specialize in the discovery of 'social crises' that a free market and voluntary associations supposedly cannot cure. Just as private entrepreneurs may creatively come up with new products that they believe consumers have never had available to them before, the members of the welfare state nomenklatura creatively come up with new social problems needing a political cure; and, of course, they are regarded as the public-interested experts most competent to take on the new task. Their bread and butter depend upon the never-ending demonstration that freedom and the free market neither satisfactorily work nor can be fully trusted.

And as they pursue the expansion of their power over the redistribution of wealth and the regulation of private enterprise, they have need of allies and outside 'experts' to assist them in their own lobbying for increased jurisdiction and enhanced budgets. Those in the private sector who desire to use the state for their own bourgeois socialist goals of obtaining subsidies, restrictions on domestic and foreign competition, and favourable pricing or production regulations, offer their expertise to demonstrate that only through such policies can the national interest be served; their particular sectorial interests, by happy coincidence, are just what serves the public interest.

Yet the interests of the welfare state nomenklatura are not merely a reflection of private special interests of the bourgeois socialists. Their source of power is the authority to control or influence relative prices, regulate the permitted methods of production and sale of goods and services in the market, and to determine the allocation of redistributed wealth. This requires control over private enterprise and not obedient subservience to the special interest groups over whom they have or want jurisdiction.

At the same time, the desire and the need to interact with the welfare state nomenklatura further corrupt the behaviour and incentives of those private enterprisers that function in this politicized market environment. Political connections and knowing how to manoeuvre in the welfare statist environment can come to have equal or even greater significance for financial success than that of normal market acumen. What such a hyper-politicized market can come to look like was explained by Ludwig von Mises in 1932, in a description of business activity in Germany at the end of the Weimar Republic shortly before the accession of the Nazis to power:

> In the interventionist state it is no longer of crucial importance for the success of an enterprise that the business should be managed in a way that satisfies the demands of consumers in the best and least costly manner. It is far more important that one has 'good relationships' with the political authorities so that the interventions work

to the advantage and not the disadvantage of the enterprise. A few more marks' more tariff protection for the products of the enterprise, a few marks' less tariff for the raw materials used in the manufacturing process can be of far more benefit to the enterprise than the greatest care in managing the business. No matter how well an enterprise may be managed, it will fail if it does not know how to protect its interests in the drawing up of the customs rates, in the negotiations before the arbitration boards, and with the cartel authorities. To have 'connections' becomes more important than to produce well and cheaply. So the leadership positions within enterprises are no longer achieved by men who understand how to organize companies and to direct production in the way the market demands, but by men who are well thought of 'above' and 'below', men who understand how to get along well with the press and all the political parties, especially with the radicals, so that they and their company give no offense. It is that class of general directors that negotiate far more often with state functionaries and party leaders than with those from whom they buy and to whom they sell. Since it is a question of obtaining political favors for their enterprises, their directors must repay the politicians with favors. In recent years, there have been relatively few large enterprises that have not had to spend very considerable sums for various undertakings in spite of it being clear from the start that they will yield no profit. But in spite of the expected loss it had to be done for political reasons. Let us not even mention contributions for purposes unrelated to business – for campaign funds, public welfare organizations, and the like.[37]

Hubris of the Intellectuals

Political plunder, state-bestowed monopolies and forced redistribution of wealth are nothing new in human history. Yet what has been unique for more than a hundred years has been the arrogance of those who have proposed to modify the outcomes of the free society into directions that they think superior to the ones that naturally emerge out of the voluntary associations and mutually agreed upon transactions of the participants of the market. Let us turn, once more, to Richard Ely. He asked the question:

> Can we not, in our industrial life, keep what we have that is valuable and escape some of the evils which socialism has so vividly depicted? And let us frankly, fully, without equivocation, acknowledge the great services which socialism has, in this as in other respects, rendered to society. Can we not carefully, conservatively add to our social order some of the strong features of socialism, and yet keep this social order intact? It seems to the author that this is practicable, and the means for doing this he endeavors to describe as a program of practicable reform. ... Those who take up social reform at the present day, must remember that they cannot accomplish much that is permanently valuable unless they start with a full knowledge of socialism and its advantages, and attempt to realize these advantages. ... Well-directed effort has accomplished great things; and we are warranted in the belief that a thorough reformation of society, and the reduction of social evils to a very low term, if not a complete abolition, is practicable.[38]

What were the important lessons that socialism supposedly had to teach us? Karl Marx and Frederick Engels, Ely believed, had shown that, if not restrained by government controls, under a free market, 'the conditions of the wage earners would have grown more and more wretched, the concentration of wealth and the centralization of production would have been carried even further, and it is not improbable that the collapse' of capitalism would have taken place. Only enlightened state intervention and redistribution of wealth could and had prevented this from happening.

What did enlightened reformers need to do through the agency of government? 'First of all, we must seek a better utilization of productive forces,' Ely said. 'This implies, negatively, that we should reduce the waste of the competitive system to its lowest possible terms; positively, that we should endeavor to secure a steady production, employing all available capital and labor power ... In the second place, would we secure the advantages of socialism', Ely continued, 'we must so mend our distribution of wealth that we shall avoid present extremes, and bring about widely diffused comfort, making frugal comfort for all an aim. Distribution must be so shaped, if practicable, that all shall have assured incomes ... In the third place, there must be abundant public provision of opportunities for the development of our faculties, including educational facilities and the large use of natural resources for purposes of recreation.'[39]

These have been the premises and goals of the welfare state during the 20th century. Karl Marx arrogantly labelled his ideas 'scientific socialism' because he claimed to have discovered the laws of history that made the passing of capitalism and the arrival of socialism inevitable. The historical laws of capitalism's development, Marx insisted, 'proved' the coming increasing misery of the working class and the concentration of wealth and capital into fewer and fewer hands, until society had been so polarized between a small handful of private owners of the means of production and an expanding poverty-stricken working class that revolutionary upheaval would sweep away the capitalist order and usher in a radical socialist transformation of the society.

The advocates of the welfare state, through most of the 20th century, have believed Marx: capitalism, if left alone, impoverishes the many and concentrates wealth into the hands of the few. Forestalling this has been the purpose of their reforms. *The ghost of Karl Marx, in other words, has haunted social policy in the Western world. And in this crucial sense all welfare statist policies have rested on Marxian foundations.*

Having seen the future through Marx's eyes and been horrified by what they saw, the welfare statists claimed to know how to bring the power of the state to bear to correct capitalism's abuses and stop history from dragging society into the vortex of radical socialist revolution. Here emerges what Wilhelm Röpke once referred to as 'the hubris of the intellect', the almost boastful self-confidence in a capacity for social engineering.[40] While the social reformers of the welfare state have claimed that theirs is the moderate alternative to comprehensive collectivism, their confidence in social engineering can be considered even more extreme than that of the radical socialists. Revolutionary socialists believed that the existing social order could not be incrementally repaired or improved. A levelling of all the institutions of society had to precede the remaking of society from the ground up.

The welfare statist social engineer has had confidence that he can tinker with the existing order to transform it and reshape it into forms more compatible with the virtues of socialism, while preserving particular features of the older order that he deems worthy of retention. He has believed that he knows how much industrial concentration is too much and what the optimal size of enterprises should be; he has believed that he knows what conditions of work and scale of wages amount to exploitation and are inconsistent with the healthy character of labour, and therefore he knows what those conditions of work and scale of wages should be; he has believed that he knows inhuman and excessively congested city life when he sees it, so he introduces urban planning and has engineered city development; he has believed that he knows at what point people, left to themselves in the market-place, will fail to preserve sufficient wildlife and untouched nature areas, so he 'modifies' property rights to enable the introduction of a planned environment that will be 'naturally' balanced.

He has believed that he knows what family environment and private provision of education is incompatible with the fostering of well-balanced and 'progressively' educated children for a better society tomorrow, so he has imposed compulsory public schooling, and designed a 'rational' and 'politically correct' curriculum reflecting what he knows to be the proper values and social norms of conduct that every human being should have and practise.[41] He has believed that he knows what is poverty and how to cure it, and has introduced income transfers, provided public housing, created work-training programmes and modified the definition of the meaning of a 'family unit', on the basis of which subsidies of various sorts are provided that are meant to engineer the emergence of 'families' more consistent with the social reformers' approved definition.

And all the time the impression is created that, fundamentally, everything is still the same. Private enterprise goes about its business; people buy and sell in the market-place; workers pick and choose among jobs; private property is not abolished; couples meet and marry, and parents still raise their children. Yet it is no longer the same as it was before the social engineer began his pragmatic and opportunistic reforming of society. Beneath the case-by-case expediency of social policy making have been anti-capitalist, anti-freedom and anti-individualist premises. And guiding every turn of the seemingly pragmatic pattern of welfare statist reform has been a hidden compass directing the cumulative outcome towards state management, the regulated society and the making of a new collectivist – now 'politically correct' – man (or, in PC lingo, 'person')![42]

THE BANKRUPTCY OF THE WELFARE STATE

Looking east, across what had been the Iron Curtain, the failure of Soviet-style socialism is visible for all to see. Its destructive effect is evident to all except the blind or the self-deceiving. Socialism has been no less destructive in its welfare state variation; only its form and degree are less easy to articulate and identify. What many people feel is an uncomfortableness, a sense that something is very wrong, that not every social policy has produced the desired effect, that somehow people and society are not morally healthy and balanced.

In the former socialist East, it is possible to point to the principle that has failed – the total state and the centrally planned economy. But how does one put one's finger on the principle that has gone wrong in the Western welfare state, when it has no articulated principle that guides it? A hundred years ago, the Socialists of the Chair of the German Historical School said, 'The functions of the state are not susceptible of abstract, a priori deductions. Each proposal must be decided by the time and the conditions.' The only principle is expediency. Where are the philosophical or political–economic theoretical principles from which one would critically evaluate and pass judgment upon the reasons for the bankruptcy of the welfare state? After a century of prag-matic reformist social engineering in both public education and the general culture, most people find it difficult even to comprehend the possibility of any Archimedean points from which to survey the damage and its causes. This was lamented as long ago as the early 1950s by Wilhelm Röpke:

> If I were asked to say what appeared to me as one of the gravest features of our time I would answer: One of the worst things is that people do not seem to stop and think and ask themselves quietly what exactly they are doing. ... More and more people no longer know what it means to put first things first and to think in terms of the principles involved. Consequently, only a few still have a real philosophy which separates the essential from the accidental and which puts everything in its place. ... Confusion, loss of orientation and lack of philosophical insight are worse than ever, and so we are drifting on an uncharted sea. We are running after current events, instead of stopping to reach the solid grounds of principles and to ask ourselves seriously what have been the reasons why so much goodwill, energy, intelligence, time and money have been wasted or not given the result we had a right to expect.[43]

Marxism insisted that there were no permanent things; no invariable, essential aspects to human nature; no inherently appropriate institutional relationships that are more conducive to societal harmony and material prosperity, and that both our reason and historical experience could make known to us. What we take to be permanent things are really only transitory things at a particular moment of historical evolution, the Marxians insisted.

The Western world has been stripped of many of its principles concerning those permanent things. The only value judgment that we have been left with is that we are supposed to be non-judgmental.[44] We may feel outrage, shock, disapproval or disappointment, but these are merely our 'personal views'. This, more than anything, is the moral bankruptcy of the welfare state. We are not permitted to ask: 'What may be the "rights of man"? What might be the legitimate, but limited functions of a government? When is a claimed entitlement nothing more than legalized plunder? Might there be moral standards, for personal conduct in private affairs as well as in the political arena, that our reason or our religion can guide us to have an understanding of, and that would not be the mere expediencies of the moment?' We are not even allowed to ask such questions in politically correct polite society.

At the end of his book, *Socialism*, Ludwig von Mises included a lengthy section on the consequences of the welfare state. He analysed the effects from compulsory labour legislation, compulsory social insurance, trade unions, government-subsidized unemployment insurance, socialization of selected industries, and fiscal policy and inflation. This section of his book is called 'Destructionism'. In it, Mises wrote, 'Socialism is not in the least what it pretends to be. It is not the pioneer of a better and finer world, but the spoiler of what thousands of years of civilization have created. It does not build; it destroys. For destruction is the essence of it. It produces nothing, it only consumes what the social order based on private ownership in the means of production has created. ... Socialism must exhaust itself in the destruction of what already exists.'[45]

Though not as visually dramatic as in eastern Europe, socialism in the form of the welfare state has been destructive of our political, economic and cultural principles. It has been and is eating at us from the inside. And to a great extent its success has been due to the fact that, after several generations of living under it, people do not even know it for what it is. The welfare state, for many, is a 'just' and 'caring' society. It is 'The American Way'.[46]

It is time to call things by their real names. It is time to stop, and take a long view. It is time to reflect and try to rediscover some of the permanent principles that gave us the potential to be free and prosperous in the past, and which, if recaptured, might just possibly put us back on the road to a healthy civil society. If we do, then possibly all the victims of socialism in the 20th century can finally put the destructive legacy of Karl Marx behind them.[47]

NOTES

1. Ludwig von Mises, *Socialism, An Economic and Sociological Analysis* [1922] (Indianapolis, IN: Liberty Classics [1951, rev. edn] 1981) p. 15.
2. Even among the classical economists of the 19th century we can find the hope and belief in the possibility of remaking mankind, if only human beings could be enveloped by the right institutional environment. There was no greater and more respected figure among the English political economists of the mid-19th century than John Stuart Mill. In his *Principles of Political Economy, with Some of Their Applications to Social Philosophy*, Mill says: 'History bears witness to the success with which large bodies of human beings may be trained to feel the public interest their own. And no soil could be more favourable to the growth of such feeling than a communist association, since all the ambition and the bodily and mental activity, which are now exerted in the pursuit of separate and self-regarding interests, would require another sphere of employment and would naturally find it in the pursuit of the general benefit of the community. The same cause, so often assigned in explanation of the devotion of the Catholic priest or monk to the interest of his order – that he has no interest apart from it – would, under communism, attach the citizen to the community.' On the errors in Mill's views concerning redistribution of wealth and socialism, see Friedrich A. Hayek, 'The Muddle of the Middle', in Svetozar Pejovich (ed.), *Philosophical and Economic Foundations of Capitalism* (Lexington, MA: D.C. Heath and Co., 1983) pp. 89–100.
3. The next several paragraphs partly draw upon Richard M. Ebeling, 'National Health Insurance and the Welfare State', in Jacob G. Hornberger and Richard M. Ebeling (eds), *The Dangers of Socialized Medicine* (Fairfax, VA: The Future of Freedom Foundation, 1994) pp. 25–37.
4. See Gustav Stolper, *The German Economy: 1870 to the Present* (London: Weidenfeld and Nicolson [1940], revised edn, 1967) pp. 43–6.
5. William H. Dawson, *The Evolution of Modern Germany*, Vol. II (New York: Charles Scribner's Sons, 1914) p. 349.
6. For a summary of the views of the German Historical School, or the 'Socialists of the Chair', as they were also known, see Émile de Laveleye, *The Socialism of Today* (London: Field and Tuer, The Leadenhall Press, 1890) pp. 265–83; also Eugen von Philippovich, 'The Infusion of Socio-Political Ideas into the Literature of German Economics', *The American Journal of Sociology* (Sept., 1912) 145–99; John Kells Ingram, *A History of Political Economy* (London: A.&C. Black, Ltd., 1923) pp. 192–232; Charles Gide and Charles Rist, *A History of Economic Doctrines: From the Time of the Physiocrats to the Present Day* (Boston: D.C. Heath and Co., 1928) pp. 379–407; and Ludwig von Mises, 'The Historical Setting of the Austrian School of Economics' [1969], in Bettina Bien Greaves (ed.), *Austrian Economics: An Anthology* (Irvington-on-Hudson, NY: The Foundation for Economic Education, 1996) pp. 60–72.
7. While these members of the German Historical School may have rejected the radical socialist agenda for a revolutionary transformation of the entire social order, their own agenda for a comprehensive system of welfare statist programmes was entirely consistent with Marx's conception of one of the predominant functions of the state once the 'bourgeois order' had been overthrown and replaced by the socialist state, which then would undertake its responsibilities during the transition leading to communism. See Karl Marx, 'Critique of the Gotha Program' [1875], in *The Marx-Engels Reader* ed. by Robert C. Tucker (New York: W.W. Norton & Co., Inc., 1972) pp. 382–98, in which Marx argues that, in the socialist state, before the workers are given the proceeds that are derived from their respective contributions to the overall output of the society, certain amounts must first be 'deducted'. Marx explains that these deductions from the total output of the society, before the workers receive the respective products of their labour, are to fund certain activities which it will now be the responsibility of the socialist state to perform. Among these activities, Marx says, will be 'reserve or insurance funds to provide against accidents, dislocations caused by natural calamities, etc ... the common satisfaction of needs, such as schools, health services, etc ... funds for those unable to work, etc., in short, for what is

included under so-called official poor relief today'. And as these welfare statist functions are taken on by the socialist state, now that capitalism has been abolished, 'From the outset this part grows considerably in comparison with present-day society and it grows in proportion as the new society develops' (pp. 385-6).

8. William H. Dawson, *Bismarck and State Socialism* [1890] (New York: William Fertig, 1973) pp. 2-4.

9. See Elmer Roberts, *Monarchical Socialism in Germany* (New York: Charles Scribner's Sons, 1913) pp. 137-8: 'Wagner, Schmoller, Schoenberg, Schaeffle, and others, originating and supporting principles of monarchical socialism, took the middle course between the extreme socialism of Lassalle, Marx, and Rodbertus, which would have ... government do everything, and the individualism of the Manchester school, limiting the powers of government to the simplest functions of administration and defense. The endeavor of German statesmanship has been to hold to everything in existing social arrangements necessary to produce individuality in the higher orders, and yet to intervene in education, sanitation, sick, accident and old-age insurance, the physical training of youth in the army, and to participate in transportation, forestry, mining, farming, and industrial enterprises, designing thus to raise the lower orders mentally, physically, and economically, so that they too become worthier individuals, adding to the power of the state and the monarchy. The intervention of the government is to be determined by expediency. The government, guided by circumstances, is ready either to take part in phases of economic life or to let individualism remain in control of them.' See also Ralph H. Bowen, *German Theories of the Corporative State, with Special Reference to the Period, 1870-1919* (New York: Russell & Russell, [1947] 1971), Ch. IV on 'Monarchical Socialism', pp. 119-59.

10. Frederic C. Howe, *Socialized Germany* (New York: Charles Scribner's Sons, 1915) p. 162.

11. Ibid., pp. 83-5.

12. Ibid., pp. 82-3; also Dawson, *Bismarck and State Socialism*, pp. 4-6: 'No department of economic activity should on principle be closed to the state; whether it should or not participate, side by side, with private enterprise, is a matter of expediency and public interest ... It is evident that the principles of state intervention in economic affairs and state care and protection for the poorer classes being posited, it is difficult to say how far these principles should be carried. The state socialists say that this must be determined by expediency, and by circumstances of time and place. ... The bounds of the state's functions have not, like the earth's foundations, been fixed from of old, that they should not be removed. The jurisdiction of government is a matter not of principle but of expediency.'

13. Eugen von Philippovich, 'The Verein für Sozialpolitik', *Quarterly Journal of Economics* (January, 1891) 227-8.

14. Joseph A. Schumpeter, *History of Economic Analysis* (New York: Oxford University Press, 1954) p. 864, explains that a sizeable number of American economists, 'not finding in the [USA] what they wanted, continued to rely on European ideas and methods though no longer exclusively English ones - the pilgrimage to Germany, in particular, became for those who could afford it almost a regular incident of their career, something like the Cavalier's tour of old'; see also Charles F. Thwing, *The American and the German University* (New York: Macmillan and Co., 1928); Jergen Herbst, *The German Historical School in American Scholarship* (Ithaca: Cornell University Press, 1965); and Joseph Dorfman, 'The Role of the German Historical School in American Economic Thought', *American Economic Review* (May, 1955) 17-28.

15. Among them were John Bates Clark, Edwin Seligman and Henry Seager of Columbia University; Richard T. Ely of the University of Wisconsin; Arthur Twining Hadley, president of Yale University; Frank W. Taussig of Harvard University; Albion Small of the University of Chicago; Edmund J. James, president of the University of Illinois; Joseph French Johnson of New York University; Simon N. Patten of the University of Pennsylvania; Frank A. Fetter of Princeton University; Wesley C. Mitchell of the National Bureau of Economic Research; and Herbert J. Davenport of Cornell University. See Frank A. Fetter 'The Economists and the Public', *American Economic Review* (March, 1925) 13-26, for a flavour of 'the new thinking' among these German-trained American

economists, and their disapproval of the 'older' economists and businessmen who emphasized limited government involvement in market affairs.

16. Wesley C. Mitchell, *Types of Economic Theory*, Vol. II (New York: Augustus M. Kelley, 1969) pp. 233–4; see also Richard T. Ely, 'The Founding and Early History of the American Economic Association', *American Economic Review*, Papers and Proceedings (March, 1936), pp. 141–50.

17. See Arthur A. Ekirch, Jr, *Progressivism in America* (New York: New Viewpoints, 1974) pp. 19–33.

18. J. Laurence Laughlin, *The Elements of Political Economy, with Some Applications to Questions of the Day* (New York: American Book Co., 1887) pp. 265 and 268; original emphasis. See also Laughlin's *Latter-Day Problems* (New York: Charles Scribner's Sons [1907], rev. edn, 1917), in which he challenged the socialist and welfare statist arguments of his younger colleagues infused with those paternalistic German ideas. Laughlin's lonely voice was joined by his Harvard University colleague, Thomas Nixon Carver, *Essays in Social Justice* (Cambridge: Cambridge University Press, 1915) and 'Liberalism at Harvard', *Harvard Graduate's Magazine* (March, 1919) 278–88; these new paternalistic and redistributive ideas had already been criticized even earlier with great cogency by William Graham Sumner, *What Social Classes Owe to Each Other* [1883] (Caldwell, ID: Caxton Printers, Ltd, 1966).

19. Henry Seager, 'Economics at Berlin and Vienna', *Journal of Political Economy* (March, 1893) 236–62, reprinted in Seager, *Labor and Other Economic Essays*, ed. by Charles A. Gulick, Jr (Freeport, NY: Books for Libraries [1931] 1968) pp. 1–29, and in Bettina Bien Greaves (ed.), *Austrian Economics: An Anthology*, pp. 33–46.

20. Henry Seager, *Principles of Economics* (New York: Henry Holt and Co., 1913) pp. 536–612. Similar analyses and conclusions, also drawing upon the German experience, can be found in Edwin R.A. Seligman, *Principles of Economics* (New York: Longmans, Green, and Co., 1914) pp. 643–93; and Frank A. Fetter, *Modern Economic Problems* (New York: Century Co., 1916) pp. 314–64. Though often embraced as an Austrian economist because of his important contributions to the theory of value, rent, capital and interest, Frank Fetter was a proponent of welfare statist legislation, arguing that, in the areas of accident, sickness, old age and unemployment insurance, 'The state, through the public insurance office, must ultimately be the sole agency for insurance ... There should be a unification of various kinds of insurance in one general plan and under one general administration for the whole state' (p. 362). See Richard T. Ely, *Outlines of Economics* (New York: Macmillan Co., 1919) pp. 444–92 and 577–95. Even so careful a scholar as Frank Taussig of Harvard University, who in reviewing the various schemes for state-managed social insurance programmes pointed out many of their potential perverse incentives and moral hazards, and explained the superiority of many private-sector alternatives as they had been administered in both the USA and Great Britain, had nothing but praise for the German welfare statist system. Indeed, he went as far as to say, 'Hardly another country possesses the staff of trained public servants needed for planning and administering so vast a machinery for social reform; and the Germans are justly proud of what they have here achieved.' See Frank W. Taussig, *Principles of Economics*, Vol. II (New York: Macmillan Co., 1915) p. 331.

21. Henry Seager, *Principles of Economics*, pp. 622–3.

22. Cf. Chapter 6 of the present volume.

23. Cf. Chapter 1 of the present volume.

24. Richard T. Ely, *Socialism: An Examination of Its Nature, Its Strengths and Its Weaknesses, with Suggestions for Social Reform* (New York: Thomas Y. Crowell & Co., 1895) pp. 352–4.

25. See James Bovard, *Lost Rights: The Destruction of American Liberties* (New York: St Martin's Press, 1994) and *Shakedown: How the Government Screws You from A to Z* (New York: Viking Press, 1995) for numerous specific examples and case studies of such intrusions and controls of the sort mentioned in the next several paragraphs.

26. See Richard A. Epstein, *Takings: Private Property and the Power of Eminent Domain* (Cambridge: Harvard University Press, 1985); *Bargaining with the State* (Princeton: Princeton University Press, 1993); Mark L. Pollot, *Grand Theft and Petit Larceny:*

Property Rights in America (San Francisco: Pacific Research Institute for Public Policy, 1993).

27. See Nathan Glazer, *Affirmative Action: Ethnic Inequality and Public Policy* (New York: Basic Books, 1975); Terry Eastland and William J. Bennett, *Counting by Race: Equality from the Founding Fathers to Bakke and Weber* (New York: Basic Books, 1979); Walter E. Block and Michael A. Walker (eds), *Discrimination, Affirmative Action, and Equal Opportunity* (Vancouver, BC: Fraser Institute, 1982); Walter Williams, *The State Against Blacks* (New York: McGraw-Hill Book Co., 1982); Thomas Sowell, *Civil Rights: Rhetoric or Reality?* (New York: William Morrow and Co., 1984); Nicholas Capaldi, *Out of Order: Affirmative Action and the Crisis of Doctrinaire Liberalism* (Buffalo, NY: Prometheus Books, 1985); Clint Bolick, *Changing Course: Civil Rights at the Crossroads* (New Brunswick, NJ: Transaction Books, 1988); *Unfinished Business: A Civil Rights Strategy for America's Third Century* (San Francisco: Pacific Research Institute for Public Policy, 1990); Herman Belz, *Equality Transformed: A Quarter-Century of Affirmative Action* (New Brunswick, NJ: Transaction Books, 1991); and Richard A. Epstein, *Forbidden Grounds: The Case Against Employment Discrimination Laws* (Cambridge, MA: Harvard University Press, 1992).

28. Martin Anderson, *Welfare: The Political Economy of Welfare Reform in the United States* (Stanford: Hoover Institution Press, 1978); Brigitte Berger and Peter L. Berger, *The War Over the Family: Capturing the Middle Ground* (Garden City, NY: Anchor Press/Doubleday, 1983); Charles Murray, *Losing Ground: American Social Policy, 1950-1980* (New York: Basic Books, 1984); Charles Murray, *The Emerging British Underclass* (London: Institute of Economic Affairs, 1990) and *Underclass: The Crisis Deepens* (London: Institute of Economic Affairs, 1994); Patricia Morgan, *Farewell to the Family? Public Policy and Family Breakdown in Britain and the USA* (London: Institute of Economic Affairs, 1995); on the general paternalistic character of the welfare state, and its ideological and philosophical premises, see Jack D. Douglas, *The Myth of the Welfare State* (New Brunswick, NJ: Transaction Books, 1989).

29. See Terry L. Anderson and Peter J. Hill, *The Birth of the Transfer Society* (Stanford: Hoover Institution, 1980).

30. Vilfredo Pareto, 'Socialism and Freedom' [1891], in Placido Bucolo (ed.), *The Other Pareto* (New York: St Martin's Press, 1980) pp. 44 and 46-7.

31. The next several paragraphs partly draw upon Richard M. Ebeling, 'Democratized Privilege: The New Mercantilism', *Freedom Daily* (Feb., 1991) 6-10, and 'Producer Interests vs. The Public Interest: The Origin of Democratized Privilege', *Freedom Daily* (March, 1991) 6-10.

32. Adam Smith, *The Wealth of Nations* [1776] (New York: Modern Library, 1937) Book I, Chapter I, p. 5.

33. See on the role of private property as a protector of individual liberty in a system of division of labour, James M. Buchanan, *Property as a Guarantor of Liberty* (Brookfield, VT: Edward Elgar Publishing Co., 1993).

34. Wilhelm Röpke, *The Social Crises of Our Time* [1942] (Chicago: University of Chicago Press, 1950) p. 129; also see Philip Wicksteed, *The Common Sense of Political Economy*, Vol. I [1910] (London: Routledge & Kegan Paul, Ltd.), 1933) pp. 349-57; and Oskar Morgenstern, *The Limits of Economics* [1934] (London: William Hodge and Co., Ltd., 1937), Ch. IV on 'The Distribution Effects of Economic Policy', pp. 29-46, reprinted in Richard M. Ebeling (ed.), *Austrian Economics: A Reader* (Hillsdale, MI: Hillsdale College Press, 1991) pp. 655-69. In the last 30 years, the economic analysis of the incentives for and financial costs to the society from the process of special interest lobbying for governmental privileges and subsidies – politically derived profits, rather than market-derived profits – has come to be known as 'rent-seeking' behaviour; see James M. Buchanan, Robert D. Tollison and Gordon Tullock (eds), *Toward a Theory of the Rent-Seeking Society* (College Station, TX: Texas A & M University Press, 1980); Robert B. Ekelund and Robert D. Tollison, *Mercantilism as a Rent-Seeking Society: Economic Regulation in Historical Perspective* (College Station, TX: Texas A & M University Press, 1981); Robert D. Tollison 'Rent-Seeking: A Survey', *Kyklos* (vol. 35, no. 4, 1982) 575-692; David C. Collander (ed.), *Neoclassical Political Economy: The Analysis of Rent-Seeking and DUP Activities*

(Cambridge: Ballinger Publishing Co., 1984); Gordon Tullock, *The Economics of Special Privilege and Rent-Seeking* (Boston: Kluwer Academic Press, 1989); Richard E. Wagner, *To Promote the General Welfare: Market Processes vs. Political Transfers* (San Francisco: Pacific Research Institute for Public Policy, 1989); and Gordon Tullock, *Rent-Seeking* (Aldershot, UK and Brookfield, VT: Edward Elgar Publishing Co., 1993).

35. On the meaning of the nomenklatura and its political power and position in the former Soviet economic system, see Richard M. Ebeling, 'Introduction' and 'The Inevitability of Capitalism and the Problems of Privatizing the Socialist Economy', in Richard M. Ebeling (ed.), *Can Capitalism Cope? Free Market Reform in the Post-Communist World*, Champions of Freedom Series, Vol. 21 (Hillsdale, MI: Hillsdale College Press, 1994) pp. 8–9 and 34–8.

36. On the different views of the behavioural characteristics of man, as often presented by economists, political scientists and sociologists, respectively, see Karl Brunner and William H. Meckling, 'The Perception of Man and the Conception of Government', *Journal of Money, Credit and Banking* (Feb., 1977), Part I, 70–85; and Karl Brunner, 'The Perceptions of Man and the Conception of Society: Two Approaches to Understanding Society', *Economic Inquiry* (July 1987) 367–88.

37. Ludwig von Mises, 'The Myth of the Failure of Capitalism' [1932], in Richard M. Ebeling (ed.), *Selected Writings of Ludwig von Mises*, Vol. 2: *Between the Two World Wars: Monetary Disorder, Interventionism, Socialism and the Great Depression* (Indianapolis, IN: Liberty Fund, 2002) pp. 188–9.

38. Richard T. Ely, *Socialism: An Examination of Its Nature, Its Strengths and Its Weaknesses, with Suggestions for Social Reform*, p. 256.

39. Ibid., pp. 355–9.

40. Wilhelm Röpke, *Civitas Humana: A Humane Order of Society* [1944] (London: William Hodge and Co., Ltd., 1948) pp. 43–56.

41. See Sheldon Richman, *Separating School and State: How to Liberate America's Families* (Fairfax, VA: The Future of Freedom Foundation, 1994).

42. Cf. Friedrich A. Hayek, *Law, Legislation and Liberty*, Vol. I: *Rules and Order* (Chicago: University of Chicago Press, 1973) ch. 3 on 'Principles and Expediency', pp. 55–71.

43. Wilhelm Röpke, 'The Problem of Economic Order' [1951], in Johannes Overbeck (ed.), *Two Essays by Wilhelm Röpke* (Lanham, MD: University Press of America, 1987), pp. 1–2.

44. In opposition to this view, for a discussion on the role of value judgments in thinking about and debating questions concerning social theory and social policy, see Wilhelm Röpke, 'A Value Judgment on Value Judgments', *Revue de la Faculté des Sciences Economiques d'Istanbul* (Vol. III, Nos 1–2, 1942) pp. 1–19.

45. Ludwig von Mises, *Socialism*, p. 458.

46. On some of the ideas and events in 20th-century American history that have helped undermine the traditional American system and the values underlying it, see Robert Nisbet, *The Present Age: Progress and Anarchy in Modern America* (New York: Harper and Row, 1988).

47. In Chapter 1 of the present volume I have tried to explain some of the universals of the human condition, as understood by the classical economists, that are essential to and can help secure a free and prosperous society. And in Chapter 2 of the present volume, I have attempted to outline the insights of the Austrian economists concerning the nature of human action, the market economy and the spontaneous social order that are the foundation for a free and prosperous society.

8. The free market and the interventionist state: the political economy of public policy

In 1926, Austrian economist Ludwig von Mises visited the United States on a lecture tour. Upon his return to Austria, he delivered a talk on 'Changes in American Economic Policy' at a meeting of the Vienna Industrial Club. He explained:

> The United States has become great and rich under the power of an economic system that has set no limits on the free pursuit of the individual, and has thereby made room for the development of the country's productive power. America's unprecedented economic prosperity is not the result of the richness of the American land, but rather of the economic policy that understood how best to take advantage of the opportunities that the land offers. American economic policy has always rejected – and still rejects today – any protection for inferiority and uncompetitiveness over efficiency and competitiveness. The success of this policy has been so great that one would believe the Americans would never change it.[1]

But Mises went on to tell his Viennese audience that new voices were being heard in America, voices that claimed that America's economic system was not 'rational' enough, that it was not democratic enough, because the voters did not have it in their immediate power to influence the direction of industrial development. Governmental controls were being introduced, not to nationalize private enterprise, but to direct it though various regulatory methods. In comparison to Europe, America was certainly noticeably less regulated. But there were strong trends moving the nation along the same heavily interventionist path Europe had been travelling for a long time. In the America of 1926, Mises observed, 'Both political parties, the Republicans as well as the Democrats, are ready to take radical steps in this direction, in order to retain the votes of the electorate.' He concluded that 'the results from such a policy will be no different in America than from those "achieved" in Europe'.[2]

In Europe, the trend toward collectivism in the 1930s and 1940s took extreme forms. Socialism, communism, fascism and Nazism were all tried on the other side of the Atlantic. They represented total rejection of a free economy and individual liberty. In America, the collectivist trend never went to such extremes, though Franklin D. Roosevelt's first New Deal came very close to the fascist model.[3]

THE FREE MARKET ECONOMY AND INTERVENTIONISM

Socialism, communism, fascism and Nazism are now all but dead. They failed miserably. But they have been replaced by what is merely another more watered-down form of collectivism that may be called 'interventionism'. Indeed, interventionism is the predominant economic system in the world today. In 1929, Mises published a collection of essays under the title *Critique of Interventionism*. He argued,

> Nearly all writers on economic policy and nearly all statesmen and party leaders are seeking an ideal system which, in their belief, is neither [purely] capitalistic nor socialistic, is based neither on [unrestricted] private property in the means of production nor on public property. They are searching for a system of private property that is hampered, regulated, and directed through government intervention and other social forces, such as labor unions. We call such an economic policy *interventionism*, the system itself the *hampered market order*.[4]

He added, 'All its followers and advocates fully agree that it is the correct policy for the coming decades, yea, even the coming generations. And all agree that interventionism constitutes an economic policy that will prevail in the foreseeable future.'[5]

Definitions

With the demise of communism, public policy – especially in the Western world – is back to where it was when Mises wrote these words at the end of the third decade of the 20th century. Comprehensive government ownership of the means of production and a fully centralized planned economy have very few adherents left, even 'on the left'. At the same time, in spite of all the casual rhetoric about the triumph of capitalism, what is defined as a 'free market economy' contains a great deal of government intervention. The following eight points, I suggest, define the genuine free market economy:

1. All means of production are privately owned.
2. The use of the means of production is under the control of private owners who may be individuals or corporate entities.
3. Consumer demands determine how the means of production will be used.
4. Competitive forces of supply and demand determine the prices for consumer goods and the various factors of production, including labour.

5. The success or failure of individual and corporate enterprises is determined by the profits or losses these enterprises earn, based on their greater or lesser ability to satisfy consumer demand in competition with their rivals in the market-place.
6. The market is not confined to domestic transactions and includes freedom of international trade.
7. The monetary system is based on a market-determined commodity (for example, gold or silver), and the banking system is private and competitive, neither controlled nor regulated by government.
8. Government is limited in its activities to the enforcement and protection of life, liberty and property.

When government merely serves as a protector of life, liberty and property, it does not 'intervene' in the economy. It respects and protects rights of ownership. It ensures that the transfer of property only occurs through a gift or through a mutually agreed-upon exchange. It ensures that, as long as individuals do not infringe upon or violate the equal rights of others (through acts of violence or fraud), they are not molested, harmed or dispossessed of their own property.[6]

While they may be open to some refinement, the eight points outlined above comprise what Mises referred to as the 'unhampered economy'. Unfortunately, many modern politicians and academics who say they endorse such a free market economy are willing to tolerate a great deal of intervention. One notable example is Robert Skidelsky, a professor of political economy at Warwick University in England. Professor Skidelsky is the widely respected author of a multi-volume biography of John Maynard Keynes.[7] He has also written that former communist countries must move towards the establishment of market institutions if they are to stabilize their economies and raise standards of living.[8] In his book, *The Road from Serfdom*, he insightfully analyses how socialist and welfare-statist ideas came to dominate economic theory and government policy in the 20th century.[9] Many of his eloquent and powerful criticisms of these forms of collectivism are based on the writings of Friedrich A. Hayek, the famous Austrian School economist and Nobel laureate. And Professor Skidelsky declares that he is an advocate of the free market.

But when it comes to identifying the role of government in his conception of the market order, he assumes that government must be responsible for a social safety net that includes Social Security and unemployment compensation; must have discretionary monetary and fiscal powers to support desired levels of employment and output; must regulate industry to ensure 'competitive' conditions in the market and 'fair' labour conditions for workers; and must directly supply certain goods and services which the market allegedly does not provide. I do not mean to single out Skidelsky for any special criticism. He is a very careful and thoughtful scholar. His is just one very clear statement of this point of view. Indeed, many others who are 'on the right' believe that government should institute some or all of these 'public policies'. It is important to appreciate, however, that the very notion of 'public policy', as the term is almost always used, implies government intervention in the market in ways that are simply inconsistent with a genuine free market economy. Interventionism as public policy is not consistent with the free market since its very purpose, by intention, is to prevent or modify the outcomes of the market.[10] Here are the eight points of interventionism:

1. The private ownership of the means of production is restricted or abridged.
2. The use of the means of production by private owners is prohibited, limited or regulated.
3. The users of the means of production are prevented from being guided solely by consumer demand.
4. Government influences or controls the formation of prices for consumer goods and/or the factors of production, including labour.
5. Government reduces the impact of market supply and demand on the success or failure of various enterprises while increasing its own influence and control over market incomes through such artificial means as pricing and production regulations, limits on freedom of entry into segments of the market, and direct or indirect subsidies.
6. Free entry into the domestic market by potential foreign rivals is discouraged or outlawed through import prohibitions, quotas or tariffs.
7. The monetary system is regulated by government for the purpose of influencing what is used as money, the value of money and the rate at which the quantity of money is increased or decreased. And all these are used as tools for affecting employment, output and growth in the economy.
8. Government's role is not limited to the protection of life, liberty and property.

It is important to note that the 'public policies' these eight points represent must be implemented through violent means. Only the threat or use of force can make people follow courses of action that differ from the ones that they would have peacefully taken if it were not for government intervention.[11] There is really nothing 'public' about these policies after all; they are coercive policies.

Contrast these policies with the policies of a free market, or unhampered economy, as we have defined it. What is most striking is the voluntary nature of economic arrangements. The means of production are privately owned and the owners are free to determine how those means will be employed. Thus control over the means of production is *depoliticized*. Since this control is not located in one place but is dispersed among a wide segment of the society's population, it is also *decentralized*. Individuals control the means through which they can maintain and improve their own circumstances and they are not dependent upon a single political source for employment or the necessities and luxuries of life.[12] But it is not just the owners of the means of production who have a high degree of autonomy in the free market economy; consumers do, too, since they are the ones who determine what products and services will be in demand.

THE LAW OF ASSOCIATION

The basis of society, Mises always emphasized, is what he called 'the law of association'. Men can more successfully improve their individual condition through cooperation, and the means through which that cooperation can be made most productive is the division of labour. By taking advantage of individual talents and circumstances through specialization, the total quantity and quality of society's output can be dramatically improved. Individuals do not have to try to satisfy all their own wants through isolated activity.[13] And once they specialize their activities, they become interdependent; they rely upon each other for the vast majority of goods and services they desire. But it is this very interdependency that gives production its real and true social character. If men are to acquire from others what they desire, they must devote their energies to producing what others are willing to accept in trade. The fundamental rule of the market is mutual agreement and voluntary exchange. Each member of society must orient his activities towards serving the wants of at least some of the other members in an unending circle of trade. The Scottish moral philosopher Adam Smith observed over two hundred years ago:

> man has almost constant occasion for the help of his brethren, and it is in vain for him to expect it from their benevolence only. He will be more likely to prevail if he can interest their self-love in his favour, and shew them that it is to their own advantage to do for him what he requires of them. Whosoever offers to another a bargain of any kind, proposes to do this. Give me that which I want, and you shall have this which you want, is the meaning of every such offer; and it is in this manner that we obtain from one another the far greater part of those good offices which we stand in need of. It is not from the benevolence of the butcher, the brewer, or the baker, that we expect our dinner, but from their regard for their own interest. We address ourselves, not to their humanity, but to their self-love, and never talk to them of our own necessities but of their own advantages.[14]

This is what ensures that consumer demand guides the uses for which the means of production are applied. Each individual must find a way to satisfy some of the needs of others before he can satisfy his own wants and desires. As a result, the prices for consumer goods and the factors of production are not decreed by government but are formed in the market-place through the competitive forces of supply and demand. Success or failure is determined by the profits and losses earned on the basis of the greater or lesser ability to meet consumer demand in competition with rivals in the market-place.[15] In a real sense, therefore, capitalism is the only true 'public policy'. Every person's private interest in the market-place is socially oriented. Through the incentives of profit and loss, each owner of means of production must direct the use of the resources under his control into those channels which he believes will most likely best serve his fellow men. In the social system of division of labour, it is not necessary for each consumer to control directly the resources upon which his wants and desires depend. The market 'socializes' their use on the behalf of consumers by making each actual owner of the means of production dependent upon successful sales to earn his own livelihood.[16]

THE POLITICAL ECONOMY OF INTERVENTIONISM: RATIONALES AND REPLIES

Just as interventionism modifies people's behaviour through coercion, it also modifies market outcomes. Why do its advocates believe this is necessary and/or desirable? It is possible to classify their rationales under three general headings, economic theory, social justice and public interest.

Perfect Competition Theory

Neoclassical, or mainstream, economics has constructed a theory of market competition that has continued to serve as the conceptual benchmark for judging and evaluating actual market situations. 'Perfect competition' is defined as a situation in which the following conditions are assumed to exist.[17]

1. There are so many buyers and sellers on both sides of the market that no one buyer or seller believes that he can influence the price in the market in which he buys or sells. Each buyer and seller takes the market price as 'given'. And each adjusts the amount he buys or sells at that given price to maximize the utility (personal satisfaction) or profit received from his purchases or sales.
2. Each seller markets a product that is exactly like those sold by all the other sellers in the same market. So the buyer does not care from whom he buys

because each seller offers a good that can be substituted for the ones offered by his rivals.

3. There are no technological or other impediments that prevent resources from being rapidly reallocated from one industry or sector of the market to another in the face of even the smallest changes in supply and demand conditions anywhere in the economy. The instant that a profit opportunity or a loss situation arises anywhere in the market, resources are reallocated to ensure that they are exactly where they should be to assure 'optimal' output everywhere in the market.

4. All participants in the market possess perfect (or sufficient) knowledge to ensure that no buyer ever pays a higher price and no seller ever accepts a lower price than the 'objective' or 'real' market condition dictates that they should. This means that profits are not earned and losses are not suffered by the participants in the market, since buyers and sellers would not pass up profits that could be earned or suffer losses that could be avoided.

These four conditions are usually considered to constitute the standard for judging a market as being 'efficient' or 'optimal' in terms of pricing and production. It is true that during the last several decades neoclassical economists have undertaken 'immanent criticisms' of the framework, pointing out that there may be rational reasons why the conception of a 'perfect market' may not always be accurate. For example, there may be 'transaction costs' involved in consummating exchanges among market participants that produce market outcomes that are different from the pattern that would exist if such 'costs' were zero.[18] Or the market situation may be less than optimal because the costs of acquiring information at the margin may exceed the anticipated benefit from acquiring additional knowledge about possible opportunities.[19] Adding these subsidiary qualifications leads some neoclassical economists to take a 'Panglossian' view; they believe that there can be no better world than the one we are living in since whatever the world produces in terms of market supplies and demands is the best that can be hoped for, given these costs of doing business and acquiring information. And this reasoning can also be turned around so the case can be made that any existing degree of government intervention is also optimal.

Hayek argued against the entire conception of perfect competition more than 50 years ago in his essay, 'The Meaning of Competition'.[20] As defined in textbooks over the decades, perfect competition explains a state of affairs in which it is assumed that the *process* of competition has already brought about a state of fully balanced equilibrium, without any explanation of how such a state of equilibrium would have come about.[21] Another way of saying this is that in neoclassical economics the word 'competition' is used as a *noun* rather than the *verb*, it is portrayed as a static state or situation rather than as a series of actions or activities. In colloquial conversation, 'to compete' is thought of as a circumstance under which the participants act in a manner to 'do better' than their rivals. To 'do better' in the market-place means to offer a lower price or a different product or an improved and more attractive commodity or service. By necessity, to compete in this sense means to change the *price* in such a way that customers find it more profitable to buy from one particular seller rather than the next fellow. It means to *differentiate the product* from the products of rivals by offering qualities or characteristics that are more attractive. It means to *discover* or *create* profit opportunities, either by being alert to price discrepancies between the potential selling price and the cost prices that others have not noticed or by inventing less costly ways of making a product.

Ironically, according to standard textbook conceptions of competition, these types of actions are often considered the hallmarks of *anti-competitive* behaviour.[22] Interventions have sometimes been advocated in the past to prevent market competitors from competing in the name of establishing a situation resembling a condition of 'perfect competition'.[23] From the perspective of Austrian School economists like Mises and Hayek, such interventions are completely misplaced.[24] Once we drop the assumption of 'perfect' or 'sufficient' knowledge, the entire neoclassical view of competition is shown to be misdirected. Instead, competition, as Hayek has referred to it, can be regarded as a 'discovery procedure'.[25] In the actual market based on a system of division of labour, individuals inevitably come to possess not only specialized skills and productive abilities – as Adam Smith and many early classical economists forcefully argued – but also specialized knowledge as well.[26] The specialization of knowledge that naturally accompanies a division of labour means that the market participants must find some way to integrate their respective activities with each other for a mutual coordination of their plans.

Prices serve this role in the market. They do so as cost estimators and information disseminators. If resources are to be efficiently applied among their alternative uses in the market, decision makers must have some way of finding out their relative market worth in different productive uses. The resource prices that arise through the competitive process of market bids for their ownership or use are composite summaries of entrepreneurial judgments concerning their value in competing lines of production. Each employer of factors of production must weigh what resources are believed to be worth to him, given his expectations of the prices consumers might be willing to pay for finished goods after a production process is completed and a commodity or service is ready for sale. The rivalrous bids of employers on the one side and the search for the most remunerative employment by owners of the factors of production on the other side generate the prices for resources and labour.

The resulting prices that emerge from consummated transactions serve as the tools for 'economic calculation' used by decision makers concerning which combinations of resources will minimize their costs of production. Market-based pricing and resource use ensure that resources are always tending to be applied to their most highly valued uses, and never *permanently* kept in some productive application that represents a lower-valued use than some other for which they could be utilized.[27] But prices are not 'static' phenomena. Since they are reflections of 'subjective' valuations and appraisals of consumers, entrepreneurs and resource owners, anything that changes those subjective valuations and appraisals will bring about changes in market prices. And every change in prices originating in one corner of the market will then generate changes in consumer and producer plans in other corners of the market. Hayek emphasized that it is only through this process of changed price bids and offers for goods and resources that individuals can effectively inform others about new supply and demand conditions. Then the others respond by 'recalculating' the most efficient ways to undertake their consumption and production plans, given the new configuration of prices with which they are confronted in the market.

The competitive discovery procedure that Hayek described does not just concern consumption decisions and production plans, given changes in the prices of the market-place. It also concerns the profit incentives and rivalry in the market, out of which market participants and decision makers are driven to unearth new opportunities and create new possibilities. Which of these new opportunities and possibilities will pay off? Which goods and services will consumers buy? What prices and qualities will be better than some rival could offer? These questions can only be answered through the market's competitive process.[28]

The same logic applies to any endeavour that involves competition. Look at the world of sports, for example. Regardless of the facts known about the players and the win–loss records of the teams, the outcome of a game cannot be known in advance. Too many variables are involved. Each has unique and non-deterministic properties. The 'games of the market', to use Hayek's metaphor, are equally non-deterministic.[29] Competitors in the free market economy only discover their own potential by being alert to new opportunities, by imagining new ways of undertaking production, by creating new goods and services, and by responding to new incentives. How they can and will react to changing market situations – including their responses to competitors who constantly challenge them with rival innovations and creations – will only emerge in the process of finding themselves in ever-new circumstances. The responses will be the result of individuals thinking about new situations and possibilities. And no one knows their own future thoughts. If they did, those thoughts would then be today's and not tomorrow's.

What public policy should be concerned with is the clear delineation and enforcement of the rules. In the unhampered economy, this means legal recognition and enforcement of individual rights to life, liberty and property. As long as the rules are followed and each participant renounces the use of force and fraud in his dealings with others, each is left free to pursue his own ends, apply the means of production under his ownership and disposal, and interact with his fellow free men as he finds most advantageous. The overall outcomes are unplanned, and spontaneous results emerge from the actions and interactions of all the participants in the market. The rules also ensure that each participant will tend to apply his knowledge, ability and potential in ways that serve the interests of the other members of society. This allows for much greater freedom, flexibility and creativity than if government intervenes in an attempt to 'plan' the results by regulating the actions and the 'play' of the market process.[30]

From this 'Austrian' perspective, neither the market nor competition need be 'perfect' as they are usually formulated in neoclassical economic theory. Markets and competition and efficiency are working as best they can as long as (1) markets are not restricted or closed by political regulation, (2) taxes do not act as barriers to savings and capital formation, and (3) interventionist policies do not attempt to deflect market processes from the course they naturally follow guided by the profit motive in the service of consumer demand.

Social Justice

'Welfare state' interventions are typically proposed in the name of 'social justice'. The assumptions behind the appeal for 'social justice' are several. The first assumption is that an unhampered economy will tend to generate exploitation. Some members of the society will prey on others, and the state should therefore intervene to redress presumed imbalances in 'power'. The second assumption is that, even if the unhampered economy does not directly exploit individuals, it does create inequalities in income and wealth that unfairly benefit some at the expense of others. Such unfairness requires compensation through income redistribution. Third, however efficient the free market may be, its competitive flexibility introduces degrees of insecurity that need to be compensated for by state interventions that either slow down the pace of change or supply employment and income guarantees to those adversely affected by market-induced changes. Regardless of the form of the argument, all the proposed policies involve direct or indirect redistribution of income through political transfers. Unless it involves brute confiscation (he who has the political power has the 'right' to coerce the transfers he wants), every appeal to social justice must rest on some notion of 'fairness' in income distribution or employment entitlement.

The charge that workers are exploited by employers goes back to the socialist critique of capitalist society that was first developed in the early 19th century and that reached its climax in the writings of Karl Marx. It would have validity only if it could be demonstrated that some are 'forced' to work for others at terms of employment to which the 'exploited' have not freely agreed. But in a free market economy a fundamental principle upon which the system operates is the rule of voluntary agreement. No individual may be coerced into buying from another, working for another, or selling to another at terms that are not freely agreed upon. By definition, a free market excludes exploitation.

The counter-charge of modern liberals, socialists and Marxists is that the free market economy is inherently exploitative because the means of production are owned and controlled by a small minority of the members of the society. Their almost exclusive control over land, machinery, factories and financial capital means that the workers must accept whatever terms the employers dictate because they have no real choice if they are to earn a living. They may appear to be free, but, in reality, their fate is sealed. The trouble is that this is not an economic assumption; it is fatalism, pure and simple. It fails to see human beings as anything more than pawns, without brains, without resourcefulness, without dignity.

It is true that, in the division of labour, it naturally follows that only a minority of a society's members specialize in the provision of any particular good or service. But no minority can force workers to work or force buyers to buy. A minority may own the means of production, but the way in which those means are utilized is really up to the much larger consuming majorities. Barbers are a minority who enjoy a virtual 'monopoly' because they have the required skills and own the means of production. But they are not exploiting the majority simply by offering haircuts.

In the market, it will always be a minority that owns the means of production and that serves as the entrepreneurial force guiding the use of those means in various lines of production. Interest, inclination, ability, persistence and a taste for risk taking are not qualities that all men share in equal measures. Only a few have the willingness and capacity to be 'captains of industry'. Successful entrepreneurship is more a gift than a result of training. The ability to 'read' the market, to have a 'feel' for where consumer demand is shifting, to have a 'sense' of how to respond to competitors – these are not things that can be learned from textbooks or MBA programmes. And while formal education and training may provide types of knowledge that can assist and enhance an entrepreneur's potential, they cannot guarantee success. At the same time, many individuals in the society are risk-averse or unsure of their ability. They prefer the contractual salary income that assures them of a certain fixed sum every month. Others are unwilling to make the personal sacrifices that self-employment and entrepreneurship require. The individual who runs his own business or even manages a business for others can rarely afford to knock off at five o'clock. Still others are unwilling to forgo present consumption to accumulate the savings that are essential for starting up or expanding a business. And some who are willing to try simply end up making too many mistakes and go out of business. These are all aspects and consequences of the natural inequality among individuals.

Finally, the charge of economic exploitation was refuted over a hundred years ago by the economist, Eugen von Böhm-Bawerk.[31] In developing the Austrian School theory of capital and interest, Böhm-Bawerk pointed out that all processes of production involve time. If the period of production is of any significant length of time, then those who are undertaking the manufacture of a product must somehow be able to sustain themselves until the commodity being produced is ready for sale and earns a price greater than or at least equal to its costs from members of the buying public. If those employed in making this good are unwilling or unable to sustain themselves until the product is sold, someone must advance them the wages that will enable them to buy the various goods and services they may need or desire. This, Böhm-Bawerk explained, is the role of the capitalist. By saving, the capitalist forgoes consumption or other uses for which he could have applied his own wealth in the present and over the period of production. His savings represent the source of the workers' wages during the production process. What Marx called the capitalists' 'exploitative profits', Böhm-Bawerk showed to be, in fact, the implicit interest payment for performing an extremely valuable service: providing the needed savings to pay workers during time-consuming, 'roundabout' processes of production. As long as there is free competition in the market for factors of production and as long as individuals are politically unrestricted from starting their own business for purposes of self-employment, there can be no justification for a charge of 'exploitation'.

If the state intervenes in an attempt to redress what is claimed to be an imbalance of 'power' in the bargaining process of the market, it can only do so by restricting the freedom of some to benefit others.[32] If, for example, it makes trade unionism and collective bargaining mandatory, it must restrict the freedom of employers and non-union members who might otherwise have chosen to enter into mutually agreed upon terms of employment. The only way that such an abridgment of ability to contract freely can be enforced is if the state either uses its monopoly of physical force to prevent such agreements or (implicitly or explicitly) delegates such coercive power to collective bargaining trade unions.[33] Enhancing 'labour's power' in this situation means to empower some workers with the coercive ability to impose upon others terms of trade more to their liking. If all workers who might be interested in finding or maintaining employment with a particular employer or group of employers agreed with advocates of collective bargaining, political empowerment would not be needed. The employers would not be able to find any workers with the skills or experience desired who would be willing to accept the jobs that were available at the wages being offered. That coercion must be introduced to prevent competition demonstrates that there are some workers with the minimum skills and experience the employers are looking for who would be willing to accept employment at a wage that underbids the minimum wage the advocates of collective bargaining are demanding.

This, of course, does not mean that the terms accepted in an exchange are always the ones workers may most prefer. Most individuals would prefer to pay one dollar instead of 20 dollars for an excellent steak dinner in a nice restaurant. The fact that many do go to restaurants and pay a higher price for a steak dinner demonstrates that, given personal preferences and the occasion, they value the dinner in that restaurant more than the price they pay for it. The same applies to acceptance of employment; given an individual's wishes to possess income to buy certain things in the market, and given the employment opportunities prevailing in the market for his particular skills and experience, he will accept the most attractive job available.

As was indicated earlier, another rationale for social justice claims that the market generates unfair inequalities in income and wealth that require the state to rectify this 'social injustice' through economic redistribution. But what is the standard for such social justice? Hayek has argued persuasively that in a market economy there is no way to judge whether the distribution of income is just or unjust. On the one hand, the relative income shares earned by individuals in a free market can be viewed as 'just' in the sense that each individual receives what he has contracted for or earned as residual profits through the voluntary transactions of the market-place. He has not received a contractual income or profit through either force or fraud. On the other hand, Hayek points out that free market incomes are earned not on the basis of merit, but rather on the basis of the value of services rendered.[34] The fact that an individual may have worked hard and to the best of his ability does not mean that the market will reward him with an income reflecting some measurement of his industriousness. He receives the income that reflects what his employer or consumers think his product or service is worth to them. If a rival were able to make a better or cheaper product with less effort and industriousness, that rival would be likely to generate more sales and receive a higher income.[35]

Furthermore, in the free market economy, the relative income shares earned by individuals are not determined according to any economy-wide plan or design. They are the outcomes of market transactions that have no economy-wide goal or purpose. The distribution of income is actually one of the 'unintended consequences' of the overall market process. No plan or prior arrangement dictates or determines how much each will earn as a result of transactions in the market-place. Nor is income distributed among the members of the society after the production and sales processes have been completed. Earned incomes arise out of competitive buying, selling and contracting, and are the results of a continuing market process.

To redistribute income according to 'social justice' requires a standard to determine what each member of the society 'deserves'. But Hayek demonstrates conclusively that no such standard exists. Merely to refer to 'industriousness', 'goodness' and 'need' is not sufficient. How can any one of these be objectively defined and measured? How is the distributional share to be determined if an individual has 'many needs', is 'fairly industrious', but is only moderately 'good'? How does this compare with a person who has 'a few simple needs', 'oozes with goodness', but is only 'slightly industrious'? Does it matter if he has a small or large family, or 'bright' or 'dumb' children? With good cause, Hayek likened the pursuit of 'social justice' to chasing after a mirage. A mirage seems real when it lies off in the distance, but it vanishes into nothing as you approach it.

The third rationale for social justice is the assumption that the very flexibility and efficiency of the free economy are actually great drawbacks because they cause changes and insecurities in income and employment. The state needs to compensate by 'adjusting' income and making employment 'secure'. While this is a hot topic today, a summary of this rationale was given by Allen G.B. Fisher over 50 years ago, during the post-World War II period of dramatic change and readjustment to peacetime conditions:

> The problem of personal security is essentially only one aspect of the wider problem of the general stability of the economy within which the individual has to earn his living. To this wider problem there are, in general, two contrasted methods of approach. One is to examine our economy sector by sector, and probably giving priority to those which have recently suffered most from instability, and then to endeavor by piecemeal action to stabilize in turn each sector of the economy, in the hope that eventually stability for the economy as a whole may emerge as a by-product from these successive but partial stabilizing processes. From the standpoint of the individual, this means that we attempt to ensure his security by establishing or restoring him to the place in the economy to which he believes himself to have a customary right. On the other hand, we may prefer to examine the economy as a whole, more or less in the analogy of a growing, living organism, the healthy growth of which is closely dependent upon a similar condition in each part of it, and therefore set ourselves the task of fostering conditions favorable to the healthy development of the whole, in the belief that the adjustment of its several parts to the constantly recurring changes in basic conditions offers the best hopes for a reasonable degree of security in each one of them. Stability for the economy as a whole is then regarded as quite consistent with frequent and continuous changes in the places occupied in it by different individuals, and will indeed often be unattainable unless such changes are made.[36]

The importance of continuous adjustment to market change was also summarized by Allen Fisher in an earlier essay:

> The problem of production in a progressive society is the problem, then, of providing in the correct order and the proper proportions the goods and services which people with rising real incomes are likely to wish to purchase. ... For, quite apart from changes in taste or fashion, rising standards of living will inevitably cause changes in the proportions which at some earlier date seemed to be appropriate, and so long as standards of living continue to rise, there will be continuous changes in the appropriate proportions, so that the economic problem of production will be constantly requiring new solutions. Changes in the proportions between different kinds of production, in their relative importance as fields for employment and investment, are, however, impossible unless there are constant transfers of resources, of labor and of capital, from the old and well-established industries to new and more risky industries. These changes often cause inconvenience to the individuals who have to make them, the laborers who have to change their occupation, and the capitalists who have to risk the loss of capital, and in consequence the changes are resisted. But unless the changes are made, not only is there no material progress, but the whole organization of production is dislocated and jammed, and we are threatened with definite retrogression.[37]

Any change in any part of the market economy necessarily results in the need for various types of adjustments in other parts of the market. Such adjustments always carry the potential for profit or loss. A system founded on the premise of voluntary exchange is one in which each participant must accept the fact that his success or failure is dependent upon whether he has succeeded in producing and offering for sale a product that others in the society value and whether they will pay more for that product than it cost to produce. If he has misjudged what the consumers want and the price they are willing to pay for what he brings to market, he suffers a loss rather than a profit. But that loss can have an important, positive impact on his business. A loss is 'feedback' – direct information from the market-place. It tells him that he has channelled his efforts in the wrong direction. It reveals that consumers prefer some other commodity, or that his rivals can make a similar product at a lower cost or with more attractive qualities. A successful entrepreneur learns from this feedback and makes appropriate changes.[38] He is like the helmsman who uses a compass to keep his ship on the right course. Imagine what a disaster it would be if some other force (like government) were to 'adjust' his compass through intervention. He would surely end up shipwrecked or adrift.

Every innovation and improvement in the quality and available quantity of goods brought to market involves disruptions of the status quo that need adjustment, but not the kind of blind adjustment government offers. New technologies and new products replace old ones. New patterns increase consumer demand for some goods and decrease it for others. The employers' demand for certain types of labour increases for the goods in higher demand,

and decreases for those in lower demand. If an economy is to adapt easily and rapidly to changing circumstances, every individual experiencing change in his respective corner of the market must be willing to respond appropriately. He must accept what the market dictates. But this 'dictation' of the market does not involve the threat or use of force. Rather, it is merely a changing set of monetary rewards that the market offers for the performance of different activities. Each individual is free to respond as he considers best. As Edwin Cannan once expressed it, 'Modern civilization, nearly all civilization, is based on the principle of making things pleasant for those who please the market and unpleasant for those who fail to do so.'[39] If it is not the reward and punishment of profit and loss that guide people in their actions, then it will have to be some form of coercion.[40]

There are dangers when people turn to state intervention for protection and security from the winds of peaceful market change. The first is that the only way that the state can provide subsidies to support loss-making producers is through taxing those who are successful and profit-making. This weakens the incentive of the successful to be as industrious and alert to market opportunities as before. It also redistributes resources away from the production of goods that consumers actually want and for which they are willing to pay. The second danger is that, once the state becomes a mechanism through which political protections and privileges may be received, individuals will have incentives to devote their time and wealth to the acquisition of favours from the state instead of using them to manufacture products that consumers want to buy. The third danger is that those who are meant to be the recipients of assistance from the state often end up being harmed rather than helped. Saving them from their own failures and mistakes ensures that they will not learn how to adapt. Such assistance creates a politics and psychology of dependency that traps many of the poor in the status of a permanent underclass that government support was supposed to eliminate.[41]

The need for such adjustment in the face of change is often more difficult for those who are employees, and not employers, to fully appreciate. In a system based on the division of labour, those who work for a contractual salary often never come into direct contact with the consumers, the ultimate purchasers of the commodity that their labour has helped produce. The required adjustments the employer concludes he must introduce into the enterprise (on the basis of his reading of the existing and expected market conditions) often appear to the employee to be arbitrary. But they are not. It is the actual or expected buying patterns of the consumers that are imposing the necessity for change.[42] The failure to understand and appreciate this fact not only leads to resentment and unrest in the workforce, but can also cause dislocations and distortions that delay adjustments to changing market conditions and increase the very economic instability intervention is meant to prevent.

Public Interest

The third rationale for interventionism is the 'public interest'. An individual or a group of individuals desire that the state intervene to achieve some end that they believe cannot be achieved voluntarily in the market-place. There are many types of public interest pleading, but three of the most popular are based on national interest, environmental preservation and public goods.

The 'national interest' is perhaps the most commonly used type. The difficulty is that this term is as slippery as the 'general welfare' and the 'common good'. It is a concept that can mean any number of things. That is why interventionists like it so much. They find it very useful in their attempts to restrict the freedoms of others for the attainment of goals they cannot achieve without compulsion. In a free market economy, however, the national interest (if this term is to have any meaning at all) is best served when government is confined to performing its limited functions of protecting life, liberty and property. When each individual's liberty is secure, then the nation is secure. For the nation as a whole to have 'interests' requiring government intervention, it would be necessary to agree upon a hierarchy of ends and means. This just is not possible, since the essence of a complex social order is the existence of diversity and divergence of chosen ends and selected means.

One of the core virtues of a free market economy based on a principle of voluntary exchange is that each member of the society sets his own goals; he pursues them by acquiring the means to his ends through voluntary exchange. Another way of saying this is that, in the free market economy, each individual is an end in himself and a means to the ends of others. As a consumer, he sets his own goals and others serve as the means to his ends in their role as producers. And, in turn, as a producer himself, he serves as the means to their ends. In this process, there is no need for any common or general agreement among the members of the society about literally thousands of complex issues. Sometimes, of course, men do share common goals and agree about their relative importance and the best means to achieve them. Then they form associations, clubs and organizations. At the same time, those who do not share those goals, or who regard their relative importance differently, are not required to participate. They can go their own way, while respecting the right of those who choose various forms of collaboration.

'Environmental protection' is a second type of public interest pleading that rests on the false assumption that the free market economy is destroying our planet and that environmental controls must be imposed by the government. But one of the most vital functions performed by a free market economy is to assist in economizing on and preserving resources that people value and that are limited in supply. Nothing is a stronger force for conservation than the profit motive and the institution of private property. When a person is allowed to own something, he has an incentive to think twice before he wastes or abuses it. If he does waste or abuse what he owns, he directly suffers the cost because he loses the benefits that could have been his if only he had shown more care. And nothing is likely to result in greater abuse and misuse of something than when it is owned by nobody.

What is worth preserving in nature? What are the best means and methods to care for resources? Should we merely maintain what we have, or should we expand its supply? Have we set aside too much and, in fact, encroached too heavily on the attainment of other ends we also value? Even the most ardent environmentalist – unless he is one of those few extremists who would like to see man extinct in the belief that everything is worth preserving except the human race – believes that some land also must be used for residential housing, places of work and non-wildlife recreation. To live, man must grow food, raise animals and use resources for clothing, the daily amenities of life, and arts and sciences. The advantage of leaving these problems to the market-place is that it is then up to the people themselves to decide these issues.

People want more wildlife areas for aesthetic appreciation or recreational enjoyment. The greater demand for these things, as expressed in the prices that consumers are willing to pay, increases the profitability for land and resource owners to use less of what they own for other purposes and instead shift their resources into these more highly valued uses. If owners of land and resources most attractive for these purposes fail to do so, they will miss out on the higher income they could be earning. If an increased demand for housing and arts and crafts brings about an increased rate of deforestation, the remaining forests not yet touched by the woodchopper's axe will rise in price because of their increasing scarcity. This creates incentives on the part of forest owners to think ahead and replant trees at a greater rate, so the higher profits can be reaped in the future through harvesting or through other uses valued by consumers. If urban areas begin to encroach on areas of natural beauty – and if members of the society value them enough to be willing to pay for their preservation – the market will see to it that ownership of these areas passes into the hands of these people because that is where the greatest monetary return is expected.

Where are pollution problems, ecological imbalances and assaults on areas of natural beauty taking place? Invariably, they are taking place in areas in society in which private property rights have not been permitted or have not been clearly delineated. No one knows for certain 'what is mine and what is thine'. In many of these areas, the resources in question are either in a no-man's-land of non-ownership or they are under the jurisdiction of the government. Non-ownership always produces what is known as 'the tragedy of the commons'. Where there is no owner, there is no cost for excessive misuse of a resource. And when no one directly feels the cost – in the form of lost income or depleted resale value – then everyone who has access to that ownerless resource will try to get as much out of it as is possible before others do.

Where property rights are not clearly specified, people will often act in ways that do not take into consideration the full effect and cost upon others. Resources and land are wrongly or excessively used because the users do not have to weigh or pay for the consequences of their actions upon others. This is the source of practically all the pollution problems that are cause for concern today.[43] By politicizing environmental problems, interventionists undermine the market's rational and reasonable mechanisms for finding out what people really value and what they are really willing to pay for. Special interests who lobby the state for environmental regulation are interested in getting what they want at the expense of others – others to whom they are unwilling to pay the real market price for the desired land and resources. Instead, they use the government to get what they want at below full market price through interventionist methods of coercion.[44]

The third type of public interest pleading argues that 'public goods' are desirable products and services that are not adequately provided by the free market because it is simply not possible to exclude non-payers from benefiting from its provision. This 'free rider' dilemma means that private profit seekers will undersupply the product or service in question. Popular examples are streets, highways and lighthouses. Sometimes education is also listed as a public good benefiting the interests of the nation or community. And, of course, it is easy to conclude that all supposed public goods should be provided by the government.[45]

A closer examination of these examples shows that there is no logical reason why such goods and services cannot be supplied by the free market.[46] If a development corporation undertakes the construction of a residential community, it will clearly be in its own interest to construct a road system leading to and through the area. Access has a direct impact on the prospective value of the homes put up for sale. At the same time, the development corporation has incentives to include facilities such as playgrounds, swimming pools and recreational and shopping areas. Purchasing a home in this 'proprietary community' would involve contracting for the provision of such 'public services'. The development corporation would lease out the stores in the shopping areas and maintain the roads, the street lighting and other amenities that would make the area attractive, convenient and desirable as a place to live.[47]

The same principle is inherent in the 'condominium' concept in which the owners of the apartments pay a fee to the building owner for maintenance and security. It is also inherent in the concept of the 'shopping mall', which the builder wants to make attractive and safe. Malls are usually surrounded by large parking areas with easy access to nearby roads and highways. Parking, restrooms, drinking fountains, benches, paging and security surveillance are free. In traditional downtown areas, it is equally imaginable that if streets and sidewalks could be privatized there would be incentives for the owners to maintain them in good order, receiving fees from adjacent stores for providing this service. Generally speaking, streets and highways can easily be supplied with the same profit incentives. Suppliers would receive tolls in exchange for access. Unlike the present system under which the government supplies most streets and highways 'free' (that is, on the basis of taxation) with open access for all drivers, private roads could offer 'peak' and 'off-peak' toll rates that would diminish highway congestion through a system of price rationing.[48] (Movie theatres and restaurants have rationed access in this way, respectively, with different matinee and evening ticket prices for movie attendance and different lunch and dinner menu prices.) Furthermore, roads and highways would also be constructed where the market demonstrates people desire to live, work and play, and not where bureaucrats and city planners think they ought to be.[49]

THE INDIVIDUAL, MORALITY AND THE STATE

In 1936, Swiss economist and political scientist William E. Rappard delivered a lecture in Philadelphia on 'The Relation of the Individual to the State'. Looking back at the trend of political and economic events in the 19th and 20th centuries, he explained:

> The revolutions at the end of the eighteenth century ... were essentially revolts of the individual against the traditional state – expressions of his desire to emancipate himself from the ties and inhibitions which the traditional state had imposed on him. ... after the rise of individualism, which one may define as the emancipation of the individual from the state, we had the rise of democracy, which one may define as the subjection of the state to the will of the individual. In the latter half of the nineteenth century and up to the present day, the individual, having emancipated himself from the state and having subjected the state to his will, has furthermore demanded of the state that it serve his material needs. Thereby he has complicated the machinery of the state to such a degree that he has again fallen under subjection to it and he has been threatened with losing control over it. ... the individual has increasingly demanded of the state services which the state is willing to render. Thereby, however, he has been led to return to the state an authority over himself which it was the main purpose of the revolutions in the beginning of the nineteenth century to shake and to break.[50]

And looking back at the early American experience, Professor Rappard emphasized:

> no one can possibly have read either the [constitutional] debates [of 1787] or the famous state papers of the Federalists without realizing that the Fathers of your Constitution were essentially animated by the desire to free the individual from the state. I believe you went farther in that direction than anyone had ever gone in the past. And your present Constitution bears the trace of this intransigent, almost ruthless, desire of the individual to free himself from the authority of the state. ... I do not think that anyone who has seriously studied the origin of the Constitution of the United States will deny that it is an essentially individualistic document, inspired by the suspicion that the state is always, or always tends to be, dictatorial.[51]

Reflecting upon the trends he observed in the USA in the New Deal era of the 1930s, Professor Rappard concluded: 'The individual demanding that the state provide him with every security has thereby jeopardized his possession of that freedom for which his ancestors fought and bled.'

Is Soviet-style central planning now in the ash heap of history? Yes. Are masses of people in the West willing to walk in blind, lock step obedience to fascist demagogues in torchlight parades? No. And hopefully neither form of totalitarianism will ever again cast its dark collectivist shadow over the West. However, almost seven decades after Professor Rappard's observations about statist trends in America and around the world, Western democracies are still enveloped in the tight grip of the interventionist state. Private property increasingly exists only on paper.[52] And with the abridgment of property rights has come the abridgment of all the other individual liberties upon which a free society is based.[53] Our lives are supervised, regulated, controlled, directed and overseen by the state. Look around in any direction of our economic and social lives and try to find even one corner of our existence free from some form of direct or indirect government intrusion into our personal and interpersonal affairs. It is practically impossible to find such a corner. Our lives are not our own. They are the property of the state. We are the tools and the victims of public policies that are intended to construct brave new worlds concocted by intellectual and political elites who still dream the utopian dream that they know better than the people themselves how their lives should be lived.[54]

Acts of Coercion

Today, it is not free market forces but political directives that most often influence what goods and services are produced, where and how they are produced, and for what purposes they may be used. Pick up any product in any store anywhere in the USA and you will discover that hundreds of federal and state regulations have actually determined the methods by which it has been manufactured, its quality and content, its packaging and terms of sale, and the conditions under which it may be 'safely' used by the purchaser. Buy a tract of land or a building and you will be trapped in a spider's web of restrictions on how you may use, improve or sell it. Every facet of our lives is now subject to the whims of the state.

In an environment in which 'public policy' determines individual lives and fortunes, in which social and economic life has become politicized, it is not surprising that many Americans have turned their attention to politics to improve their market position and relative income share. Legalized coercion has become the method by which they get ahead in life. And make no mistake about it: every income transfer, every tariff or import quota, every business subsidy, every regulation or prohibition on who may compete or how a product may be produced and marketed, and every restraint on the use and transfer of property is an act of coercion. Political force is interjected into what would otherwise be a system of peaceful and voluntary transactions.

Over time, interventionism blurs the distinction between what is moral and what is not. In ordinary life, most people take for granted that certain forms of conduct are permissible while others are not. These are the Golden Rules they live by. Government's task in society is to enforce and protect these rules, which, as I have already indicated, are summarized in two basic principles: (1) neither force nor fraud shall be practised in dealings with others, and (2) the rights and property of others must be respected. In the moral order that is the free market economy, these principles are the wellspring of honesty and trust. Without them, America is threatened with ultimate ruin, with a war of all-against-all in the pursuit of plunder. When individuals began to ask government to do things for them, rather than merely secure rights and property, they began asking government to violate others' rights and property for their benefit. Their demands on government have been rationalized by intellectuals and social engineers who have persuaded them that what they wanted but did not have was due to the greed, exploitation and immorality of others. Basic morality and justice have been transcended in the political arena in order to take from the 'haves' and give to the 'have nots'. Theft through political means has become the basis of a 'higher' morality – social justice, which is supposed to remedy the alleged injustices of the free market economy.

Moral Bankruptcy

But once the market became politicized in this manner, morality began to degenerate. Increasingly, the only way to survive in society is to resort to the same types of political methods for gain as others are using or to devise ways to evade controls and regulations. More and more people have been drawn into the arena of political intrigue and manipulation or violation of the law for economic gain. Human relationships and the political process have become increasingly corrupted. In the 1920s, Mises explained a crucial aspect of this corruption of morality and law:

> By constantly violating criminal laws and moral decrees [people] lose the ability to distinguish between right and wrong, good and bad. The merchant who began by violating foreign exchange controls, import and export restrictions, price ceilings, etc., easily proceeds to defraud his partners. The decay of business morals ... is the inevitable concomitant of the regulations imposed on trade.[55]

Mises was, of course, repeating the lesson that French classical economist Frédéric Bastiat had attempted to teach in the 1850s in his famous essay 'The Law'.[56] When the state becomes the violator of liberty and property rather than its guarantor, it debases respect for all law. Society develops an increasing disrespect and disregard for what the law demands. It views the law as the agent for immorality in the form of legalized plunder for the benefit of some at the expense of others. And this same disrespect and disregard sooner or later starts to creep into dealings between individuals. Society stands on the brink of lawlessness, and the attitude grows that 'anything goes' in human relationships.

Bastiat predicted the moral bankruptcy that has been brought on by the interventionist state. But are we condemned to continue down this path of moral and political corruption? Many thoughtful observers shake their heads and conclude that the answer is 'yes'. But it is worth recalling that, in 1951, Mises wrote an essay called 'Trends Can Change'. He was replying to those who despaired over the trend toward socialist central planning. At the time, the situation did seem irreversible; political, economic and social trends all seemed to be heading in the direction of comprehensive collectivism:

> One of the cherished dogmas implied in contemporary fashionable doctrines is the belief that tendencies of social evolution as manifested in the recent past will prevail in the future too. Any attempt to reverse or even to stop a trend is doomed to failure. ... The prestige of this myth is so enormous that it quells any opposition. It spreads defeatism among those who do not share the opinion that everything which comes later is better than what preceded, and are fully aware of the disastrous effects of all-round planning, i.e., totalitarian socialism. They too meekly submit to what, the pseudo-scholars tell them, is inevitable. It is this mentality of passively accepting defeat that has made socialism triumph in many European countries and may very soon make it conquer in this country [the United States] too. ... Now trends of evolution can change, and hitherto they almost always have changed. But they changed only because they met firm opposition. The prevailing trend toward what Hilaire Belloc called the servile state will certainly not be reversed if nobody has the courage to attack its underlying dogmas.[57]

The trend towards totalitarian socialism *was* reversed. It was reversed by its own inherent unworkability. It was reversed by the faith of millions of people in the Soviet bloc who would not give up the dream of freedom and by a courageous few in those countries who were willing to risk imprisonment or their lives to make freedom a reality. And it was reversed by friends of freedom in the West who helped prevent its triumph in their homelands and who provided an intellectual defence of liberty and the free market.

Interventionism in America in the early 21st century is a trend that can also be reversed. Its own inherent unworkability and strangulation of the wealth-creating mechanisms of the market has already started the reversal process. But that is not enough. We must rekindle our belief in and desire for freedom. And we have to speak out and refute the rationales for interventionism. We need to share with our fellow citizens a clear and persuasive vision of the free society and the unhampered market economy. If we succeed, the great trend of the 21st century will be towards greater individual freedom, an expanding global market-place and rising standards of living for all. That future can be ours, if only we have the courage to defend freedom and oppose the interventionist dogmas of our time.

NOTES

1. Ludwig von Mises, 'Changes in American Economic Policy' [1926], in Richard M. Ebeling (ed.), *Selected Writings of Ludwig von Mises*, Vol. 2: *Between the Two World Wars: Monetary Disorder, Interventionism, Socialism and the Great Depression* (Indianapolis, IN: Liberty Fund, 2002) p.160.
2. Ibid., p.162.
3. For a comparison of the similarities between New Deal America and Nazi Germany in the 1930s, see Robert Skidelsky, *The Road From Serfdom: The Economic and Political Consequences of the End of Communism* (New York: Viking Penguin, 1996) pp.60–63; for an excellent contemporary account of the statist aspects of American economic policy in the 1930s, see A.S.J. Baster, *The Twilight of American Capitalism: An Economic Interpretation of the New Deal* (London: P.S. King & Son, 1937); also John T. Flynn, 'Whose Child Is the NRA?' [1934], in *Forgotten Lessons: Selected Essays by John T. Flynn* (Irvington-on-Hudson, NY: Foundation for Economic Education, 1995); and for an overview of the economic thinking of those involved in Roosevelt's administration, see William J. Barber, *Designs within Disorder: Franklin D. Roosevelt, the Economists, and the Shaping of American Economic Policy, 1933–1945* (New York: Cambridge University Press, 1996).
4. Ludwig von Mises, *Critique of Interventionism: Inquiries into the Economic Policy and the Economic Ideology of the Present* [1929] (Irvington-on-Hudson, NY: Foundation for Economic Education, 1996) p.xi.
5. Ibid., p.1.
6. Ibid., pp.2–3; see also Thomas Nixon Carver, *The Present Economic Revolution in the United States* (London: George Allen & Unwin, 1926) pp.5–6.
7. Robert Skidelsky, *John Maynard Keynes: Hopes Betrayed, 1883–1920* (London: Macmillan, 1983); *John Maynard Keynes: The Economist as Saviour, 1920–1937* (London: Macmillan, 1992); and *John Maynard Keynes: Fighting for Britain, 1937–1946* (London: Macmillan, 2000).
8. Robert Skidelsky (ed.), *Russia's Stormy Path to Reform* (London: Social Market Foundation, 1995).
9. Robert Skidelsky, *The Road from Serfdom: The Economic and Political Consequences of the End of Communism* (New York: Viking Penguin, 1996).

10. Oskar Morgenstern, *The Limits of Economics* [1934] (London: William Hodge and Co., 1937) p.1; and Ludwig von Mises, *Human Action, Treatise on Economics* [1949] (Irvington-on-Hudson, NY: Foundation for Economic Education, 4th edn, 1996) p.718: 'The system of interventionism or of the hampered market economy ... does not want to eliminate the market altogether. It wants production and consumption to develop along lines different from those prescribed by an unhampered market, and it wants to achieve its aims by injecting into the working of the market orders, commands, and prohibitions for whose enforcement the police power and its apparatus of violent compulsion and coercion stand ready.'

11. Cf. Mises, *Human Action*, p.719: 'It is important to remember that government interference always means either violent action or the threat of such action ... Government is in the last resort the employment of armed men, of policemen, gendarmes, soldiers, prison guards, and hangmen. The essential feature of government is the enforcement of its decrees by beating, killing, and imprisoning. Those who ask for more government interference are asking ultimately for more compulsion and less freedom.' See also Murray N. Rothbard, *Power and Market: Government and the Economy* (Menlo Park: Institute for Humane Studies, 1970) pp.9–11; and Sanford Ikeda, *Dynamics of the Mixed Economy: Toward a Theory of Interventionism* (New York: Routledge, 1997) p.35.

12. See James M. Buchanan, *Property as a Guarantor of Liberty* (Aldershot, UK and Brookfield, VT: Edward Elgar Publishing, 1993). On the history and general importance of private property rights, see Gottfried Dietze, *In Defense of Property* (Baltimore: Johns Hopkins University Press, 1963); Tom Bethell, *Noblest Triumph: Property and Prosperity Through the Ages* (New York: St Martin's Press, 1998); and Richard Pipes, *Property and Freedom* (New York: Alfred A. Knopf, 1999); see also Samuel L. Blumenfeld (ed.), *Property in a Humane Economy* (LaSalle, IL: Open Court, 1974).

13. Mises, *Human Action*, pp.159–66.

14. Adam Smith, *The Wealth of Nations* [1776] (New York: Modern Library, 1936) p.14.

15. Mises, *Human Action*, pp.257–397; and Murray N. Rothbard, *Man, Economy and State: A Treatise on Economic Principles* [1962] (Los Angeles: Nash Publishing, 1970).

16. Ludwig von Mises, *Socialism, an Economic and Sociological Analysis* [1922] (Indianapolis, IN: Liberty Classics [3rd rev. edn, 1951], 1981) pp.30–32; see also John Bates Clark, *The Philosophy of Wealth* [1887] (New York: Augustus M. Kelley, 1967) pp.38–9: 'The individual man ... produces for the market. Every producer is serving the world, and the world is serving every consumer. ... Society holds two distinct relations toward every man; it is the object of his efforts; he is the object of its efforts. He produces for the general market; it is his study to ascertain a public want, and to create to supply it. He buys from the general market; he informs himself concerning the goods of many producers, and buys wherever the things offered are adapted in quality and price to his necessities.'

17. In its modern standard form, the conditions for a state of 'perfect competition' to be present was first formalized by Frank H. Knight, *Risk, Uncertainty and Profit* [1921] (New York: Kelley & Millman, Inc., 1957), Part 2 on 'Perfect Competition', pp.51–194; however, several years before publishing this book, in an article on 'Neglected Factors in the Problem of Normal Interest', *Quarterly Journal of Economics* (February 1916) 283, Knight referred to 'the impossible conditions of ideally perfect competition, where time and space were annihilated and universal omniscience prevailed'. See also Helmut Arndt, *Economic Theory vs. Economic Reality* (East Lansing, MI: Michigan State University Press, 1984) pp.37–65.

18. See, for example, Ronald H. Coase, *The Firm, the Market, and the Law* (Chicago: University of Chicago Press, 1988); and Oliver E. Williamson and Scott E. Masten (eds), *The Economics of Transaction Costs* (Cheltenham, UK/Northampton, MA: Edward Elgar, 1999).

19. See, for example, George J. Stigler, 'The Economics of Information' [1961], in *The Organization of Industry* (Chicago: University of Chicago Press, 1968) pp.171–90.

20. Friedrich A. Hayek, 'The Meaning of Competition' [1946], in *Individualism and Economic Order* (Chicago: University of Chicago Press, 1948) pp.92–106.

21. For a detailed critique of many of the assumptions that are the foundation of neoclassical equilibrium theory that is written by a prominent Austrian School economist of the inter-war

period, see Hans Mayer, 'The Cognitive Value of Functional Theories of Price' [1932], in Israel M. Kirzner (ed.), *Classics in Austrian Economics*, Vol. 2 (London: William Pickering, 1994) pp. 55–168; and for a modern reformulation, see Robin Cowan and Mario J. Rizzo, 'The Genetic-Causal Tradition and Modern Economic Theory', *Kyklos*, Vol. 49, No. 3 (1996) pp. 273–317.

22. For a critical analysis of the neoclassical conception of competition from a modern Austrian School point of view, see Dominick T. Armentano, *Antitrust and Monopoly: Anatomy of a Policy Failure* (New York: John Wiley & Sons, 1982) pp. 13–48; see also Israel M. Kirzner, 'The Driving Force of the Market: The Idea of "Competition" in Contemporary Economic Theory and in the Austrian Theory of the Market Process', in Richard M. Ebeling (ed.), *Austrian Economics: Perspectives on the Past and Prospects for the Future*, Champions of Freedom, Vol. 17 (Hillsdale, MI: Hillsdale College Press, 1991) pp. 139–60; and Mark Addleson, 'Competition', in Peter J. Boettke (ed.), *The Elgar Companion to Austrian Economics* (Aldershot, UK and Brookfield, VT: Edward Elgar Publishing, 1994) pp. 96–102.

23. For Austrian School criticisms of such policy proposals, see Stephen C. Littlechild, *The Fallacy of the Mixed Economy: An 'Austrian' Critique of Conventional Economics and Government Policy* (San Francisco: Cato Institute, 1979); W. Duncan Reekie, *Markets, Entrepreneurs, and Liberty: An Austrian View of Capitalism* (New York: St Martin's Press, 1984); and D.T. Armentano, *Antitrust: The Case for Repeal* (Washington, DC: Cato Institute, 1986). For a critical analysis of the 'operational' assumptions underlying many interventionist policy proposals, see Robert Formaini, *The Myth of Scientific Public Policy* (New Brunswick, NJ: Transaction Books, 1990).

24. For summaries of the ideas of the Austrian School economists in contrast to the ideas of other schools of economic thought, see Ludwig M. Lachmann, 'The Significance of the Austrian School of Economics in the History of Ideas' [1966], in Richard M. Ebeling (ed.), *Austrian Economics: A Reader*, Champions of Freedom, Vol. 18 (Hillsdale, MI: Hillsdale College Press, 1991) pp. 17–39; Chapter 2 of the present volume; and Israel M. Kirzner, 'Entrepreneurial Discovery and the Competitive Market Process: An Austrian Approach', *Journal of Economic Literature* (March 1997) 60–85, and *How Markets Work: Disequilibrium, Entrepreneurship and Discovery* (London: Institute of Economic Affairs, 1997).

25. Friedrich A. Hayek, 'Competition as a Discovery Procedure' [1968], in *New Studies in Philosophy, Politics, Economics and the History of Ideas* (Chicago: University of Chicago Press, 1978) pp. 179–90; see also E.G. West, *Adam Smith and Modern Economics* (Aldershot, UK and Brookfield, VT: Edward Elgar Publishing Co., 1990) pp. 21–3.

26. See Friedrich A. Hayek, 'The Use of Knowledge in Society' [1945], in *Individualism and Economic Order*, pp. 77–91. On the classical economists' view of the market economy in comparison to the view of most 20th-century economists, see Chapter 1 of the present volume.

27. See Mises, *Human Action*, pp. 200–217, on the meaning and significance of economic calculation.

28. The logic and process of such entrepreneurial 'discovery' has been the theme of most of the writings of Israel M. Kirzner; see *Competition and Entrepreneurship* (Chicago: University of Chicago Press, 1973); *Perception, Opportunity, and Profit: Studies in the Theory of Entrepreneurship* (Chicago: University of Chicago Press, 1979); *Discovery and the Capitalist Process* (Chicago: University of Chicago Press, 1985); *Discovery, Capitalism, and Distributive Justice* (New York: Blackwell, Publishers, 1989); and *The Meaning of Market Process: Essays in the Development of Modern Austrian Economics* (New York: Routledge, 1992).

29. Friedrich A. Hayek, *Law, Legislation, and Liberty*, Vol. 2: *The Mirage of Social Justice* (Chicago: University of Chicago Press, 1976) pp. 115–20.

30. See Norman P. Barry, *The Invisible Hand in Economics and Politics: A Study in the Two Conflicting Explanations of Society: End-States and Processes* (London: Institute of Economic Affairs, 1988).

31. Eugen von Böhm-Bawerk, *Capital and Interest* [1914], Vol. 1 (South Holland, IL: Libertarian Press, 1959) pp.241–321; 'Unresolved Contradiction in the Marxian System' [1896], in *Shorter Classics* (South Holland, IL: Libertarian Press, 1962) pp.201–302; also H.W.B. Joseph, *The Labour Theory of Value in Karl Marx* (London: Oxford University Press, 1923).

32. The classic essay on this theme is Eugen von Böhm-Bawerk, 'Control or Economic Law' [1914], in *Shorter Classics*, pp.139–99.

33. On the economic effects of coerced collective bargaining, see W.H. Hutt, *The Theory of Collective Bargaining, 1930-1975* (London: Institute of Economic Affairs, 1975); *The Strike-Threat System: The Economic Consequences of Collective Bargaining* (New Rochelle, NY: Arlington House, 1973); Sylvester Petro, *The Labor Policy of the Free Society* (New York: Ronald Press, 1957); Gustavo R. Velsaso, *Labor Legislation from an Economic Point of View* (Indianapolis, IN: Liberty Fund, 1973); Morgan O. Reynolds, *Power and Privilege: Labor Unions in America* (New York: Universe Books, 1984); and Howard Dickman, *Industrial Democracy in America: Ideological Origins of National Labor Relations Policy* (LaSalle, IL: Open Court, 1987).

34. Hayek, *Law, Legislation and Liberty*, Vol. 2, pp.62–100.

35. Students sometimes resent the fact that their grade is solely dependent upon on how well they have 'delivered the goods', that is, answered the questions on an exam with correct and complete answers, and not on the basis of how 'hard' they have studied. It bothers some students that someone for whom the material 'comes easy' gets an 'A', while someone who studied for long hours is 'given' a lower grade.

36. Allen G.B. Fisher, 'More Stabilization: Less Stability', *Kyklos*, Vol. 1, No. 1 (1947) 3–4.

37. Allen G.B. Fisher, 'The Economic Implications of Material Progress', *International Labor Review* (July 1935) 7–8; on this general theme, see Allen G.B. Fisher, *The Clash of Progress and Security* [1935] (New York: Augustus M. Kelley, 1966).

38. See Mises, *Human Action*, pp.289–94 and Mises, 'Profit and Loss' [1951], in *Planning for Freedom* (South Holland, IL: Libertarian Press, 4th rev. edn, 1980) pp.108–50, on the nature and role of profit and loss in the free market economy.

39. Edwin Cannan, *An Economist's Protest* (London: P.S. King & Son, 1927) pp.vii–viii.

40. Mises, *Human Action*, pp.599–600.

41. This theme is developed in great detail in Dwight R. Lee and Richard B. McKenzie, *Failure and Progress: The Bright Side of the Dismal Science* (Washington, DC: Cato Institute, 1993).

42. See Edwin Cannan, *Economic Scares* (London: P.S. King & Son, 1933) pp.21–41.

43. Mises, *Human Action*, pp.654–61.

44. See Richard L. Stroup and John A. Baden, *Natural Resources: Bureaucratic Myths and Environmental Management* (San Francisco: Pacific Institute for Public Policy Research, 1983); Walter E. Block (ed.), *Economics and the Environment: A Reconciliation* (Vancouver, BC: Fraser Institute, 1990); Terry L. Anderson and Donald R. Leal, *Free Market Environmentalism* (Boulder, CO: Westview Press, 1991); Roy E. Cordato, *Welfare Economics and Externalities in an Open Ended Universe: A Modern Austrian Perspective* (Boston: Kluwer Academic Press, 1992); Joseph Bast, Peter J. Hill and Richard C. Rue, *Eco-Sanity: A Common-Sense Guide to Environmentalism* (Lanham, MD: Madison Books, 1994); Terry L. Anderson (ed.), *Breaking Environmental Policy Gridlock* (Stanford: Hoover Institution, 1997).

45. An example of such a rationale for subsidized public education is Charles Murray, *What it Means to be a Libertarian: A Personal Interpretation* (New York: Broadway Books, 1997) pp.90–101; however, on the advantages of a fully privatized system of education, see Sheldon Richman, *Separating School and State: How to Liberate America's Families* (Fairfax, VA: The Future of Freedom Foundation, 1994).

46. For a refutation of the claim that lighthouses are an obvious public good, see Ronald H. Coase, 'The Lighthouse in Economics' [1974], in *The Firm, The Market and the Law*, pp.187–213.

47. See Spencer Heath, *Citadel, Market and Altar* (Baltimore, MD: Science of Society Foundation, 1957) and Spencer MacCullum, *The Art of Community* (Menlo Park, CA:

Institute for Humane Studies, 1970); on the general refutation of the public goods argument along these lines, see Fred Foldvary, *Public Goods and Private Communities: The Private Provision of Social Services* (Aldershot, UK and Brookfield, VT: Edward Elgar Publishing, 1994); also Mark Pennington, *Liberating the Land: The Case for Private Land-Use Planning* (London: Institute of Economic Affairs, 2002).

48. See John Hibbs, *Transport Without Politics* ...? (London: Institute of Economic Affairs, 1982); Eammon Butler (ed.), *Roads and the Private Sector* (London: Adam Smith Institute, 1982); Gabriel Roth and Eammon Butler, *Private Roads Ahead* (London: Adam Smith Institute, 1982); see also Francis A. Walker, *Political Economy* (New York: Henry Holt and Co., 1888) p.520: 'Public roads and bridges also exhibit the socialistic character in a highly marked degree.'

49. See Jane Jacobs, *The Death and Life of Great American Cities* (New York: Vintage Books, 1961).

50. William E. Rappard, 'The Relation of the Individual to the State', *Annals of the American Academy of Political and Social Science* (January 1937) 215–18.

51. Ibid.

52. See Richard A. Epstein, *Takings: Private Property and the Power of Eminent Domain* (Cambridge, MA: Harvard University Press, 1985); and Mark L. Pollot, *Grand Theft and Petit Larceny: Property Rights in America* (San Francisco: Pacific Research Institute for Public Policy, 1993).

53. See Bernard H. Siegan, *Economic Liberties and the Constitution* (Chicago: University of Chicago Press, 1980).

54. See Bertrand de Jouvenel, 'The Attitude of Intellectuals to the Market Society', *The Owl* (January 1951) 19–27; and Thomas Sowell, *The Vision of the Anointed: Self-Congratulation as a Basis for Social Policy* (New York: Basic Books, 1995).

55. Mises, *Critique of Interventionism*, p.13.

56. Frédéric Bastiat, 'The Law' [1850], *Selected Essays on Political Economy* (Princeton: D. Van Nostrand, 1964) pp.51–96; see Richard M. Ebeling, 'Bastiat: Champion of Economic Liberty', *Ideas on Liberty* (June 2001) pp.27–31.

57. Ludwig von Mises, 'Trends Can Change' [1951], *Planning for Freedom*, pp.173–4, 179.

9. The limits of economic policy: the Austrian economists and the German ORDO liberals

THE POLITICAL AND ECONOMIC CRISIS OF THE 20th CENTURY

The century that has recently come to an end was one of the darkest and cruellest in human history. Twenty million people were killed in World War I; 50 million more lost their lives in World War II. The communist experiment in the Soviet Union cost the lives of 64 million. The Nazi experience in Europe took, separate from war combatants, another 25 million lives. The years of Mao Tse-tung's reign in communist China may have taken up to 80 million lives. Overall, and separate from wars, it has been estimated that governments in the 20th century may have killed more than 270 million people.[1]

Many of the most cherished and hard-won freedoms and constitutional protections of human liberty acquired during the 18th and 19th centuries have been either weakened or, in some countries during various periods of time, denied and abolished in our time. The economic liberties of open competition and free trade, that were the hallmark of many if not most of the Western economies at the beginning of the 20th century, have been replaced by government regulation and redistributive welfarism, and state-managed trade between nations and regions of the world.[2]

At the height of this political–economic darkness, in the 1930s and 1940s, there were many who wondered if human freedom, democratic government and a free economy were going to perish under the onslaught of totalitarian collectivism.[3] Even with the end of the Nazi era in 1945, and separate from the cold war with communism for the 45 years following the close of World War II, the West has been plagued by the encroachment of moderate collectivism in the form of the interventionist and welfare state.[4]

Only now, at the end of this brutal one hundred years, are the assumptions of collectivism – in all its forms – being challenged and reconsidered. But this reconsideration is not occurring in an intellectual vacuum. In spite of collectivism's triumphs, even in its most victorious decades during the 1930s and 1940s, there were important voices raised against it. These voices spoke out against both the assumptions and the policies of collectivism and offered in their place alternative visions of a free and prosperous society.

Two groups were especially outstanding in their criticisms of collectivism and their defences of the free society: the Austrian economists and the German ORDO liberals. In 1948, two of the leading German liberal economists, Walter Eucken and Franz Böhm, published the first issue of the *Yearbook for the Order of Economy and Society (ORDO)*. The yearbook became the focal point for a growing number of German economists convinced of the superiority of a market economy over all types of socialism; they developed various arguments for the defence of the market order and what they considered the necessary supporting political and social institutions for the preservation of a free society. Many of these German liberals had been opponents of socialism and Nazism in the 1920s and 1930s. In the post-World War II era, they wished to see a new democratic Germany with a 'social market economy'.[5]

THE COMMON ENEMIES AND COMMON PREMISES OF THE AUSTRIANS AND THE GERMAN LIBERALS

Throughout the 1920s, 1930s and 1940s, the Austrians and the German liberals shared a group of common enemies: historicism, positivism and collectivism. They were common enemies because the Austrians and the German liberals possessed a set of common premises from which they generally looked at the world.

At the level of economic theory, the Austrians and the German liberal economists were advocates of 'laws of economics' derived from an understanding of the human condition under circumstances of scarcity.[6] They rejected the German Historical School's insistence that economic relationships were determined by and limited to changing historical forces. They also rejected the idea that the collectivist state has the potential to mould and transform interpersonal relationships and market outcomes in ways considered superior to merely leaving the market to follow its own course.

For the Austrians and the German liberals, the attempt to violate the laws of the market could only lead to disaster. Thus both groups strongly opposed the most extreme form of a violation of the market: socialist central planning. For effective coordination of human activities there was no substitute for market competition and price-guided production and resource allocation. In the 1920s, Ludwig von Mises had demonstrated the 'irrationality' of a centrally planned economy once private property had been nationalized, monetary transactions and market exchange had been abolished and a central planning agency had the authority to determine the allocation of resources, the relative quantities of final goods to be manufactured with those resources, and the remunerations that each factor of production was to receive. Without market prices and entrepreneurial competitive bids for factors of production, there was simply no way of knowing whether the means of production were being applied to their most highly valued uses and at minimum costs of production.[7]

Indeed, for both Austrians like Ludwig von Mises and German liberals like Franz Böhm, the private entrepreneur was the creative, motor force of a dynamic market economy. Without the free entrepreneur, innovation, effective coordination of market activity and the incentives for efficient production would be albeit impossible.[8]

The types of theoretical arguments made by Mises and his Austrian colleague, Friedrich A. Hayek,[9] against socialism were not merely echoed by the German liberals - they were extended by them. Wilhelm Röpke, for instance, argued forcefully that the central planning mentality was indicative of the 'hubris of the intellectual' who believed that it was in his power to engineer human society into any shape he deemed preferable to the one he found man currently living in. Nothing could be further from the truth, Röpke insisted. Social engineering would not only fail to achieve the ends promised, it would lead to decay and destruction of human society.[10]

In his exposition of different types of economic order, Walter Eucken demonstrated, along lines parallel to Mises', that beyond that most elemental primitive social order, a centrally planned society would lack the methods necessary to record and register effectively the relative scarcities of goods and resources, so as to estimate correctly their relative values in alternative uses. The competitive market finely and continually registered changes in each of the multitudes of supplies and demands throughout a complex economy through movements in prices, that then served as the coordinating tools for the economy-wide interdependency of all sectors of the economy.[11] In this argument, Eucken was complementing and reinforcing the analysis that Hayek gave in his famous essay on 'The Use of Knowledge in Society'.[12] Furthermore, Eucken applied his critique of the centrally planned economy to the historical experience of the Nazi command economy. Everything that the Austrians and German liberals had said, 'in theory', about the impossibility and inefficiencies of central planning was shown by Eucken to have been, in fact, the case in the Nazi economic order.[13]

The Austrians and the German liberals were no less united in their arguments against many of the activities of the interventionist state. Both emphasized the interdependency of the economic order. State interventions introduced in particular corners of the market - whether they were price or production controls - inevitably brought about imbalances, not only in the market in which the intervention had been introduced, but over time in related markets with which the initially affected sector of the economy had relationships of product and price complementary and substitution.[14] It was these types of price and wage interventions that Austrians and many of the German liberals saw as a reason for the intensity and duration of the Great Depression.[15] (Some of the German liberals, most notably Wilhelm Röpke, however, believed that a 'secondary depression', having more to do with perverse expectations and cumulative contractions of income and output, had created a situation in which wage and price flexibility was not enough to generate an economic recovery.)[16]

But most importantly, what the Austrians and the German liberals were especially united in was their shared sense of modern collectivism's philosophical and moral threat to the free and open society. Mises emphasized that the Marxian and Nazi revolutions represented revolts against reason, with their respective premises of class and race-based logic and consciousness. These, in Mises' view, were reactionary movements attempting to take society back to an anti-rational, tribal past.[17] Hayek argued that historicism and collectivism represented rejections of both methodological and political individualism, that not only led to wrong theories concerning the nature of man and society, but threatened a return to the slave society, as well.[18]

But the moral dangers of these ideological and philosophical trends in the early and middle decades of the 20th century were emphasized most strongly, among the German liberals, by Wilhelm Röpke and Alexander Rüstow.[19] The sickness of the 20th century did not have its cause in the economic crisis that began in 1929 or in the growth of dictatorships and the total state. These were symptoms for deeper diseases in the social body.[20] Scientism conceptually reduced man to manipulatable quantitative matter, stripped of any spiritual and a moral qualities; the triumphs of the natural sciences, in giving man increasing mastery over nature, had generated an arrogance of knowledge and power among intellectuals, leading them to believe that society could be reconstructed according to a preferred design, with the individual reduced to a mere cog in the machine. Scientism and historicism were twin forces undermining all conceptions of morality and truth outside and beyond the external observations of the laboratory experiment.

'It is a type of thought which relentlessly ignores mankind as a spiritual and moral entity and which knows almost nothing of these eternally human and social values,' Röpke insisted. These forces create a 'combination of scientific hubris and engineering mentality which hoped to be able to do just as it pleased with Man and society,' and generated a 'tendency to cultivate the moral sciences according to the methods of the natural sciences and to limit oneself to what can be measured, weighed and documented'.[21]

But while the Austrians and German liberals shared the same outlook and concerns about the general trends and dangers from scientism, historicism and collectivism in the 20th century, their visions of the good and free society to put in place of these dark forces, while often running on parallel lines, were not the same. A large part of the reason for these differences had to do with their diagnoses of the causes of the maladies of society. And these differences in diagnoses were based upon their differing interpretations of the history and consequences of industrial capitalism in the 19th and early 20th centuries.

AUSTRIAN AND ORDO LIBERAL INTERPRETATIONS OF THE HISTORY AND CONSEQUENCES OF INDUSTRIAL CAPITALISM

If collectivism and totalitarianism were the enemies against which the Austrians and German liberals were united, they also believed that the only alternative to secure both liberty and prosperity was the market economy and a constitutional order that restrained government and protected individual freedom. Only the market could provide the institutional arrangements for economic coordination through competition and the price system. The market economy also was an indispensable mechanism for decentralizing power, both private and governmental.

There remained, however, the issue of what were to be the functions of the state, even in a social order predominantly built around the institutions of the market. On this question the commonalty of views among the Austrians and the German liberals began to break down. A central reason for the divergence of views at this point had to do with their respective interpretations of the history of industrial capitalism.

The members of both schools of thought considered the emergence of capitalism and industrialism as immensely beneficial to the average, common man. Capitalism freed man from the oppressive status society of earlier ages and generated expanding opportunities for individual improvement and rising standards of living. Liberal capitalism restrained governments and widened the circles of human life that were depoliticized and private. An Austrian like Ludwig von Mises and a German liberal like Wilhelm Röpke could both wax eloquent on the benefits of the freer society that liberal capitalism had opened up for 'the common man' in the 19th century.[22]

But the world that liberal capitalism had built in the 19th century was not without its flaws. Private power in the forms of monopolies and cartels had begun to emerge in the Western economies in the last third of the 19th century. Significant discrepancies in wealth and income persisted among groups in the society. Industrial life was often harsh and demanding for those who found new employments in the factory system. Industrial cities became congested and unaesthetic in the eyes of many.

The analysis of the nature, causes and cures for these conditions separated

Austrians like Mises from German liberals like Röpke, Eucken and Rüstow. For Mises, the problem of monopolies and cartels was one that had its origin in continuing state intervention in the market. Legally unrestricted entry into the market was the best guarantee against 'private power'. The persistence or emergence of monopolies and cartels in the market, Mises argued, had primarily arisen from the continuing ability of the state to bestow entry-limiting privileges upon some producers in the market. The liberal solution, in Mises's view, was to repeal these privileges and prevent the state from introducing any such restrictions in the future. Monopoly power in the market, argued Mises, could only arise if a producer could acquire exclusive control of a vital resource, without which neither a particular product nor any close substitutes could be offered to consumers. Mises was convinced that there were few resources or raw materials possessing such unique qualities and in such a limited supply that it had been or was possible for a private producer to obtain such 'private power' on the free market. The only essential anti-monopoly policy for any government was non-intervention in the market.[23]

German liberals like Walter Eucken and Wilhelm Röpke took a different view. On the one hand, they agreed that a fundamental flaw in governmental policy in the late 19th and early 20th centuries, especially in Germany, had been either to tolerate or to foster the establishment of cartels and monopolies over certain industries. But in Eucken's view there was a distinction between free competition and freedom of contract. Unless restrained by law, participants in the market could enter into contracts that could establish cartels, and thus constrain competition on the market. The government, therefore, needed to do more than merely abstain from intervention in the market; it needed actively to prevent private actions that potentially would restrict market choices and options.[24]

Röpke agreed with Eucken, and also argued further that 'bigness' itself on the market, and the striving for and the worship of the 'colossal' in industry as well as in government, had been a flow in 19th-century capitalism. Röpke, good economist that he was, understood the advantages of economies of scale for the very mass production that had raised the standard of living of the 'masses', but gigantism in industry and manufacturing distorted the social order and created the potentials for private abuse of power on the market. He, too, therefore, concluded that government needed to limit the growth of industrial giants that might overpower the markets in which they functioned.[25]

Rüstow shared Eucken's and Röpke's views, arguing that monopoly in the 19th century became more of an ideal among private producers, with government openly and secretly fostering the formation of cartels. Only an active government policy to prevent these tendencies could help to stop one of the forces producing 'capitalist degeneration'; but his emphasis was more on the need for government to resist pandering to the privileges and subsidies demanded by private producers from the state.[26]

Austrians like Mises also drew different conclusions than their German liberal colleagues about the effect of industrial capitalism on the standard of life and the living conditions of the 'working class'. In Mises' view, the market economy in the 19th century had been the great liberator of the poor. The free market had deproletarianized the lowest social strata of society by raising standards of living to such a point that even 'the masses' became 'bourgeois' in their thoughts and deeds.[27] Industrial capitalism had freed women from dependency and implicit bondage to their fathers or husbands. The market economy, with its rule of contract rather than status, had enabled women to be free agents with increasingly equal rights before the law.[28] The factory system, while involving long hours and tiring work, had been the saviour of untold numbers of children, who otherwise would have died from famine or the low standard of living in the climatic uncertainty of rural life. Legal restrictions on child and female labour, therefore, were, in fact, anti-children and anti-women.[29]

This was not, in general, a view held by many of the German liberals, especially Röpke. They argued that industrialization and urban life, regardless of its economic benefits, had created the 'proletarianization' of masses of people. They were cut off from their roots of family, community and tradition; they were grey masses working in giant grey factories, residing in grey urban housing complexes. Culture and beauty were lost in this environment.[30]

Not all German liberals took as dark a view of industrial society as Röpke, just as not all Austrians took as non-interventionist a view as Mises. Yet, in general, these were the lines of alternative interpretation of the fruit of industrial capitalism in the two schools of thought. (While Friedrich Hayek would be considered, not only an 'Austrian', but a follower of Mises on most policy views, in fact, he held many policy positions that could be considered closer to the German liberals than to Mises.)[31]

THE GERMAN ORDO LIBERALS, THE SOCIAL MARKET ECONOMY AND ITS CONSEQUENCES

The German liberals believed that the free society had to contain a degree of government intervention far greater than many of the Austrians considered desirable. But in the eyes of the German liberals, these interventions should be of a particular type, with very special purposes in mind. In the early 1930s, Rüstow had suggested a system of liberal interventionism.[32] Röpke took this idea and formalized it in the context of comfortable and non-conformable interventions. The distinction referred to whether the interventions distorted and unbalanced market relationships, and therefore made more interventions necessary to redress the negative effects of the first interventions; or whether the interventions were consistent with the general laws of market relationships, while only modifying certain industrial or income patterns to generate an overall outcome more consistent with certain social and moral standards deemed desirable for societal harmony.[33]

In the context of their criticism of the shortcoming of the unregulated market economy, in the years immediately after World War II some of the German liberals developed a theory of economic policy under the heading of the 'social market economy'. This term was coined and explained in terms of governmental functions by Alfred Müller-Armack in the late 1940s.[34] An elaboration of the types of 'social' policies needed to maintain a free and healthy market economy was also laid out by Walter Eucken.[35] Müller-Armack explained the purpose and the goal of the social market economy:

> The aim must be to establish a market economy tempered by social safeguards which are consistent with free-market principles. ... What we need is an all-embracing system which unites intellectual and personal freedom with social security. ... The ideals of freedom and social justice can indeed be linked together on the foundation of the market economy.[36]

In the free society, according to Müller-Armack, Eucken and Röpke (though, in fairness, each placed different emphases on these points, and several of them were not listed in Eucken's elaboration of the responsibilities of the government), the duties of the state would include the following:

1. regulation of the sizes of industries to prevent concentration of economic power;
2. redistribution of income through the tax system to modify unacceptable or socially destabilizing inequalities of wealth;
3. a series of social insurance programmes to meet certain minimal requirements for some segments of the society;
4. centralized monetary control to help establish and maintain a stable market order;
5. occupational training for better planning of a skilled workforce to meet the needs of industry;
6. influencing the degree of industrial versus self-employment through use of the tax incentives;
7. environmental regulation and control of natural resources;
8. urban and rural planning to direct and control industrial and residential patterns for a 'balanced' living environment.

In the view of the German liberals, these economic policies, while inconsistent with the older, 19th-century classical liberal conception of the state's functions, were necessary to preserve a functioning market economy in the long run, and represented interventions that were conformable with the market order.

However, by 1950, a mere two years after the beginning of the German economic reforms, Röpke asked, 'Is the German Economic Policy the Right One?' He still defended the 'social market' interventionist state, but he was worried that state expenditures on various social programmes were already getting beyond the bounds of conformable interventionism.[37] Later in the 1950s, Röpke expressed his deep concern that the welfare functions of the government, in Germany and the West in general, were expanding so much that the individual was rapidly become a ward of the state, losing all sense of responsibility for himself and his family.[38] Alexander Rüstow expressed the same fears in a paper suggesting that the social market economy in Germany and other Western economies was in danger of following 'the other road to serfdom', through a growing state welfare dependency by the people.[39] Similar fears and concerns were expressed by proponents of the German liberal approach in the 1970s and 1980s.[40] Not only had the government increasingly extended its welfare statist controlling functions, but state intervention in industrial and market activity was being used more and more to serve special interests at the expense of market freedom and consumer choice.

The general consensus among many of the German liberals on why this perverse turn of events was occurring was that government policy had been captured by those ideologically further to the left; and economic policy increasingly was coming under the influence, if not control, of various special interest groups who wished to use the state's redistributive and regulatory powers for their own benefit.

Christian Watrin, for example, said that the social market economy's maintenance and success were dependent upon a fundamental consensus among the population of a country that the system was desirable and worth defending.[41] But the consensus that government should intervene 'this far, but not further', had broken down as an increasing portion of the population wanted more from the state than the German liberals had wanted the government to do. That the social market economy could be used for various purposes and with greater or lesser degrees of intrusive intervention had been understood in the 1940s by Müller-Armack.

How had the German liberals expected to prevent this expansion of the state's 'social' functions beyond the limits that they thought desirable? They were not ignorant of the power of special interests, indeed they considered the influence of such interests on policy as the reason why state intervention so often led to outcomes damaging to the health and prosperity of society.[42] What they seemed to count on was the 'strong state'; that is, a state powerful enough to resist the pressures and temptations of special interests, and a state managed by 'statesmen' and professional civil servants who would be guided by a conception of the 'good of society' according to the types of ideas held by the German liberals concerning what the government should and should not do in terms of its power to intervene into market affairs.[43] Their hopes have turned out to be not well founded.

THE AUSTRIAN ECONOMISTS AND THE LIMITS OF ECONOMIC POLICY

At the end of his book on *Socialism*, Ludwig von Mises included a section on what he called, 'Destructionism'. This was his term for what has become known as the welfare state. Among the types of economic policies that he considered destructive in their effect on the social order were compulsory social insurance, unemployment insurance, taxing policies that were used either to confiscate income and wealth or to influence its distribution among segments of the society, and labour legislation favouring unions or controlling the conditions and hours of work.[44]

These are the types of policies that slowly eat at the moral and economic fibre of a society. Through them individuals lose their sense of self-responsibility and increasingly look for ways for personal gain, not through the market, but by use and manipulation of the political rules of the game. With every step away from the market determining the use of resources, the direction of production and the incomes earned by participants in the exchange-based system of division of labour, the state increases its influence and control over these matters. They are politicized to the degree that the state intervenes in market affairs. Relative income shares are determined to that degree by politics, rather than the market.[45] And, for this reason, Mises considered all such interventions as stepping-stones on the road to socialism, the 'other road to serfdom' to which Rüstow referred.

From this perspective the distinction that many of the German liberals made between conformable and non-conformable interventions loses its significance. State intervention for industrial regulation or income redistribution along the lines advocated by Röpke, Müller-Armack and Eucken are no less disruptive and distortive than the types of more direct interventions in the price system, against which they were such articulate opponents.[46] It is just that the disruptive and distortive effects are more subtle, indirect and time-consuming in having their full effect.

Long before the public choice theorists offered their insightful analysis of the economics of the political process, the Austrians explained many of the same phenomena. In his 1934 book on *The Limits of Economics*, Oskar Morgenstern devoted a chapter to the problem of 'The Distribution of Effects of Economic Policy'.[47] All government economic policy, Morgenstern stated, has as its purpose the bestowing of some economic benefits on groups who would not acquire various net gains if not for the intervention.

But the full impact of the intervention is never felt immediately by all segments of the economic community. As with any change in market conditions, its influence is first felt in the sectors of the economy in which the interventions have been 'injected' into the system, and then they slowly work their way from one part of the economy to the next. This creates, Morgenstern explained, a pattern of biased influences among different sectors of the economy, which has become known more recently through the public choice literature as the process of the 'concentration of benefits and diffusion of costs' due to the introduction of political interventions within the market.

As the effect of an intervention sequentially has an impact on first one sector of the economy and then another, a widening circle of groups in the social system of division of labour have their material interest affected by it. More and more groups have 'an interest' in the intervention's impact upon them. The introduction of redistributive income transfers to ameliorate supposed inequalities in wealth do not only have importance for those groups immediately affected positively by the transfer. As these beneficiaries expend their politically transferred income, various sectors of the market become dependent upon this now increased spending stream as a source of additional revenue, and they have an incentive to want it to continue in the future. There emerges an expanding circle of interest groups who have an incentive and a profit motive to lobby and pressure for its continuance and its increase. Thus income transfers, even of the 'modest' and 'limited' type that had been advocated by the German liberals, slowly build up a larger and larger constituency for politically based economic gain. Hence the special interest politics that the German liberals had considered to be the scourge of many of the bad policies of the past were reinforced rather than weakened by the very income transfer policies they proposed. This helped create the momentum for the politicization of the market-place they protested against as the post-World War II decades went by.

This same logic applied to their 'social market' policies for industrial and environmental regulation, urban and rural planning, social insurance and occupational training programmes, and indicative planning to influence employment patterns through the tax code.[48]

In his proposal for a 'social market economy', Müller-Armack had called for the 'ideals of freedom and social justice' being 'linked together on the foundation of the market economy'. But what is 'social justice'? To this question, Friedrich Hayek has given the answer: it is a mirage that has no tangible substance and actually serves as a philosophical and ideological cover for income transfers and redistribution of power from individuals to the state.[49]

Indeed, the fundamental mistake that the German liberals made on this point was implicitly to accept the socialist critique of income distribution under capitalism. The old classical liberals of the 19th century had not denied that income might be 'unjustly' acquired or maintained. But their argument was that the injustice had its origin in the fact that the recipients of these income shares had obtained them by political means rather than through offerings of market-valued goods and services to consumers. Their answer was repeal of the privileges or barriers to market competition that had established these unjust relationships among groups in society.[50]

But the German liberals had implicitly accepted the socialist idea that one could have a policy norm for the distribution of income other than, and different from, the relative income earnings resulting from the market competition between suppliers and demanders. They may very well have had a conception of the appropriate floors and ceilings that should be established for minimum and maximum incomes in the society, but how could they prove that theirs was the appropriate, or 'more just', degree of redistributed income shares, compared to more egalitarian advocates to their political left? Besides which, philosopher-kings do not dictate social and economic policy in a democracy, it is 'the people', in the form of coalitions of special interest groups. And as long as the state is endowed with the authority and power to take the wealth and income of some and transfer it to others through the political process, then the 'socially just' distribution of wealth will be determined by those coalitions of sectorial interests.

Indeed, the only way in which the 'social market economy' could have been kept within the bounds of interventionist discretion preferred by the German liberals would have been through an authoritarian state controlled by themselves or those who had like minds. Yet it was to escape from the nightmare of dictatorial government in Germany that they advocated the re-establishment of a democratic order and a market economy after World War II. They were caught in a dilemma from which there was no escape, given the prevalence of ideological advocates and various special interests with economic policy visions and goals different from their own.

In the revised, second edition of *Human Action*, Ludwig von Mises added some remarks on the 'social market economy' worth quoting:

> The supporters of the most recent form of interventionism, the German 'soziale Marktwirtschaft' [social market economy], stress that they consider the market economy to be the best possible and most desirable system of society's economic organization, and they are opposed to the government omnipotence of socialism. But, of course, all these advocates of a middle-of-the-road policy emphasize with the same vigor that they reject Manchesterism and laissez-faire liberalism. It is necessary, they say, that the state interfere with the market phenomena whenever and wherever the 'free play of the economic forces' results in conditions that appear as 'socially' undesirable. ... If it is in the jurisdiction of the government to decide

whether or not definite conditions of the economy justify its intervention, no sphere of operation is left to the market. ... For as soon as the outcome brought about by the operation of the unhampered market differs from what the authorities consider 'socially' desirable, the government interferes. That means the market is free as long as it does precisely what the government wants it to do. It is 'free' to do what the authorities consider to be the 'right' things, but not to do what they consider the 'wrong' things; the decision concerning what is right and what is wrong rests with the government.[51]

The German liberals devised the idea of the 'social market economy' and its accompanying policy tool of 'conformable' interventionism as a 'third-way', between the tragedy and failure of comprehensive collectivism and what seemed to them to be the unacceptable harshness of *laissez-faire* liberalism. Yet now, at the beginning of the 21st century, it is clear that this third way does not offer a stable and market-conformable alternative to both socialist central planning and *laissez-faire* liberalism. Its unintended consequences tend to result in its degeneration into a system of inconsistent and often contradictory interventions manipulated by special interests (including the interests of the political authorities themselves) and susceptible to the political influences of ideological pressure groups. Once having accepted the premise that the state should and can intervene to redress supposed abuses, injustices and anti-social market outcomes, there really remains no corner of the market free from governmental inspection and control.

The Austrians, and especially Ludwig von Mises, seem, therefore, to have been right: there is no alternative to the unhampered market economy of *laissez-faire* liberalism. This is a difficult conclusion for many in society to accept. In spite of the demise of communism, the socialist critique of capitalist society still implicitly dominates the thinking of most intellectuals and many in the general population. Capitalism is harsh, potentially exploitive and unjust when left to its own natural course, this socialist critique of the market economy argued. This is still the view of many, and the rationale for the view that the market cannot be left unregulated and unsupervised by the state. This is the myth that must be given up, a myth that was perpetuated by, among others, these German liberals who sincerely wanted to preserve a free society.

Myth breaking is no easy task, especially when it is propounded in the government-run schools, in the mass media and in the popular histories of the 19th and 20th centuries. But if a truly free society is to be possible in the 21st century, it is a task that must be successfully accomplished.

NOTES

1. See R.J. Rummel, *Death by Government* (New Brunswick: Transaction Books, 1994) for a comprehensive summary of the human cost of statism and collectivism around the world in the 20th century.

2. See Chapter 6 of the present volume, and Richard M. Ebeling, 'Free Trade, Managed Trade and the State', in Richard M. Ebeling and Jacob G. Hornberger (eds), *The Case for Free Trade and Open Immigration* (Fairfax, VA.: The Future of Freedom Foundation, 1996) pp.7–27.
3. See William Henry Chamberlin, *Collectivism: A False Utopia* (New York: The Macmillan Co., 1938) and William E. Rappard, *The Crisis of Democracy* (Chicago: University of Chicago Press, 1938), for examples of analyses of the crisis of the inter-war period by two classical liberals expressing these types of fears.
4. See Chapter 7 of the present volume.
5. On the historical background and ideas of the Austrian Economists, see Chapter 2 of the present volume, and Ludwig M. Lachmann, 'The Significance of the Austrian School of Economics in the History of Ideas' [1966], in Richard M. Ebeling (ed.), *Austrian Economics: A Reader* (Hillsdale, MI: Hillsdale College Press, 1991) pp.17–39. On the historical background of the German ORDO liberals and their ideas, see Konrad Zweig, *The Origins of the German Social Market Economy – the Leading Ideas and their Intellectual Roots* (London: Adam Smith Institute, 1980); and A.J. Nicholls, *Freedom with Responsibility: The Social Market Economy in Germany, 1918–1963* (Oxford: Oxford University Press, 1994).
6. The Austrians and the German liberals, of course, were not alone in defending the universality of general laws of economics; see, for example, the clear statement on this matter by the Swedish economist, Eli Heckscher, 'A Plea for Theory in Economic History', *Economic History* (Jan., 1929) 525–34, and the most influential formulation of the general 'logic of choice' during this period in English by Lionel Robbins, *An Essay on the Nature and Significance of Economic Science* [1932; 2nd rev. edn, 1935] (London: Macmillan, 1971).
7. Ludwig von Mises, 'Economic Calculation in the Socialist Commonwealth' [1920] in F.A. von Hayek (ed.), *Collectivist Economic Planning* (London: George Routledge and Sons, Ltd., 1935) pp.87–130; and Mises, *Socialism: An Economic and Sociological Analysis* [1922, 2nd rev. edn, 1932] (Indianapolis, IN: Liberty Classics [3rd rev. edn, 1951] 1981).
8. Ludwig von Mises, *Human Action, A Treatise on Economics* [1949] (Chicago: Henry Regnery, 3rd rev. edn, 1966) pp.257–326; 'Profit and Loss' [1951], in *Planning for Freedom* (South Holland, IL: Libertarian Press, 1980) pp.108–50; Franz Böhm, 'Rule of Law in a Market Economy', in *Germany's Social Market Economy: Origins and Evolution*, Alan Peacock and Hans Willgerodt (eds) (London: Macmillan, 1989) pp.46–67.
9. F.A. Hayek, *Individualism and Economic Order* (Chicago: University of Chicago Press, 1948) pp.119–208.
10. Wilhelm Röpke, *The Social Crisis of Our Time* [1942] (Chicago: University of Chicago Press 1950) pp.83–99 and 153–9; *Civitas Humana: A Humane Order of Society* (London: William Hodge and Co., Ltd., 1948) pp.11–24 and 45–9.
11. Walter Eucken, *The Foundations of Economics: History and Theory in the Analysis of Economic Reality* [1940] (Chicago: University of Chicago Press, 6th rev. edn, 1950) pp.117–220; 'What Kind of Social and Economic System?' [1948], in *Germany's Social Market Economy: Origins and Evolution*, Alan Peacock and Hans Willgerodt (eds) (London: Macmillan, 1989) pp.27–45.
12. F.A. Hayek, 'The Use of Knowledge in Society' [1945], in *Individualism and Economic Order* (Chicago: University of Chicago Press, 1948) pp.77–91.
13. Walter Eucken, 'On the Theory of the Centrally Administered Economy: An Analysis of the German Experiment', Parts I and II, *Economica* (Feb. and Aug., 1948) 79–100 and 173–93.
14. Ludwig von Mises, *Critique of Interventionism* [1929] (Irvington-on-Hudson, NY: The Foundation for Economic Education, 1996); Wilhelm Röpke, *Economics of the Free Society* [1937] (Chicago: Henry Regnery Co., 9th rev. edn, 1961) pp.142–6; Walter Eucken, 'What Kind of Economic and Social System?', pp.29–31.
15. Ludwig von Mises, 'The Causes of the Economic Crisis' [1931], in *On the Manipulation of Money and Credit* (Dobbs Ferry, NY: Free Market Books, 1978) pp.173–203; 'The Myth of the Failure of Capitalism' [1932], in Richard M. Ebeling (ed.), *Selected Writings of Ludwig von Mises*, Vol. 2: *Between the Two World Wars: Monetary Disorder, Interventionism, Socialism, and the Great Depression* (Indianapolis: IN: Liberty Fund, 2002) pp.182–91; Franz Böhm, 'The Non-State ("Natural") Laws Inherent in a Competitive Economy' [1933],

in Wolfgang Stützel, Christian Watrin, Hans Willgerodt and Karl Hohmann (eds), *Standard Texts on the Social Market Economy* (New York: Gustav Fischer, 1982) pp. 107-14.

16. Wilhelm Röpke, *Crises and Cycles* (London: William Hodge and Sons, Ltd., 1936) pp. 119-34.

17. Ludwig von Mises, *Human Action*, pp. 72-91.

18. F.A. Hayek, *The Counter-Revolution of Science* [1942] (Glencoe, IL: The Free Press, 1955); *The Road to Serfdom* [1944] (Chicago: University of Chicago Press, 1967).

19. See Daniel Johnson, 'Exiles and Half-Exiles: Wilhelm Röpke, Alexander Rüstow and Walter Eucken', in *German Neo-Liberals and the Social Market Economy*, Alan Peacock and Hans Willgerodt (eds) (London: Macmillan, 1989) pp. 40-68.

20. Wilhelm Röpke and Alexander Rüstow, 'A Note on the Urgent Necessity of Re-Orientation of Social Science', prepared for the Walter Lippmann Colloquium sponsored by the International Institute for Intellectual Cooperation held in Paris, August, 1938; Alexander Rüstow, 'General Sociological Causes of the Economic Disintegration and Possibilities of Reconstruction', an appendix in Wilhelm Röpke, *International Economic Disintegration* [1942] (Philadelphia, PA: Porcupine Press, 1978) pp. 267-83; Wilhelm Röpke, 'A Value Judgment on Value Judgments', *Revue de la Faculté des Sciences Economiques d'Istanbul*, Vol. III, Nos 1-2 (1942) 1-19; *The Social Crisis of Our Time* [1942] (Chicago: University of Chicago Press 1950); *Civitas Humana: A Humane Order of Society* (London: William Hodge and Co., Ltd., 1948).

21. Wilhelm Röpke, *Civitas Humana*, pp. 55-6.

22. Ludwig von Mises, *Liberalism* [1927] (New York: The Foundation for Economic Education, 1985); Wilhelm Röpke, *The Social Crisis of Our Time*, pp. 100-13.

23. Ludwig von Mises, *Liberalism*, pp. 90-95; *Human Action*, pp. 357-79.

24. Walter Eucken, *This Unsuccessful Age, or the Pains of Economic Progress* (London: William Hodge and Co., Ltd., 1951) pp. 31-6.

25. Wilhelm Röpke, *The Social Crisis of Our Time*, pp. 62-71 and 117-21.

26. Alexander Rüstow, *Domination and Freedom: A Historical Critique of Civilization* (Princeton, NJ: Princeton University Press, 1980) pp. 454-7. This work originally appeared in three volumes in German in the 1950s. The differences between Mises, on the one hand, and Röpke and Rüstow, on the other hand, on this point came out clearly in a discussion of the causes of monopoly and monopoly power during a conference in Paris in 1938 devoted to the causes of the decline and the conditions required for the revival of classical liberalism; see Louis Rougier (ed.), *Compte-Rendu des Séances du Colloque Walter Lippmann, 26-30 Août 1938* [*Report of the Sessions of the Walter Lippmann Colloquium, August 26-30, 1938*] (Paris: Librairie de Médicis, 1938) pp. 35-42.

27. Ludwig von Mises, *Human Action*, p. 669.

28. Ludwig von Mises, *Socialism*, pp. 76-83.

29. Ludwig von Mises, *Human Action*, pp. 614-23. Hayek, in the 1950s, edited a collection of essays, based on papers delivered at a meeting of the Mont Pelerin Society, that tried to rectify the myths surrounding the industrial revolution; see F.A. Hayek (ed.), *Capitalism and the Historians* (Chicago: University of Chicago Press, 1954). Röpke took partial exception to this revisionist view of the industrial revolution; see Wilhelm Röpke, 'Der "Kapitalismus" und die Wirtschafts-historiker' ['"Capitalism" and the Economic Historian'] *Neue Zücker Zeitung*, No. 614 (16 March 1954).

30. Wilhelm Röpke, *Civitas Humana*, pp. 131-49; *A Humane Economy: The Social Framework of the Free Market* [1958] (Chicago: Henry Regnery Co., 1960) pp. 36-89. Mises and Rüstow argued over the issue of capitalism's effect on social life and unity at the 1938 Walter Lippmann Colloquium; see, Louis Rougier (ed.), *Colloque Walter Lippmann*, pp. 77-98.

31. See, especially, the sections of *The Road to Serfdom*, pp. 32-42, 119-22 and *The Constitution of Liberty* (Chicago: University of Chicago Press, 1962), Part III, pp. 253-394, devoted to the role of government in the free society and the welfare state; on this point, see Richard M. Ebeling, review of *Hayek on Hayek* in *Freedom Daily* (Sept., 1994) 39-44.

32. Alexander Rüstow, 'Liberal Intervention' [1932], in *Standard Texts on the Social Market Economy*, pp. 183-8.

33. Wilhelm Röpke, *The Social Crisis of Our Time*, pp. 184–91; *Civitas Humana*, pp. 36–4.
34. Alfred Müller-Armack, 'The Social Aspect of the Economic System' [1947], in *Standard Texts on the Social Market Economy*, pp. 5–22; 'The Meaning of the Social Market Economy' [1956], in *Germany's Social Market Economy: Origins and Evolution*, pp. 82–6; and 'The Second Phase of the Social Market Economy: An Additional Concept of a Humane Economy' [1960], in *Standard Texts on the Social Market Economy*, pp. 49–62.
35. Walter Eucken, 'A Policy for Establishing a System of Free Enterprise' [1952], in *Standard Texts on the Social Market Economy*, pp. 115–31.
36. Müller-Armack, 'The Social Aspect of the Economic System', pp. 18 and 22.
37. Wilhelm Röpke, 'Is the German Economic Policy the Right One?', in *Standard Texts on the Social Market Economy*, pp. 37–47.
38. Wilhelm Röpke, *Welfare, Freedom and Inflation* [1957] (Auburn, AL: University of Alabama Press, 1964); also *The Humane Economy*, pp. 151–90.
39. Alexander Rüstow, 'Welfare State or Self-Responsibility', paper delivered at The Mont Pelerin Society in West Berlin, Aug.–Sept., 1956.
40. Walter Hamm, 'The Welfare State at Its Limits' [1981] and Hans Otto Lenel, 'Does Germany Still Have a Social Market Economy?' [1971], in *Germany's Social Market Economy: Origins and Evolution*, pp. 171–94 and 261–72; Christian Watrin, 'How Jeopardized is the Social Market Economy?' [1978], in *Standard Texts on the Social Market Economy*, pp. 91–100.
41. Christian Watrin, 'How Jeopardized is the Social Market Economy?', p. 96.
42. Röpke, *The Social Crisis of Our Time*, pp. 124–34.
43. Alexander Rüstow, 'Liberal Intervention', pp. 185–6; Röpke, *The Social Crisis of Our Time*, pp. 191–4.
44. Ludwig von Mises, *Socialism*, pp. 424–52.
45. Mises, 'The Myth of the Failure of Capitalism', pp. 188–90.
46. For Austrian analyses of the negative effects that follow from government regulation of market activity, see Murray N. Rothbard, *Power and Market: Government and the Economy* (Menlo Park, CA: Institute for Humane Studies, 1970); Donald C. Lavoie, 'The Development of the Misesian Theory of Interventionism', in *Method, Process, and Austrian Economics: Essays in Honor of Ludwig von Mises*, Israel M. Kirzner (ed.) (Lexington, MA: Lexington Books, 1982) pp. 169–83; Israel M. Kirzner, 'The Perils of Regulation: A Market-Process Approach', in *Discovery and the Capitalist Process* (Chicago: University of Chicago Press, 1985) pp. 119–49; Sanford Ikeda, *Dynamics of the Mixed Economy: Toward a Theory of Interventionism* (London/New York: Routledge, 1997). And for an Austrian theoretical and historical analysis of the antitrust laws in the United States, see Dominick T. Armentano, *Antitrust and Monopoly: Anatomy of a Policy Failure* (New York: John Wiley & Sons, 1982), and *Antitrust Policy: The Case for Repeal* (Washington, DC: Cato Institute, 1986).
47. Oskar Morgenstern, *The Limits of Economics* [1934] (London: William Hodge & Co., Ltd., 1937) pp. 29–46; this chapter is also reprinted in Richard M. Ebeling (ed.), *Austrian Economics: A Reader* (Hillsdale, MI: Hillsdale College Press, 1991) pp. 655–69.
48. On the nature of indicative planning, see Vera Lutz, *Central Planning for the Market Economy* (London: Longmans, Green and Co., Ltd., 1969).
49. Friedrich A. Hayek, *Law, Legislation and Liberty*, Vol. 2: *The Mirage of Social Justice* (Chicago: University of Chicago Press, 1976).
50. See Ludwig von Mises, 'The Clash of Group Interests' [1945], in Richard M. Ebeling (ed.), *Money, Method and the Market Process, Essays by Ludwig von Mises* (Norwell, MA: Kluwer Academic Publishers, 1990) pp. 202–14.
51. Mises, *Human Action*, pp. 723–4; also 'Economic Freedom in the Present-Day World' [1957], in *Economic Freedom and Interventionism* (Irvington-on-Hudson, NY: The Foundation for Economic Education, 1990) p. 240: 'The German Ordo-Liberalism is different only in details from the *Sozialpolitik* of the Schmoller and Wagner school. After the episodes of Weimar radicalism and Nazi socialism, it is a return to the *Wohlfahrtstaat* [welfare state] of Bismarck and Posadovsky.'

10. The global economy and classical liberalism: past, present and future

THE UNITED STATES IN THE GLOBAL ECONOMY

Reading the headlines of the daily newspapers or watching the evening television news, the world seems like an extremely dangerous place. If a visitor from another planet were to try to draw conclusions about what human existence on earth is all about just from looking at the popular news sources, he would easily have the impression that our world is filled with nothing but wars, civil wars, ethnic conflicts, terrorist acts, organized criminal activity and random violence.

Unfortunately, these things are occurring in many places around the world and they create a degree of suffering, hardship, destruction and cruelty that is often beyond the human imagination to fully comprehend. Many people do live in social environments that truly represent a human existence that is often 'nasty, brutish, and short'.

But there is another world, one that does not fill the newspaper headlines every day and which is not as frequently depicted in the flickering pictures that cross our television screens. This is the world of commerce, industry and international exchange. For probably almost half the population of the world, and especially in western Europe, North and South America, Australia and increasing portions of Asia and eastern Europe, life is relatively peaceful and orderly. Production, not plunder, envelops the affairs of daily life. Precisely because of its common and mundane routine, it does not receive the same attention as do violent acts. The world has a lot of peace and prosperity; it just goes unnoticed unless we stop and think about what we take for granted around us. This is the world of everyday life that the United States participates in and with which it is increasingly interdependent. Perhaps some numbers will make this more obvious:[1]

- In spite of passport requirements and visa restrictions, 45·4 million people visited the USA in 1994, 43·4 million in 1995 and 48·8 million in 1998; they spent almost $78 billion in 1994, $61·1 billion in 1995 and $71 billion in 1998 during their travels in the country.
- Direct US investment around the world totalled over $621 billion in

247

1994, $711 billion in 1995, $1 trillion in 1998 and $1·13 trillion in 1999. In 1999, half was invested in Europe and about one-sixth was invested in the Asia–Pacific region, including Japan.

• Direct foreign investment in the US totalled over $502·4 billion in 1994, $560 billion in 1995, $793 billion in 1998 and $986 billion in 1999. In 1999, Europeans invested almost 60 per cent of this sum and Asians, including the Japanese, invested less than 20 per cent.

• Between 1994 and 1999, US direct investment around the world increased by 82 per cent, while foreign direct investment in the US rose by about 95 per cent.

• In 1994, the USA exported over $512 billion in goods, while importing more than $663 billion in goods. (Of total exports in 1994, about $45 billion was in the form of agricultural products, while over $402 billion was in manufactured goods.) In 1999, the US exported more than $695 billions in goods, while importing about $1 trillion in goods. (In 1999, of total exports, agricultural products amounted to almost $47 billion, while manufactured goods made up $565 billion of the total.)

• Between 1994 and 1999, US exports rose almost 37 per cent and imports rose almost 50 per cent.

The USA and many other nations have truly become an increasingly interdependent global economy, one in which goods move across borders far more often than do armies.

THE TRIUMPH OF FREE TRADE IN THE 19th CENTURY

In appreciating the fact that the world has become an increasingly global market-place, it is worth keeping in mind that this is a relatively new phenomenon in modern human history. Two hundred years ago, the dominant nation states of Europe were imbued with the ideology of mercantilism, the 18th century's version of the regulated and planned economy.[2] The mercantilist system began to be systematically challenged only in the middle of the 18th century. The challenge was mounted on the European continent by the French physiocrats and in Great Britain by the Scottish moral philosophers led by David Hume and Adam Smith. Adam Smith's *The Wealth of Nations* has justly come to be considered one of the intellectual fountainheads of modern economic liberty. With a brilliant combination of logic and historical example, Smith demonstrated, as few others had up to his day, that governmental controls, regulations and restrictions on economic freedom were the fundamental causes of extensive poverty, misuse of resources and pervasive political corruption. He declared that what Great Britain – and, indeed, any country – needed if it desired increased prosperity for all, wise use of its resources and greater justice in human relationships was a 'system of natural liberty'. Under such a system, Smith argued, 'Every man, as long as he does not violate the laws of justice, is left perfectly free to pursue his own interest his own way, and to bring both his industry and capital into competition with those of any other man, or order of men. ... The sovereign is completely discharged from a duty ... of which no human wisdom or knowledge could ever be sufficient; the duty of superintending the industry of private people, and of directing it towards employments most suitable to the interest of society.'[3]

The government, in Smith's view, would be limited to three functions: (1) the protection of the citizenry from foreign aggression; (2) the protection of the citizenry from domestic robbery and murder, which meant establishing a judicial system to administer justice; and (3) the provision of a number of limited public works that Smith believed might not be profitable for private citizens to provide but which might have a wider usefulness for the society.

But in spite of the eloquence and rigour with which Smith demonstrated the harm and futility of the mercantilist forms of planning and regulation in his day, he despaired that economic freedom would ever be triumphant. 'To expect, indeed, that the freedom of trade should ever be entirely restored to Great Britain,' he said, 'is as absurd as to expect that an Oceana or Utopia should ever be established in it. Not only the prejudices of the public, but what is much more unconquerable, the private interests of many individuals irresistibly oppose it.'[4]

And, in fact, the next several decades following Adam Smith's death in 1790 seemed to bear out his pessimism. While, under the prime ministership of William Pitt in the 1780s, Great Britain moved in directions more in line with the types of trade policies advocated by Smith, this trend reversed in the 1790s after the start of the wars that Britain began to fight with first revolutionary and then Napoleonic France. New protectionist trade barriers were imposed in the name of the war effort. Britain and France tried to enforce naval blockades against each other. Only a pervasive network of smuggling throughout Europe prevented many from going without food or clothing.[5] As Francis Hirst explained in his book, *From Adam Smith to Philip Snowden: A History of Free Trade in Great Britain*, 'When peace came in 1815 it found Great Britain exhausted by 22 years of war and protection.'[6]

But instead of reversing the controls and regulations, the British Parliament passed the Corn Laws of 1815, which were meant to ensure a protected market for British agricultural interests. No foreign wheat could be imported into the British Isles unless the domestic price were to reach an exorbitantly high level. This condemned the low-income industrial workers of British towns and cities to a meagre and expensive diet. The trade barriers also acted as restraints on the development of the emerging British manufacturing industries.

In 1820, a group of British industrialists issued a 'Merchant's Petition', declaring that they were 'against every restrictive regulation of trade, not essential to the revenue, against all duties merely protective from foreign competition'. In 1830, Sir Henry Parnell, a long-time Chairman of the Finance Committee of the House of Commons, published *On Financial Reform*. In this book he declared, 'If once men were allowed to take their own way, they would very soon, to the great advantage of society, undeceive the world of the error of restricting trade, and show that the passage of merchandise from one state to another ought to be as free as air and water. Every country should be as a general and common fair for the sale of goods, and the individual and nation which makes the best commodity should find the greatest advantage.'[7]

In 1836, an Anti-Corn Law Association was formed in London, which in 1839 was renamed the Anti-Corn Law League in Manchester. For the next seven years, under the masterful and powerful leadership of Richard Cobden and John Bright, the League fought unstintingly for the repeal of the Corn Laws and the establishment of total free trade in the British Empire. Throughout the cities, towns, and villages of Great Britain, Anti-Corn Law League chapters were opened. Hundreds of thousands of pounds were collected as voluntary donations to fund rallies, meetings, public lectures and debates. They organized a vast publishing campaign of books, monographs and pamphlets advocating the repeal of all protectionist restrictions and the freeing of all trade and commerce from government control.

From the beginning, Richard Cobden, in making his case for free trade, saw the breaking down of trade barriers as a powerful avenue for depoliticizing human relationships; by privatizing all market transactions between individuals of different countries, free trade would assist in removing many of the causes of war. 'As little intercourse as possible between Governments,' Cobden declared, 'as much connection as possible between the nations of the world.' To emphasize this, the slogan of the Anti-Corn Law League became 'Free Trade, Peace, and Good-Will Among Nations'.

Furthermore, Cobden and the Anti-Corn Law League made theirs the case for *unilateral* free trade: 'We came to the conclusion that the less we attempted to persuade foreigners to adopt our trade principles, the better,' Cobden explained in later years, 'for we discovered so much suspicion of the motives of England, that it was lending an argument to the protectionists abroad to incite the popular feeling against the free-traders ... To take away this pretence, we avowed our total indifference whether other nations became free-traders or not; but we should abolish Protection for our own selves, and leave other countries to take whatever course they liked best.'[8]

In 1841, Sir Robert Peel became prime minister; he was determined to maintain the Corn Laws as a cornerstone of British foreign economic policy, but, through one of those ironies of history, the man appointed to lead the defence of protectionism ended up presiding over the abolition of protectionism in Great Britain. Over a period of years, Peel's government lowered and in some cases eliminated many of the trade restrictions on manufacturing and industrial goods, but it baulked at reducing the trade barriers on agriculture. Under the unrelenting arguments of the free traders, Peel finally admitted, during a debate in the House of Commons in 1843, 'I am bound to say that it is our interest to buy cheap, whether other countries will buy cheap or no.' In 1845, of the 813 commodities on the import tariff restriction list, 430 were moved to the free trade list. But, still, Peel was unwilling to give way on the Corn Laws.

Then, in the autumn of 1845, the worst rains in living memory hit the British Isles and the domestic food crops were devastated. Food supplies declined, bread prices rose dramatically, and the potato harvest was destroyed in Ireland, threatening mass starvation. Young boys could be heard in the cities saying, 'I be protected and I be starving.' Daniel O'Connell led demonstrations in Ireland in which a cannon would be dragged through the streets to which was attached a sign saying, 'Free trade or this'. In November 1845, the leaders of both the Tory and Whig parties came out for repeal of the Corn Laws. In January 1846, Robert Peel told the House of Commons that the Corn Laws would be abolished. On 27 February, the resolution was approved, and the Corn Importation Bill left the House of Commons on 16 May, after passing on the third reading. The Duke of Wellington speedily ushered the bill through the House of Lords, and free trade became the law of the land in Great Britain on 26 June 1846.

Angered by his surrender to the free traders, the protectionist Tories forced Robert Peel to resign from the prime ministership the very same day free trade was triumphant in Britain. In his final public address, Peel declared that he hoped that whatever government was formed it would continue the 'application of those principles which tend to establish a freer intercourse with other nations'. And he went on to say:

If other countries choose to buy in the dearest market, such an option on their part constitutes no reason why we should not be permitted to buy in the cheapest. I trust the Government ... will not resume the policy which they and we have felt most inconvenient, namely, the haggling with foreign countries about reciprocal concessions, instead of taking the independent course which we believe conducive to our own interests. Let us trust to the influence of public opinion in other countries – let us trust that our example, with the proof of practical benefit we derive from it, will at no remote period insure the adoption of the principles on which we have acted, rather than defer indefinitely by delay equivalent concessions from other countries.[9]

Within three years, by 1849, not only were the Corn Laws gone, but so were the remaining Navigation Acts carried over from the 18th century that had required goods being imported into Britain to be carried on British ships. From then on, both goods and merchant vessels from any land could arrive in Great Britain 'as free as air and water', as Henry Parnell had wished it to be in 1830.

On 26 June 1846, Great Britain became the first country in the world to institute a unilateral policy of free trade. For the rest of the 19th century, indeed, until the dark forces of collectivism enveloped Europe during World War I, the British Empire was open to all the world for the free movement of men, money and goods. Its economic success served as a bright, principled example to the rest of the globe, many of whose member countries followed the British lead in establishing, if not completely free trade, at least regimes of much greater freedom of trade and commerce.[10]

The triumph of free trade in 1846 in Great Britain was one of the shining jewels in the crowning achievements of 19th-century classical liberalism. But not only did it represent the opening of the door to material prosperity among an expanding group of nations of the world, it also heralded an epoch of greatly depoliticized relationships that, in fact, made international trade the private affairs of individuals and not concerns of the state.[11] What type of international order was created in those last decades of the 19th century under the increasing adoption of free trade, free markets, low taxes and limited government by more and more countries in the 'civilized world' of Europe and North America? Here is one description, by the Austrian economist Oskar Morgenstern:

Before 1914 there was freedom of travel without passports, freedom of migration, and freedom from exchange control and other monetary restrictions. Citizenship was freely granted to immigrants. Short-term or long-term capital could move unsupervised in any direction, and these movements took any form. Direct foreign investments were common and welcome; securities of other countries were freely traded on most stock markets. Transfer of profits was unhampered and foreign investments were not confiscated after they had begun to show yield. Monetary standards in most countries were firmly established in gold. ... Indeed the monetary systems of some countries were tied together even more firmly by international monetary unions – for example, the Latin Union – organized so that the money of each member state could circulate freely at par in all other member states. Gold coins of all countries found their way easily in all directions. ... It is also noteworthy that international financial and commercial transactions before 1914 were among individuals (and corporations) and rarely among countries dealing as a whole. ... National boundaries were thus of small importance, as was the fact that most countries had different currencies. ... There were colonial wars, but they did not leave deep scars. There were also other wars such as the Spanish–American, the Russo–Japanese, and the Balkan war, but they were localized and occurred at the periphery of economic centers.[12]

COLLECTIVISM, FULL EMPLOYMENT, THE WELFARE STATE AND STATE MANAGEMENT OF GLOBAL TRADE

The emergence of socialism and neomercantilism towards the end of the 19th century eventually brought about the end of the classical liberal era and its epoch of free trade, free markets and free men. Beginning in the 1880s, Imperial Germany led the way in bringing about the demise of free trade, with its establishment of the welfare state and its growing drive for territorial self-sufficiency.[13] The rest of the world followed suit during World War I, when, under the argument of wartime national emergencies, every one of the belligerent nations introduced trade barriers, migration restrictions, exchange controls, national planning and abridgments of civil liberties. And the world never recovered from the repoliticizing of economic life during the war. The 'return to normalcy' in the 1920s, both in the USA and in Europe, still left intact a heavy legacy of government controls, expanded welfare statism and a new ideology of economic nationalism.[14] The Great Depression in the 1930s only intensified the growth of economic nationalistic tendencies in the general climate of political collectivism that dominated practically all the leading countries of the world.[15]

In the totalitarian countries of the inter-war period (fascist Italy, Nazi Germany and the Soviet Union) the ideology of collectivism dictated the repoliticizing of international trade. In the total state there was no domain of the private individual untouchable by the supreme political authority. As Benito Mussolini clearly expressed it: 'Against individualism, the Fascist conception is for the State. ... Fascism reaffirms the State as the true reality of the individual. ... Fascism is ... for the only liberty that can be a real thing, the liberty of the State. ... Therefore, for the Fascist, everything is in the State, and nothing human or spiritual exists, much less has value, outside the State. In this sense Fascism is totalitarian. ... Outside of the State there can be neither individuals nor groups.'[16]

In the Soviet Union, there could be no question of private trade, commerce or international exchange; the government had nationalized all the means of production and placed them under the direct control of the central planning authority, which determined, in the interests of the 'dictatorship of the proletariat', the importation and exportation of any commodities or raw materials in terms of whether or not it would serve the goals of the socialist state's 'Plan'. In fascist Italy and Nazi Germany, private trade, commerce and exchange was made subordinate to the interests and goals of 'the nation' or 'the race', respectively, for the achievement of which the state dictated the direction of production, regulated wages and prices, and controlled the flows of imports and exports.

At the same time, while not having the same extreme political implications or consequences, the interventionist-regulated economy that came to dominate the major Western democracies in the 1930s meant that international trade could not be viewed as the private affairs of various individuals, either.[17] Governments were increasingly charged with responsibility for the maintenance and stability of various national aggregates – the levels of total employment, output, and wages and prices – within their respective national borders. Keynesian economics played a crucial role in cementing this conception of the role and responsibility of governments. It was argued, by Keynes and those who developed his theoretical edifice in the 1940s, that it was possible for governments through the right mix of monetary and fiscal policies to influence the levels of national employment and output. Maintaining sufficient 'aggregate demand' to ensure continuous 'full employment' became the central principle advocated by proponents of the 'new economics'.

For the German-language edition of *The General Theory of Employment, Interest and Money*, Keynes wrote a special foreword in September 1936. He told the economists of Nazi Germany that, 'the theory of output as a whole, which is what the following book purports to provide, is much more easily adopted to the conditions of a totalitarian state, than ... under conditions of free competition and a large degree of laissez faire'.[18] I am not suggesting that Keynes was a Nazi sympathizer or an advocate of totalitarianism; such a charge would be extremely unjust. But I do suggest that Keynes did see very clearly that, if his set of policy proposals for government monetary and fiscal intervention to maintain full employment was to work, then the market forces beyond government control or direct influence had to be kept to a minimum.

One primary market force that has the potential to undermine a national policy of full employment is international trade. Government attempts to increase aggregate demand and generate greater employment can be foiled by consumers; that is, if they are free to buy foreign goods that they find more attractive or less expensive than the domestic versions for sale. The free entry of less expensive foreign commodities can undermine government attempts to maintain high domestic aggregate demand and artificially high wages and labour demands. Government attempts to stimulate domestic investment by artificially lowering interest rates through monetary expansion can also be blocked, if the savers and lenders in that country are at liberty to transfer their loanable funds to foreign markets where they can find interest rates higher than those now prevailing on the domestic market.[19]

If Keynesian 'solutions' to supposed employment problems were to work, then governments needed to have within their authority the right to raise tariffs, control the quantity of imports and exports, restrict the free flow of financial capital across borders, and influence exchange rates between currencies. The more successfully the government could control any such private sector 'leaks' out of the national economy, the greater the effect that government could hope to have over the aggregate levels of domestic output and employment. But the more the government extended its power over private sector choices and options concerning the direction of national economic activity, the narrower, necessarily, had to become the arena of strictly market-determined outcomes. And logically, therefore, the greater the 'total' control by the state over that nation's economy. Keynes was quite right (and quite honest) when he told the Nazi economists of the mid-1930s that his policy prescriptions might be more effectively applied in their fascist version of the planned economy than in the increasingly regulated but still freer market economies of the Western democracies.[20]

Seymour Harris, one of the most ardent and prolific popularizers of Keynesian economics in the 1940s and 1950s, pointed out, 'In the twenties, Keynes had made up his mind that independence in monetary policy was a *sine qua non* for sensible domestic policy; and that independence and laissez faire were not compatible. ... [In the 1940s] he now said and reiterated that Great Britain would not subject its economy to controls from without; that a country pursuing prudent policies at home must not be embarrassed by strains originating abroad; that domestic policies of each country are the primary concern.'[21]

It should be clear, however, that if every country were to follow this policy prescription, government controls, regulations and prohibitions on international trade would be the rule and not the exception. International trade frictions would be inevitable as each nation suspiciously watched the export and import policies of their neighbours for signs of danger to their respective domestic policy goals.

The global expansion of the welfare state earlier in the 20th century also required the repoliticizing of international trade. The essence of the welfare state is the redistribution of wealth. The welfare state includes direct income transfers between various groups in the society; state provision of retirement plans and healthcare insurance and services; in-kind provision by the state of various goods and services to eligible groups in the society; the guaranteeing or influencing of various relative income shares earned by different groups in the society through minimum wage laws, regulatory practices, licensing procedures, workplace health and safety standards, subsidies and direct government expenditures for various goods and services. And these are just a few of the methods and goals in a welfare state! International trade can undermine or weaken the ability of the state to fulfil any number of these redistributive purposes. Every one of these programmes requires massive amounts of tax revenues and detailed regulatory practices. Taxes siphon off private sector wealth that otherwise could have been used for savings, investment and capital formation. Taxes retard private capacities for research and development or, through government spending, redirects research and development away from strictly market-determined channels into those to which the government assigns greater political importance. Minimum wage laws, workplace health and safety rules, and regulatory restraints and procedures for the manufacture and sale of goods and services all reduce market flexibility and responsiveness to changing circumstances, both in the domestic and the international market.

The implementation of the 'safety net society', both in terms of government provision of 'social programmes' and of government guarantees of protected relative income shares, cannot be as fully assured if international trade is free and unrestricted. Goods may come in that outcompete minimum wage sectors of the economy; foreign goods may incorporate technologies and features attractive to the buying public, but which the domestic producers cannot readily match. Why? Because taxes have prevented the accumulation of the savings that could have enabled relevant private sector research and development; or because research and development is now found to have been shunted down a wrong track owing to government influence on the direction taken by R & D; or because domestic producers' shares of their nation's market may be reduced because the regulatory rules and procedures diminish their ability to match their foreign competitors' offerings to the consumers of that society. And this, in turn, can affect government welfare spending and tax receipts if, in the face of loss of market share, sectors of the domestic economy must 'downsize'. At the same time, alternative employment and investment opportunities will not be easily found or moved into, precisely because the market-place rules, regulations and restrictions imposed by the interventionist welfare state preclude relatively rapid adjustment to the changed circumstances of domestic and global supply and demand.[22]

During World War II, the Allied countries, led by the USA, decided that a return to the autarkic and beggar-thy-neighbour policies of the period between both world wars would be a disaster.[23] International trade and commerce, global access to raw materials and the opportunity for foreign investment were considered essential elements if a new world order was to be constructed; this new world order was planned to be superior to the economic nationalism of the inter-war period.[24]

But the new world order that arose out of the ashes of World War II was not like the world order before 1914. The new international economic order was not grounded in the older classical liberal notion of free trade. As the German free market economist Moritz J. Bonn pointed out in 1945, 'International economic relations can be carried out in three different ways: exclusively by private individuals and corporations; exclusively by governments; or by private persons and corporations on the one side and by governments and government institutions on the other side.'[25] Before World War I, while not completely free of government control and influence, international commerce and trade had predominantly been the affairs of private individuals.[26] In the period between the wars, international trade had fallen extensively under government control.[27] In the post-World War II period, international trade became an admittedly fairly liberal, but nonetheless intergovernmental, system of managed and controlled trade.[28]

The global economy was based upon and managed in the context of a set of international governmental organizations. The late David Osterfeld summarized this political order of international economic relations:

> The three pillars of the postwar economic world were the World Bank, intended to make long-term loans for the reconstruction of a Europe ravaged by war and to Third World countries to stimulate economic development by the creation of wealth; the International Monetary Fund, designed to insure monetary stability through the use of short-term loans; and the General Agreement on Tariffs and Trade, whose purpose was to promote an open international trading order. Together, it was thought, the three institutions would prevent a return to the economic nationalism that characterized the depression years of the 1930s when many nations engaged in 'competitive depreciation' of their currencies in order to stimulate exports while enacting tariffs in an effort to prevent imports, thereby, it was hoped, stimulating domestic production and reducing unemployment.[29]

What were the consequences in the postwar era? Looking back on the three decades after 1945, Gottfried Haberler stated, 'There is virtually general agreement that the first twenty-five or thirty years after World War II were a period of unprecedented growth and prosperity. Compared with the interwar period, the entire postwar period ... must be judged a great success. ... World trade grew by leaps and bound.'[30] And it is the continuing legacy of that fairly liberal system of managed trade that is the basis for the continuation in the growth of trade and investment outlined in the opening section of this chapter.

But beginning in the 1970s, the general trend began to be away from more liberal and freer trade to greater controlled and managed trade. The methods employed were less the traditional ones of tariff barriers and import restrictions, and more of a different kind. The techniques were explained by Jan Tumlir in the 1980s:

> The new protectionism is a very different animal. It has been growing gradually. Industries have used intelligent, long-term planning creating an expanded system of protection. The expansion proceeds sectorally; instead of an effort to reduce all imports as much as possible, we are witnessing the construction of industrial protection systems, each tailored to the special needs of the industry in question, each administered by a highly specialized bureaucracy, often co-opted into public service from the respective industry association. The system coordinates several instruments – trade restrictions, subsidies, explicit or tacit exemptions from competition or antitrust law, and elements of direct government regulation. The protectionism of the 1930s was openly adversary; the new one, however, builds on negotiations, indeed, is in a perverse way the result of international cooperation. As

a result, the new protectionism is politically stronger because it accommodates a broader range of interests. Where earlier forms of protection created vested interests in the importing country only, the new protectionism has built up almost equally strong vested interest on the export side as well. ... For all these reasons the new protectionism will be much more difficult to roll back.[31]

How has this trend come about? It is explained primarily by the factors discussed earlier. While proclaiming a belief in free trade and globalized commerce, the world in the postwar period increasingly became enveloped in the spider's web of welfare statist programmes that required governments to secure redistributive shares of income and market shares for selected and privileged sectors of their respective economies. Given the institutional responsibilities that modern governments have taken upon themselves in the name of the 'social good', the 'national interest' and the 'general welfare' as the 20th century progressed, and most especially during the last seven decades, the state's use of domestic as well as international policy tools to serve special interests feeding at the trough of the government has been inevitable.[32]

The international institutions established after 1945 have reflected this ideological, political and economic trend. Whether it be the International Monetary Fund (IMF), the World Bank or the General Agreement on Tariffs and Trade (transformed in 1995 into the World Trade Organization), the purpose has been for governments to oversee, manage and direct the pattern of international trade and investment. The IMF and the World Bank have expanded and extended their activities to more greatly influence the distribution of loanable funds to both governments and private investors, especially in Third World countries. They have also taken upon themselves the responsibility of tying such loans and credits to guidelines for economic policy reform in the recipient nations. During their almost six-decade histories, the IMF and the World Bank have followed the various interventionist and collectivist fads and fashions that have dominated public policy, whether in the industrialized countries or the Third World nations: financial support of nationalized industries, below-market interest rate loans for loss-making sectors of the economy, billion-dollar credit lines for Third World governments, sponsorship of land and income redistribution, planning schemes to foster 'balanced growth' and balanced-budget plans that tie IMF and World Bank money to tax increases.[33]

As we saw, during the first several decades of international trade relations under the General Agreement on Tariffs and Trade (GATT), global commerce was noticeably liberalized, with tariff barriers and import restrictions being significantly lowered. Yet this was not the result of free trade but rather of the particular pattern of politically managed trade agreed upon by the leading international trading players. It remained in effect only for as long as the member governments in this international organization continued to regulate the global market in the direction of freer trade.

Since the 1970s, however, the world has increasingly come to be dominated by a different set of ideas about the circumstances when international trade can be considered 'fair' and 'just'.[34] The central problem with an idea like 'fair trade' is that it is as empty and ambiguous a term as 'social justice', being able to mean almost anything that the user of the concept wishes it to.[35] As Jagdish Bhagwati has pointed out, under the heading of 'fair trade' nearly anything that one country does in terms of its domestic and trading policies can be rationalized by another government as involving 'unfair' trade practices that negatively affect or threaten its domestic industries' market circumstances. 'If everything becomes a question of fair trade,' Professor Bhagwati has pointed out, '"managed trade" will then be the outcome, with bureaucrats allocating trade according to what domestic lobbying pressures and foreign political muscle dictate.'[36]

Will the World Trade Organization (WTO) – which is an outgrowth of the GATT – be any better? The preamble of the agreement establishing the WTO states that the joint purpose of the member governments is to 'raise standards of living, ensuring full employment and a large and steadily growing volume of real income and effective demand, and expanding the production of and trade in goods and services, while allowing for optimal use of the world's resources in accordance with the objective of sustainable development, seeking both to protect and preserve the environment and to enhance the means of doing so in a manner consistent with their respective needs and concerns at different levels of development'.[37]

In the WTO's own summary of its duties and responsibilities as an international institution representing the member governments of the world, it is stated that, 'The WTO is not the "free-trade" institution it is sometimes described as – if only because it permits tariffs and, in limited circumstances, other forms of protection. It is more accurate to say it is a system of rules dedicated to open, fair and undistorted competition. ... The WTO agreement on agriculture [for example] is designed to provide fairness in farm trade.' And as a carry-over of previous GATT provisions, 'industrial countries' are 'encouraged' to 'assist developing nation members "as a matter of conscious and purposeful effort" in their trading conditions'. In other words, the WTO is delegated the responsibility to oversee the negotiation and administration of international trade agreements that have the task of reconciling the irreconcilable: the liberalization of international trade relations among the nations of the world in the political–economic context of national policies of welfare statism, interventionism, protectionism and indicative planning to foster the maintenance and growth of privileged industrial and agricultural sectors of the respective national economies of the various member nations.

All that can be expected from the WTO, therefore, is a continuation of the same types of policies that have up to now stood in the way of an actual international order of liberal free trade.

The World Trade Organization is headquartered in Geneva, Switzerland, at 154, rue de Lausanne, at the Centre William Rappard. It is highly probable that most of the executives and employees at the WTO know very little about the ideas of the man in whose name the building in which their offices are housed has been dedicated. Yet William Rappard, an economist and political scientist by training (and a long-time friend of Ludwig von Mises), was one of the most knowledgeable and respected proponents of individual freedom, free trade and democratic government in the period between the two world wars. In numerous writings he explained the disastrous consequences that must always result from collectivism, totalitarianism, economic nationalism and protectionism.[38]

In one of his finest essays, 'The Common Menace of Economic and Military Armaments', delivered in London as the Richard Cobden Lecture of 1936, after lucidly demonstrating all of the dangers and costs of economic nationalism and political collectivism, William Rappard concluded that 'the only hope of humanity therefore lies in a return to the Cobdenite ideals of individual freedom within each nation, and of economic cooperation, peace, and goodwill among all nations'.[39] He believed that a return to a regime of limited government and free enterprise was the only true path to a world in which the individual would be secure in his liberty against that greatest threat to human freedom: the state. In his brilliant 1938 book summarizing the history of democracy through the ages and the totalitarian threats it faced in the 20th century, Rappard explained why economic freedom was so important. If political freedom was to be preserved and restored, he argued,

> Our efforts would tend to relieve the state of many of the burdens under which it is staggering today and under which it cannot remain either responsive to the will of the people or respectful of their primary liberties. As we see it, the defense of democracy demands a return to greater economic freedom, without which no state, however organized, can give its citizens more than the illusion of governing themselves. If the political will of the people is again to become supreme, it must be content to assert itself over a more limited domain. It is, therefore, not only because we believe private enterprise to be more creative, more progressive, more efficient, and consequently productive of greater general prosperity than that of the state, that we venture to advocate a limitation of the latter. It is also because we believe that no state that has been allowed to become totalitarian in its activities can fail to become totalitarian in its claims on the subservience of its subjects. Our plea for more private liberty is, therefore, political no less than economic.[40]

With the end of the Soviet Union in 1991, the world saw the end of the last of the totalitarian states that originally emerged out of the wreckage of World

War I. Democratic government ended the 20th century triumphant against all the earlier collectivist and totalitarian rationales for denying people representative participation in the political process. Yet the collectivist premises still dominate domestic and international economic policy, as is clearly enunciated in the preamble to the establishment of the WTO: governments are responsible for increasing standards of living, full employment, rising real income, environmental regulation, 'optimal' resource use, and 'sustainable development'. International trade is to be pursued and regularized among the nations of the world in the context of each country pursuing these stated national objectives. Both individual freedom and a peaceful, open regime of free trade are to be subservient to these interventionist and welfare-statist goals.

In a 1937 essay, Rappard defined nationalism as 'the doctrine which places the nation at the top of the scale of political values, that is above the three rival values of the individual, of regional units, and of the international community. ... If we wished to define economic nationalism by its underlying purpose, we should say that it was a doctrine destined to serve the nation by making it not richer, but freer, by promoting not its material welfare, but its independence of foreign influences'.[41] By this definition, while not totalitarian in its compass, the world is still ruled by economic nationalism. For, as demonstrated earlier, once the state takes on responsibility for income maintenance and redistribution, welfare state 'safety nets', secured market shares for both its domestic and foreign trade sectors, and the growth of industries earmarked for privileged subsidized development – all national goals within the confines of the boundaries of the nation state – it by necessity places these goals above the liberty of its own individual citizens and an open international order. Until these last vestiges of collectivism and nationalism are set aside, the attainment of a real global economic system will be impossible. And it is clear that the World Trade Organization, on the basis of its own statement of purpose, represents little of the fundamental political–economic principles of individual liberty and free trade that were advocated by the man in whose name the building is dedicated in which the WTO has its headquarters.[42]

A FREE GLOBAL ECONOMY FOR THE 21st CENTURY

In 1927, Ludwig von Mises wrote:

> [Classical] liberalism is, from the very outset, a world-embracing political concept, and the same ideas that it seeks to realize within a limited area it holds to be valid also for the larger sphere of world politics. ... The starting point of [classical] liberal thought is the recognition of the value and importance of human cooperation ... The ultimate ideal envisioned by [classical] liberalism is the perfect cooperation of all mankind, taking place peacefully and without friction. [Classical] liberal ...

thinking is cosmopolitan and ecumenical, it takes in all men and the whole world. [Classical] liberalism is, in this sense, humanism; and the [classical] liberal, a citizen of the world, cosmopolite.[43]

The good news for classical liberals today is that the last vestiges of collectivism and interventionist welfare statism that continue to hold the world in its grip have lost their ideological and philosophic underpinnings. The brave new worlds promised by communism, fascism and Nazism – and in pursuit of which the 20th century was made a brutal nightmare for millions of people – have lost their euphoric appeals. The interventionist welfare state that grew out of a general acceptance of the Marxian and socialist critique of capitalist society has been reduced to a financially crushing political game of special-interest politics for privilege and redistributive favours.[44] The present-day political rhetoric about racism, genderism and environmentalism is merely the latest variation on the old Marxism theme of 'class conflict', that is, supposed irreconcilabilities between groups: racial groups, sexual groups, man versus animal, and plant-life groups.[45]

It is time to go beyond these reactionary, anti-individualist ideas of the recent past. It is time to pick up the threads of the ideas of classical liberalism that were broken by the opening shots of World War I. A better, freer, more prosperous world can be ours. What would such a world look like? Mises once gave an outline of such a free world, and it is worth quoting it at length:

[Classical] liberalism's proposals for the coexistence and cooperation of nations and states are only a part of the total [classical] liberal program. They can be realized, they can be made to work only within a [classical] liberal world. The main excellence of the [classical] liberal scheme of social, economic, and political organization is this – it makes the peaceful cooperation of nations possible ...

In order to grasp the meaning of this liberal program we need to imagine a world in which [classical] liberalism is supreme. Either all the states in it are [classical] liberal, or enough are so that when united they are able to repulse an attack of militarist aggressors. In this [classical] liberal world, or [classical] liberal part of the world, there is private property in the means of production. The working of the market is not hampered by government interference. There are no trade barriers; men can live and work where they want. Frontiers are drawn on the maps but they do not hinder the migrations of men and shipping of commodities. Natives do not enjoy rights that are denied to aliens. Governments and their servants restrict their activities to the protection of life, health, and property against fraudulent or violent aggression. They do not discriminate against foreigners. The courts are independent and effectively protect everybody against the encroachments of officialdom. Everyone is permitted to say, to write, and to print what he likes. Education is not subject to government interference. Governments are like night-watchmen whom the citizens have entrusted with the task of handling the police power. The men in office are regarded as mortal men, not as super-human beings or paternal authorities who have the right and the duty to hold the people in tutelage. Governments do not have the right to dictate to the citizens what language they must use in their daily speech or in what language they must bring up or educate their children.

Administrative organs and tribunals are bound to use each man's language in dealing with him, provided this language is spoken in the district by a reasonable number of residents.

In such a world it makes no difference where the frontiers of a country are drawn. Nobody has a special material interest in enlarging the territory of the state in which he lives; nobody suffers a loss if a part of this area is separated from the state. It is also immaterial whether all parts of the state's territory are in direct geographical connection, or whether they are separated by a piece of land belonging to another state. It is of no economic importance whether the country has frontage on the ocean or not. ...[46]

For [classical] liberalism there is no problem here at all. Private railroads, if quite free of government interference, can traverse the territory of many states without any trouble. If there are no tariff boundaries and no limitations on the movement of persons, animals, or goods, then it is of no consequence whether a train ride in a few hours crosses the borders of [several] states more or less often. ... An inland country believes that it needs a 'corridor' to the sea in order to keep its foreign trade free of the influence of the interventionist and [statist] policies of the countries whose territories separate it from the sea. If free trade were the rule, it would be hard to see what advantage an inland country could expect from the possession of a 'corridor'. ...[47]

There would be no more wars because there would be no incentive for aggression. War would not pay. Armies and navies would be superfluous. Policemen would suffice for the fight against crime. In such a world the state is not a metaphysical entity but simply the producer of security and peace. It is the night-watchman. ...

The reality in which we have to live differs very much from this perfect world of ideal [classical] liberalism. But this is due only to the fact that men have rejected [classical] liberalism for [statism]. They have burdened the state, which could be a more or less efficient night-watchman, with a multitude of other duties. Neither nature, nor the working of forces beyond human control, nor inevitable necessity has led to [statism], but the acts of men.[48]

If Mises' imagery of a perfect world of ideal classical liberalism seems 'radical' and 'politically impossible' or 'realistically unattainable', it is worth remembering, as we saw, that in its essence that was the world before World War I. Not perfect and not as 'pure' as outlined as an ideal by Mises, but very close, and certainly a lot closer than what most of the world experienced in the 20th century.[49]

How can we return to freedom's road in the 21st century? We must dismantle the interventionist welfare state and all of the institutions upon which it is maintained.

The Dismantling of the Welfare State as a Precondition for a Liberal International Order

The welfare state is unreformable and can never be made compatible with a civil society of peaceful and voluntary human relationships. It is in its essence what the 19th-century French free market economist Frédéric Bastiat called a system of 'legalized plunder', in which the wealth and income of one segment of society is forcibly redistributed to another segment of society as the unending product of a war of all-against-all between special interest groups of sundry sorts in the arena of democratic politics.[50]

It is vital to revive a historical memory of how, in the 19th and early 20th centuries, it was the private sector that developed charitable and for-profit methods to alleviate the human problems of a complex and changing society that in our time are considered to require intrusions by the state into the private and interpersonal affairs of the citizenry.[51] Indeed, it was only following the emergence of the state's growing intrusion into these matters that the private sector was increasingly 'crowded out'; the private sector was unable to match the government's 'unfair competition' of being about to offer the provision of these 'social' services at zero or heavily subsidized prices by taxing the general public and, at the same time, depriving the private sector of the financial resources needed to continue to offer alternative charitable options in the magnitudes required.

Furthermore, there can be no lasting hope for the development of an international order of open, free trade for as long as the state makes the provision and maintenance of such programmes matters of fundamental 'national interest'. As the German free market economist Wilhelm Röpke clearly explained, the welfare state is a major creator and reinforcer of the nationalist spirit that runs counter to such an international order:

> Since the national government is both the organizer of welfare and the compulsive agent, the fact that economic and social life become objects of political action means that they are nationalized themselves, which, in turn, means that an excessive social integration grows up within the framework of the national state, making all the more difficult the process of international integration. The more frequently appeals are made to the 'solidarity' of people who share the same passport or the same national residence the more they are forced into a self-supporting, economically isolationist 'national community', the more complete is the 'nationalization' of human beings at the expense of the free international community of nations and of international solidarity. ... While saving and private insurance are forms of provision which belong to the sphere of economics, the market, private law and freedom, and are not, therefore, confined by national boundaries, public provision belongs to the realm of politics, collectivist organization, public law and compulsion and, therefore, tends to lock people up within their national boundaries.[52]

The Abolition of the Regulated Economy as a Precondition for a Liberal International Order

When the classical liberals and free market economists in the early and middle decades of the 19th century advocated the dismantling of the 18th-century system of economic controls and regulations known as mercantilism, it was not only because they believed that such an interventionist system was incompatible with the individual's right of free, peaceful interaction with his fellow men for mutually beneficial gain. They also argued that no government, or its administrative officials, had the knowledge or ability to order and direct the affairs of private citizens better than those private persons could do for themselves. And, furthermore, they argued that the productive results of free men interacting in pursuit of their respective self-interests would generate a greater and more widely dispersed wealth of nations than under any state supervision.[53]

In our time, the interventionist system has returned in a much more comprehensive form than ever experienced before the triumph of free trade in the mid-19th century. Every facet of market activity is under the regulation, licensing and approval of the state. In the political arena, economic regulation has become the primary mechanism for those who wish to limit or eliminate competition in their respective corners of the market.[54] Furthermore, the economic theories that predominantly underlie the rationales for government regulation present a distorted understanding of the actual, dynamic market process out of which arises the creative entrepreneurial competition that generates the continual coordination of supply and demand, as well as a never-ending stream of new and improved goods and services for the consuming public.[55]

In addition, the greater the extent of domestic regulation, the more unrestricted foreign competition threatens to undermine the goals for which the regulations have been established in the first place – and the more the state must oppose free trade. This has been explained with great clarity by Mises:

A nation's policy forms an integral whole. Foreign policy and domestic policy are closely linked together, they are but one system. Economic nationalism is the corollary of the present-day domestic policies of government interference with business and national planning as free trade was the complement of domestic free trade. There can be protectionism in a country with domestic free trade, but where there is no domestic free trade, protectionism is indispensable. A national government's might is limited to the territory subject to its sovereignty. It does not have the power to interfere directly with conditions abroad. Where there is free trade, foreign competition would in the short run already frustrate the aims sought by the various measures of government intervention with domestic business. When the domestic market is not to some extent insulated from the foreign markets, there can be no question of government control. The farther a nation goes on the way to public regulation and regimentation, the more it is pushed toward economic isolation.[56]

A Sound Monetary System as a Precondition for a Liberal International Order

In the 19th century, classical liberals considered the gold standard as the monetary corollary to free trade and free markets. Having experienced the harmful consequences of paper money and inflation during the Napoleonic wars, the classical liberals were extremely suspicious of allowing governments unrestrained and discretionary control over money. By limiting the issuance of paper money to a fixed ratio of the gold left on deposit in banks, the classical liberals believed that a check would be placed on the possibility of an over-issue of depreciating currency. A sound monetary system, they argued, would serve as the financial backdrop for savings, investment and capital formation.[57] And, indeed, the gold standard of the 19th and early 20th centuries served just that valuable role. As Melchior Palyi explained:

> The gold standard was 'sacrosanct' to the generations brought up on the Adam Smith ideals of free markets, from arbitrary and discriminatory interventions of governmental powers. Indeed, it was an essential instrument of economic freedom. It protected the individual against arbitrary measures of the government by offering a convenient hedge against 'confiscatory' taxation, as well as against the depreciation or devaluation of the currency. It was an instrument of 'mobility' within and beyond national borders. Above all, it raised a mighty barrier against authoritarian interferences with the economic process. ... The gold standard in the classical sense was part and parcel of an economic order. It was a keystone of the system of public law, social customs and institutions, called 'capitalism' ... a system that rested on what appears in perspective as virtually unlimited freedom of consumer choice, business enterprise, and markets. ... The role of gold in unifying the economy of the civilized world can scarcely be overestimated. It was the condition *sine qua non* of the international capital flow, both short-term and long-term, a basic instrument in 'opening up' the world to economic progress and diffusing modern civilization.[58]

Governments in the 20th century destroyed the gold standard: first, during World War I, as each of the belligerent powers wanted the unlimited power of printing money to finance their respective war expenditures, and then during the early 1930s, as most of the major European and North American governments wanted, again, unlimited power to issue paper money as a panacea to 'cure' the mass unemployment and falling industrial production experienced during the Great Depression.[59] All of the major countries of the world became practitioners of *monetary nationalism*.[60]

Under the gold standard, each nation's currency was linked to the world supply of gold and its distribution among various countries.[61] The world's supply of gold was determined by the profitability of mining gold, given the monetary and non-monetary uses for the metal relative to the costs of mining it out of the ground. The distribution of the world's supply of gold among the nations of the world was determined by the demands for the metal in various parts of the world as reflected in its price. If the demand for gold – for whatever purposes – increased or decreased in any particular country, this set in motion a change in its distribution, with gold moving into the country in which its value had risen and flowing out of the country in which (in comparison) its value was now lower. Prices and wages tended to rise in the country into which gold flowed, and prices and wages would tend to decline in that country out of which the gold was moving. The long-term movement of gold would continue until prices had sufficiently risen in one country and declined in the other to again create a condition of equilibrium: that is, the purchasing power of a unit of gold over goods and services would be more or less equivalent in both countries. As a result, there would no longer exist any profit incentive for moving gold from one country to the other.

This is what made the gold standard an *international* monetary system. The various currencies and price structures of the major countries of the world were interconnected and interdependent through their use of gold as the common 'anchor' of the respective national currencies. This is what made the gold standard relatively independent of the changing currents and influences of national politics. As long as a country was on the gold standard and the government of that country followed 'the rules of the game' (of only expanding or contracting the quantity of its currency and bank deposit money in circulation to reflect any increases and decreases in the quantity of gold in that nation's economy), that government had no or very limited direct monetary control over the structure of prices and wages in its country.

But it was precisely this monetary control that governments wanted, especially beginning in the 1930s. The major governments of the world, including the USA, discarded the gold standard and its limitations for the purpose of instituting *national monetary planning*. Governments wanted the authority to manipulate the quantity of money in circulation so as to have the power to try to 'plan' the optimal level of prices and wages in the name of stimulating industrial expansion and full employment. And governments have continued this usurpation of authority over money in their national economies ever since. Such usurpation creates regimes of monetary nationalism, because the primary influence on both the level of, and any movements in, prices and wages in general in the various countries of the world is then controlled by the respective monetary central planners.[62]

To the extent that the respective national currencies of the world are still interconnected, this is now a matter of the various governments of the world agreeing to set limits on the movements in the foreign exchange rates between their respective currencies and to follow various domestic monetary and fiscal policies to set floors and ceilings on their respective rates of monetary expansion.

The national monetary central planners may choose on their own, or in mutual agreement with their governmental partners in other countries, to follow a conservative policy that prevents the expansion of their respective national currencies to a point at which serious inflationary processes are set in motion; but, if this is done, it is completely dependent upon the decisions of the political policy makers. There no longer exists an external check to limit monetary expansions in the same way as under the old pre-World War I gold standard.[63]

If it has generally come to be accepted that the end of communism and 'the great socialist experiment' in the Soviet Union demonstrated the unworkability and failure of economic central planning in general, why should it be thought that it is in the wisdom and power of governments (or their designated administrative agencies) to succeed in carrying out *monetary central planning*? Because that is what government management of national monetary systems really is in its essence. The government decides what shall be legally designated money. The government plans the quantity of money that shall be in circulation in the national economy. It is the government, on the basis of various policy objectives, that sets targets for what it thinks the trend in prices and wages should be, and what the level of (at least, short-term) interest rates should be, as intermediary steps to influencing investment, employment and production in the economy. Governments have neither the knowledge nor the dispassionate rationality to do these things successfully, any more than the central planners in Moscow had the knowledge or ability to plan successfully the production and distribution of shoes, hats or milk.

The classical liberal agenda for the 21st century, therefore, must include a vision of a non-governmental monetary order. The monetary order of the future should be based on a market-generated system of free banking; a free banking system would replace government central banking and with it end any government control of the money supply.[64] With the end of central banking would also come the end of monetary nationalism. The monetary system will have been privatized, with the normal market forces of supply and demand determining which commodity is selected as the money good (most likely gold and/or silver, if history is any judge); the market-determined profitability of the commodity's production, worldwide, would establish the quantity of the commodity supplied for monetary purposes. Governments would no longer have the power or the authority to manipulate the monetary standard in the name of national economic goals. In its place would arise a new monetary internationalism, a system that could generate the sound monetary foundation for a new century of global trade and prosperity.

Unilateral Free Trade as an Avenue for Moving towards the New Global Economy of the Future

Can a classical liberal global order be created in a political environment in which the governments of the world all practise in various ways, for various purposes, a vast array of interventionist–welfare statist policies? Must the first steps towards such a free trade global economy for the 21st century wait until a sizeable number of countries all come to the same political–philosophical and political–economic conclusions more or less simultaneously, so that the necessary policies can all be implemented at the same time and to the same extent across several international borders?

Quite simply, no. The British free traders of the 19th century set themselves the goals of opening the British Isles to unregulated free markets and free trade, in spite and regardless of the fact that all the other nations with which Great Britain traded and competed had chosen to retain their mercantilist and protectionist barriers against open international commerce.

For example, suppose the USA were to follow such a unilateral free trade policy. Every lowering of a tariff or import restriction immediately benefits the American consumer. Goods bought at a higher price because of the previous import duty are now purchased for less. Depending on how elastic the demand is for the foreign goods at the lower per unit price, consumers may now spend more or less than before on the larger quantities purchased. If the demand is fairly inelastic, consumers will buy more, but their total expenditures on these goods will be less. This will leave more money in their pockets to increase their demand for things that they could not afford when the imported goods were sold at the past higher tariff prices. If consumer demand is fairly elastic, when the larger quantities of these goods are purchased at the lower free trade prices, total consumer expenditures will be greater for these goods; the additional revenues earned by the foreign sellers will increase their financial ability to buy more American exports. Either way, the result is the outcome of the free market choices of the American consuming public. And, either way, demand for American goods goes up, either because of an increased demand by Americans now that they have saved some money on less expensive imports or because of the increased demand of foreign sellers who now have a greater dollar income with which to purchase American goods.

What if the government of the other country now selling more exports to America keeps its trade barriers in place and will not allow their own citizens to import more American goods? Then the dollars they have earned will either be kept in the USA and used for direct or indirect investments in the American economy or those dollars will be sold to someone on the foreign exchange market who is interested in acquiring dollars precisely because he wishes either to buy American goods or to invest in the American economy. Either way, markets are benefited in the USA.

What if the USA opens its borders to unrestricted trade and the government of another country decides to take advantage of this by subsidizing some privileged industries so they can sell more in the USA at prices below the actual market costs of production? The effect for the American consumer is the same as if the foreign manufacturer had an actual lowering of its costs of production: the good is available for less, the American buyers can purchase more and maybe save some money in the process. Some domestic American manufacturers may see a falling off in their business due to this lower-cost foreign competition, but there is always work to be done and investment that can be profitably undertaken, if only those who have capital to invest and if those who have hands to hire are willing to adjust their activities to reflect the changed market conditions. Who should complain about the subsidized exports to the USA? Surely it should be the taxpayers in the country providing those subsidies to selected and privileged segments of the foreign country's industries. It is those foreign taxpayers who suffer a redistribution of their income and wealth to the privileged special interest groups in their own country.

What if another country, in spite of the US free trade policy, decides to raise its tariffs and import restrictions against American goods? This may well reduce the market for and sales of American goods in that country, resulting in lowered profitability and diminished employment opportunities in the affected export sectors of the US economy. But what is to be done? Retaliate and raise the import duties on that country's goods that are sold in the USA? What are the consequences? The foreign exporters now earn less from sales because Americans purchase a smaller amount at the raised tariff price; this, in turn, means that those foreign manufacturers buy fewer American exports because their dollar earning will have gone down as a result of the US retaliatory conduct. At the same time, it is the American consumer who pays the higher price for the imported goods now that the tariff has been raised. American exporters lose business and the American consumer is poorer to the extent of the increase of the tariff.

More than a hundred years ago, in 1896, British economist Henry Dunning MacLeod analysed the consequences of retaliatory trade policies, using an example in which France is presumed to raise its tariffs against British goods and then Britain retaliates by raising its tariffs against French goods. He picturesquely concluded: 'By the method of retaliatory duties, when the Frenchman smites us on one cheek, we immediately hit ourselves an extremely hard slap on the other. The Frenchman, by his duties, does us an injury, and we, by retaliating, immediately do ourselves a great deal more.' MacLeod suggested that 'the *true way to fight hostile tariffs is by free trade*'.[65]

Can the USA end its regulation of or subsidies to sectors of the American economy in a world in which other governments continue to regulate and subsidize? Regulatory intervention harms (a) the American manufacturer, who is hindered or prevented from investing or utilizing his financial and real capital in ways he thinks would most likely earn him profits from better producing and marketing goods which he believes consumers desire and for which they would be willing to pay; and (b) the American consumer, who is prevented from having the variety of goods and competitive alternatives that an open, unhampered market would tend to provide. To the extent that such regulatory or licensing restrictions are repealed the American market is made potentially more open, responsive and productive in an ever-changing environment of shifting supply and demand, including that in the arena of international trade.

The elimination of subsidies to all sectors of the American economy will immediately change the configuration of profitable investments and resource uses, from those artificially created by the government's distortion of prices and costs through the subsidy programmes into a pattern of investment and resource utilization that reflects the actual market opportunities at home and abroad. And this can only improve the efficiency with which resources are applied, goods are manufactured and consumer wants are satisfied.

To the extent that other nations subsidize selected industries for purposes of advancing research and technological development, the American manufacturer is saved part of the costs he might otherwise have had to incur. He can 'jump into the market' on the back of the foreign developer who, through the tax dollars dispersed to that sector of the foreign economy, has 'worked out' the bugs and refined the technological potentials. Any investments in similar or improved technologies the American competitor finds it privately profitable to pursue will therefore have the potential to be more cost-efficient and improved versions. Rather than being left behind because a foreign government is subsidizing various 'high-tech' sectors of its economy, the American competitor can potentially leap ahead, not burdened with real capital incorporating the earlier versions that are being made obsolete with each new turn of the research and production experimentation process.

From practically every angle, therefore, the USA could follow a path of unilateral free trade and reap the benefits from doing so both in the short and the long run. Furthermore, the advantage of following such a unilateral course is that America's pace of progress towards free trade would not be controlled by or confined within the context of multilateral agreements of reciprocal tariff and other trade barrier reductions.

The USA hurts no other nation by going its own way. The governments of other nations can choose to buy high and sell low; they can surround their own citizens with protectionist walls that retard improvements in their standards of living; they can impose onerous taxes on their people in the pursuit of privileges and subsidies for some at the expense of others; they can conjure up any ideological fantasies they want to rationalize their economically irrational policies as a means to justify their actions to the citizens who must endure and bear the costs of what they do.

The example that the USA could create by pursuing a policy of unilateral free trade and radically liberated markets at home could serve as the same type of model for the world in the 21st century that Great Britain's heroic jump into unilateral free trade did for Europe and North America in the 19th century. In the late 1840s, Nassau Senior, one of the most respected British economists of his time, argued:

> For centuries, the government has labored to fetter and misdirect the industry of the people. Instead of confining itself to its true task of defending its subjects from foreign and domestic violence and fraud, it has taken on itself the task of rendering them, or of rendering certain classes of them, rich. It has dictated to them what they shall produce, and to whom they shall sell, and what they shall purchase, and to whom they shall sell, and what they shall purchase, and to what markets they shall resort. It has considered the whole body of consumers as a prey to be sacrificed to any class, or to any section of a class, that chose to ask for a monopoly ...
>
> The advocate of freedom dwells on the benefit of making full use of our own particular advantages of situation, wealth, and skill, and availing ourselves to the utmost of those possessed by our neighbors. ... He observes, in the words of Adam Smith, that it is the maxim of every prudent master of a family, never to make at home what it will cost him more to make than to buy. The tailor does not make his own shoes, but buys them of the shoemaker. The shoemaker does not make his own clothes, but buys them of the tailor. The farmer attempts to make neither the one nor the other, but employs those different artificers. All of them find it in their interest to employ their whole industry in ways in which they have some advantage over their neighbors, and to purchase, with a part of its produce, whatever else they have occasion for. And he infers, that what is prudence in the conduct of every private family, can scarcely be folly in that of a great kingdom.[66]

The world today, no matter how 'free' it seems on the surface, is fettered with the very same types of rules, regulations, controls and commands that classical economists such as Nassau Senior spoke out against more than a century-and-a-half ago. And the advocate of freedom again reminds politicians and the general public that the greater wisdom is to allow each man to have the liberty and discretion to find his own best place in a market system of division of labour, out of which can come far greater wealth and prosperity than any politically controlling hand could ever produce. If this is true, if Adam Smith and others like Nassau Senior were right, then there is no need for or use in allowing the follies of others to delay freedom in the USA, and through freedom in the USA, a new beacon light of liberty for the rest of the world.

CLASSICAL LIBERALISM AND A GLOBAL ECONOMY OF THE FUTURE

On 15 January 1846, as the battle for free trade in Great Britain was reaching its conclusion, Richard Cobden spoke before a vast crowd of 9 000 people in Manchester, England. Assuring his listeners that their goal of abolishing protectionism and establishing a regime of free trade was now finally at hand after many years of effort, Cobden at the end of his address chose to reflect on the wider and more far-reaching consequences that he believed were ahead, following the triumph of freedom of trade:

> I can say that I have taken as large and great a view of the effects of this mighty principle [of free trade] as ever did any man who dreamt over it in his own study. ... I see in the Free Trade principle that which shall act on the moral world as the principle of gravitation in the universe – drawing men together, thrusting aside the antagonism of race, and creed, and language, and uniting us in the bonds of eternal peace. I have looked even further. ... I believe that the effect will be to change the face of the world. ... I believe that the desire and the motive for large and mighty empires; for gigantic armies and navies ... will die away; I believe such things will cease to be necessary, or to be used, when men become one family, and freely exchanges the fruits of his labor with his brother man.[67]

A dream? Perhaps. But free trade and its classical liberal underpinning did change the world in ways that, while not as fantastic as in Cobden's prevision of the future, were nonetheless momentous, as we have seen. The accomplishment of more of Cobden's dream was cut short by the counter-revolution of collectivism in its socialist, interventionist and welfare statist forms in the 20th century. The counter-revolution has now petered out. Classical liberal ideas concerning human freedom, the crucial importance of private property, the value of individual self-responsibility and the need to limit government to a narrow 'night-watchman' function are beginning to have a renewed life following the wreckage of statism. And if it is triumphant, the global economy of the 21st century may very well bring with it a world of individual liberty, international peace and cosmopolitan prosperity. What a reward after the agony of the 20th century, if only we have the understanding and the will to try!

NOTES

1. These statistics are taken from the 1995, 1996 and 2001 editions of *The World Almanac and Book of Facts* (Mahwah, NJ: Funk & Wagnalls); see also the data on the pattern of world trade and investment during the last several decades in Douglas A. Irwin, *Free Trade Under Fire* (Princeton, NJ: Princeton University Press, 2002) pp. 5–20.
2. The next several pages on the history of the success of the free trade movement in

274   *Austrian Economics and the Political Economy of Freedom*

19th-century Great Britain draw on Richard M. Ebeling, 'Free Trade, Peace and Goodwill Among Nations: The Sesquicentennial of the Triumph of Free Trade', *Freedom Daily* (June 1996) 10–17.

3. Adam Smith, *An Inquiry into the Nature and Causes of the Wealth of Nations* [1776], Edwin Cannan edn (New York: Modern Library, 1937) p.651.
4. Ibid., pp.437–8.
5. See Eli F. Heckscher, *The Continental System: An Economic Interpretation* [1922] (Gloucester, MA: Peter Smith, 1964) for a detailed study of the mercantilist-protectionist polices during the Napoleonic wars.
6. Francis W. Hirst, *From Adam Smith to Philip Snowden: A History of Free Trade in Great Britain* (London: T. Fisher Unwin, Ltd., 1925) p.13; for histories of the free trade movement in Great Britain, see Archibald Prentice, *History of the Anti-Corn-Law League* [1853] (New York: Augustus M. Kelley, 1968); Francis W. Hirst (ed.), *Free Trade and Other Fundamental Doctrines of the Manchester School* [1903] (New York: Augustus M. Kelley, 1968); George Armitage-Smith, *The Free-Trade Movement and Its Results* [1903] (Freeport, NY: Books for Libraries Press, 1969); John Morley, *The Life of Richard Cobden* (London: T. Fisher Unwin, 1903); and Norman McCord, *The Anti-Corn Law League, 1838–1846* (London: Unwin University Books, 1968). For a history of free trade ideas throughout the ages, see Douglas A. Irwin, *Against the Tide: An Intellectual History of Free Trade* (Princeton, NJ: Princeton University Press, 1996).
7. Quoted in Francis W. Hirst, *From Adam Smith to Philip Snowden*, p.22.
8. Quoted in J.A. Hobson, *Richard Cobden: The International Man* [1919] (London: Ernest Benn, Ltd., 1968) p.41.
9. Norman McCord (ed.), *Free Trade: Theory and Practice from Adam Smith to Keynes* (Newton Abbot, UK: David and Charles, 1970) pp.91–2.
10. Charles F. Bastable, *The Commerce of Nations*, 2nd edn (London: Methuen & Co., 1899); Frank W. Taussig, *Free Trade, the Tariff and Reciprocity* (New York: The Macmillan Co., 1920) pp.1–2; and Gustav Stolper, *This Age of Fable: The Political and Economic World We Live In* (New York: Reynal & Hitchcock, 1942) pp.7–8.
11. Wilhelm Röpke, *International Order and Economic Integration* (Dordrecht-Holland: D. Reidel Publishing Co., 1959) pp.72–9; and Richard M. Ebeling, 'World Peace, International Order and Classical Liberalism', *International Journal of World Peace* (December 1995) pp.47–68.
12. Oskar Morgenstern, *International Financial Transactions and Business Cycles* (Princeton, NJ: Princeton University Press, 1959) pp.17, 19, 21; also see John Maynard Keynes, *The Economic Consequences of the Peace* [1919] (New York: Harper & Row, 1971) pp.10–12; Gustav Stolper, *This Age of Fables: The Political and Economic World We Live In* (New York: Reynal & Hitchcock, 1942) pp.7–9; and Joseph A. Schumpeter, 'An Economic Interpretation of Our Time: The Lowell Lectures' [1941], in *The Economics and Sociology of Capitalism* (Princeton, NJ: Princeton University Press, 1991) pp.339–40.
13. See Wilhelm Röpke, *German Commercial Policy* (London: Longmans, Green and Co., 1934); Constanino Bresciani-Turroni, '"Living Space" versus an International System', *Al Qanoun Wal Iqtisad*, Vol. X, Nos 1–2 (1940) pp.35–68; Arcadius Kahan, 'Nineteenth-Century European Experience with Policies of Economic Nationalism', in Harry G. Johnson (ed.), *Economic Nationalism in Old and New States* (Chicago: University of Chicago Press, 1967) pp.17–30; and Richard M. Ebeling, Chapter 8 of the present volume.
14. See Gustav Cassel, *Recent Monopolistic Tendencies in Industry and Trade: Being an Analysis of the Nature and Causes of the Poverty of Nations* (Geneva: League of Nations, 1927); 'From Protectionism Through Planned Economy to Dictatorship' [Richard Cobden Lecture, 1934], reprinted in *Planned Society:Yesterday, Today and Tomorrow*, ed. Findley MacKenzie (New York: Prentice-Hall, 1937) pp.775–98; William E. Rappard, 'The Common Menace of Economic and Military Armaments' [Richard Cobden Lecture, 1936], reprinted in *Varia Politica: Publiés ou Réimprimés à l'occasion du soixante-dixieme anniversaire de William E. Rappard* (Zurich: Editions Polygraphiques, 1953) pp.76–100; 'Economic Nationalism', in *Authority and the Individual, Harvard Tercenterary Conference of Arts and Sciences* (Cambridge, MA: Harvard University Press, 1937) pp.74–112;

Post-War Efforts for Freer Trade (Geneva: Geneva Research Center, 1938); Allen G.B. Fisher, *Economic Self-Sufficiency*, Oxford Pamphlets on World Affairs, No. 4 (Oxford: Clarendon Press, 1939); Michael A. Heilperin, *Studies in Economic Nationalism* (Geneva: Librairie E. Droz, 1962); also Robert Higgs, *Crisis and Leviathan* (Oxford: Oxford University Press, 1987) pp. 123–94, and Robert Nisbet, *The Present Age* (New York: Harper & Row, 1988) pp. 1–83.

15. Moritz J. Bonn, *The World Crisis, and the Teaching of the Manchester School* [The Third Cobden Lecture] (London: Cobden-Sanderson, 1931); Ludwig von Mises, 'The Causes of the Economic Crisis' [1931], in *On the Manipulation of Money and Credit* (Dobbs Ferry, NY: Free Market Books, 1978) pp. 173–203; 'The Disintegration of the International Division of Labor' [1938], in *Money, Method and the Market Process: Essays by Ludwig von Mises*, Richard M. Ebeling (ed.) (Norwell, MA: Kluwer Academic Press, 1990) pp. 113–36; Lionel Robbins, *The Great Depression* (London: Macmillan Co., Ltd., 1934); *Economic Planning and International Order* (London: Macmillan Co., 1937); Fritz Machlup, *Führer durch die Krisenpolitik* (Vienna: Julius Springer, 1934); Gottfried Haberler, *Liberale und Planwirtschaftliche Handelspolitik* (Berlin: Junker und Dunnhaupt, 1934); and Wilhelm Röpke, *International Economic Disintegration* [1942] (Philadelphia: Porcupine Press, 1978).

16. Benito Mussolini, 'The Doctrine of Fascism' [1932], in *Communism, Fascism, and Democracy: The Theoretical Foundations*, Carl Cohen (ed.) (New York: Random House, 1962) pp. 351–2; see also Michael A. Heilperin, 'Totalitarian Trade', *World Affairs Interpreter* (January 1941) 1–8.

17. For a brief summary of the common features of economic policy in Hitler's Nazi Germany and Franklin Roosevelt's America under the first New Deal, see Robert Skidelsky, *The Road from Freedom: The Economic and Political Consequences of the End of Communism* (New York: Allen Lane, Penguin Press, 1996) pp. 60–63.

18. John Maynard Keynes, *The General Theory of Employment, Interest and Money* [1936] (Cambridge: Macmillan Press, Ltd., 1973) p. xvi.

19. Cf. Ludwig von Mises, 'Economic Nationalism and Peaceful Economic Cooperation' [1943], in Richard M. Ebeling (ed.), *Money, Method, and the Market Process: Essays by Ludwig von Mises* (Norwell, MA: Kluwer Academic Press, 1990) pp. 158–9.

20. See Wilhelm Röpke, 'The Economics of Full Employment' [1952], in *The Critics of Keynesian Economics*, Henry Hazlitt (ed.) (Princeton, NJ: D. Van Nostrand, 1960) esp. pp. 381–4; Michael A. Heilperin, *The Trade of Nations*, 2nd edn (New York: Alfred A. Knopf, 1952) pp. 88–105, 123–33; *Studies in Economic Nationalism*, pp. 97–128; and Henry Hazlitt, *The Failure of the 'New Economics': An Analysis of the Keynesian Fallacies* (Princeton, NJ: D. Van Nostrand, 1959) pp. 337–73.

21. Seymour E. Harris, 'International Economics: Introduction', in Seymour E. Harris (ed.), *The New Economics: Keynes' Influence on Theory and Public Policy* (New York: Alfred A. Knopf, 1947) pp. 253 and 259.

22. See Melvyn B. Krauss, *The New Protectionism: The Welfare State and International Trade* (New York: New York University Press, 1978), for a detailed and insightful analysis of the incompatibility of an international order of free trade and the intrusive and extensive modern welfare state.

23. Cf. Norman Angell, *This Have and Have-Not Business: Political Fantasy and Economic Fact* (London: Hamish Hamilton, Publishers, 1936), for a critical study of the errors in the idea that nations can permanently improve their economic well-being by monopolizing control of natural resources at the expense of their potential trading partners. See also Eugene Staley, *Raw Materials in War and Peace* (New York: Council on Foreign Relations, 1937), and Ludwig von Mises, 'The League of Nations and the Raw Materials Problem' [1937], in Richard M. Ebeling (ed.), *Selected Writings of Ludwig von Mises vol. 2. Between the Two World Wars: Monetary Disorder, Interventionism, Socialism and the Great Depression* (Indianapolis, IN: Liberty Fund, 2002) pp. 307–14.

24. On the actions and policies of the 'Big Three' – the United States, Great Britain and the Soviet Union – that made the post-World War II political and economic world order, see Richard M. Ebeling, 'Covering the Map of the World – the Half-Century Legacy of

the Yalta Conference', in Richard M. Ebeling and Jacob G. Hornberger (eds), *The Failure of America's Foreign Wars* (Fairfax, VA: The Future of Freedom Foundation, 1996) pp. 151-98.

25. Moritz J. Bonn, 'International Economic Relations between Governments: A Source of World Peace or Friction?', *Proceedings of the Academy of Political Science* (May 1945) 123.

26. See Richard M. Ebeling, 'World Peace, International Order, and Classical Liberalism', *International Journal of World Peace* (December 1995) esp. 47-54; on the extent and types of government influences on international investment decisions in the pre-World War I period, see Herbert Feis, *Europe: The World's Banker, 1870-1914* [1930] (Clifton, NJ: Augustus M. Kelley, 1974); and Eugene Staley, *War and the Private Investor* [1935] (New York: Herbert Fertig, 1967).

27. See James G. Smith, *Economic Planning and the Tariff* (Princeton, NJ: Princeton University Press, 1934).

28. Henry Hazlitt, 'The Coming Economic Pattern: Free Trade or State Domination?', *The American Scholar* (Winter 1944-5) pp. 9-10. The difference between the two systems of international economic order was explained by Henry Hazlitt toward the end of World War II:

> Freedom of trade, in the eyes of Adam Smith and his 19th-century successors in the liberal tradition, meant freedom from government interference. ... They wanted a removal of prohibitions and of nearly all tariffs. But they did not ask for positive 'encouragement' or artificial stimulants. They were as much opposed to bounties as they were to barriers. What the older liberals meant by freedom, in short, was the freedom of the individual citizen. ... The world barriers to international trade in the 1930s, for which every large nation was in part responsible, but in the erection of which the totalitarian governments went to the greatest lengths, brought about such chaos that few responsible persons now undertake to defend them. High tariffs, import quotas, export subsidies, competitive currency depreciation, blocked currencies, bilateral arrangements, forced barter – all these are today deplored by lip in all respectable circles. The demand now is for International Cooperation. But when the concrete proposals for this international cooperation are examined, it turns out to be something radically different from the international cooperation hoped for by the older liberals. It is not the freedom of the private citizens of any country to trade with the private citizens of any other. It is not primarily the cooperation among private citizens of different countries at all. It is primarily cooperation among governments. As in the thirties, it is governments that are going to take matters in hand. But instead, as in the wicked thirties, of restricting trade and making economic war upon each other, this time, we are told, the governments are going to direct and stimulate trade in the interests of peace. It is a pleasant fantasy; but there are the gravest reasons for doubting that it will ever be realized. ... For government officials, even when they really understand (which is very rarely) the basic economic forces they are trying to control, are almost never disinterested. They are almost certain to reflect the special interests of some pressure group. The interests of the pressure groups represented by the bureaucrats of one nation are certain to clash with those of the pressure groups represented by the bureaucrats of another. And these conflicting interests, precisely because they are represented by their representative governments, are far more likely to clash openly, directly and politically than in a world of genuine free trade.

29. David Osterfeld, 'The World Bank and the IMF: Misbegotten Sisters', in Peter J. Boettke (ed.), *The Collapse of Development Planning* (New York: New York University Press, 1994) p. 186.

30. Gottfried Haberler, 'The Liberal International Economic Order in Historical Perspective', in Ryan C. Amacher, Gottfried Haberler and Thomas D. Willett (eds), *Challenges to a Liberal International Economic Order* (Washington, DC: American Enterprise Institute, 1979) pp. 49-50; see also Jagdish Bhagwati, *Protectionism* (Cambridge, MA: MIT Press, 1988) pp. 1-15.

31. Jan Tumlir, *Protectionism: Trade Policy in Democratic Societies* (Washington, DC: American Enterprise Institute, 1985) pp.38-9; see also Jan Tumlir, 'The New Protectionism, Cartels and the International Order', in *Challenges to a Liberal International Economic Order*, pp.239-58.

32. 'Public choice' theory has cogently shown how the political arena can be understood as a market in which redistributive privileges are given to successful special interest groups that have sufficient incentives to expend scarce resources in the process of political lobbying; at the same time, those holding political office have an incentive to 'sell' favours, subsidies and redistributions in exchange for votes and financial contributions; and, as well, those who work in the bureaucracies have incentives to rationalize extensions of government regulation and control to enhance their own power and position in the society. For applications of the public choice approach to the problems of government intervention and management in international trade, commerce and investment, see Charles K. Rowley, Willem Thorbecke and Richard E. Wagner, *Trade Protection in the United States* (Aldershot, UK and Brookfield, VT: Edward Elgar, 1995); also Roland Vaubel, 'The Political Economy of the IMF: A Public Choice Analysis', in Doug Bandow and Ian Vasquez (eds), *Perpetuating Poverty: The World Bank, the IMF, and the Developing World* (Washington, DC: Cato Institute, 1994) pp.37-55.

33. The essays in *Perpetuating Poverty, supra*, note 32, document the political philosophy guiding and deleterious consequences following from the policies of the IMF and the World Bank on developing nations around the world. Development economist Peter T. Bauer has for years analysed the ideas behind and the effects resulting from the programmes instituted by these international organizations, as well as various foreign aid programmes provided by Western governments; see, for example, his books, *Equality, the Third World and Economic Delusion* (London: Weidenfeld and Nicolson, 1981) and *Reality and Rhetoric: Studies in the Economics of Development* (Cambridge, MA: Harvard University Press, 1984). See also Karl Brunner (ed.), *The First and the Third World: Essays on the New International Economic Order* (Rochester, NY: University of Rochester Policy Center Publications, 1978); Melvyn B. Krauss, *Development Without Aid: Growth, Poverty and Government* (New York: McGraw-Hill, 1983); Deepak Lal, *The Poverty of 'Development Economics'* (Cambridge, MA: Harvard University Press, 1985); *The Limits of International Cooperation* (London: Institute of Economic Affairs, 1990). On the World Bank, see Bryan T. Johnson, *The World Bank and Economic Growth: 50 Years of Failure* (Washington, DC: Heritage Foundation, 1996); *Backgrounder* No. 1082; and Mark Skousen, 'Austrian Capital Theory and Economic Development in the Third World', in Richard M. Ebeling (ed.), *Austrian Economics: Perspectives on the Past and Prospects for the Future*, Champions of Freedom Series, Vol. 17 (Hillsdale, MI: Hillsdale College Press, 1991) pp.355-78.

34. See James Bovard, *The Fair Trade Fraud* (New York: St Martin's Press, 1991) for a critical analysis of the notion of 'fair trade' instead of free trade and its manipulation to serve the goals of special interest groups.

35. Friedrich A. Hayek, *Law, Legislation and Liberty*, Vol. II: *The Mirage of Social Justice* (Chicago: University of Chicago Press, 1976).

36. Jagdish Bhagwati, *The World Trading System at Risk* (Princeton, NJ: Princeton University Press, 1991) p.22.

37. From 'About the WTO', 'WTO Home Page' (www@wto-org).

38. William Rappard (1883-1958) founded the Graduate Institute of International Studies in Geneva, Switzerland, in 1928. Under his supervision, especially in the years between the two world wars, the Institute brought together, either as permanent faculty or as visiting professors and lecturers, some of the finest scholars of the times. Among the faculty in the 1930s, for example, were Paul Mantoux, Ludwig von Mises, Wilhelm Röpke, Michael A. Heilperin, Guglielomo Ferrero, Hans Kelsen and Paul Guggenheim. For a concise appreciation of Rappard's contributions as an economist, political scientist, historian and world peace advocate, see Richard M. Ebeling, 'William E. Rappard: An International Man in an Age of Nationalism', *Ideas on Liberty* (January 2000) 33-41. For an overview of the Institute's work for free trade, democratic government and world peace during the period that Rappard was the director, see the 40-year anniversary volume, *HEI, 1927-1967*

(Geneve: Institut Universitaire de Hautes Etudes Internationales, 1967). It is, perhaps, interesting to note that, when Rappard was 25, he spent the 1908-9 semester studying at the University of Vienna with the then leading members of the Austrian School of Economics.

39.   William E. Rappard, 'The Common Menace of Economic and Military Armaments' [1936], reprinted in *Varia Politica* (Zurich: Editions Polygraphiques, 1953) p. 100.

40.   William E. Rappard, *The Crisis of Democracy* (Chicago: University of Chicago Press, 1938) pp. 267-8.

41.   William E. Rappard, 'Economic Nationalism', in *Authority and the Individual: Harvard Tercentenary Conference of Arts and Sciences* (Cambridge, MA: Harvard University Press, 1937) pp. 78 and 83-4; see also the valuable essays on this topic in Michael A. Heilperin, *Studies in Economic Nationalism* (Geneva: Librairie E. Droz, 1962).

42.   In fairness, it should be pointed out that, in a series of recent speeches, Mr Renato Ruggiero, the former Director-General of the WTO, forcefully argued for what he called a 'borderless world', that would represent 'a free global market and a free global trading system.' He warned of the danger 'of a power-based system [of] competing [regional trading] blocs' that 'attempt to regionalize the global economy' and which would be a threat even to the degree of liberalized world trade that currently exists. As Mr Ruggiero also correctly pointed out, 'It comes down to a question of the sort of world we want to live in.' See his addresses, 'Implications for Trade in a Borderless World', delivered to the World Trade Congress, Singapore, 24 April 1996, and 'The Road Ahead: International Trade Policy in the Era of the WTO', The Fourth Annual Sylvia Ostry Lecture, Ottawa, Canada, 28 May 1996 (www.wto.org/, press releases 46 and 49). But this is precisely the problem. While the rhetoric used, including Mr Ruggiero's, resonates with the language of free trade, open markets and global competition, the reality of the policies advocated and implemented by the member states of the WTO, and the statement of actual principles underlying the purpose of the WTO, are inconsistent with any real depoliticized, privatized system of freedom of trade, commerce and investment around the world. The governments of the world do not want free trade; they want managed trade that is 'liberal' when and to the extent that it is considered consistent with, or supportive of, their respective interventionist–welfare-statist domestic policies.

43.   Ludwig von Mises, *Liberalism in the Classical Tradition* [1927] (Irvington-on-Hudson, NY: Foundation for Economic Education, 1985) pp. 105-6; and Edwin R.A. Seligman, *Principles of Economics*, 6th edn (New York: Longmans, Green, and Co., 1914) p. 569: 'The essence of free trade is cosmopolitanism; the essence of protectionism is nationalism'.

44.   See Chapter 7 of the present volume.

45.   Cf. Paul Craig Roberts and Lawrence M. Stratton, *The New Color Line: How Quotas and Privileges Destroy Democracy* (Washington, DC: Regnery Publishing, Inc., 1995) pp. iii, 165: 'Critical Race Theory and radical feminism are Marxist to the core. [Critical Race Theorists] see American democracy as an unjust combination by whites to oppress blacks. Feminism applies the same denial of goodwill to the genders. ... The determinism of the new Marxism allows whites no more escape from their racial consciousness than the old Marxism allowed the bourgeoisie to transcend their class consciousness.' Also Richard M. Ebeling, 'Collectivist Myths and Racial Prejudices', *Freedom Daily* (October 1991) 6-10.

46.   Ludwig von Mises, *Omnipotent Government: The Rise of the Total State and Total War* (New Haven: Yale University Press, 1944) pp. 91-2; *Liberalism in the Classical Tradition*, pp. 112-13.

47.   Ludwig von Mises, *Liberalism in the Classical Tradition*, pp. 112-13.

48.   Ludwig von Mises, *Omnipotent Government: the Rise of the Total State and Total War*, p. 92.

49.   See Chapter 6 of the present volume.

50.   Frédéric Bastiat, 'The Law', in *Selected Essays on Political Economy* (Princeton, NJ: D. Van Nostrand Co., Inc., 1964) pp. 51-96.

51.   Histories of the private sector's successful handling of 'social services' in the past in America and Great Britain have begun to appear, most notably, Marvin Olasky, *The Tragedy of American Compassion* (Washington, DC: Regnery Gateway, 1992); and David Green, *Reinventing Civil Society: The Rediscovery of Welfare Without Politics* (London: Institute

of Economic Affairs, 1993); see also Robert Whalen, *The Corrosion of Charity: From Moral Renewal to the Contract Culture* (London: Institute of Economic Affairs, 1996).

52. Wilhelm Röpke, *Welfare, Freedom, and Inflation* (Auburn, AL: University of Alabama Press, 1964) p.29; see also John Torpey, *The Invention of the Passport: Surveillance, Citizenship and the State* (Cambridge University Press, 2000).

53. See Chapter 1 of the present volume; also Richard M. Ebeling, 'Free Trade, Managed Trade and the State', in Richard M. Ebeling and Jacob G. Hornberger (ed), *The Case for Free Trade and Open Immigration* (Fairfax, VA: Future of Freedom Foundation, 1995) pp.2-29.

54. Public choice theory, as pointed out in note 32, has insightfully demonstrated the nature and workings of special-interest politics in democratic society; see James M. Buchanan, Robert D. Tollison and Gordon Tullock (eds), *Toward a Theory of the Rent-Seeking Society* (College Station, TX: Texas A & M University Press, 1980); Robert E. McCormick and Robert D. Tollison, *Politicians, Legislation, and the Economy: An Inquiry into the Interest-Group Theory of Government* (Boston: Martinus Nijhoff Publishing, 1981); Gordon Tullock, *The Economics of Special Privilege and Rent Seeking* (Boston: Kluwer Academic Publisher, 1989); and Fred S. McChesney and William F. Shughart (eds), *The Causes and Consequences of Antitrust: A Public Choice Perspective* (Chicago: University of Chicago Press, 1995).

55. See Israel M. Kirzner, 'The Perils of Regulation: A Market-Process Approach', in *Discovery and the Capitalist Process* (Chicago: University of Chicago Press, 1985) pp.199-249; also reprinted in Richard M. Ebeling (ed.), *Austrian Economics: A Reader*, Champions of Freedom Series, Vol. 18 (Hillsdale, MI: Hillsdale College Press, 1991) pp.618-55; see also Dominick T. Armentano, *Antitrust and Monopoly: Anatomy of a Policy Failure* (New York: John Wiley and Sons, 1982); *Antitrust Policy: The Case for Repeal* (Washington, DC: Cato Institute, 1985); S.C. Littlechild, *The Fallacy of the Mixed Economy: An Austrian Critique of Economic Theory and Policy* (London: Institute of Economic Affairs, 1978); also Robert W. Poole (ed.), *Instead of Regulation: Alternatives to Federal Regulatory Agencies* (Lexington, MA: Lexington Books, 1982).

56. Ludwig von Mises, 'Autarky and Its Consequences' [1943], in Richard M. Ebeling (ed.), *Money, Method and the Market Process: Essays by Ludwig von Mises* (Norwell, MA: Kluwer Academic Publishers, 1990) p.145; see also Mises, *Omnipotent Government*, p.3.

57. Ludwig von Mises, *The Theory of Money and Credit* [1924, rev. edn, 1953] (Indianapolis, IN: Liberty Classics, 1981) pp.453-75.

58. Melchior Palyi, *The Twilight of Gold, 1914-1936: Myths and Realities* (Chicago: Henry Regnery Co., 1972) pp.5 and 9; see also Wilhelm Röpke, *International Order and Economic Integration* (Dordrecht: D. Reidel Publishing Co., 1959) pp.75-7.

59. On the monetary mismanagement of Great Britain, France, Germany, and the USA during World War I, see J. Laurence Laughlin, *A New Exposition of Money, Credit, and Prices*, Vol. II (Chicago: University of Chicago Press, 1931) pp.515-626; Edwin W. Kemmerer, *Money: The Principles of Money and Their Exemplification in Outstanding Chapters of Monetary History* (New York: Macmillan Co., 1935) pp.271-318; on the period leading up to and during the Great Depression, see Friedrich A. Hayek, 'The Fate of the Gold Standard' [1932], in *Money, Capital, and Fluctuations: Early Essays* (Chicago: University of Chicago Press, 1984) pp.118-35; Lionel Robbins, *The Great Depression* (New York: Macmillan Co., 1934); Frederic Benham, *British Monetary Policy* (London: P.S. King and Son, Ltd., 1932); H.F. Fraser, *Great Britain and the Gold Standard* (New York: Macmillan Co., 1933); C.A. Phillips, T.F. McManus and R.W. Nelson, *Banking and the Business Cycle* (New York: Macmillan Co., 1937); and Melchior Palyi, *The Twilight of Gold*.

60. See F.A. Hayek, 'Monetary Nationalism and International Stability' [1937], reprinted in Stephen Kresge (ed.), *The Collected Works of F.A. Hayek*, Vol. 6: *Good Money, Part II, The Standard* (Chicago: University of Chicago Press, 1999) pp.37-100; Lionel Robbins, *Economic Planning and International Order* (London: Macmillan, 1937) pp.280-99; and Lawrence H. White, *Monetary Nationalism Reconsidered* (Oakland, CA: Independent Institute, 1996).

61. Moritz J. Bonn, 'The Gold Standard in International Relations', in *Problems of Peace*, 8th Series, ed. William E. Rappard [1934] (Freeport, NY: Books for Libraries Press, 1968)

pp.163–79; and T.E. Gregory, *The Gold Standard and Its Future*, 3rd edn (New York: E.P. Dutton & Co., Inc., 1935) pp.1–29.

62. See Friedrich A. Hayek, *Monetary Nationalism, and International Stability* [1937] (New York: Augustus M. Kelley, 1971); Lionel Robbins, *Economic Planning and International Order* (New York: Macmillan Co., 1937) pp.280–301; Michael A. Heilperin, *International Monetary Economics* (London: Longmans, Green and Co., 1939); *Aspects of the Pathology of Money: Monetary Essays from Four Decades* (London: Michael Joseph, 1968).

63. The case has been made, for example, by Richard B. McKenzie and Dwight R. Lee, *Quicksilver Capital: How the Rapid Movement of Wealth Has Changed the World* (New York: Free Press, 1991), that the recent development of computerized global capital markets has served to introduce a new external check on discretionary monetary and fiscal policies by national governments, because any adverse economic policy anticipated or introduced in a particular country immediately results in financial capital fleeing from that nation into alternative markets around the world – at the mere pressing of a computer key. Computer technology and the integration of global financial markets certainly do provide financial capital investors with greater and quicker mobility. But while the 'corridor' of national governmental discretion may have been narrowed owing to these market developments, this still has not eliminated the power or the domestic policy interests of governments in attempting to manipulate domestic interest rates, foreign exchange rates and the general level of prices and wages in their respective countries. The policy makers now must merely more carefully weigh the costs of (perhaps significant) marginal capital outflows and their impacts on interest rates, foreign exchange and the availability of loanable funds for both government and private sector borrowing in comparison to the domestic political benefits from implementing the particular policy in question. Furthermore, while financial capital can take 'flight' in the face of expected or actual 'negative' policies, real capital (physical plant and equipment) and the labour force cannot. Those buying the financial assets being sold by those who wish to take their 'quicksilver capital' and flee will view the purchase of titles to the real capital up for sale as bargains (at least in the short run); after all, those desiring to flee can only do so if they find a willing buyer, and that will be a function of the price at which those wishing to flee are willing to sell. For a useful, earlier discussion of this topic, see Fritz Machlup, 'Die Theorie der Kapitalflucht' ['The Theory of Capital Flight'] *Weltwirtschaftliches Archiv*, Vol. 36 (1932) 512–29; see also David F. DeRosa, *In Defense of Free Capital Markets* (Princeton, NJ: Bloomberg Press, 2001) and Forrest Capie, *Capital Controls: A 'Cure' Worse Than the Problem?* (London: Institute of Economic Affairs, 2002).

64. On the possibilities and workability of a market-generated monetary order and system of free banking, see Ludwig von Mises, 'Monetary Stabilization and Cyclical Policy' [1928], in *On the Manipulation of Money and Credit* (Dobbs Ferry, NY: Free Market Books, 1978) pp.138–40; *Human Action, A Treatise on Economics*, 3rd rev. edn (Chicago: Henry Regnery Co., 1966) pp.440–48; *The Theory of Money and Credit*, 3rd rev. edn (Indianapolis, IN: Liberty Classics [1953] 1981) pp.434–8; Chapter 5 of the present volume; Lawrence H. White, 'Mises on Free Banking and Fractional Reserves', in *A Man of Principle: Essays in Honor of Hans F. Sennholz*, John W. Robbins and Mark Spangler (eds) (Grove City, PA: Grove City College Press [1992]) pp.517–33; Vera C. Smith, *The Rationale of Central Banking and the Free Banking Alternative* [1936] (Indianapolis, IN: Liberty Press, 1990); Friedrich A. Hayek, 'Denationalization of Money – the Argument Refined' [1978], in *Economic Freedom* (New York: Blackwell Publishers, 1991) pp.125–235; Lawrence H. White, *Free Banking in Britain: Theory, Experience, and Debate, 1800-1845* (Cambridge, MA: Cambridge University Press, 1984); *Competition and Currency: Essays on Free Banking and Money* (New York: New York University Press, 1989); George A. Selgin, *The Theory of Free Banking: Money Supply Under Competitive Note Issue* (Totowa, NJ: Rowman & Littlefield, 1988); Hans Sennholz, *Money and Freedom* (Cedar Falls, IA: Center for Futures Education, Inc., 1985); Kevin Dowd, *Private Money: The Path to Monetary Stability* (London: Institute of Economic Affairs, 1988); *The State and the Monetary System* (New York: St Martin's Press, 1989); *Laissez Faire Banking* (New York: Routledge, 1993); Kevin Dowd (ed.), *The Experience of Free Banking* (New York: Routledge, 1992); Steven

Horwitz, *Monetary Evolution, Free Banking and Economic Order* (Boulder, CO: Westview Press, 1992); Murray N. Rothbard, *The Case for a 100 Percent Gold Dollar* [1962] (Auburn, AL: Ludwig von Mises Institute, 1991); and Mark Skousen, *Economics of a Pure Gold Standard* (Auburn, AL: Ludwig von Mises Institute, 1988).

65. Henry Dunning MacLeod, *The History of Economics* (London: Bliss, Sands and Co., 1896) pp. 82 and 84 (italics in original); also see Henry Fawcett, *Manual of Political Economy*, 4th edn (London: Macmillan and Co., 1874) pp. 389-90.

66. Nassau Senior, *Industrial Efficiency and Social Economy*, Vol. II (New York: Henry Holt and Co., 1928) pp. 159 and 193.

67. Francis W. Hirst (ed.), *Free Trade and Other Fundamental Doctrines of the Manchester School* [1903] (New York: Augustus M. Kelley, 1968) p. 229.

Index